Studies in Ecological Economics

Volume 5

Series editor
R. Kerry Turner, University of East Anglia School of Environmental Sciences, Norwich, UK

The series "Ecological Economics" aims to present monographs and edited volumes that offer fresh perspectives and overviews on a range of topics in Ecological Economics. Special attention will be given to integrative research methods and techniques and to pluralistic approaches. Fundamental and critical discussions are invited of: theoretical assumptions, ethical starting points, behavioural models, (co) evolutionary change, integration concepts, the ecosystem approach and ecosystem services environmental macroeconomics, industrial ecology, spatial dimensions, thermodynamics and production functions, policy goals and instruments, international policy dimensions, alternative welfare measures, valuation and benefits transfer. Particular emphasis will be placed on the interaction between valuation, modelling and evaluation in a multidisciplinary setting; the link between ecology, biodiversity, ecosystem services, economics politics and environmental management; the incorporation of physical flows in economic models; and the interface between development, poverty, technology and sustainability. In addition, applied and policy oriented research is welcomed, addressing specific resources, substances, materials, regions, sectors, countries or environmental problems. International comparative studies are also encouraged. The ultimate aim of this series is to present a rigorous but broad perspective on contemporary and future environmental policy questions.

More information about this series at http://www.springer.com/series/6526

Karl Seeley

Macroeconomics in Ecological Context

Springer

Karl Seeley
Hartwick College
Oneonta, NY, USA

ISSN 1389-6954
Studies in Ecological Economics
ISBN 978-3-319-51755-1 ISBN 978-3-319-51757-5 (eBook)
DOI 10.1007/978-3-319-51757-5

Library of Congress Control Number: 2016963149

Printed on acid-free paper

This Springer imprint is published by Springer Nature
The registered company is Springer International Publishing AG
The registered company address is: Gewerbestrasse 11, 6330 Cham, Switzerland

For Joe, who taught me a lot, including my first lesson in economics, though he didn't remember that.

To my parents, Bob and Char, who raised my siblings and me in an environment of intellectual openness and curiosity.

Preface

This book arose out of my efforts to take something resembling conventional macroeconomics and root it in physical reality.

My path into economics had been unconventional, via Fritz Schumacher's *Small Is Beautiful* and the essays of Vàclav Havel, which linked the economy, political system, and environmental situation of Czechoslovakia under communism.

Then in the macroeconomics classes I took, there were labor, capital, and technology—and that was it. Resources and the environment were a specialized subdiscipline in economics, and they were essentially absent from macroeconomics. I gravitated toward ecological understandings of the economy, but the more I learned about the field, the more I came to see that an approach based solely on resources left too much unexplained. Havel's view of the economy was inspiring, but he was, after all, not an economist, and there was a lot to learn from people who had actually made a career of studying the economy.

When I started teaching macroeconomics regularly at Hartwick College in 2002, an additional consideration entered the picture. I wanted my students to understand the environmental context of the economy, but I knew they also needed to be able to work with standard macroeconomic tools so they'd be prepared for future coursework, graduate school, or work situations where their colleagues had learned "normal" macroeconomics.

My classroom approach was initially an ad hoc discussion of resources tacked on at the end of a standard course, but eventually I figured out and developed the approach used here, this particular way of integrating resources into the production function.

The connections between the environment and the economy show up most clearly in Chaps. 1 and 2 and Parts II and IV. Part III is in some ways a more conventional approach to understanding business cycles, with aggregate demand, IS-LM, and the Phillips curve, but it is grounded in an understanding of money that is influenced by endogenous money, because I have found that approach to lend itself most readily to connecting the strange social phenomenon that is money to the physical world that money influences.

In a sense, this does not aim to be a complete textbook, covering every last facet of the topic that someone might consider important for a college student at the intermediate level to know. The goal, rather, is a tool kit of clear models for understanding the long run and the business cycle, in a context where resource supply and availability are meaningful for the economy. Indeed, many economists will see it as outdated to use the IS-LM framework, or the Phillips curve, or perhaps even the production function and equilibrium approach of Part II. At the same time, there are plenty of economists—including textbook writers—who still use those tools. Apparently, we lack a strong consensus as to what should constitute "conventional macroeconomics." So, for instance, if you have no patience for the IS-LM model, perhaps you can use the discussion of it in Part III to see how to adapt the resource insights here to a different conventional macroeconomic framework more to your liking.

Just as the book doesn't aim to be complete, it doesn't claim to be an authoritative last word. Indeed, how could such a thing be possible in our time? Eight years ago, on the brink of the great financial crisis, there was a kind of consensus around a neoclassical synthesis. Of course there were dissenters on the "conservative" side tending toward real business cycles, microfoundations, and rational expectations and dissenters in a more liberal direction arguing for more active fiscal policy. But there was a broad middle where "we knew" that fiscal policy was to be avoided as clumsy, monetary policy was a nimble tool for managing the economy, and greater global integration and market liberalization had increased the stability of the global economy. That partial consensus has now been blown away, and it seems ill-advised to present the vision of any one person or even any one group as a definitive way of understanding the economy.

What I offer is a way of truly integrating resources and the environment into macroeconomics while preserving what macroeconomists have already learned.

My hope is that, in an era when resources are more and more an object of our attention, this particular addition to our tool kit comes at an opportune time and that others can adapt it to their own purposes.

A brief note on the practicalities of using the book: Part III is significantly longer than the others. It may work for you to have an exam after Parts I and II, another after Part III, and then a third exam after Part IV, which you can flesh out with additional readings of your choosing. Also, Chap. 3 is a long and potentially dry treatment of several key concepts; depending on one's teaching and/or learning style, it may be more useful to only skim the chapter at first and then revisit specific parts of it as they become useful to you.

Oneonta, NY, USA Karl Seeley
June 2016

Acknowledgments

My most immediate thanks go to my "family" in the Economics Department at Hartwick College. Dr. Larry Malone, Dr. Carli Ficano, and Dr. Kristin Jones are smart, they're excellent economists and teachers, they create an environment that is supportive and open to new ways of thinking about economics and teaching it, and they're simply a pleasure to be around and work with. In short, they are ideal colleagues, and it's unlikely this book or the ideas in it would have come to fruition without my having had the good fortune to land among them at Hartwick.

During my sabbatical year in Prague, Dr. Josef Seják of J.E.Purkyně University in Ústí nad Labem was a wonderfully stimulating intellectual sparring partner. There's a direct line from our conversations there to the framing of Part III. Similarly, Dr. Ilona Švihlíková formerly from the College of International and Public Relations Prague, now at J.A. Komenský University, provided the impetus and the venue for a talk which helped me further work out an ecological take on macroeconomics. Those Prague connections were enabled by my academic "host," Dr. Vlastimil Černý in the International Relations Department of the College of Management at the Czech University of Life Sciences. Ing. Václav Vacek was instrumental in making that situation happen and was also wonderfully hospitable to me and my family during our Prague sojourn.

Closer to home, in 1994, an old family friend clued me in to Charlie Hall's co-authored book *Energy and Resource Quality* [1], which I promptly devoured. The book had a formative impact on my thinking about economics and the environment at a time when I was relatively new to the field. In 2008, I sent Charlie the first version of the model that became Part II of this book. He sent it back with copious comments and invited me into a new venture he was starting, a series of meetings on what he called "biophysical economics." My involvement in those meetings provided a sympathetically critical sounding board for fleshing out my own take on that set of ideas.

I have to thank many springs' worth of Hartwick College students in macroeconomic theory who provided real-time feedback on the approach embodied in this book. In addition, Jordan Liz and Patrick Thompson both provided valuable assistance as summer student assistants.

Fritz Schmuhl at Springer Verlag took an early interest in the work and was enthusiastic and infinitely patient in the face of my slowness in getting it figured out enough to actually be a book.

Last but hardly least, my wife Kate has been a source of continual encouragement throughout the process.

Reference

1. Hall, C. A. S., Cleveland, C. J., & Kaufman, R. (1986). *Energy and resource quality: The ecology of the economic process*. New York: Wiley.

Contents

Acronyms

ABM	Agent-Based Modeling
AD	Aggregate Demand
ARRA	American Recovery and Reinvestment Act, a fiscal stimulus program passed in February, 2009
AS	Aggregate Supply
BAU	Business As Usual
BEA	Bureau of Economic Affairs
BLS	Bureau of Labor Statistics
Btu	British thermal units
CBO	Congressional Budget Office
CO_2	Carbon Dioxide
CPI	Consumer Price Index
CPI-U	Consumer Price Index for All Urban Consumers
CRS	Constant Returns to Scale
CZK	Czech crowns (currency unit)
ECB	European Central Bank, the monetary-policy authority for the Eurozone
EROEI	Energy Returned On Energy Invested
EROI	Energy Return On Investment
EU	European Union
FDIC	Federal Deposit Insurance Corporation
FOMC	Federal Open Market Committee
GDP	Gross Domestic Product
ICE	Internal Combustion Engine
IPCC	Intergovernmental Panel on Climate Change, an organization under the auspices of the United Nations, established to present an international consensus on the science of climate change
IRS	Internal Revenue Service
IS	Investment-Savings
IV	Initial Value
kWh	kilowatt hours
LM	Liquidity-Money

MBS	Mortgage-Backed Securities
MPE	Marginal Propensity to Expend (on domestic output)
MPK	Marginal Product of Capital
MPN	Marginal Product of Labor
MPRF	Monetary Policy Reaction Function
MZM	Money of Zero Maturity
NAIRU	Non-Accelerating Inflation Rate of Unemployment
NIPA	National Income and Product Accounts
OPEC	Organization of Petroleum Exporting Countries
PC	Phillips Curve
ppm	parts per million
PPP	Purchasing Power Parity
PV	Photovoltaic
QE	Quantitative Easing
R&D	Research and Development
RBC	Real Business Cycle (theory)
TFP	Total Factor Productivity
TOE	Tonnes of Oil Equivalent
USD	United States Dollars
ZIRP	Zero Interest-Rate Policy
ZLB	Zero Lower Bound

Part I
Building Blocks

This part of the book sets the economy in its physical context of the wider world—so that we can do macroeconomics as if the real world existed. It starts with a very general look at the connections between the economy and the world, then moves to a more specific treatment of ecosystems, how they function, and how an economy relates to them. The part ends with an overview of some key macroeconomic concepts and terms that will be used throughout the rest of the book and includes a discussion of the data for the general concept of "resources."

Chapter 1
The Economy in the World

Abstract We begin by looking at the physical steps needed for a plate of pasta Bolognese to appear on your table. This serves as a template for the way the economy is grounded in the physical world. We then consider what distinguishes the *economic* perspective on humans' use of nature from those of other disciplines, and then what distinguishes macroeconomics from its cousin microeconomics.

1.1 The History of Pasta

Think about the most recent meal you ate. How did it get to your table? Let's say it was a plate of spaghetti with Bolognese sauce—a pretty simple affair. To keep things easy, let's focus just on the pasta itself, leaving the sauce aside.

A farmer grew some wheat, using a tractor, a combine, some fertilizer and pesticides, and maybe irrigation water. The tractor and combine used fuel (almost certainly derived from petroleum).

The machinery and the chemical inputs were made in factories away somewhere. The machinery factory used steel, made from iron ore and coal, and the factory itself used more coal and some electricity, which came perhaps from burning still more coal somewhere, or from a hydroelectric dam, or from a nuclear power plant, or from a natural-gas-burning turbine, or maybe even from a wind turbine (though just in statistical terms that's not particularly likely, since as of 2015 a growing but still small portion of electricity in the U.S. comes from wind power). The chemical factory used petroleum and natural gas as inputs, and electricity and more petroleum as inputs (and we've already seen where the electricity comes from).

If there's no irrigation, the farm is located in a place where the environment provides enough precipitation over the course of the year to produce a decent crop. If there is irrigation, some serious work has been done to make that possible. Perhaps the farm has a pump that brings water up from an aquifer—an action that is only possible if the water is there in the first place. And the pump itself is another piece of machinery whose story is essentially like that of the tractor and the combine. The pump runs either by petroleum or electricity. (70 years ago the iconic farm windmill was pulling water up from underground, but those things weren't nearly as powerful as the motorized pumps that have replaced them.) Or maybe the water comes from

K. Seeley, *Macroeconomics in Ecological Context*, Studies in Ecological Economics 5, DOI 10.1007/978-3-319-51757-5_1

off-farm through an irrigation canal, which means the water had to exist somewhere else in the first place. And then people had to build the irrigation canals, which at a minimum means digging them out with machinery (see above for the production of machines), but may also mean lining parts of the canal with concrete or encasing it in steel (see above for the production of steel). The concrete is another whole process, starting from mining limestone, through heating it, combining it with crushed rock and water—energy and raw materials at every step of the way. The irrigation system probably involved a dam somewhere to impound water and make it more predictably available. If it's a small dam it might be made just of earth, pushed around with machinery (see above) powered by petroleum. If it's a big "mainstem" dam (in the path of a major river), it's probably got a lot of concrete and steel in it, too. And if we're really unlucky, the water doesn't get from the dam to the farm by gravity alone, but must be lifted first, maybe as much as 1,000 ft—more machinery to do that, and more electricity to power it.

The machinery and the chemical inputs were brought to the farm on trains and trucks driven by petroleum or, in the case of the train, maybe electricity. The harvested wheat leaves the farm the same way.

The wheat goes to a mill, where it is turned into flour. The flour goes to another factory where it is turned into pasta. The pasta goes to a warehouse and from there to your college's kitchen, or to a grocery store and to your home. All of this transportation depends on petroleum, with maybe some electricity for parts of the route covered by train. The mill, the factory, and the warehouse all use electricity to operate or just to keep the lights on when people are in there. The cook (maybe that's you) boils some water, using either natural gas or electricity. In goes the pasta, wait 10 min, and it's ready to eat.

Except that we forgot about the sauce, which has beef, pork, tomatoes, wine, milk, carrots, onion, and celery. Each of those inputs has its own story, differing from the wheat in its details but sharing the same outlines.

So much for the inputs. What about the outputs (other than the spaghetti ala Bolognese, that is)? Depending on each farmer's practices, there's more or less erosion from the fields, carrying soil particles, fertilizer, and pesticides into waterways. The erosion also reduces the field's fertility and ability to retain water, effects that are counteracted with the application of fertilizer and irrigation water.

The manure from the cows and the pigs may be stored in manure "lagoons" blighting their neighborhoods and occasionally bursting, spilling their noxious contents into the nearest river. Or it may be spread on fields to fertilize the next year's crop. If it's spread too thick, much of it washes off with the rain into the nearest river, or percolates down into the groundwater. And if the animal feedlots are highly concentrated, the manure has to be carried significant distances to where it can be put on fields—trucks and petroleum again. Or maybe the cows and pigs are from small farms where the ratio of animals to land is low so the manure doesn't have to be carried anywhere and the soil can readily absorb it before it reaches an aquifer or a river.

The mines that produce the coal and iron ore and the wells that produce the petroleum and the natural gas all have their impacts on the land. And the combustion of coal, petroleum, and natural gas all produce carbon dioxide that changes the atmosphere and alters the climate. (The cows release methane, having some of the same effect.)

The irrigation has its own set of effects. If water is drawn out of a river, that may reduce the amount of water available downstream to support fish stocks or marshes. If the irrigation water does make its way back to the river, it is probably carrying some mix of soil, fertilizer, pesticides, manure, and salts that it has picked up on its way through the farm, and it brings all these "gifts" to the river. It's also probably warmer than the water that stayed in the river, so it raises the temperature, further changing the mix of what thrives and what dies. If the irrigation depends on a dam, that implies another set of effects. Running water has been turned into a slack pool. Riparian areas (lands along a stream or river) have been turned into the bottom of a lake. Fish migration has been impeded or blocked entirely.

Irrigation from aquifers is a simpler set of impacts, the main one being that the water level in the aquifer drops over time as you pump lots of water out, so each year you have to bring water up from further down, requiring more electricity, and periodically requiring an upgrade to a more powerful pump. But aquifers don't exist in splendid isolation; sometimes their contents seep out of hillsides and feed streams in lands that would otherwise be arid. As the aquifer level goes down, the seepage is reduced and the stream flows become erratic or dry up entirely.

So that's one plate of pasta. But of course, that's unfair.

If all we wanted was a single plate of pasta, we'd have someone plant some wheat with a digging stick, carry water from the stream in a gourd, cut the wheat by hand with a stone scythe, grind it between hand-held stones, and cook it in a "pot" made of a cow's stomach suspended from branches over a wood fire. But we're not interested in having just a few plates of pasta. The vast apparatus described above is necessary because we want to provide billions of pasta servings every year, and year after year. And that same apparatus brings us all our other foods. It brings us the cars we drive, the clothes we wear, the movies we watch, the medical services we use, the computer games we play, the books we read, and so on through the rest of the endless catalog of things we use.

Each of these things has its own story, and each story can be picked apart in at least as much detail as the pasta story above. It's useful to keep the pasta story in mind, because it reminds us that all production ultimately stars four actors: labor, capital, technology, and—at the root of them all—resources. We'll get into those four actors in Chap. 2, but for now think back on the pasta story and generalize it to all other goods. Then take a breath and realize that:

An economy is a social organization for taking the materials of the physical world and transforming them to suit our purposes.

1.2 The Economic Perspective

Economics is certainly not the only discipline to look at this process. Anthropology, sociology, and psychology all have insights on how and why humans use nature, and toward what ends. Various technological fields look for ways of using nature better (with "better" being defined in different ways). Scientific disciplines inform the technologists and study the effects we have when we transform the physical world. Each discipline brings its own lens to the question. And the particular lens that economics uses has to do with its assumptions about how people behave.

Economics starts with the observation that people face tradeoffs—more of one desirable thing usually means less of another. The particular tradeoffs people face are shaped by technology and the economy's resource base.

A place that receives 50 in of rain a year and has a long growing season might grow corn or wheat, but if the corn gets a higher price, the choice of growing wheat means giving up valuable corn.

Another place might get 30 in of rain and have a shorter growing season. Corn may not be viable, so people have to decide between wheat and pasture.

Further on, only 15 in of rain falls in a year, and the growing season is only 3 months. Wheat is viable in good years, but pasture starts to look a lot more attractive. But how intensively should you pasture? If you raise two cows per acre, you can keep the pasture going forever. If you raise ten cows per acre, you'll get a lot more profit for a few years, but after that you'll only be able to feed half a cow on an acre. And maybe you made that choice consciously, or maybe you didn't understand that you were exhausting the land.

On the other hand, if you make meat popular enough, even that farm that receives 50 in of rain a year will switch to pasture, or at least feed its corn to its cows.

And who are you growing food for? If transportation is expensive, you only grow the things that your neighbors want to eat, in quantities they're able to consume. Relatively light foods that don't spoil easily—like wheat—you can grow far away from population centers. Perishable items like tomatoes had better be grown close to where people are going to eat them. But as the price of transportation comes down, your options about what to grow in a given place start to have more to do with the soil and the weather and less to do with where other people live.

So **people make tradeoffs shaped by the economy's resource base and its technology**, and **they make those choices subject to preferences** (their own and other people's) **and their information about those tradeoffs**. (If you don't know that pasturing 10 cows per acre will ruin your pasture, you'll probably do it; if you know, you *might* do it, as long as you think the present gain is worth the future loss.) **The economic perspective focuses on those tradeoffs and tries to understand how and why people make the decisions they do. It also tries to understand the consequences of those tradeoffs, and the ways that people's options change over time.**

1.3 Macroeconomics vs. Microeconomics

So that's the big picture of what economics is about. But this is a book specifically about macroeconomics, so it's important to define our subject matter. Start with what macroeconomics isn't—that is, start with microeconomics.

Microeconomics looks at individual goods, individual firms, and individual consumers. You might study the market for gasoline, or oranges, or movies, or blockbuster movies, or movie talent, or pretty much anything.

Within these markets you might look at individual firms. Why did this one close down and another one open up? Why did Firm A build a new factory? Why did Firm B layoff 20% of its workforce?

You can also look at individual consumers. How will people respond to a program of food stamps that subsidize grocery purchases for households with low incomes? What shapes people's decisions about going to college, or saving for retirement, or engaging in addictive behavior?

The focus of microeconomics is on individual markets and on individual actors in the economic game.

Macroeconomics is about aggregates. Rather than the market for gasoline and whether more is produced or less, we're interested in the production of everything (which we call Gross Domestic Product, or GDP).

Rather than the hiring and firing decisions of individual firms or employment in a given line of work, we're interested in the overall level of employment or unemployment.

Where microeconomics might look at interest rates and how they affect individual saving or borrowing decisions, macroeconomics treats interest as an important endogenous part of the whole economy, arising from current economic conditions and shaping behaviors that will influence future possibilities.

And macroeconomics looks at the change in prices overall, rather than the price of any particular good.

These four building blocks are used to build two basic macroeconomic stories. The first is about **long-run growth**, where over time an economy is able to produce more stuff, and produce more stuff *per capita*.

The other story concerns the **business cycle**, that unpredictable alternation between periods of economic growth, when GDP is rising rapidly, and periods of economic contraction, known as recessions or, in extreme cases like the 1930s, depressions. In addition to a shrinking GDP, recessions are characterized by high unemployment, which gives policy-makers a strong interest in understanding them and, if possible, ameliorating them. For a while recessions were also associated with prices that were rising slowly or even falling, rather than rising quickly, but in recent decades that link has weakened.

In telling both these stories macroeconomics also makes use of the interest rate and the idea of investment.

One thing macroeconomics has not been about, for more than a century, is resources. A key premise of this book is that this neglect of resources has been a fundamental error for the field of macroeconomics. In microeconomics you can leave resource questions aside—they can always be part of some other market than the one you're examining. The abundance or scarcity of some resource may affect the market you're analyzing, but that can be perfectly well brought in as an exogenous factor. If growing wheat takes petroleum, you can ask, "What if petroleum got cheaper, or more expensive?" and do your analysis from there. It's also reasonable to ignore the effect that any one particular market has on the state of resources in general.

Although an economy as a whole is a system for taking resources from the physical world and altering them for our purposes, when looking at a particular good it's reasonable to assume that the extraction has happened in some other part of the system and just focus on the labor and the capital involved in its further modification. You can look at the economics of the extraction of some particular resource, or the emission of some particular pollutant, and you can bring all those issues into your microeconomic analysis, but you don't have to. You can reasonably do microeconomics without incorporating environmental factors into your thinking, leaving them instead to specialists in resource economics.

Macroeconomics is different, because resources are an integral part of the story. While many individual economic processes can be understood without considering the physical resources involved, **the aggregate economic process is impossible without resources**. While under certain conditions (discussed later in the book) it's harmless to ignore resources, in more general terms **the aggregate economic process cannot sensibly be analyzed in isolation from resources**. Think of the pasta story again. We can treat resources as exogenous when we look at the individual parts of the story. Coal and iron ore are available at certain prices; what kind of steel factory do you want to build and how many workers do you want to hire? The same for the transportation, or the irrigation, or the choice to have Bolognese or a vegetarian sauce.

But step back and look at not just the pasta story, but all the other stories like it that make up the aggregate economy, the macroeconomy. Take away the resources and the whole thing just stops dead in its tracks. Change the resources and the whole thing is fundamentally altered.

In a world without fossil fuel, countries with really short growing seasons will eat crops like barley and have scarce populations; countries with moderate growing seasons will eat wheat and have more people; countries with long growing seasons will eat corn and greatly outnumber their barley-growing neighbors. A world that doesn't know about coal or oil will farm with draft animals and travel rarely. A world that invents the steam engine *and* has access to coal will travel extensively and increase farmers' yields with abundant steel implements. A world that discovers petroleum *and* invents the internal combustion engine will farm with tractors, travel 10,000 miles per person per year, and eat bell peppers grown 4,000 miles away. And people in countries with short growing seasons might eat anything they like, because even if they can't grow it where they live, they can bring the food from wherever it *does* grow. And if they can take oil and do something with it that others value, they can even be densely populated, despite the difficulty they have growing large quantities of food.

The economic choices available to people always result from the interaction among resources in the world, the techniques people have figured out for using those resources, and the tools and machines they have built that embody those techniques.

The course of macroeconomic change is not determined strictly by the economy's resource base—human ingenuity and human choices are fundamental parts of the story. But those choices and that ingenuity don't occur in a natural vacuum; they occur in the context of what nature offers us, and the way that our ancestors' choices have altered what is available.

1.4 What Is an Economy For?

If you listen to economic or business news or public discussions of economics, you'll find frequent mention of the Gross Domestic Product, of growth, of jobs, of unemployment, of growth, of interest rates, and of growth yet again. The unstated assumption behind this is that unemployment is bad and that economic growth is good. Just ask anyone who has lost their job how much hardship can come from being unemployed. And as for growth, just listen to an election campaign to identify the holy grail of our general economic thinking.

The case for unemployment being bad is pretty strong, as people rarely benefit from losing their jobs, and even the wider society is in some ways made worse off when significant numbers of people are involuntarily unemployed. The benefits of growth are in certain respects undeniable: the general level of material comfort enjoyed in the world's richer countries is the result of decades or centuries of economic growth. But it is a more ambiguous phenomenon than unemployment, with some negative effects accompanying its positive ones (for an extensive discussion of the downsides, see [2]). Yet you will be hard-pressed to find a news item about the GDP that doesn't assume that bigger is better.

But if growth isn't always good, how can we tell when it is and when it isn't? The best way to do that is to step back and ask what an economy is for. My answer—and I hope you'll agree—is that an economy should support the well-being of the people whose economy it is. That in turn raises the question of what makes for human well-being.

First off, let's admit that human well-being is hard to measure, and with that admission out of the way, we can think about what contributes to human happiness, unfettered by whether or not we can turn any of it into numbers.

One component is certainly material consumption: we need adequate food, water, clothing, and shelter. We apparently like to have *more* than adequate amounts of these things, and many other things as well. These material goods are partly produced by humans (as when we grow food or build a house), based on inputs from the environment (the land on which the food grows, the trees from which the house's lumber is cut). They also come more directly from nature, as when environmental conditions influence the quality of the water we drink or put on our crops.

A second obvious thing to include is health. Presumably we can agree that, all else being equal, populations who experience high rates of disease and short life spans are worse off than healthy, long-lived people. And health, like the previous material items, results from a combination of environmental conditions and things people produce. On the human-produced side there is not only good medical care and all the tools that help in its provision, but also the quantity and quality of the food people have available, and the systems in place to control the spread of infectious diseases. The environmental influences include things like clean air, whose absence is usually, of course, a product of human action, but they can also be non-human-influenced factors such as whether a given locale is hospitable for germs or disease-carrying organisms.

While consumption and health are both directly about our physical well-being, environmental quality straddles the physical and psychological areas. On the physical side, it influences both our health and the ease of producing the things we consume. But to the extent that we get aesthetic enjoyment from the environment, it also plays a role in our psychological well-being, in our happiness distinct from our material consumption and our health.

Everything we've looked at so far has been measured on the individual scale, but humans, like other primates, are a social species, and a part of how well we're doing depends on our social surroundings. A particular level of material consumption and state of health can be consistent with greater or lesser happiness, depending in part on whether we feel ourselves to be part of vibrant communities with social networks we can draw on for connection, companionship, and even for material support. These communities and networks can range from the atmosphere at our place of employment or our involvement in some voluntary organization, down to the level of our closest relatives and friends.

Another slippery piece of the puzzle, but apparently fundamental, is our sense of worth, our sense that what we do is important. For many people this comes from their employment, as people take pleasure in a job worth doing and a job well done. It can also come from our households, whether that's keeping things running with cleaning and cooking, or helping one's children grow up well. Another source of worth can be volunteer activities, with charities, at our houses of worship, in schools, coaching youth sports, helping people hindered by age or disability. Whatever the source, people tend to report more satisfaction with life and better mental health when they have reason to think that they improve someone else's well-being. (For related ideas, see [5] and [7].)

Lastly, there is culture, which is another multi-faceted factor. It is partly cultural products, such as art, and journalism. A well done play or movie, a great piece of music, a wonderful book, a fantastic painting, a riveting story—all contribute in real though intangible ways to our quality of life. Culture in this sense requires some kind of material foundation, since there has to be enough food and shelter for some people to be able to devote some or even lots of their time to "making" culture. But great culture can be created on far less material wealth than we currently take for granted in the rich countries, as evidenced by Bach, Shakespeare, Swift, Aristophanes, the Parthenon, and may more—artists and art we still admire today, produced by societies that we would consider poor.

The other aspect of culture that's relevant here is a much subtler one, having to do with day-to-day mores and beliefs, views of the world that we absorb from our cultural surroundings, without even realizing that that's what's happening. And this cultural inheritance can shape how we relate to things, and thereby affect how much happiness we get from the things we have. We all have some material desires, grounded in our simple need for survival. But beyond that, our preferences are not arbitrary; they develop over time in response to our experiences and the messages we pick up from our culture. It's possible for a culture to focus people's attention on their material possessions and acquisitions and inculcate the expectation that ever greater happiness comes from ever more things, and that if one is unhappy, the problem has a material solution. (On the formation of preferences, see [1] and [4].) Yet many causes of unhappiness are spiritual or social in nature, and efforts to solve them with things will inevitably fall short. And while new possessions bring some initial happiness, we seem to revert to our prior level of contentment before too long, so the pursuit of bliss through purchases likewise consistently falls short. A culture that focuses people's attention on their things and away from addressing non-material sources of happiness and misery will thus systematically reduce the well-being people get from their consumption.[1]

Quite a list: consumption, health, environmental quality, social networks, sense of worth, cultural output, cultural norms. It's not a complete list, but it gives a sense of the range of factors that play into how well we're doing. Now let's look at the standard criteria for "success" in macroeconomics.

1.5 What Economics Actually Measures

The goals of standard macroeconomics can be summed up as:

- High consumption
- Low unemployment
- High GDP
- Continually growing GDP
- Inflation that is low and stable

High consumption was on our list above, fitting in as part of human-created material well-being. Note that we often focus on the *average* level consumption, so that whether everyone has the same consumption, or some have much while others little, the measured level of success will be the same.

[1]For a deeper analysis of a related idea, see [6].

Low unemployment is good, both because employment supports a household's ability to purchase goods to consume, and because of the psychological impacts of joblessness on the unemployed.

A high level of GDP per capita supports high consumption.

Continually growing GDP per capita is good because it makes it easier for poor people to get out of poverty or to make comfortable people wealthy. It's also important for employment: if technology is making the average worker more productive, then the economy won't be able to employ the whole labor force unless there is ever-increasing demand for output to match.

Inflation should be stable, because unpredictable inflation is disruptive to people's economic plans. It should be low, because higher inflation tends to be more volatile, and people seem to dislike inflation (even if their wages are keeping up with prices).

Compare this list to the "good life" sketched out in Sect. 1.4 above. High consumption is on both. For similar reasons (loss of consumption and psychological cost), low unemployment is on both. Other than that, everything on the standard macroeconomics list is there to support high consumption (with a little nod to people's dislike of inflation). And all of the other factors contributing to well-being are missing: environmental quality, culture (other than what is included in consumption), community, family, sense of purpose (other than what is conveyed by employment), our culture's ability to help us gain enjoyment from what we have, or its tendency to train our eyes always on what we lack. None of that is in the standard treatment.

Traditional economics has a reason for its approach, and it's a serious one: macroeconomics counts success in things that can actually be measured. If you focus on elements that are measured sporadically or very unreliably, then you are limited in testing whether what you're saying about the economy matches up with reality.

This isn't an argument to be dismissed lightly, but it's also insufficient. It's true that the data on those other factors aren't as concrete as the items macroeconomics usually looks at, nor are they gathered with anything like the regularity of economic statistics. Yet the evidence from psychology and other disciplines is quite strong, that consumption is an inadequate measure of human well-being and satisfaction.[2] If the pursuit of increased consumption sacrifices large amounts of the other virtues, the result will not be a better society, so we have to remember the relationship between the things we can measure and the things we ultimately care about.

With that caveat, this book will nonetheless deal primarily with the indicators that show up in other macroeconomics books. Although GDP isn't the be-all and end-all of economic life, it does matter, not least because it is linked with the functioning of money and of the government. And although consumption is far from the only

[2]This is part of the idea behind the "Easterlin paradox," which refers to the finding that increasing income has a positive impact on happiness in the short run but little to none in the long run (e.g., [3]; for a contrary view see [8]).

important factor in how good people's lives are, it does still have something to do with their behavior. Also, even if we look more skeptically at the goal of growth than in most texts, consumption, investment, prices, unemployment are all real things that affect people's lives, so it's important to understand them.

But it is crucial to remember that, while we'll look at what tends to cause GDP and consumption to increase, we're not necessarily equating those outcomes with success, and particularly in Part IV we'll be getting into situations where the traditional goals of macroeconomic policy can actually be directly opposed to increased well-being.

1.6 A Look Ahead

This book starts with resources at the center of its attention. Chapter 2 lays out more formally the role that resources play in the economy, while Chap. 3 wraps up Part I by presenting the major terms and concepts used.

Part II covers the long-run model, starting with the production function in Chap. 4, which also introduces the markets for resources and for labor. Chapter 5 breaks down output into its major components and lays out how they're related. Chapter 6 ties together the two preceding chapters into the model of long-run equilibrium and looks at policy implications. Chapter 7 analyzes the way economic growth happens and explains the "conditional equivalence" between this approach and a more conventional one which omits resources—in other words, the circumstances under which you can safely ignore the role of resources in the economy, thereby simplifying the analysis.

The long-run model tells us something useful about growth, but it comes up empty in dealing with the business cycle, which is addressed in Part III, starting with an explanation of money: what it is and how it functions, including the workings of the banking system overall and the central bank within that. The natural consequence of money's nature and function is the Keynesian concept of the expenditure multiplier, whether applied to spending by government or the private sector. This leads in turn to Chap. 12 on monetary policy, which operates through the central bank's influence on interest rates and the money supply, followed by fiscal policy in Chap. 13, which explains the tools for trying to stabilize the economy through changes in taxation and government spending. Succeeding chapters deal with some of the standard models for understanding the business cycle: The IS-LM system connecting changes in interest rates with changes in output, and the model of aggregate demand and aggregate supply. Chapter 17 closes this part of the book with a look at arguments about monetary and fiscal policy and evidence for how well they work.

Part III had some strong similarities with other textbooks; the emphasis on money first is unusual, but like them, it treats the business cycle as something divorced from questions of resource availability. That's because it takes the conditional equivalence from the end of Part II and runs with it, which simplifies the analysis of business cycles. Part IV then brings resources back into consideration. First, Chap. 18 provides an idiosyncratic synthesis of the long- and short-run views of the economy, a cousin of the standard model, then briefly considers alternative perspectives that don't focus on resources, from the Minsky model of fundamental instability to the real-business-cycle theory. Chapter 19 revisits the material from Chap. 2 on the resource perspectives developed by Howard Hotelling and M. King Hubbert. It then discusses the evidence that our resource situation is getting fundamentally tighter and introduces the concept of energy return on energy invested, or EROI. Chapter 20 looks at how the long-run model behaves when resource supply can't be easily expanded, and also classifies the different possible responses to that situation. Chapter 21 reconnects the resource-based model and the business-cycle material from Part III in order to understand the behavior of a business cycle driven by changes in the resource situation. It also explores ways of adapting the Keynesian lessons on policy to a resource-constrained world. Chapter 22 wraps things up by laying out the deep structural similarities between the conventional model and this resource-based one, while pointing out the different garb that those traditional structures put on in this new setting.

Problems

1.1 Choose any product you use on a daily basis. Try to think through the chain of production, starting with resources out in the world, passing through various types of factories or other facilities, using various types of labor, until the product comes into your hands.

Make a list of the material components that are in the good or are necessary to provide the service. For those material components, what steps are involved in turning raw materials into the product or into the components of the product or into the tools or machines that allow the service to be provided?

1.2 Consider the famous essay "I, pencil" by Leonard E. Read, available at http://www.econlib.org/library/Essays/rdPncl1.html.

(a) Make a list of all the places that resources enter the narrative. Try to think of places that they lurk unremarked.
(b) Why is delivering a half-ounce of mail to a house different from delivering four pounds of oil?
(c) What tradeoffs are being made in providing service to and from all parts of the country with a single price for a first-class stamp, rather than different prices to reflect the different conditions of moving mail different distances and in different conditions?
(d) How does the decision to have a single price for all postal customers affect the price for customers in urban settings?

1.3 Look at the Human Development Index calculated by the Human Development Programme of the United Nations (at http://hdr.undp.org/en/statistics/hdi/).

(a) In what ways do you think their measurement is a useful indicator of true human well-being?
(b) What problems do you see in their approach, either at a broad conceptual level or in the specifics of how they carry out the calculations?

References

1. Bowles, S. (1998). Endogenous preferences: The cultural consequences of markets and other economic institutions. *Journal of Economic Literature, 36*(1), 75–111.
2. Daly, H. E., & Cobb, J. B. (1994). *For the common good: Redirecting the economy toward community, the environment, and a sustainable future*. Boston: Beacon Press.
3. Easterlin, R. A., McVey, L. A., Switek, M., Sawangfa, O., Zweig, J. S. (2010). The happiness-income paradox revisited. *Procedings of the National Academy of Sciences, 107*(52), 22463–22468.
4. Layard, R. (2003). What is happiness? Are we getting happier? Lionel Robbins Memorial Lectures 2002/3, 2003. http://cep.lse.ac.uk/events/lectures/layard/RL030303.pdf. Accessed July 17, 2014.
5. Moynihan, D. P., DeLeire, T., & Enami, K. (2013). A life worth living: Evidence on the relationship between prosocial values and happiness. *The American Review of Public Administration, 45*, 311–326.
6. Schor, J. B. (1999). *The overspent american: Why we want what we don't need*. New York: Harper Perennial.
7. Schwartz, C., Meisenhelder, J. B., Ma, Y., & Reed, G. (2003). Altruistic social interest behaviors are associated with better mental health. *Psychosomatic Medicine, 65*(7), 778–785.
8. Stevenson, B., & Wolfers, J. (2008). Economic growth and subjective well-being: Reassessing the Easterlin paradox. NBER working paper 14282. http://www.nber.org/papers/w14282. Accessed July 17, 2014.

Chapter 2
Resources and Economic Processes

Abstract The starting point for placing the macroeconomy in an ecological context is to understand some basics of how ecosystems function and how energy moves resources around within them. "Resources" are then generalized to "gradients," followed by making the distinction between renewable and nonrenewable resources and a consideration of the major types of renewable resources. There is discussion of the rational use of exhaustible resources, but a more detailed treatment is left for Chap. 19. The final part of the chapter looks at the relationship between technology and resource use.

2.1 Ecosystems and Resource Use

If we're going to understand the economy in the context of the physical world, we need to start with some tools to help us interpret that world. We need some way of taking the baffling complexity that's out there and reducing it to the point that we can get our heads around it, but not simplify it so much that it ceases to mean anything. What we need is a basic ecological framework, which we'll then flesh out with a fuller understanding of how a few particularly important types of resources work.

The keystone of all resources will turn out to be energy. The other resources matter, because if they're abundant and well situated, you don't need to use as much energy to make them economically useful. But energy is still uniquely important, for two reasons.

First, while different economic processes use different resources, *every* economic activity uses some amount of energy. If a particular resource becomes hard to get, you can probably find some other resource to use as a substitute, and the more technologically advanced you are, the more easily you'll be able to adapt other inputs to your purposes. So it's usually impossible to say that any one resource is absolutely crucial, so long as substitutes are available. In contrast, while some ways of accomplishing a task may use *less* energy than others, every task requires *some* energy.

Note that some important resource substitutions in the past were substitutions among ways of obtaining energy to drive economic activity. There are plenty of significant exceptions: petroleum replacing whale-oil as a lubricant; wood fiber

K. Seeley, *Macroeconomics in Ecological Context*, Studies in Ecological Economics 5, DOI 10.1007/978-3-319-51757-5_2

replacing rags in paper-making; fiber-optic cable (i.e., sand) replacing copper wire in the transmission of information (and transmitting far *more* information per unit of energy than was possible over copper wires); etc. But technological change has been marked by key substitutions among energy sources. When fuel wood was becoming hard to get for the European economies, they figured out how to substitute coal. This new resource was still abundant when people worked out the application of petroleum, but the substitution went forward anyway, since there are ways that oil is preferable to coal. Now that we're facing uncertainties in future oil supplies, a major focus is substitutions away from oil, whether it be back to coal, further into nuclear power, to biofuels, or increased use of wind and solar energy.

The second reason for the importance of energy is that it's a kind of universal substitute among grades of other resources, as explained below in Sect. 2.2 on "Gradients". If you have a high-grade iron-ore deposit, that's nice because it takes relatively little energy to gather the rock and extract the iron. But you can still extract iron from lower grades as long as you have enough energy to do the work of concentrating the iron. In principle, with enough energy you could "mine" iron from seawater, though in practice that's likely to always entail an impossibly large amount of energy.

To start developing an understanding of energy flows, we'll look at a very simplified picture of a prairie. This picture will exclude plenty of organisms and relationships, but it will include some important ones and illustrate the behavior of energy in an ecosystem and set up our understanding of the role of energy in an economy.

Our simplified ecosystem (see Fig. 2.1) starts with the sun, which provides the energy that makes the grass (and other plants) grow. Birds, insects, rodents, and bison all eat various parts of the grass. Some of the birds also eat some of the insects. Birds of prey eat some of the insects and some of the rodents. Every time

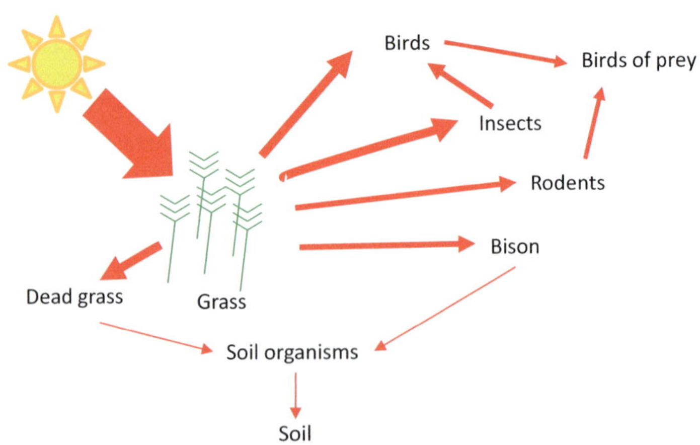

Fig. 2.1 Simplified energy flow through a prairie ecosystem

one animal eats another, in addition to getting the various nutrients and molecules it needs to build and maintain its body, it's capturing energy, all of which was originally captured from the sun by plants.

Not all the grass gets eaten, and parts of what is eaten end up not in a bison, but in bison feces (and other animals' excrement as well). The dead grass and the feces have some energy (and nutrient) value of their own, so there are "decomposers" which consume those resources and eventually turn them into soil. Figure 2.1 shows these relationships diagrammatically.

In addition to illustrating some important prairie-ecosystem relationships, this diagram indirectly demonstrates part of the **First Law of Thermodynamics**:

Energy can be neither created nor destroyed, but only transformed.

In particular, the diagram illustrates the part of the law that says that energy can't be created, because if you look at the energy available to any organism in the system, it can ultimately be traced back to solar energy captured by green plants. Without that initial step of capture, it's not available to anything else in the system.

Useful as it is for that purpose, however, the diagram doesn't do so well with the other piece of the first law, which says that energy can't be destroyed, because if you were to look quantitatively at the energy used by the birds of prey, you'd find that it's less than the energy captured by the things that they eat. And if you look at the energy in the dead grass and in everything that eats the live grass, it's less than the energy captured by the grass originally. If that's a puzzle, the answer comes from the **Second Law of Thermodynamics**:

Every time energy is transformed, some of it is dissipated as low-grade heat that's not available for doing anything useful.

In terms of Fig. 2.1, the transformations are when organisms *use* the energy they capture from the previous link in the energy chain. The bodies of plants contain only some of the energy they've captured from the sun, because they use a lot of the captured energy to operate the process of respiration and to move molecules around as they build their bodies. Similarly, birds' bodies contain far less energy than the food they consume, because they use energy to do the work of *building* their bodies—not to mention the work of pumping blood around, using their brains, and, well, flying. This pattern repeats at every stage of the ecosystem, with organisms taking most of the energy they consume and dissipating it in the simple act of living. Figure 2.2 illustrates this dissipation.

But even if you tracked all of those transformative losses and added them up, and added up the energy content of all the organisms along the energy chain, you still wouldn't account for all the energy originally captured by the grass, so we still seem

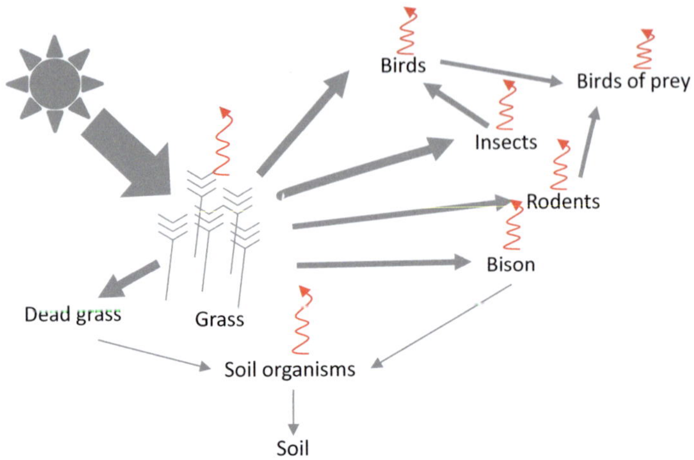

Fig. 2.2 Dissipation of energy by every ecosystem component

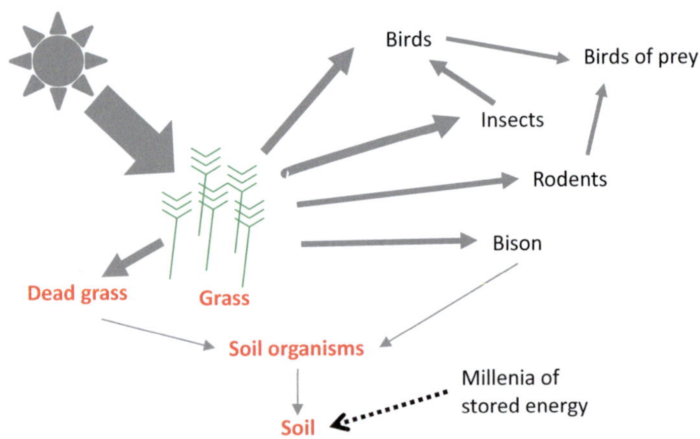

Fig. 2.3 Major points of energy storage in a prairie ecosystem

to be in violation of the "can't be destroyed" part of the First Law. Where did the missing energy go? The answer is the soil, which may store up millennia of energy not dissipated by the other parts of the system. It also embodies millennia of work arranging molecules and nutrients in ways that support plant growth.[1] Additional significant stores (though not as big as a healthy, long-developing soil), are the grass itself and possibly dead grass not yet consumed by the decomposers. This is all illustrated in Fig. 2.3.

[1]These two attributes—energy content and nutrient arrangements—help make virgin soils so productive when first converted to agriculture. Their value is a function of the "work" nature did before humans started using them for farming.

A convenient way to summarize all this information is with a diagramming language developed by Howard T. Odum (see [6]). Energy flows from left to right, out of one node into the next, or down into a "sink." A partial list of symbols Odum used includes:

- A circle represents a source of energy outside the boundary of the system being studied;
- A rectangle with a rounded right end is a plant performing photosynthesis;
- A hexagon is a "self-sustaining unit" such as an animal species, that cycles energy through itself in order to maintain itself and to obtain more energy;
- The shape with a rounded bottom and a peaked "roof" is a store of energy;
- An arrow leading down to three lines is a heat sink;
- Energy flows from left to right or in at the top and out at the bottom along the lines connecting the other shapes in the diagram.

With those symbols one can summarize the information of Figs. 2.1, 2.2 and 2.3 in Fig. 2.4.

Through careful study of a particular ecosystem, actual units of energy can be estimated for every connection from one node to another and into heat sinks. If this were a complete diagram of a prairie ecosystem, the First Law of Thermodynamics tells us that, because energy can be neither created nor destroyed, everything that enters the system from the sun must either end up going into one of the heat sinks or into the storage node in the soil.[2] The Second Law of Thermodynamics is about the unavoidable losses when transforming energy and thus tells us that the heat sinks can't be eliminated and can't even be reduced all that much.

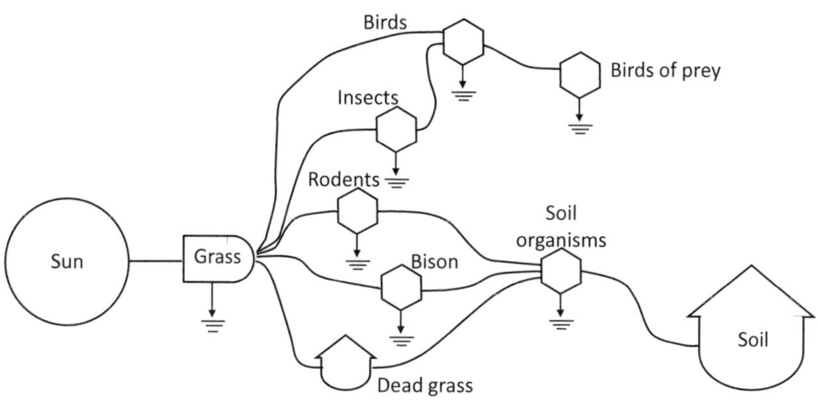

Fig. 2.4 Simplified prairie ecosystem using Odum's symbolic language

[2]If we were to extend the time frame of the analysis, the energy in the soil would also eventually go *somewhere*. Similarly, if a fire sweeps across the prairie, much of the energy in both the dead plants and the live grass will be quickly converted to heat and dissipated to the air.

Such energy-flow diagrams are one way of describing ecosystems (and an important one), but there are others. Similar diagrams could be built to track the flow of key materials such as nitrogen. We can measure the total biomass, or living material, in an area. We can look at the biodiversity, or the range of different living things. Biodiversity may relate to the complexity of relationships among components of an ecosystem. Complexity in turn has a connection to the number of times energy is passed from one node to another before being fully dissipated into heat sinks.

All of these perspectives relate to how a system responds to shocks from the outside, such as a fire or a flood. But by itself an ecosystem doesn't really have a "purpose," so it's hard to say when it's "succeeding." If we introduce humans into the picture, it's a different story. We start by bringing ourselves in as we once were, small parts of the ecosystems we inhabited. Being omnivores, we drew food from various parts of the environment (see Fig. 2.5). We altered that environment in certain important ways,[3] but we couldn't draw more than a limited amount of the system's energy for our own purposes—the functioning of the system required most of the energy to remain in paths that didn't directly serve us, in order to maintain the parts of the system that we *did* draw from.

As soon as you have humans, even small populations of gatherer-hunters, you have the beginnings of an economy, as people learn how to make tools and alter their environment and develop ways of sharing or exchanging food and other

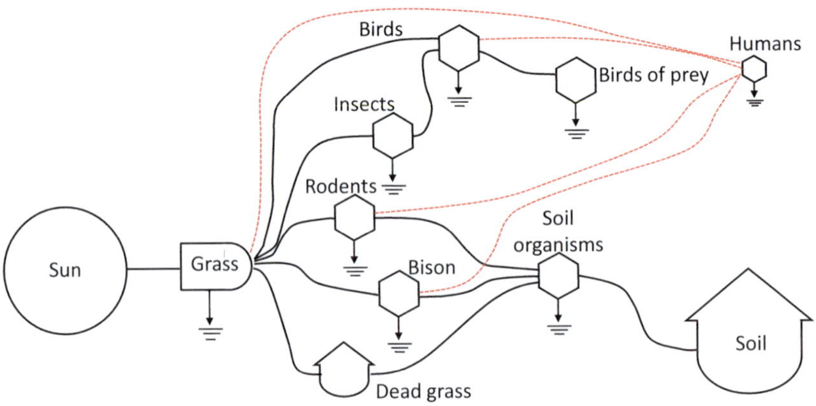

Fig. 2.5 Position of hunter-gatherer humans in an ecosystem

[3]In North America, for instance, the first European explorers were struck by the "natural" parklands of large pine trees relatively far apart with sparse underbrush, seemingly made by God to be perfect deer-hunting grounds; in fact, the native peoples of the area co-created that habitat by periodic controlled burns that left the large trees intact while clearing out the understory and prompting the growth of new shoots; the shoots attracted deer, while the absence of understory made them easy to hunt (see [3]).

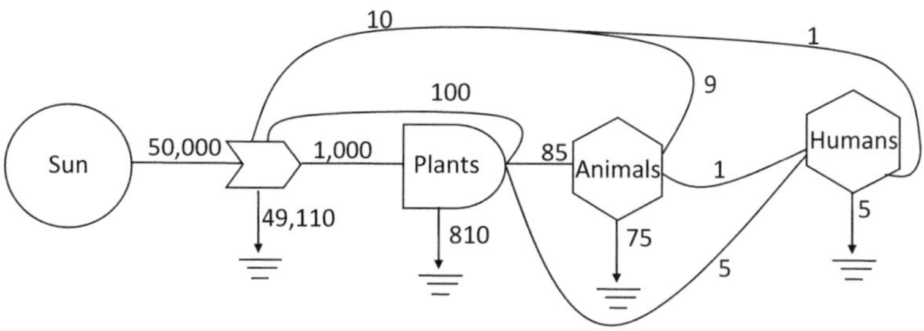

Fig. 2.6 Simplified energy flow in a hunter-gatherer economy

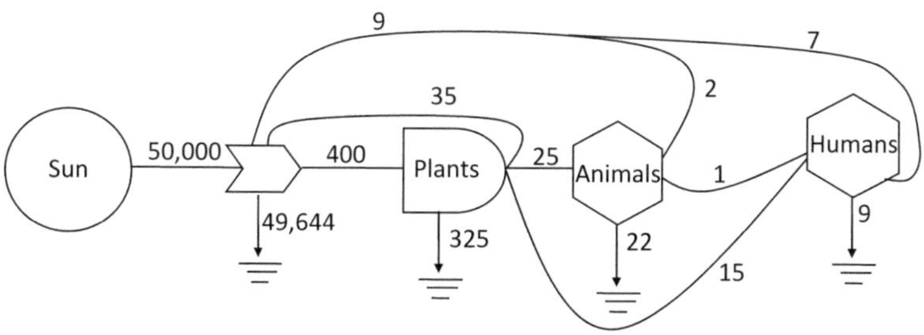

Fig. 2.7 Simplified energy flow in a primitive agricultural system

items. And now that we have humans in our ecosystem, we also have a more emotionally resonant measure of "success," which is how well human activity accomplishes human purposes. In macroeconomics that purpose is routinely equated with economic growth; that's a problematic equivalence, for reasons that will be explored later in the book, but for now it's useful to accept it for what it can help us see about the relationship between economies and ecosystems. We've just seen this basic human economy come into existence, and its growth is limited by the ability of the local ecosystem to provide sustenance. If the economy grows too large, the ecosystem will be damaged and the human population will be forcibly reduced by a simple lack of food.

One response to that is a more thoroughgoing rearrangement of the ecosystem, essentially what we know as agriculture. A comparison of Figs. 2.6 and 2.7 illustrates the transitions from small humans in an ecosystem to primitive agriculture.

The numbers of units of energy flowing through the system are purely illustrative. The somewhat arrow-like shape between the sun ant the plants depicts a "work gate," where one or more flows of energy do no work themselves but control or contribute to the work done by some other flow of energy. In this instance, the work gate represents the photosynthetic process, diagrammed distinct from the plants themselves simply for expositional purposes.

In Fig. 2.6, note first of all that most of the solar energy striking the area is not captured by photosynthesis but lost directly to the heat sink. Of the 1,000 units actually captured, the majority (810) serve the plants' own metabolic needs before going to the heat sink; the other 190 are embodied in plant biomass available for other purposes. Eighty-five of those feed animals, while five feed humans. The other 100 die and decay, and in doing so enhance the growth of other plants, which increases the photosynthetic capture of solar energy; those 100 units are thus depicted flowing back to the work gate as one of the "controlling" flows, and on out into the work gate's heat sink. The humans eat one unit of energy in the form of animal biomass, and the humans and animals take various actions that enhance the photosynthetic process (intentional or unintentional distribution of seeds; grazing by bison that accelerates grass growth; etc.).

Figure 2.7 represents a shift to primitive agriculture. There has been a massive redirection of the ecosystem's energy flows toward humans and thus away from other animals. In concrete terms, other animals have largely been excluded (except those that humans deem useful), and the mixed plant biome of a prairie or forest has been replaced by a relatively small number of crops that are of particular interest to humans. In this instance note that, while far more energy is available to humans than before, far less energy is captured by plants in the first place. This reflects the stylized fact that primitive farming reduces the overall biological productivity of an area, even as it produces more food specifically for humans from a given area (see, e.g., [7]).

Notice also the change in the disposition of human energy. Before agriculture a relatively small portion of our energy contributed to improving the success of the plants on which we depended (that's the 1 that flows back from humans to the work gate between the sun and the plants). In primitive agriculture a much larger share is devoted to operating the farm (in Fig. 2.7 it's the 7 flowing back to the work gate, out of the 16 ingested): getting unwanted plants and animals out and keeping them out is hard work; in addition, those energy flows from plants and animals back to the photosynthetic work gate were useful functions of ecosystem maintenance that were being done for us. As hunter-gatherers, we couldn't extract large quantities of energy from the system, but the jobs of dispersing seeds, maintaining the soil, and controlling infestations were almost entirely done without great effort on our part. When we shifted to agriculture and excluded all the plants and animals we didn't want, we thereby got rid of the species that had been doing all that work for us; with them gone, we had to do it ourselves. This shifting use of human energy reflects another tendency: while agriculture tends to support more people per acre than does a gatherer-hunter society, it also requires that a much greater part of the day be spent in activities directed toward the provision of sustenance (see, e.g., [2]).

Figure 2.8 represents a much later further development of the agricultural system. Fossil fuel is used to manufacture fertilizer and transport it to the farm. And though the energy content of the fertilizer is only 500 units, it allows the photosynthetic capture to increase from the mere 400 of primitive agriculture to 2,000; this new level is much higher than even the 1,000 units of photosynthetic capture in the pre-agricultural ecosystem. The fertilizer is in effect "leveraging" the solar energy: while the actual energy captured by the plants' leaves is from the sun, the plants are able to capture far more than before because of the abundant nutrients the fertilizer makes available.

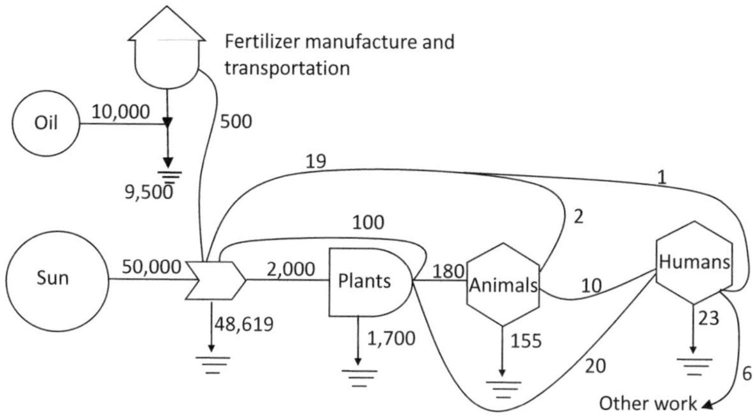

Fig. 2.8 Simplified energy flow in a modern agricultural system

With plants capturing so much solar energy, humans can eat a lot and simultaneously support a very large animal population, using that population in turn as a significant source of food. While it's not shown on the diagram, fossil fuel is also helping with much of the field work, which can now be done with less human energy than before. Significant amounts of human energy can now be devoted to other work, as in modern economies taken as a whole, where a very small minority grows enough food for all, and the great majority of the workforce is engaged in other activities.

When we first introduced humans back in Fig. 2.5, that gave us the rudiments of an economy. Now with three more figures under our belts, we have the material for three rough observations about the relationship between resources and economic activity.

1. Economic activity is bounded by the availability of resources. Human inventiveness may find ways of using those resources more effectively or ways of obtaining more resources, or ways of using things that hadn't previously been thought of as resources. But with a given technology, a bigger economy requires more resources.
2. An important way of obtaining larger flows of energy (or other resources) for human purposes is the rearrangement of ecosystems so that a larger portion of what's there flows toward us. This presumably has good effects for humans, at least in the short run. And as for its impact on other species, it is presumably "good" for those we find useful and "bad" for most others (the population of cows has boomed over the last two centuries, while the bison was almost wiped out), while on balance likely rendering the system less biologically productive than before.
3. Fossil fuels are a game-changer. In addition to leveraging solar resources by enabling larger capture of solar energy, they allow solar resources already in use to be redirected to other purposes. This takes the form of more land growing

food for humans instead of growing food for animals to plough our fields or drive us around, as well as more land being available for non-agricultural purposes, whether that's wilderness or urban development. Finally, fossil fuels are a concentrated energy source, available in quantities that—while supplies last—are determined more by human effort than by the steady but slow influx of solar radiation.

Our introduction to ecosystems has brought us fairly far, but to better understand the role that resources in general play in the economy, as well as the differences between renewable and exhaustibles, the next concept we need is that of gradients.

2.2 Gradients

In a steam engine, there's a pressure difference between the high pressure inside the boiler and the relatively low pressure in the air around the machine. The steam engine is designed to take advantage of this difference by channeling the escaping steam through a piston or a turbine, where it will do some work on its way to the outside.

A piece of steel is different from a lump of iron ore or a random piece of the Earth's crust. The iron has been gathered together and combined with just enough carbon to give the steel its particular properties. The steel is a specific concentration and organization of matter, different from the matter around it.

The pressure in the boiler and the iron and carbon in the steel are both examples of "gradients." For a definition of the idea, you can think of it as "a measurable difference across a distance of temperature (the classic thermodynamic gradient which runs heat engines), pressure, chemical concentration, or other variables" [9, p. 174].

The connection between this idea and economics was developed at length by Nicholas Georgescu-Roegen [8], then taken further by Charles A.S. Hall, Cutler J. Cleveland, and Robert Kaufmann [4], but it can best be understood with some tangible examples.

To start, think of wood available for burning. When the wood burns, it releases useful energy that can be applied to various purposes, such as cooking your food or heating your house. The wood itself represents a gradient, an organized collection of chemical bonds that contain a great deal of potential energy. When you burn it, you turn it to ash, a less ordered state, containing less potential energy. You *reduce* the gradient embodied in the wood.

Think of another specific use for that wood, burning some of it to make charcoal, and in turn burning the charcoal to make steel. In the first step, some of the wood is turned into charcoal, a fuel that will burn hotter than the original wood—it thus embodies a more powerful gradient than does the wood. But in order to create that larger gradient in one part of the system, there had to be an even larger *reduction* of a gradient somewhere else—namely, in the part of the wood that was turned to ash. (This follows from the 2nd Law: the transformation of one part of the wood to ash and another part to charcoal had to involve a net loss of available energy.)

Then the charcoal is used in metalworking. We start with iron ore, which is a gradient of sorts, because the iron atoms are more concentrated in the ore than they are in a random piece of rock, but those atoms of iron are still combined with lots of other elements, and that prevents the iron from being useful. We turn the ore into iron, thereby creating a larger gradient—we've increased the concentration of iron in the ore from 30% or 70% toward something close to 100%. Then we give the iron even more order by getting the carbon ratio just right to improve the metal's qualities. Finally the steel (or sometimes the iron) is turned into the actual useful implements, whether horseshoes or tools. At each step of the way, the order and usefulness of the inputs has been increased—we have created a series of ever-larger gradients. Starting from the process of making charcoal, the continual upgrading of the iron from ore to implement has been made possible by turning a large quantity of wood into ash and waste heat. In other words, one set of indirectly useful gradients (the wood) has been reduced, in order to build up another set of more directly useful gradients (the iron, steel, and implements).

The next question is how the wood got to be a gradient in the first place. It's made up of carbon and hydrogen atoms combined in ways that will release energy when combined with oxygen. The tree took as its working materials water and atmospheric oxygen, and work had to be done to transform those into the more organized form of the tree's matter. If work was done, there had to be some gradient that could power the initial assembly of the tree's carbohydrates. The source of that gradient is, obviously, the sun. Most of the solar radiation landing on the forest was dissipated as waste heat, but some of it was absorbed by the leaves of trees and other green plants. Of the energy that the leaves captured, some was used to power the plants' metabolic processes. A little of it (about 1% of the total that fell on the forest) ended up embodied in the biomass of the forest plants, including the wood of the trees, available for humans to build with or to burn.

The big picture is that a vast gradient—the solar energy landing on the earth—is turned into the much more modest gradient of wood, plus a lot of waste-heat. Then we transform these modest gradients in the wood into the small gradients of warm houses and useful cooked food, and lots of ash and waste heat. The modest gradient in the wood can also become *very* small quantities of the gradient embodied in iron and steel implements, and a very large quantity of ash and waste heat.

Note the constraints that the simple laws of thermodynamics are imposing here. Heating and cooking are hard because gathering wood is hard. Making iron is harder—it takes a lot of work to retrieve ore and crush it, and a *lot* of wood is needed to melt that crushed ore to extract the iron. Making steel is *really* hard: first you have to make iron, then you have to use a lot of wood to make a modest amount of charcoal, and then the iron plus the charcoal gives you a little steel.

Coal is similar to wood in being a thermodynamic gradient (it's made up of hydrocarbons rather than carbohydrates, but it's roughly the same idea of energy stored in bonds of carbon and hydrogen). And it has a similar fate in that you can heat or cook with it. You can also turn lots of coal gradient into a little steel and lots of ash and waste heat.

The present use of coal is different from wood because it's generally more energy-dense and found in large deposits. The energy density means you don't have to gather as much of it to accomplish the same thing as with wood, and that fact there's more energy per pound means that you can carry energy around more easily. The large deposits mean you can find a lot in one place to start with—it comes pre-gathered.

Another significant difference is that it's not the accumulation of a year's sunlight, as with an annual crop, or a few decades' sunlight in the immediate past, as with a tree. A coal bed is a deposit of a small fraction of millions of years of sunlight in the far distant past. The same process that stored the energy in the tree also stored energy in other forms of biomass hundreds of millions of years ago, and rather than decomposing, some of those carbon-hydrogen bonds were buried in anoxic (oxygen-free) environments, preserved from decomposition, and transformed into coal.

This attribute of coal is behind two key differences from wood. First of all, the gradient embodied in a forest is being continually restored by the action of the sun, whereas the gradient embodied in a coal deposit will not be restored on a time scale that is of any use to humans. However, *until* that coal gradient is all reduced, you can use any quantity of it you can get your hands on, rather than being limited by recent solar capture.

- An annual crop allows you to use as much as all of a year's solar energy at once.
- A forest allows you to use several decades' accumulation of solar energy in a big pulse (though then you'll have to wait several decades until a similar pulse is available).
- Coal allows you to use millennia of solar energy at one time, year after year—for a while.

The next big resource to consider is oil. It is similar to coal in being a portion of biomass from tens or hundreds of millions of years ago, but the source of biomass and the path from there to being a fossil fuel are slightly different from coal, resulting in a different outcome. On the positive side, oil is more energy-dense than coal. Also, as a fluid it's easier to get out of the ground and transport.[4]

[4]Strictly speaking, that statement is only true of what's called "conventional oil," that you can get out of the ground with a relatively simple pump. A small but growing fraction of our liquid fuels comes from "unconventional oil" such as tar sands or oil shale, where the oil is thicker and more

It's also easily transformed into liquid fuel for internal combustion engines or flying, and the energy density makes flying feasible.

The one downside of conventional oil, the stuff that's easiest to get out of the ground and easiest to refine, is there's not nearly as much of it as there is of coal. There are much larger quantities of "unconventional" oils found in tar sands, oil shales, deposits of heavy oil, and far underneath deep sea floors, but these are either hard to get to (particularly the deep-sea deposits) or hard to refine, or both.

As suggested with the example of iron, the concept of a gradient can be generalized beyond energy sources to resources more generally. Metal ores come in varying concentrations: hematite and magnetite are around 70% iron (Hematite, Geology.com, http://geology.com/minerals/hematite.shtml. Accessed January 19, 2017; Magnetite, Geology.com, http://geology.com/minerals/magnetite.shtml. Accessed January 19, 2017); taconite is about 25% to 30% iron (Magnetite, Geology.com, http://geology.com/minerals/magnetite.shtml. Accessed January 19, 2017); while the iron concentration in the Earth's crust is about 5% (Lutgens, F. K. & Tarbuck, E. J. (2000). Abundance of elements in the Earth's crust (Chapter 2). In *Essentials of geology* (7th ed.). Prentice Hall. cited in http://hyperphysics.phy-astr.gsu.edu/hbase/Tables/elabund.html. Accessed January 19, 2017). In seawater iron can be found at a concentration of 0.0034 ppm (parts per million), or 0.00000034% [1]. In principle, iron can be derived from any of these sources, as long as you have at your disposal enough energy to do the work of concentrating the resource. Taconite, with its 20% of iron, is referred to as a "low grade" ore because it takes a lot more work to turn it into useful metal than is required with better grades. Extracting iron from average soil is impractical, and concentrating it out of seawater is orders of magnitude less possible. From an iron perspective, a deposit of hematite is a fairly powerful gradient, while taconite is a weaker but still acceptably strong gradient, and seawater represents essentially no gradient at all, the iron being thoroughly mixed in with other things (mostly water, of course). The more concentrated the ore (the more order it has from your perspective of looking for iron), the less energy you need to turn it into something you can use, and so the more useful a resource it is for the economy.

Whole ecosystems can be looked at in this same way. In a healthy, productive ecosystem, diverse species feed each other and perform roles for each other such as concentrating nutrients, propagating plants, and so on. Humans can extract food or lumber or clean water or fiber from such an ecosystem with relatively little work. As the ecosystem is degraded, the challenge of getting resources out becomes larger; you can still extract useful things from it, but you will have to expend more energy, perhaps settling for smaller trees, or ranging over a larger area to gather the same amount of food. A degraded ecosystem has less order or less powerful gradients, and so you have to make up for that by greater expenditure of energy.

---

closely bound to the rock in which it's found, requiring more arduous extraction techniques than just pumping.

In agriculture, soils can be exhausted by careless or overly intensive farming. You can still get a crop, but for the same number of trips over the field planting seeds, fighting weeds, and harvesting, you'll produce less. You can keep the yield up by adding more fertilizer, but again, that's a greater energy input. The healthy agricultural soil is a useful gradient requiring relatively small inputs of work in order to produce a crop, while the degraded agricultural soil is a smaller gradient.

Different kinds of oil can be understood through the same lens. A petroleum product like gasoline can be made from a variety of raw resources, ranging from light sweet crude from Saudi Arabia (flows easily from the ground, has relatively low sulfur content) through Venezuelan crude (more sulfur) to tar sands (much harder to extract and process). But with each step along the scale, the total energy used to get the desired product increases. From the perspective of oil used for human purposes, the light sweet crude is the most powerful gradient, while the tar sands are a relatively weak one (though still powerful enough to be somewhat profitable to extract and burn).

Liquid fuels can even be made from coal—by the end of World War II the German Luftwaffe depended on coal-to-liquids, and South Africa, facing trade sanctions during the later years of Apartheid, invested heavily in the process [5]. But it's a lot more work than making liquid fuels out of petroleum, so it's only been done on a serious scale where war or international sanctions made it impossible to get adequate amounts of petroleum.

Resources of all types differ in how easily they can be turned into something humans want or used to accomplish something humans would like to do.

The scale from more powerful gradients to less powerful can be understood as a measure of "resource quality," as used in Hall, Cleveland and Kaufmann [4].

2.3 Renewable vs. Exhaustible Resources

After the idea of gradients or resource quality, the next important thing to understand about resources is the distinction between renewable and exhaustible. Each of these types has its useful aspect. In some obvious sense renewables are preferable because they are (of course!) renewable. If we're worried about running out of oil, or natural gas, or coal, why not move away from these resources toward things that we can't run out of?

Renewability is an important resources attribute, but for the last 200 years it has usually been outweighed by two characteristics of exhaustible resources. First, renewable resources are infinite over time (if you wait around long enough, you can obtain from them any quantity of energy you could practically desire), but they are strictly limited *at a given time*. (This is explored further in Sect. 2.4

Table 2.1 General characteristics of resources by type

	Over infinite time (stock)	In a finite period (flow)	Degree of concentration
Renewable	Infinite	Limited	Low
Exhaustible	Limited	Expandable in response to human effort[a]	High

[a]As long as the resource's stock limit is sufficiently far away

below.) Exhaustible resources have limits, of course, but as long as those limits are sufficiently far away, the flow of these resources can be continually expanded through human effort.

Second, many of the applications in a modern industrial economy require relatively high concentrations of energy (a lot of heat in one place to smelt metal; a lot of kinetic energy in one place to move cars, trucks, trains, airplanes). Fossil fuels (which are exhaustible) come pre-concentrated, courtesy of pressure and heat applied over millions of years by geological processes, through no effort of ours. Renewable resources, in comparison, tend to be much more diffuse, inherently requiring more work by humans to concentrate them for industrial purposes (Table 2.1).[5]

2.4 Major Types of Renewable Resources

To better understand the economic implications of renewable resources and their application, it's useful to have a little more background on their characteristics. Consider the following list:

- Fish
- Lumber
- Ethanol and biodiesel (liquid fuels made from plants)
- Animal dung (burned as a fuel in many poor countries)
- Working animals (e.g., horse-drawn wagons or ploughs)
- Wind power
- Photovoltaic [PV] cells (materials that convert sunlight directly into electricity)
- Solar hot water
- Passive solar heat
- Hydroelectric power

The items on the list could be divided up in various ways, but the one that matters here is the distinction between biological and non-biological.

[5]Note that if you are carrying out non-industrialized agriculture, the diffuse nature of solar-derived sources is not a problem; you are working with a system that has been shaped by natural selection and by humans to make good use of the solar resource as it is found "in nature."

All renewable resources are driven ultimately by the sun.[6] But the first five items on the list differ from the others in being dependent on photosynthesis and on ecosystems. In that subset, the way that the solar energy is initially captured is by green plants absorbing it and using it to manufacture sugars. From there the energy can be turned into ethanol. Or the plant can use the energy to manufacture oil which humans then turn into biodiesel. Or the plant can use the energy to assemble the more complicated molecules that make up wood (both a store of energy and a useful material). Or the plant is eaten by animals, thus supporting a marine food chain leading ultimately to fish we eat. Or the plant is eaten by animals, and some of the energy shows up in the dung, while another part of the energy is available in the animals' ability to do work.

And in order for the plants to be abundant and able to do their photosynthetic work, there have to be ecosystems that are at least somewhat functioning. The ecosystems are also necessary to support those parts of biological energy systems that are made up of animals.

The lower part of the list, starting with wind power, is a different kettle of fish, if you will. These are all just as dependent on the sun as the biological systems, but they are generally *in*dependent of ecosystems and the presence any given species, or of any species at all. Sun strikes a PV array, and electricity is produced. Sun heats different parts of the Earth differently, and air moves around in response, creating winds that can drive windmills. Sun evaporates water which then falls as snow and rain in the mountains, creating flows of water that can drive water wheels and hydroelectric turbines. Capturing energy from these processes depends only on the devices we have built to take advantage of them and is independent of the health of the ecosystems in which they happen.

Note that, despite this distinction between biological and non-biological, both types are generally characterized by having potentially infinite stocks over time, flows that are naturally slow and expensive to speed up, and concentrations that are low.

This distinction between biological and non-biological renewable resources influences the ways we are likely to use them. The disadvantage of the biological type is that we are prone to overharvesting them or damaging the ecosystems on which they depend. At a minimum, that means that greater use now (including greater carelessness in how we treat ecosystems) means less use at some later time, even if the total flow over infinite time is still infinite. If we fish an area too hard or farm a piece of ground too intensively, at some point we must back off and allow the resource to recover, as it is likely to do if we give it a chance. If we *don't* back off, we run into the more extreme consequence of actually turning a renewable resources into, in effect an exhaustible one: driving a species extinct, or doing so much damage to a piece of soil that it doesn't come back within a time frame that is meaningful for humans.

[6] The validity of this statement depends on whether you count geothermal energy in the category of renewables. If you do, then it is an exception to the statement.

Non-biological renewable resources don't suffer from this limitation. No matter how much sunlight and wind and water we harness in a given year, the sun will shine just as brightly next year, and it will drive about the same amount of wind and lift about the same amount of water. The non-biological resources can be thought of as "robust" compared to the biological ones that we are all too capable of damaging.[7]

However, the biological resources have one big advantage over the non-biological ones: they tend to be easier (i.e., cheaper) to get hold of. In the extreme, people walking past nut trees or a berry patch can harvest some solar energy with nothing more than their own hands. Hunter-gatherers and pre-industrial agriculturalists use tools that, while sometimes very elegant and sophisticated and perhaps requiring substantial human time to make, do not require a lot of material input. And once the fish is caught or the tree is cut, there isn't a lot of additional processing required. Ecosystems have already done the work of turning solar energy into something close to what we actually want.[8]

In contrast, all non-biological resources require some kind of machinery, some kind of capital, if they are to be harnessed. Water power requires at minimum a water wheel, quite possibly a diversion channel, usually a dam; wind power requires a windmill or wind turbine, etc. So we have a contrast between relatively indestructible non-biological resources that require significant capital up front, and biological resources where harvests today can impair harvests tomorrow, but the capital costs tend to be lower.

Another kind of renewable resource is the biosphere's capacity to absorb the wastes we dump into it. This may not feel like an input, the way wood is an input to a house or petroleum is an input to flying. In fact, it's related to an output, rather than an input, though that output is unintentional. Even so, the similarity to an input is there.

You can't make a house without using some sort of material, like wood or stone or adobe. You can't fly a plane without using petroleum. And you can't burn coal without using up some of the biosphere's ability to absorb the soot and CO_2. So we can think of that absorptive capacity as an input. The biggest difference is in how its limits make themselves known to us.

[7]Another exception: Some hydropower systems, such as in the Pacific Northwest of the U.S., have been built in places where the twentieth-century weather pattern included large winter snowpacks. These acted as natural reservoirs, releasing the winter precipitation throughout the spring melt into June or July. In the warmer twenty-first century, the snowpacks are smaller and they melt sooner. To get the same level of summer electricity production as in the twentieth century, we're going to need larger human-made reservoirs than before. Droughts related to climate change make the problem worse.

[8]The same can be said of agroecosystems, the ecosystems created by humans in our farming endeavors.

When we catch the last fish, we can't catch any more. When we pull the last chunk of coal out of a mine, we can't mine coal there anymore.[9] But when we overload the environment's absorptive capacity, we can keep going. The fact that the environment can't absorb any more waste doesn't mean that we're physically incapable of dumping any more. The only way to *force* us to stop dumping is to stop *us*.[10]

Nature imposes limits on our harvest of fish by killing the fish. She imposes limits on our dumping of waste by killing us.

2.5 The Rational Use of Exhaustible Resources

With a renewable resource, "sustainability" is easy to define: the amount that can be used year after year, without impairing the ability to use the same amount the year after. But if we start thinking in similar terms about nonrenewable resources, we run into a particular kind of economic puzzle.

In one sense, there is no "sustainable" level of exhaustible resource use, because such resources are, well, exhaustible. Any level of use, continued for long enough, will result in the resource being used up, and if the economy has come to depend on that resource, you've got a big problem. On the other hand, for the reasons discussed above, these are incredibly useful resources, so it hardly seems to make sense to simply ignore them.

A standard tool for understanding how a non-renewable resource *should* be priced and extracted is what's known as the Hotelling Rule. We'll get into that in Chap. 19 when we look at the question of limitations on fossil-fuel extraction, along with two other approaches, known as the Hartwick Rule and the Hubbert Curve.

For now, as will be discussed in more detail in Chap. 4, we'll treat nonrenewable resources as being a normal sort of good: there's a demand curve based on people's uses for them, and there's a supply curve based on the state of technology and capital, interacting with the geology of the resource. Rather than trying to figure out what people *should* do with the resource, we'll assume that people use them as they can get their hands on them and pay for them.

---

[9]In reality, there's almost always *some* coal left, stuff that it's simply not practical to get out. And the definition of "practical" shifts with our technology and our desperation. But with that caveat we can modify the sentence to say, "when we pull the last chunk of practically mineable coal."

[10]This is discussed further in Sect. 19.3.

2.6 Technology and Resource Use

Unlike resources, which are generally neglected in macroeconomic models, technology is widely acknowledged to play a key role. Given that resources actually are important, it's worth considering what technology is and how it relates to resource use.

A very general definition could be that:

Technological improvement allows humans to do more of whatever we consider useful, given the inputs available.

This is normally understood in a particular way, as meaning that technological progress allows us to get more output from a given quantity of inputs, and there certainly are innovations that have that effect.

- A more efficient car engine delivers the same amount of power to the wheels while using less gasoline.
- When locomotives switched from steam power to diesel engines, a lot more of the fuel's chemical energy was turned into useful motion, and less into waste heat.
- When you replace incandescent light bulbs with fluorescent lights, a lot more of the electricity you use gets turned into light and a lot less gets turned into heat.
- Decades ago a coal-fired power plant was about 20–30% efficient (that much of the coal's energy was turned into electricity, while the rest became waste heat); the newest ones approach 50% efficiency.

Other innovations, however, aren't about doing more with less, but about doing more by figuring out ways to do *more*. As a paradigmatic example, think of the change from carriages and carts drawn by horses and oxen to trains pulled by steam locomotives.

With animal traction, a driver or two with a team of perhaps four horses could move at most several tons of freight or maybe as many as 10 passengers, for a distance of 20, or perhaps 30 miles in a day. By the time the steam locomotive was well developed in the second half of the nineteenth century, a train crew of five or six men could move hundreds of tons of freight or hundreds of people, in greater comfort, over a distance of hundreds of miles in a day. Even if you figure in all the other people who work for the railroad—the crews maintaining the tracks and rolling stock, the ticket agents, the station masters, the switch operators—the amount of transportation provided, divided by the number of workers, far outpaced the productivity of the teamster with his horses.

You can even figure in the increased capital. Say your horse-drawn wagons provided 10 units of transportation using 2 units of labor and 1 unit of capital, and the railroad provides 10,000 units of transportation, using 50 units of labor and

100 units of capital. Your output went up by 1,000 times, while your (labor times capital) only went up by a factor of 500. There's been an increase in your "total factor productivity" (TFP), the amount of output you get given *all* your inputs.

The traditional way of viewing this kind of change is that it is a combination of innovation and investment. People invented steam engines, converted the output to rotary motion, and attached that to a vehicle. Wheel profiles were improved for safer, faster operation. Higher quality steel allowed better rails and more powerful locomotives. And then there was the massive investment of building all those tracks and engines and cars.

And all of that is true, but it's leaving out something big, because the locomotive doesn't run on ingenuity. The horses that preceded the train could only move because they had ingested food that contained energy that plants had captured from sunlight. The locomotive, pulling far more weight at much higher speeds, needs correspondingly a much larger quantity of energy than does a team of horses. And regardless of whether that energy comes from wood or from coal, one of the things the steam locomotive did was allow the average transportation worker to control a much larger flow of energy. Where the teamster controlled the modest energy of a team of four horses, the railroad engineer and his crew of four or five were controlling hundreds of horsepower. Viewed that way, it's no surprise that they got a lot more done.

Innovation is tied to resources in other ways. The internal combustion engine (ICE) was truly a breakthrough: compared to a steam engine it has a higher ratio of power to weight, which allows for more powerful and more flexible sources of traction. But it required a liquid fuel with relatively high energy density.[11] Airplanes are a similar innovation, requiring the internal combustion engine itself, combined with improved understanding of aerodynamics. But again, without an energy-dense liquid fuel, all the aerodynamics in the world wouldn't have brought us heavier-than-air flight.

It's worth pointing out one last broad characteristic of innovation: just as technology in general is often about finding a way for humans to control a greater flow of resources, many innovations involve ways of replacing renewable resource inputs with fossil or other nonrenewable inputs. The shift from horse-drawn carriage to coal-driven train was not just a massive increase in energy flow, it was also the replacement of a renewable resource by an exhaustible one. The same goes for metal and plastic replacing wood in a broad range of uses, from toys to construction materials. And also the way that petroleum fuels crowded out ethanol for the internal combustion engine. Even the replacement of metal with plastic is a related phenomenon: of course iron ore is an exhaustible resource, as is the coal burned to turn the ore into a useful product. But as long as oil is cheap enough, the plastic replacements are a useful innovation.

[11] Ethanol—a form of alcohol derived from plants—was widely used early in the history of the automobile. For various reasons, it was displaced by gasoline, derived from petroleum, a fossil fuel.

In this context it is worth reemphasizing three attributes of fossil fuels relative to the biological resources they have significantly replaced. First, they are energy-dense: a given weight of fossil fuel holds a relatively large amount of energy. This makes them more practical for transporting over long distances, since not as much energy needs to be devoted to moving a given amount of energy. In a related vein, it gives them an advantage as transportation fuels: a vehicle will usually need to bring along its energy source, so the lighter the energy source, the better.[12] Second, they are typically found in large deposits, which means that a useful quantity can be obtained in one place, rather than having to range over large distances to gather the amounts needed for industrial or transportation purposes. Third, because they are stored solar energy from the distant past, not dependent on recent inflows of solar energy, they can be applied at any scale that humans desire, so long as we build the machinery to extract and utilize them—and as long as supplies last.

If innovation and investment are often about obtaining and applying an increased flow of resources—energy in particular—then fossil fuels are the natural handmaiden of innovation and investment. The potential for abundant supplies is a strong incentive to take the steps needed to make those supplies actually available. As we encounter difficulties increasing our extraction of these inputs, it will be interesting to see whether some new class of substances can be found with comparable or preferable attributes or, if not, how human innovation will respond to a situation of decreased resource availability.

Problems

Problem 2.1 Why is energy's role in the economy different from the role of other resources?

Problem 2.2 How has the human relationship to ecosystems changed since prehistoric times?

Problem 2.3 Which system is more efficient: hunter-gatherer societies, or primitive agriculture? Which system is more effective?

Problem 2.4 How do biological and non-biological renewable resources differ?

Problem 2.5 What limits are there on our ability to increase our use of renewable resources?

Problem 2.6 What are two economic advantages of fossil fuels over renewables?

[12]The obvious exception is electric trains, trolleys, and trolleybuses, which don't carry their energy source but pick it up along the way from wires or electrified rails. But note that these are currently the only widespread applications of electric vehicles—the on-board delivery systems for electricity are so heavy as to make them weak competitors so far for fossil fuels.

Problem 2.7 What is an economic disadvantage of fossil fuels compared to renewables?

Problem 2.8 Does innovation allow us to use resources, or replace resources?

Problem 2.9 Can you think of an innovation not mentioned in the text that entails increased resource use?

Problem 2.10 Can you think of an innovation not mentioned in the text that entails increased efficiency of resource use?

Problem 2.11 Footnote 12 mentions electric trains, trolleys, and buses. What physical traits of these technologies make it economically challenging to spread them much beyond their current extent?

References

1. Anthoni, J. F. (2006). The chemical composition of seawater. Online; Accessed July 18, 2014; table cited is from Turekian, K. K. (1968). *Oceans*. Prentice-Hall.
2. Boserup, E. (1981). *Population and technological change: A study of long-term trends*. Chicago: University of Chicago Press.
3. Cronon, W. (1983). *Changes in the land: Indians, colonists, and the ecology of New England*. New York: Hill and Wang.
4. Hall, C. A. S., Cleveland, C. J., & Kaufman, R. (1986). *Energy and resource quality: The ecology of the economic process*. New York: Wiley.
5. National Energy Technology Laboratory. (2011). Fischer-Tropsch fuels. Online; Accessed July 18, 2014.
6. Odum, H. T. (1970). *Environment, power, and society*. New York: Wiley.
7. Redman, C. L. (1999). *Human impact on ancient environments*. Tucson: University of Arizona Press.
8. Roegen, N. G. (1971). *The entropy law and the economic process*. Cambridge: Harvard University Press.
9. Sagan, D., & Whiteside, J. H. (2004). Gradient-reduction theory: Thermodynamics and the purpose of life. In S. H. Schneider, J. R. Miller, E. Crist, & P. J. Boston (Eds.), *Scientists debate Gaia: The next century* (pp. 173–186, chapter 15). Cambridge: MIT Press. http://www.ldeo.columbia.edu/~polsen/nbcp/sagan_whiteside_05_sm.pdf.

Chapter 3
Key Variables

Abstract This chapter introduces the key conventional terms for measuring and describing the macroeconomy: GDP, inflation, unemployment, interest rates, the balance of payments, and the exchange rate. Unusually for a macroeconomics text, it also looks at measures of resource use. Distinctions are repeatedly made between real and nominal values of different variables. The concept of the GDP is linked back to the reduction of gradients described in Chap. 2.

3.1 GDP

The gross domestic product, or GDP, is the most frequently used yardstick for how "the economy" is doing. Economists look at both the total GDP and the GDP per capita, or per person, which is simply the GDP divided by the population. A country with a high GDP per capita is considered better off than one with a low GDP per capita, and a country with a rapidly growing GDP is considered better off than one with a GDP that is growing only slowly or even declining.

GDP is the measure of all **final** goods and services produced in the economy in a given period of time, usually a year or a quarter. In simplest terms, that amounts to adding up the value of everything sold to final users. These "final uses" are broken into four broad categories:

1. Consumption—stuff that households buy for themselves, like cars, food, heating oil, medical care, rent, etc.
2. Investment (technically, "Gross domestic private investment")—businesses building new capital (factories, machinery, office buildings); construction firms building new houses; additions to inventory.
3. Net exports—the amount of stuff we make here and sell to foreign consumers, businesses and governments, minus the amount of stuff made elsewhere and sold to U.S. consumers, firms, and governments (all levels: Federal, state, and local).
4. Government (technically, "Government consumption expenditures and gross investment")—the key with this category is to exclude transfers such as food

K. Seeley, *Macroeconomics in Ecological Context*, Studies in Ecological Economics 5, DOI 10.1007/978-3-319-51757-5_3

stamps and Social Security (see below about double counting). Government consumption expenditures are things like money spent on police, courts, regulatory agencies, military salaries, and legislatures. Government investment is money spent on things like military hardware and roads and other infrastructure.

3.1.1 Don't Double-Count

If the goal is to get an accurate picture of how much economic production there is, we obviously don't want to count the same thing twice, or treat the same production process differently if its ownership structure happens to change.

As an example of the first problem, consider the case of rubber sold to a tire-manufacturer, who sells the finished tires to a car company, which then puts the tires on a car it sells to you. The price you pay for the car must be enough to compensate the car company for the tires (and everything else in the car); the amount the car company paid the tire-maker must be enough to compensate the tire company for the rubber (and everything else that went into the tires); and the money paid by the tire-maker must be enough to compensate the producer of the rubber for everything involved in providing that product. So if we were to add up the cost of the rubber and the cost of the tires, in addition to what you paid for the car, we would be counting the tires twice and the rubber three times. The rubber and the tires are **intermediate goods**; they certainly matter, but their value gets included in the GDP via the final goods they end up in.

As for changes in ownership structure, consider these three independent companies (rubber producer, tire maker, car company) being combined into one vertically integrated firm. Whereas before we saw each step from rubber to auto showroom as an independent transaction, now all we see is the finished car. So if we'd been counting each transaction, this merger would make our measure of economic output go down without any change in what was actually being produced.

The exclusion of transfer payments (like food stamps and Social Security) from the category of "Government" also has to do with avoiding double-counting. When the government buys cement to build a road, that's an expenditure on a final good. When it sends your grandmother a Social Security check, she turns around and spends that money on final goods and services. If the Social Security check were counted as part of government expenditure, the money would have been counted twice.

3.1.2 GDP, Value Added, and Resources

Look at that car-manufacturing process another way. When sand is turned into glass, it is made more valuable. When the glass is installed in the car, it is again made more valuable. Each of those steps also involves the reduction of some gradient:

the use of some energy plus—usually—the creation of waste in connection with the improvement of some material (think of the improvement of iron ore into steel, leaving behind slag and coal ash). The same is true for every step in the manufacture of the car, and for every step of every economic process.

The GDP is measuring the sum of all value added across the economy, and since it is impossible to add value without reducing a gradient (i.e., using resources of some sort), the GDP must in a rough way be linked to resource use, though the relationship is not fixed over time, nor even identical at a given time across all activities or across all economies.

3.1.3 What GDP Isn't

It is common but incorrect to treat GDP as an indicator of how well-off a society is overall. It's true that there is a broad correlation between higher GDP per capita on the one hand and more favorable levels of many of the things that shape people's quality of life on the other. If you compare any rich country such as the U.S., Canada, Japan, or countries in western Europe, with a middle-income country like Mexico or a poor country like Pakistan, you find that, as you climb the GDP ladder, a country's citizens have, on average, better health, longer lives, more education, more leisure, more stuff, and a smaller portion of the population living in abject poverty.

But among countries with broadly similar income levels, the correlation between GDP per capita and other measures of well-being is practically non-existent. The U.S. has higher GDP per capita than most countries in western Europe, yet we typically have shorter life expectancy, higher rates of disease, more violent crime, and less leisure. Our relatively unfavorable health outcomes aren't for lack of trying, as we spend more per capita on health care than other rich nations. Nor is our relatively high crime rate for lack of trying, as we spend more on police and prisons.

There are even exceptions to the correlation between the quality of life and the broad groups of "rich," "middle income," and "poor". The state of Kerala in India has a per capita GDP that is lower than the average for India as a whole, and India's level in 2012 was less than 1/12th of the U.S.'s (that's by a measure that accounts for differences in prices of basic goods between the two countries [4]; if you just convert India's GDP at the official exchange rate, the difference is even larger). Yet if you only examined its literacy rate, life expectancy, and health, you would guess that Kerala had practically a First-World economy (see [11]).

GDP *is* a measure of how *the economy* is doing—as opposed to the society as a whole—but even for this it's a less-than-perfect measure. In the first years of the twenty-first century, the U.S. GDP grew at a relatively fast rate, producing more stuff each year than the year before, suggesting that the economy was doing great. At the same time, wages were stagnating and many households were only keeping up by taking on unmanageable levels of debt, suggesting that the economy wasn't working all that well. The financial crisis that started in 2007 was partly a result of those tensions.

In the end, there's only so much that a single number can tell you. GDP measures economic activity, and it does it pretty well. It's also an indicator—though only one among several—of how *the economy* is doing overall. And it is routinely misused as an indicator of how *the society* is doing overall, a role for which it is only weakly suited.[1]

3.2 Resource Use

For all its problems, GDP does sum an important aspect of the economy in a single number. To include resource-use in our understanding of the macroeconomy, it would be helpful to have a similar number with relation to resources. Unfortunately, no such number exists, though two useful overall numbers are aggregate energy use and ecological footprints.

3.2.1 Aggregate Energy Use

As explained in Sect. 2.1, energy is the keystone of all the economy's resources. Various public and private entities track various aspects of energy use in individual countries, in regions, and around the world.

In the U.S. the main governmental source is the Energy Information Administration, part of the Department of Energy. It focuses on U.S. data but has global data as well. The Organization for Economic Cooperation and Development (a group of 34 countries, roughly the world's wealthy democracies) runs the International Energy Agency, which keeps detailed data for all the member states as well as information on most other countries in the world. On the private side, the energy company British Petroleum publishes its annual *Energy outlook*, with coverage of energy use for many individual countries as well as a global picture. They also provide an annual time series of petroleum prices going back to 1869.

In all of these data sources, there are issues of how to add up different forms of energy. Oil is measured either in barrels or in tonnes (a metric ton, or 1,000 kg). Coal is often measured in tonnes or tons (U.S. tons, or 2,000 pounds, about 9% less than a tonne), but a tonne of coal doesn't contain as much energy as a tonne of oil—and even within coal there are different grades, with different energy densities (energy per tonne). Natural gas is measured in Btu's (British thermal units) or in a volume, such as cubic feet (or trillion cubic feet). In principal, those problems can be gotten around by converting everything into some common unit like Btu's, joules (a metric unit of energy, analogous to Btu's) or tonnes of oil equivalent (TOE). But electricity presents other problems.

[1]For a more thorough discussion of the GDP's weaknesses, see [2].

In many countries a large portion of the energy comes from some combination of coal, natural gas, and oil, so if we've already measured the use of those fossil fuels we shouldn't also count the electricity produced from burning them. But some electricity comes from nuclear power (in France, fission power accounts for 75% of all electricity produced, and over 40% of energy overall [5, 6]). In other countries, hydropower is a significant source, and though wind and solar are still relatively small in the U.S., they're increasingly important and are already significant in some countries.

Electricity has an energy content, so we could count the kilowatt hours (kWh) produced from non-fossil sources, convert that to Btu's, and add it to our fossil-fuel number. But that might undercount the importance of the electricity, because if we get 100 Btu's of electricity from wind, we would have had to burn 200 or 250 Btu's of coal to produce it in a coal-fired power plant, because coal-fired plants are generally 50% efficient or less. So should we count the electricity at its energy content, or at the quantity of fossil fuel that, on average, we would have burned to produce it?

A further issue involves the "quality" of different energy sources. Petroleum's liquidity and density makes it more useful than coal, and electricity's ease of transport and essential role in electronics and communications gives it a value that in some way exceeds its energy content, and calculations of total energy use can be adjusted to account for those differences, as in [1]. In using such conversions, you have to balance the gain in how well the data reflect the reality you're trying to describe, against an unavoidable element of arbitrariness in the size of the conversion factor you use.

In addition to electricity, you have to add in biofuels (wood, whether burned in houses or in electric power plants and factories; ethanol made from crops like corn or sugar cane; biodiesel from palm, soy, canola, or other plant source of oil), geothermal, and other small sources.

3.2.2 Ecological Footprints

Energy data provide a very important measure of resource use, because every economic activity involves some energy, and even the extraction of other resources, from lumber to iron ore, requires applying energy. Nonetheless, looking at energy alone gives an incomplete picture of the use of resources overall.

Ecological footprints are in some ways a more comprehensive measure. They count the land used for growing food and animal products, including crop land, orchards, and pasture. They count acreage used to provide lumber, paper inputs, or firewood. They count water areas being harvested for fish. They count acreage occupied by buildings and roads—the built environment that we create around ourselves. And they count fossil fuel use, but in an indirect way.[2]

[2]For an early description of the methodology, see [12]; more current info and country estimates are at [8].

All the other units discussed are directly in acres (or hectares, to use the metric version), but fossil-fuel use is trickier to convert to those units. If you're operating an oil well or an underground coal mine, the surface area disturbed by your extraction operation is relatively small compared to the amount of energy you're providing to the economy. Yet the environmental impact of *using* that energy is far-reaching (see Sect. 19.3).

Footprint analysis has a way around this. If you know how much of a given fossil fuel was burned, you know how much CO_2 was emitted, and that can be converted into an area of land that would have to be devoted to growing new plants in order to absorb that quantity of CO_2. That area of plants is then the footprint of your fossil-fuel use.

This is clever but it's also a problematic solution. First, when you use an acre of land to grow crops or build houses, you're actually using that acre. If you're currently using half the world's potential cropland, you can't do more than double your crop acreage. In contrast, when you emit a ton of carbon, nothing compels you to set aside the corresponding acreage to absorb it. And we *don't* set that acreage aside. So by this methodology it's possible for the global economy to use an acreage that accounts for one-and-a-half Earths, as the Footprint Network found in 2014 [10, p. 32]. Second, it's not clear that it's the right conversion. We want to know the effect we're having on the Earth; the acreage needed in order to have *no* impact is not necessarily the same as the damage done by the impact we *are* having. That said, it's hard to know what the right conversion methodology would be. In the absence of a better approach, the one used by the Footprint Network is reasonable; people using the data simply need to remember how they are produced.

A last point about ecological footprints is the way that they're related to countries. If industries in China use 2.73 trillion tonnes of oil equivalent, all of that energy use is counted as China's in energy-use data. But much of that energy is used to produce steel which will be exported to make cars and buildings in other countries, and another part of the energy is burned to make consumer goods that will be exported to other countries. That energy use, in some sense, is part of the footprint of the country that buys the consumer goods and uses the steel. Ecological Footprint reports follow that logic: if China emits 10.3 billion tons of CO_2, only some of that is counted as part of China's footprint, while the rest is divvied up among the countries that bought China's exports. There's a case to be made for the "country of emission" approach used in energy data, and also for the "country of final use" approach in the footprints data. Either one is reasonable, as long as the person using the data understands what is behind the numbers.

3.3 Inflation

Where microeconomics concerns itself with changes in *relative* prices (Did gasoline get more expensive relative to orange juice, or shoes, or rent?), macroeconomics looks at the overall price level: does it take more dollars to buy stuff in general than it did last month, or last year? The method for answering those questions is to construct a price index, then use it to convert nominal prices to real prices and to measure the rate of inflation.

3.3.1 Price Indexes

The government tracks prices in various ways, but the two most important for our purposes are the consumer price index (CPI) and the implicit GDP deflator.

The CPI is the most commonly cited measure of inflation. It is based on a basket of goods representing what a statistically average consumer spends. As the prices of the various goods in the basket change, the CPI tells you how much more or less money you would need to spend to keep buying that same basket of goods.

One way to think about the implicit GDP deflator is that it turns the methodology of the CPI around. The CPI defines a basket of goods, then keeps that fixed as prices change. The implicit GDP deflator looks at what was actually produced in each year (rather than measuring a predetermined basket), but then applies a fixed set of prices. The appendix provides examples of how to construct both measures.

While the construction and use of these two inflation measures is arithmetically straightforward, there are three important cautions against their mindless use: the substitution effect; the fact that most people aren't statistically average (some people are quite radically different from average, in important ways); and the problem of new products and quality changes.

Substitution For the purposes of the price index, the basket of goods that you're tracking has to stay the same, but as prices change, people's actual behavior will change along with them. Even if you were "average" in the year the basket was defined, meaning that you bought those goods in the proportions specified, when the prices changed you would substitute away from things that had gotten more expensive (you'd buy less of them) and towards things that had gotten cheaper. This flexibility means that the price index overstates the impact of inflation on an average person.

The implicit GDP deflator is actually not affected by this problem; it measures what's actually produced in a given year, and so it takes account of whatever substitutions are actually occurring in people's behavior.

Being far from average Let's say the "average" person likes movies and candy about the same. If you like movies a lot and don't much care for candy, your basket will look significantly different from the one the statisticians at the Bureau of Labor statistics are tracking. So if movies were to go up in price while candy got cheaper, you'd be hurt a lot by price changes—more than the change in the price index would suggest.

On the other hand, if you really like candy and never go to the movies, you're actually experiencing deflation, as the cost of the basket you buy has gone down. In this case, the price index overstates the impact of inflation.

In the real world, the elderly are a classic example of a group for whom the CPI probably understates the impact of inflation. The elderly spend a relatively large portion of their income on health care, the prices of which are going up faster than other things. If the average person spends 10% of income on health care, but you spend 25%, then large increases in health-care costs leave you worse off than the inflation index suggests.

New goods and quality changes Looking first at the CPI, there are obviously important items in the average consumer's "basket" in 2012 that didn't exist in 1982: cell phones, personal computers, broadband access fees, etc. The longer you keep the statistical "basket" around, the less well it reflects what people are actually buying. You can continue tracking the changing prices of bread, shirts, and apartments that you put in your basket in, say, 1984, but the absence of things like consumer electronics makes the result less useful.

In contrast to the CPI, new products make it hard to even calculate the real GDP. We know how many cell phones and cell-phone packages were bought in 2013, and we know their 2013 prices, so we can get the nominal GDP without a problem. But the products didn't exist in 1993, so if you're using 1993 as your "base" year, there is no base-year price by which to measure the real GDP.

A related issue is changes in quality. TVs existed in 1993, but the "average" TV today is arguably of better quality than the average one made 20 years ago. If the price has gone from $200 to $250, but the quality is 30% better, has the price *really* gone up? And how do you measure "30% better"?

Other goods may actually have gone *down* in quality. Ground beef today is almost exclusively from cows raised in feedlots rather than on pasture, and slaughtered in large, highly mechanized packing plants. This results in meat with lower quantities of important nutrients like omega-3 fatty acids, higher quantities of hormones and antibiotics used on feedlot cattle, and a higher risk of *E. coli* contamination. It's just as hard to quantify this reduced quality as it is to put a number on the increased quality of consumer electronics.

The best answer to both issues (i.e., new products and quality changes) is "**chaining**." Rather than keeping one basket or one set of prices fixed for several years, use only pairs of adjacent years, then string them together to get a longer series. This limits the distortions from new goods and quality changes, as well as from substitutions (though it still can't address the problem of being far from average). When you apply chaining, you end up with **chained CPI**, or calculations of real GDP in **chained dollars** of 2009, or whatever year you're using as your base year.

3.3.2 Applying a Price Index

Once you have a price index, you can use it to convert nominal prices or GDP levels to real (inflation-adjusted) prices or GDP levels. Changes in real values are more meaningful guides to economic conditions than are changes in nominal values.

The table below shows the nominal price for gasoline in January 2001 and again in January 2011. It also provides the corresponding values for a price index, and then the real price.

To get the real price, you divide the nominal price by the same year's value of the price index, then multiply by 100. So the Year 1 real price is calculated as

Real price = $1.56 / 175.1 × 100 = $0.891.

Using just the nominal prices, you would say that gasoline had gotten 101% more expensive (slightly more than doubling):

$$\begin{aligned}\%\text{ change in price} &= (\text{New price})/(\text{Old price}) - 1\\ &= \$3.14/\$1.56 - 1\\ &= 2.013 - 1\\ &= 1.013\\ &= 101.3\%.\end{aligned}$$

But applying the same formula to the price level tells the amount of inflation over that same time, which was 25.7%.

Applying the formula again, this time to the real prices, we can see that the increase in real price was only 60.1%.

A large piece the increase in gasoline prices was real—gas got more expensive faster than things did in general—but the other part was related to a general increase in prices.

The real prices are in terms of whatever the base year is for the price index you're using. In the example here, the CPI is indexed to the period 1982–1984, so the prices that you calculate using it are in terms of dollars from that period. The price of gasoline in January 2011, in terms of dollars with the purchasing power of dollars in the early 1980s, was $1.427.

3.3.3 *Calculating Inflation*

As implied in Sect. 3.3.2 above, the amount of inflation between any two periods is simply the percent change in the CPI over that span. As an example, use the CPI values from Table 3.1:

Table 3.1 Converting nominal prices to real

Period	Nominal price	CPI 1982–1984 = 100	Real price in $ of 1982–1984
Jan. 2001	1.56	175.1	0.891
Jan. 2011	3.14	220.1	1.427
Change in %	101.3%	25.7%	60.1%

$$\begin{aligned}\text{Amount of inflation} &= (\text{Later CPI value})/(\text{Earlier CPI value}) - 1\\ &= 220.1/175.1 - 1\\ &= 1.257 - 1\\ &= 0.257\\ &= 25.7\%.\end{aligned}$$

To get the annual *rate* of inflation over a period, you have to do a slightly more complicated calculation. The question you're answering is, At what rate would something have to grow, for as long as it grew, to achieve the total growth that was observed?

If a quantity grows at $100x\%$ per period, for t time periods, the ratio of the new quantity to the original one will be:

$$(1+x)^t.$$

If we observe the new quantity, y_{new}, and the old quantity, y_{old}, then we can define the percentage rate we're looking for with the equation:

$$(1+x)^t = \frac{y_{\text{new}}}{y_{\text{old}}}.$$

We can get rid of the t exponent on the left by raising both sides to the $1/t$:

$$1+x = \left(\frac{y_{\text{new}}}{y_{\text{old}}}\right)^{1/t}.$$

Now we subtract 1 from both sides, and we have the periodic percentage rate of growth over the span:

$$x = \left(\frac{y_{\text{new}}}{y_{\text{old}}}\right)^{1/t} - 1.$$

Applying it to the CPI numbers from Table 3.1 above:

$$\begin{aligned}\text{Average inflation rate} &= (220.1/175.1)^{1/10} - 1\\ &= 1.257^{1/10} - 1\\ &= 1.0231 - 1\\ &= 0.0231\\ &= 2.31\%. \qquad (3.1)\end{aligned}$$

If prices had grown at 2.31% every year from January 2001 to January 2011, the cumulative effect would have been the 25.7% total increase that was actually observed.

3.4 Unemployment

In principle, the unemployment rate is quite a simple concept. You define the labor force: all those people who *could* be working, whether or not they actually are. Then you define the unemployed: those members of the labor force who *aren't* working. Once you have those pieces, the unemployment rate is then:

$$u = U/L,$$

where u is the unemployment rate, in percent, U is the number of unemployed, and L is the number of people in the labor force.

The labor force can be defined in terms of the unemployed (U) and the employed (call them E), so we have

$$L = E + U$$

and

$$u = \frac{U}{E + U}$$

Simply as a matter of algebra, the following are true:

- When U grows, the unemployment rate increases.
- When E grows, the unemployment rate decreases.
- When U and L increase by the same amount, that will raise the unemployment rate; conversely, anything that lowers U and L by the same amount will reduce the unemployment rate.

The trick comes with defining U and L more precisely. The Bureau of Labor Statistics gives the following brief definitions (from [7]):

Civilian noninstitutional population: Persons 16 years of age and older residing in the 50 states and the District of Columbia, who are not inmates of institutions (e.g., penal and mental facilities, homes for the aged), and who are not on active duty in the Armed Forces.

Civilian labor force: All persons in the civilian noninstitutional population classified as either employed or unemployed.

Employed persons: All persons who, during the reference week (week including the 12 day of the month), (a) did any work as paid employees, worked in their own business or profession or on their own farm, or worked 15 h or more as unpaid workers in an enterprise operated by a member of their family, or (b) were not working but who had jobs from which they were temporarily absent. Each employed person is counted only once, even if he or she holds more than one job.

Unemployed persons: All persons who had no employment during the reference week, were available for work, except for temporary illness, and had made specific efforts to find employment some time during the 4 week-period ending with the reference week. Persons who were waiting to be recalled to a job from which they had been laid off need not have been looking for work to be classified as unemployed.

This is a good start. The definition of "employed" is fairly straightforward, but notice in the definition of "unemployed persons" that they need to have made "specific efforts to find employment some time during the 4 week-period ending with the reference week." When you lose your job, you move from "employed" to "unemployed," but you stay in the definition of the labor force: U goes up with no change in L, so the measured unemployment rate goes up. If after some time you give up looking for work, you are no longer counted as unemployed, so you are removed from both the "unemployed" and from the labor force. U and L go down by the same amount, so the measured unemployment rate goes down.

Some other implications to consider:

- If an unemployed person joins the armed forces or is sent to jail, U and L drop by the same amount, so the measured unemployment rate goes down.
- If someone without a job but not looking for one—and therefore not defined as "unemployed"—joins the armed forces, there is no change in the measured unemployment rate: they weren't in the civilian labor force before, and they aren't now.
- If an employed person joins the military, U is unchanged but L goes down, so the measured unemployment rate goes up.
- In addition to the institutionalized population (jail, long-term care, mental hospitals, etc.) and the military, another large group is implicitly not counted in the civilian labor force: students (unless of course a student actually has a job or is looking for one).

The definition of unemployment really does have an impact on the measured unemployment rate as the following table illustrates (Table 3.2).

The labels "U-1" through "U-6" refer to different ways of defining who is unemployed, or as the table puts it, "Alternative measures of labor underutilization." The "official" rate of unemployment is U-3 (it's also referred to as the "headline" rate, since if a news outlet is going to discuss just one of these numbers, it's almost certainly U-3).

The most restrictive definition is U-1, which is "Persons unemployed 15 weeks or longer, as a percent of the civilian labor force." In other words, you have to have been out of work for about 3.5 months before you get included in U-1.

Table 3.2 Various measures of unemployment over time

	Jan. 2013	Sep. 2013	Oct. 2013	Nov. 2013	Dec. 2013	Jan. 2014
U-1	4.2	3.8	3.8	3.7	3.6	3.4
U-2	4.3	3.7	4.0	3.7	3.5	3.5
U-3	7.9	7.2	7.2	7.0	6.7	6.6
U-4	8.4	7.7	7.7	7.4	7.2	7.1
U-5	9.3	8.6	8.6	8.2	8.1	8.1
U-6	14.4	13.6	13.7	13.1	13.1	12.7

Data from [3]

At the other end of the spectrum is U-6, which is "U-6 Total unemployed, plus all persons marginally attached to the labor force, plus total employed part time for economic reasons, as a percent of the civilian labor force plus all persons marginally attached to the labor force." The phrase "marginally attached" refers to "discouraged" workers who have stopped looking because they keep not finding anything; it also includes people who aren't looking *much*. If you are "employed part time for economic reasons," that means you have part-time work, so you're not unemployed, but you would rather have a full-time job, so your labor is being underutilized.

As the table illustrates, the different measures paint very different pictures of the labor market. People sometimes refer to U-6 as the "real" unemployment rate, as if the government were hiding something by making such a big deal out of the U-3 with its smaller numbers. One problem with this argument is that the government itself calculates—and publishes!—the U-6 along with the U-3 and the others. A second problem is that none of the measures in the table is inherently "right." Each of them provides a different angle on a complex situation.

There are two other important measures of the state of the labor market.

The **employment-population ratio** is just what it sounds like: the number of people employed, divided by the (civilian noninstitutional) population:

Employment-population ratio = E / Population.

In the short term this goes up or down with improvement or deterioration in the labor market. In the long term it's shaped by demographic changes such as the increasing tendency of women to be in the labor market or the changing portion of the population that is of retirement-age.

The **labor-force participation rate** is the ratio of people in the labor force to the total population:

Labor-force participation rate = L / Population

This is shaped by the same short-term and long-term factors as the employment-population ratio. In addition, it reflects a psychological factor. When people are optimistic about their job prospects, they start looking for jobs and may move from being out of the labor force to being in the labor force, thus raising the participation rate. If they're quickly successful in finding jobs, the employment-population ratio will go up and the unemployment rate will go down. If they're not immediately successful, the employment-population ratio will be unchanged, but the unemployment rate will go *up*.

The moral of the story is that sometimes you need to look at a range of employment data to get an accurate picture of the labor market.

3.5 Interest Rates

In economic theory there is often discussion of "*the* interest rate," as if there were a single rate that applied to the entire economy. Other times, particularly in the business press, there will be references to "interest rates." This at least reflects the reality that there are many different rates depending on the borrower's situation and the lender's assessment of the borrower's credit-worthiness, but it still leaves a lot of vagueness. The most important distinction is between interest rates set as a matter of policy by the central bank (in the United States, that's the Federal Reserve, colloquially known as "the Fed"), and interest rates set by the market.

Chapter 6 will introduce a highly stylized way of thinking about market-determined rates in the long run, a version of what can be called a "loanable funds market." Chapter 10 embeds interest rates in a more concrete view of the role of banks and the process of money creation and extension of credit. For now we merely identify the major categories of interest rates.

Economic agents want to lend and borrow for varying lengths of time—even the Federal government borrows money at terms ranging from 3 months to 30 years. And borrowers vary widely in their credit-worthiness. There's an essentially universal assumption that the U.S. government will not default on its loans (if it did, the consequences for the global economy would likely be stunning—and not in a good way). Historically it was true that a family buying a home was unlikely to go bankrupt and become unable to continue paying its mortgage, but the chance was never zero. And an individual with a small income or a history of defaults will be assumed to be a high-risk borrower (the same goes for poorly run countries and companies whose business prospects are perceived to be deteriorating). The riskier the borrower, the higher an interest rate the market will make the borrower pay, in order to compensate the lenders for the chance of losing all or part of their money.[3]

Market-determined interest rates include mortgages (determined by how many people want to buy houses, and who wants to lend to them to do so), car loans (car companies sometimes reduce interest rates—increase their willingness to lend—in

[3]One of the things that happened in housing in the first decade of this century was that mortgage brokers often took "an individual with a small income or a history of defaults" and turned him or her into "a family buying a home." Logically, that meant that families buying homes were no longer a group with such a low risk of default. But banks continued to treat all mortgages, even those to people with bad credit scores, as loans that were highly likely to be repaid. Oops. But they did still charge high interest rates, so hey, no biggie. A very readable narrative of part of what happened is [9].

order to sell more cars), corporate bonds (how much do companies want to borrow, and how willing are people to lend to them), and government bonds (how big a deficit is the government covering and how willing are people to step up at the bond auctions the government regularly holds).

In the U.S., there are two policy-driven interest rates—that is, rates that are not the result of supply and demand in a market, but simply determined as a matter of policy by the Federal Reserve: the discount rate, and the Federal Funds rate. These are rates used only between the Fed and the banks that are members of it, and among those members.

The details of how these rates are set are left to the discussion of monetary policy in Chap. 12. For now, the important thing is that the central bank, through the rates it controls, can't determine the rates set in the market, but it does have an influence on them. Lower interest rates set by the Fed will tend to bring about lower interest rates elsewhere in the economy. But the effect is stronger or weaker at different times, and sometimes it hardly exists at all.

3.5.1 Real vs. Nominal Interest

Nominal interest is the number you see on your savings account (for anyone who still puts their money in savings accounts). If something pays 6% nominal interest per year and you put in $100, a year from now you'll have $106. But like elsewhere in economics, you're more interested in what that $106 can buy you than with the number $106 itself, and that depends on how much inflation there's been in the year while your money's been sitting in the bank.

If both the interest rate and the inflation rate are small (no more than about 10%), you can approximate the real interest rate by subtracting the inflation rate from the nominal interest rate. If nominal interest is 7% and inflation is 4%, then the real interest rate is about 3%: if you put aside $100 in January 2005, you'll end up with $107 in January 2006, but prices will have gone up too, so that $107 in 2006 will buy you about the same as $103 would have in 2005. The appendix derives the formula for calculating the exact real interest rate.

The trick with real interest rates is that you don't know what they are when you make your lending and borrowing decisions. When you decide to lend money, you commit to a nominal interest rate—you agree that you'll give someone $100 now and they'll give you back, say, $107 a year from now. But neither you nor the borrower knows what the inflation rate will be. You have some expectation of it: perhaps you expect inflation to be 3%, so a 7% nominal interest rate gives you about 4% real and you might decide that's a good deal. You have an *ex ante* ("from before") real interest rate of 4%. And maybe the borrower expects inflation to be 3.5%, giving her an ex ante real interest rate of about 3.5%, which she also thinks is an acceptable deal for her purposes. But *ex post* ("from after"), you're both likely to have been wrong to some extent. If inflation turned out to be 5%, then the *ex post* real interest rate was only about 2%; you didn't do so well and the borrower got a good deal. If the inflation rate was only 1%, the *ex post* real interest rate is 6% and you did significantly better than expected while the borrower has to pay more (in real terms) than she'd thought she would have to. If inflation turns out to be 10%, the real interest rate is roughly *negative* 3%. You got shafted and the borrower got a great deal, paying you back less (in purchasing power) than you gave her.

Though inflation is impossible to forecast perfectly, in a low-inflation regime (such as the U.S. since about 1982), it doesn't jump around too erratically. So while people get a little more or a little less real interest than they expected, they're never too far off. As inflation rises, it tends to get more erratic, making it more likely that participants in credit markets will make serious errors in their inflation forecasts. And fundamental shifts in inflation, for instance from a period of high inflation to a period of low inflation, can leave some interest rates "stranded." In the late 1970s, U.S. inflation hovered around 10% for a few years. Nominal interest rates rose to about 15% in response, in order to preserve a decent positive real interest rate. Some of those loans were for 5, 10, or more years. In 1982 inflation was reduced significantly, down to the low single digits, but people were still committed to loans with nominal interest rates in the teens, resulting in real interest of about 10%. For people who happen to have saved money in long-term instruments in the late 1970s, this was a welcome windfall, as they enjoyed high real returns during the 1980s. Anyone who had borrowed at the same time, however, found themselves paying far more than they expected.

3.6 Foreign Affairs

The trade deficit gets a fair amount of attention, but it's merely the most talked-about part of a larger system of international transactions. The components we'll focus on are:

<u>Trade deficit</u> This is simply the difference between imports and exports. If you read that we have a trade deficit of $600 billion in some year, that means that we imported $600 billion more than we exported. This is the same as a trade *balance* of −$600 billion (notice the "minus" sign: it's negative $600 billion). A positive trade balance is a trade surplus.

<u>Balance of payments</u> The trade deficit is part of a whole system of international accounts. The two major components are the *current account* and the *financial account*. By definition, these two along with the smaller components are supposed to balance out, and together they make up the *balance of payments*.

<u>Current account</u> As the name suggests, the current account tracks payments related to current expenditure. The largest part of this is trade in goods and services, but it includes income sent from one country to another. Exports are entered in the current account as a positive number, because the money associated with the export is flowing into the U.S. For the same reason, if you own a company in Germany and bring some of the income from that into the U.S., that also enters into the current account as a positive number, because the money is flowing into the U.S.

The value of imports is counted on the negative side of the ledger, as are U.S. government aid to other countries, income from properties and companies in the U.S. owned by people elsewhere, and "private remittances," such as when someone from Latin America works here and sends money to their family back home.

Financial account Let's say you've got $2.1 trillion going out, buying imports and going to other countries as income payments, aid, and private remittances, and you've only got $1.5 trillion coming in as payment for imports and income earned on American-owned properties abroad, that means you have got a current account deficit of $600 billion (your current account shows up as −$600 billion), and you have to make that up somehow. The way you do it, more or less, is sell to foreigners assets equal to your shortfall in traded goods. It's as if I sent you $60 worth of stuff out of my current production and you sent me $100 worth of stuff out of your current production. I've got to either give you $40, or give you other stuff worth $40—maybe some land, maybe a factory, maybe a bond or some shares of stock. Transactions in assets like these are entered in the financial account.[4]

As with the current account, positive entries in the financial account represent net flows of money into the U.S. This includes events such as (the terms in brackets are the relevant categories as named by the Bureau of Economic Affairs in its balance-of-payments data):

- a German citizen buys stock shares in an American company ["Other foreign assets in the United States/U.S. securities other than U.S. Treasury securities"];
- a Japanese company builds a factory in the U.S. ["Other foreign assets in the United States, net/Direct investment"];
- the People's Bank of China finances the U.S. federal government deficit by buying U.S. bonds ["Foreign official assets in the United States, net/U.S. Government securities/U.S. Treasury securities"].

Negative entries in the financial account represent flows of money out of the U.S.: when Americans buy foreign stocks or bonds; when U.S. companies build factories abroad, etc.

3.6.1 Interpreting the Balance of Payments

It's common to bemoan a large trade deficit, and it would probably be common to bemoan a large current-account deficit if more people knew the term. While current-account deficits have consequences, it's important to understand both sides of the coin.

[4]Some sources call this the "capital account." I'm following the usage of the Bureau of Economic Analysis, the agency that compiles the data on international transactions for the U.S.

If others are selling us more stuff than we're selling them, we have to hand over income-producing assets to make up the difference. If they don't want more of our cars, corn, movies, and banking services, we have to instead give them more of our factories, land, stocks, and bonds. That means that in the future, the income from those factories etc. will go to foreigners (and become negative entries in some future year's current account). So that's the downside of running a negative current account balance and therefore needing to run a positive financial account balance.

On the other hand, if foreigners are willing to, in effect, lend us money, we can undertake more investment than if we had to finance all our activity out of our own means. Also, foreigners may be choosing to acquire assets in the U.S. economy because they think that the economic climate here will make those assets highly productive in the future—a vote of confidence, if you will. But by the nature of the balance of payments, if foreigners want to accumulate U.S. assets, that has to be financed by them running trade surpluses against us, which is the same as us running a trade deficit.

3.7 Exchange Rates

Just as with prices and interest rates, there are also two kinds of exchange rates: nominal and real.

The nominal exchange rate is what you see in the business pages of the newspaper: how much of one currency does it take to buy a unit of another currency. The nominal exchange rate is denoted in this book by e, and describes the amount of your currency you have to give up to purchase a unit of some other currency. Thus an increase in e describes a situation where you have to give up more of your currency than before to obtain a unit of some foreign currency. This often described as your currency getting "weaker."

The real exchange rate adjusts the nominal exchange rate for differences in price levels between any pair of countries. So changes in the real exchange rate describe changes in the *quantity of goods made in one country* that you have to give up to get a fixed *quantity of goods made in another country*. We will denote the real exchange rate by ε, and when it gets bigger, that means there's been an increase in the quantity of goods and services produced in your country that you need to give up to get a given quantity of goods and services produced in some other country.

Note that while e has units (dollars per euro, pounds per yen, roubles per rupee), ε is unitless. It is, rather, an index which only has meaning relative to some other time period. Choose some base year—say, 2004. Let P^D be the domestic price level (the price level in your own economy) and P^F be the foreign price level (the level in the country you're comparing yourself to for purposes of the exchange rate). Then e_0, $P^D{}_0$, and $P^F{}_0$ are the nominal exchange rate, domestic price level, and foreign price level for 2004, while e_t, $P^D{}_t$, and $P^F{}_t$ are the values of those same variables for some other year, denoted t.

Set ε_0 to any arbitrary level. (It could be 100, but it doesn't matter; as with price indexes, we're ultimately interested in proportional changes, not in absolute levels.) Then the general formula for ε_t is

$$\varepsilon_t = \varepsilon_0 \times \frac{P^F{}_t/P^F{}_0}{P^D{}_t/P^D{}_0} \times (e_t/e_0). \quad (3.2)$$

Despite their differences, the real exchange rate ε shares a property with the nominal exchange rate e, which is that a higher value of ε (or of e) means a weaker currency in real (or nominal) terms. It is important to note that this particular meaning of a larger ε or e is not a universal usage; you will likely encounter sources in which a larger value of the real or nominal exchange rate means a stronger currency rather than a weaker one. When working with data on nominal exchange rates, pay close attention to whether the data are, for example, dollars per euro or euros per dollar. In the case of real exchange rates, it's helpful to have a familiar "signature" in the data. For dollar exchange rates you can use the period immediately after September, 2008. The collapse of Lehman Brothers caused people to worry about global economic security and so they sought "safe harbor" in the U.S. economy by buying assets denominated in U.S. dollars. This caused the dollar to strengthen significantly. If you're using data that show a falling exchange rate right after September, 2008, then your source is using the same convention as in this book; if the real exchange rate is rising, then it is using the opposite approach. It doesn't matter which you use, as long as you are clear with yourself and with your audience, and consistent within any given setting.

Change in nominal exchange rate without change in prices What happens if the dollar appreciates relative to the euro but dollar prices of goods in the U.S. and euro prices of goods in Europe remain unchanged? That is, the dollar is "strengthening" against the euro in nominal terms, with no change in prices in the two economies. Specifically, one dollar will buy more euros than before, or it doesn't take as many dollars as before to buy one euro. Since prices within each country are unchanged, this makes it easier for people in the U.S. to import goods and services from abroad, so the dollar has strengthened in real terms.[5]

Change in prices without change in nominal exchange rate Now imagine that there's inflation in both countries but it's higher in the U.S. than in Europe, so it takes a lot more dollars to buy stuff in the U.S. while it only takes a few more euros in Europe. When an American spends a dollar buying euros, she's giving up a lot less stuff than before (because high dollar inflation means her dollar doesn't buy as much as it used to) whereas the euros she gets are worth almost as much as they used to be (due to Europe's low inflation). This makes it easier for the American to buy foreign stuff. The dollar has strengthened in real terms, conveyed by a drop in ε.

[5]The same would be true if, rather than remaining unchanged, the price level in both economies had changed by the same amount in percentage terms.

Disparate inflation rates and pressure on nominal exchange rates The scenario described just above may seem like a free lunch. Inflation here makes it easier for us to buy stuff from abroad. But that was predicated on the nominal exchange rate not changing. Assume that $\varepsilon = 120$ is in some sense the "right" real exchange rate—that is, the rate that correctly reflects productivity, expected growth, perceived stability, etc. of the two economies.

What happens if the current nominal exchange rate causes the real exchange rate to be $\varepsilon = 110$ instead of $\varepsilon = 120$? The dollar is "too strong," making it "too easy" for Americans to import from Europe, or "too hard" for Europeans to import from America. Looking at Eq. 3.2 we can see that a period of particularly low inflation in the U.S., or particularly high inflation in Europe, would solve the problem. If neither of those things happens, then markets will put pressure on the nominal exchange rate to rise (more dollars per euro), which would also move the real exchange rate in the right direction.

3.7.1 Exchange Rates and Interest Rates

The real exchange rate is driven ultimately by demand for all dollar-denominated items, whether they're physical products, services, or financial assets. If real interest rates in the U.S. are higher than real interest rates in Europe then, all else being equal, people will want to park their money in the U.S. economy. That requires dollars, increasing the demand for dollars and putting downward pressure on the real exchange rate. So for any relative prices in goods, a higher interest rate in the U.S. will result in a lower real exchange rate (a "stronger" dollar).

3.7.2 Exchange Rates and the Overall Investment Climate

People and companies make investments in expectation of profits, and various institutional factors make business profits more likely. From a conservative perspective, one might point to: relatively little government regulation of the economy; weak labor unions; a productive labor force. A liberal might counter that intelligent regulation can improve the economy, and that sometimes unions improve working conditions in ways that make the labor force more productive, so weak unions may help profits directly but hurt them indirectly. The two sides would likely agree that profits are helped by a stable and transparent legal system and a high rate of GDP growth.

Whatever factors *actually* make companies more profitable, they act the same way as a high real interest rate: to the extent that they exist, they make investment in the U.S. economy more attractive than otherwise. This investment requires dollars, so these factors increase demand for dollars and drive down the real exchange rate.

Appendix: Price Indexes

To see how the CPI is constructed, imagine a simple basket with only two goods: movie tickets and magazines. We do some surveys and learn that each month the average consumer goes to three movies and buys four magazines. Movie tickets cost $8 and magazines cost $5. Table 3.3 shows this consumer basket, along with the prices (in the row "p_1"), the amount of expenditure on each good, which is the quantity of that good times its price (in the "Expenditure" row) and the total cost of the basket (in the "Basket cost" column). If we take the current period as the base period, then we arbitrarily set the index value to 100.

Then we come back at a later time and find that prices have changed. Movies have gone up by 25% to $10, while magazines have only gone up by 5% to $5.25. We assume the same basket as originally and see how much it costs to buy now. The index value is our new cost, divided by our old cost, times the base level of the index, which is 100, so the calculation in this specific case is $51/44 \times 100$. The two different items in the basket have gone up by different amounts, but the overall price level is summarized by the movement from 100.0 in Table 3.3 to 115.9 in Table 3.4.

For the implicit GDP deflator, imagine a simple economy that produces only cars and orange juice. In 1993 it produced 100 cars at $20,000 each, and 1,000,000 cans of OJ at $1.00 each. The nominal GDP is simply the output times the price (Table 3.5).

Ten years later, the economy has grown, with production of both cars and OJ up, but prices have also increased (Table 3.6).

Table 3.3 Costing out a simple consumer basket

	Movies	Magazines	Basket cost	Index value
Quantity	3	4		
p_1	8	5		
Expenditure	24	20	44	100.0

Table 3.4 The basket's cost with new prices

	Movies	Magazines	Basket cost	Index value
Quantity	3	4		
p_2	10	5.25		
Expenditure	30	21	51	115.9

Table 3.5 An initial GDP calculation

	Quantity, 1993	Price, 1993	Expenditure
Cars	100	$20,000	$2,000,000
OJ	1,000,000	$1.00	$1,000,000
Nominal GDP			$3,000,000

Table 3.6 A later nominal GDP calculation

	Quantity, 2003	Price, 2003	Expenditure
Cars	110	\$25,000	\$2,750,000
OJ	1,050,000	\$1.05	\$1,102,500
Nominal GDP			\$3,852,500

Table 3.7 Calculating real GDP

	Quantity, 2003	Price, 1993	Expenditure
Cars	110	\$20,000	\$2,200,000
OJ	1,050,000	\$1.00	\$1,050,000
Nominal GDP			\$3,250,500

The nominal GDP is up by 28%, increasing from \$3 million to more than \$3.8 million, but some portion of that is just price increases and doesn't reflect an increase in actual output.

The implicit GDP deflator filters out inflation by using a constant set of prices to evaluate a changing output. In this case, we add up the actual output from 2003 using the prices from 1993 (Table 3.7).

So the real GDP for 2003, in 1993 prices, is \$3,250,000, as opposed to the nominal 2003 GDP of \$3,852,500. Real GDP only increased by 8.3% (from \$3 million to \$3.25 million), rather than 28%.

The last step is to see how much inflation there was between 1993 and 2003. You do that by comparing the nominal and real GDP figures for 2003. The nominal GDP for that year is 18.5% higher than the real figure, so over those 10 years, prices rose by 18.5%, as measured by the implicit GDP deflator.

Appendix: Real and Nominal Interest Rates

Let i be the nominal interest rate, π be the rate of inflation, and r the real interest rate.

As mentioned in Sect. 3.5.1, the approximate real interest rate is just the nominal rate minus the inflation rate:

$$r \cong i - \pi.$$

The exact formula takes your changed number of dollars after you've earned the nominal interest rate, and divides that by the changed number of dollars needed to buy the same stuff as before.

The changed number of dollars is simply whatever you started with (call it IV, the "initial value") times $1 + i$ (that is, one plus the interest rate), or $IV \times (1 + i)$.

The changed amount of dollars needed now per dollar before is $1 + \pi$ (that is, one plus the rate of inflation).

Meanwhile, the real interest rate represents the gain in what you can actually buy, so the changed amount of what you can buy is the initial value times $1 + r$, or $IV \times (1 + r)$.

So the real interest rate, represented as the changed amount of dollars, divided by the changed amount of dollars needed is described by the equation:

$$IV(1 + r) = \frac{IV(1 + i)}{1 + \pi}$$

We can get rid of the IV by dividing it into both sides. Then to see the relationship to the approximation above, we can do a little algebraic manipulation. Modify the numerator by adding and subtracting π:

$$1 + r = \frac{(1 + i) + \pi - \pi}{1 + \pi}$$

We reorganize the numerator:

$$1 + r = \frac{i - \pi + (1 + \pi)}{(1 + \pi)}$$

We note that $(1 + \pi)/(1 + \pi) = 1$ and rewrite again:

$$1 + r = \frac{i - \pi}{(1 + \pi)} + 1$$

If we subtract 1 from each side, we get the exact equation for the real interest rate:

$$r = \frac{i - \pi}{1 + \pi}$$

Looking back at the approximation, the only difference is the denominator of $(1 + \pi)$. If inflation is low, then π is close to 0, and $(1 + \pi)$ is close to 1, so the approximation is close to the exact figure. As inflation gets larger, $1 + \pi$ gets very different from 1, so the approximation overstates the exact value significantly.

Appendix: Real Exchange Rates

This appendix walks you through a numerical example that is meant to compliment the conceptual overview in Sect. 3.7.

Imagine that some standard kind of Ford car sells for $18,000 in the U.S., and that some standard sort of Volkswagen sells for €20,000 in Europe. Let's say the

Table 3.8 Examples of changing real exchange rates

Row	Ford price (in \$)	VW price (in €)	Nominal exch. rate (e)	VW price (in \$)	Fords per VW	Real exch. rate (ε)
A	18,000	20,000	1.20	24,000	1.33	100.0
B	18,000	20,000	1.10	22,000	1.22	91.7
C	25,000	24,000	1.20	28,800	1.15	86.5
D	25,000	24,000	1.39	33,333	1.33	100.0

nominal exchange rate (denoted e) is \$1.20/€—that is, getting one euro costs you \$1.20.

In this artificial example, the real exchange rate (denoted ε) is the quantity of Fords you need to give up to get one VW. Getting a VW requires €20,000, and at \$1.20/€, that takes \$24,000. To get \$24,000 requires giving up 1.33 Fords (1.33 × $\$18,000 = \$24,000$). Since the real exchange rate is a unitless index that only has meaning relative to its own value in some other period, we can arbitrarily say that at this point $\varepsilon = 100$. See row A of Table 3.8.

Row B reflects the scenario of a change in the nominal exchange rate with no change in prices. Let's say the new nominal exchange rate is e = \$1.10/€. Now it only requires \$22,000 to buy a VW (€20,000 × \$1.10/€= \$22,000). And \$22,000 is equivalent to 1.22 Fords. In other words, instead of needing 1.33 Fords to buy a VW, you only need 1.22, so the real exchange rate has fallen from 100.0 to 91.7.

Another way of saying that is that it takes fewer of our goods to get a unit of foreign goods, which is reflected in the drop in ε.

Row C illustrates higher inflation in the U.S. than in Europe. The price of a Ford rises from \$18,000 to \$25,000, while the price of a VW rises from €20,000 only to €24,000. At the same time, the nominal exchange rate is still e = \$1.20/€, as it was in row A.

Getting a VW now requires \$28,800 (€24,000 × \$1.20/€= \$28,800). That in turn requires giving up 1.15 Fords (\$28,800 per VW, divided by \$25,000 per Ford, gives 1.15 Fords) instead of 1.33. So the real exchange rate has fallen from $\varepsilon = 100$ to $\varepsilon = 86.5$ As explained in the main text, a falling exchange rate means that imports are cheaper because a given quantity of foreign goods requires the sacrifice of a smaller quantity of American goods (or exports are more expensive, because a given quantity of foreign goods doesn't get you as large a quantity of American goods as before).

This makes a certain amount of sense. If prices here rise faster than prices abroad, but nominal exchange rates don't adjust, it becomes harder for foreigners to buy our stuff.

In terms of disparate inflation and pressure on the nominal rate, in the Ford/VW example of this appendix assume that $\varepsilon = 100$ is was the "right" level. That is, given the relative demand for Fords and VWs, the market clears when you have to give up 1.33 Fords to get one VW, or you have to give up 0.75 VWs to get one Ford. At the real exchange rate of $\varepsilon = 86.5$ in row C, American goods are too expensive, so people are buying too many VWs and not enough Fords. If European inflation doesn't catch up with American inflation, the only way to bring the relative prices of these two goods back to their equilibrium level is through changes in the nominal exchange rate, *e*.

Specifically, we need a value of e such that giving up 1.33 Fords at \$25,000 each gives you enough euros to buy one VW at €24,000 each. So

$$€24{,}000 \times e\$/€ = 1.33 \times \$25{,}000,$$

or

$$\begin{aligned} e &= \$33,333/€24{,}000 \\ &= \$1.39/€. \end{aligned}$$

The adjustment is unlikely to be instantaneous, but all else being equal, higher inflation here than abroad creates pressure to "weaken" the dollar—that is, it creates pressure for a nominal exchange rate such that one dollar doesn't buy as many euros as it used to. Relatively low inflation here has the opposite effect.

Appendix: Data Links

GDP The Gross Domestic Product is published by the Bureau of Economic Analysis, at www.bea.gov, under the "National" tab. You're looking for "NIPA", or National Income and Product Accounts. Note that BEA publishes the data in many different forms: annual vs. quarterly; quarterly data seasonally adjusted vs. not seasonally adjusted; period-to-period percentage change; current dollars vs. constant (inflation-adjusted) dollars. Each form has its use, but for many purposes the most helpful is Table 1.1.6 of the BEA's National Data, giving GDP in chained dollars (a form of inflation adjustment).

Resources Energy data are available from many sources, including the Energy Information Administration of the U.S. Department of Energy (http://www.eia.gov/; look for the data attached to the Monthly Energy Review or the Annual Energy Review), the International Energy Agency run by the Organization for Economic Cooperation and Development (http://www.iea.org/), and the annual *Statistical review of world energy* produced by British Petroleum (http://www.bp.com/en/global/corporate/about-bp/energy-economics/statistical-review-of-world-energy.html). Ecological footprint data are available from http://www.footprintnetwork.org/.

Inflation Price statistics are issued by the Bureau of Labor Statistics at www.bls.gov. The most commonly cited rate is based on the Consumer Price Index for All Urban Consumers (CPI-U), but numerous other measures are available. In addition, BLS provides price information on a limited list of representative goods, such as gasoline and ground beef.

Unemployment Labor statistics are kept, not surprisingly, by the Bureau of Labor Statistics, at www.bls.gov. They provide figures on unemployment rates, labor-market participation, the employment-population ratio, number of jobs, and numerous breakdowns by gender, race/ethnicity, age, and economic sector.

Interest rates The Federal Reserve provides a selection of U.S. interest rates in its Table H.15, available at http://www.federalreserve.gov/econresdata/default.htm.

International transactions Trade figures can be derived from the GDP tables referred to above, because the presentation of GDP includes imports and exports as separate components. The broader set of international transactions, however, is available from the Bureau of Economic Analysis at www.bea.gov under the "International" tab.

FRED: Federal Reserve Economic Data The St. Louis bank of the Federal Reserve makes available a vast range of data from numerous agencies. The interface takes some getting used to, but once you're comfortable with it you can pull together data from disparate source in a consistent format.

Problems

Problem 3.1 Table 3.9 provides GDP and population for six countries. The GDP numbers are in millions of dollars, adjusted for purchasing power parity (PPP)—that is, they take account of the differences in prices of basic goods between countries.

(a) Use the data in the table to calculate GDP per capita. Note that total GDP is given in millions of dollars, whereas population is given in people (not millions of people), so you'll have to adjust one or the other so that your answer will come out in dollars per person, not millions of dollars per person.
(b) Which measure of GDP tells you more about how important a country is in the world economy?
(c) Which measure of GDP tells you more about the quality of life a country's inhabitants probably enjoy?

Table 3.9 GDP and population, various countries

Country	GDP	Population	GDP per capita
Norway	255,022	4,993,700	
U.S.	14,526,550	313,020,000	
Germany	2,944,352	81,796,000	
China	10,119,896	1,339,724,852	
Indonesia	1,032,952	237,641,326	
India	4,057,787	1,210,193,422	

GDP data from International Monetary Fund, via Wikipedia
Population data from national censuses, via Wikipedia

Table 3.10 Nominal prices and price index

	Nominal price	Price index (2011 base)	Real price (in 2011 dollars)
September 2002	2.065	80.5	
May 2011	3.277	100.5	
Cumulative inflation			
Annualized inflation			

Table 3.11 Data for unemployment problem

Pd	Population	Employed	Unemployed	Labor force	Unemploy-ment rate	Employment population ratio	Labor force participation rate
1	160	100	9				
2	170	105	8				

Problem 3.2 Table 3.10 gives the nominal price of ground chuck, and a price index that has been indexed to 2011. Fill in the real price, in 2011 dollars, the cumulative inflation from September 2002 to May 2011, and the annualized rate of inflation over that same span. (Note that years can be denoted in decimal or fractional terms, e.g., 1 year and 3 months can be written as 1.25 years, or as 15/12 years.)

Problem 3.3 Go to the bls.gov site and get data on the employment-population ratio and the participation rate, for the last 10 years. Either through the website or by downloading the data to a spreadsheet program such as Excel, make a chart of the two data series. What does each suggest about when the economy was doing well or poorly?

Problem 3.4 Repeat Problem 3.3, but using the unemployment rate instead of the other measures specified in that problem.

Problem 3.5 Table 3.11 below gives numbers for population (i.e., adult, civilian, non-institutionalized population), the number of people employed, and the number of people unemployed.

(a) Fill in the labor force, the unemployment rate, the employment-population ratio, and the labor-force participation rate, across two different periods (1 and 2).
(b) Which item(s) give evidence of the labor market improving?
(c) Which item(s) give evidence of the labor market getting worse?

Problem 3.6 Let's say you lend out money at 6% nominal interest for 1 year. When you make the loan, you expect the inflation rate to be 2% over that year, but it turns out to be 3%.

(a) What was your ex ante real interest rate, using the approximation?
(b) What was your ex ante real interest rate, using the exact formula?
(c) What was your ex post real interest rate, using the approximation?
(d) What was your ex post real interest rate, using the exact formula?
(e) Did things work out better for you than you expected, or worse?

Problem 3.7 Say you borrow money at 10% nominal annual interest, for 3 years. It is to be paid back in a lump sum at the end of 3 years (that is, it's different from a mortgage, where you pay some interest and some principal every month until all the principal has been paid off). You expect inflation to be 5% per year in all three years. It turns out to be 2% the first year, 2% the second year, and 11% the third year.

(a) What's your ex ante approximate annual real interest rate?
(b) What's your ex ante exact annual real interest rate?
(c) What's your ex post exact average annual interest rate? (This is tricky. You have to look at the total amount your dollars grew, based on the nominal interest rate, and compare it to the total amount that prices grew, based on the actual inflation rate. Then apply the technique of annualizing the growth rate.)

Problem 3.8 Say the nominal exchange rate between the US dollar and the Czech crown is 0.05 USD/CZK (you pay 5 cents to get one Czech crown). Apples in a Czech grocery store cost 49 crowns per kilo.

(a) Convert the Czech apple price to U.S. dollars: In dollar terms, how much does a kilo of apples cost in that store?
(b) Now the nominal exchange rate changes, becoming 0.06 USD/CZK. What's the new dollar price of that kilo of Czech apples?
(c) In going from 0.05 USD/CZK to 0.06 USD/CZK, has the dollar strengthened or weakened against the crown?
(d) Now assume that, at the same time as the nominal exchange rate changes from 0.05 to 0.06, there has been a total of 30% inflation in the U.S. and none in the Czech Republic. In real terms, has the dollar strengthened or weakened against the Czech crown?

Problem 3.9 Table 3.12 below shows seven items from the international transactions accounts, along with their amounts. Put each one in the correct column of either the current account or the financial account. Remember that money amounts flowing into the U.S. go in the "positive" column, while money amounts flowing out go in the "negative" column. The amount for sale of U.S. Treasury bonds is not given, but since the financial account and the current account have to balance each other out (at least in theory), you can figure out what it's supposed to be.

The items that you put in the "negative" columns can be left as positive numbers; if you do that, then be sure to subtract all the negatives in the current account from all the positives in the current account, and all the negatives in the financial account

Table 3.12 Numbers for balance-of-payments exercise

		Current account		Financial account	
		Positive	Negative	Positive	Negative
Exports	450				
Imports	550				
Payments of interest on bonds of U.S. companies held by people outside the U.S.	45				
Receipt of income on foreign bonds held by people in the U.S.	70				
Construction of a Toyota factory in Kentucky	15				
Sale of U.S. Treasury bonds to the Bank of China					
Purchase of Greek bonds by people in the U.S.	5				
Balance on current account or financial account					

from all the positives in the financial account in getting the balance within each account. If you enter the "negative" items as negative numbers, then you add up everything in each account.

References

1. Cleveland, C. J., Costanza, R., Hall, C. A. S., & Kaufmann, R. (1984). Energy and the United States economy: A biophysical perspective. *Science, 225*, 890–897.
2. Daly, H. E., & Cobb, J. B. (1994). *For the common good: Redirecting the economy toward community, the environment, and a sustainable future*. Boston: Beacon Press.
3. Employment situation, table a-15. (2014). Alternative measures of labor utilization. Accessed February 8, 2014.
4. Feenstra, R. C., Inklaar, R., & Timmer, M. P. (2015). The next generation of the Penn World Table, available for download at www.ggdc.net/pwt.
5. International Energy Agency. (2015). France: Electricity and heat for 2012. http://www.iea.org/statistics/statisticssearch/report/?year=2012&country=FRANCE&product=ElectricityandHeat.
6. International Energy Agency. (2015). France: Indicators for 2012. http://www.iea.org/statistics/statisticssearch/report/?year=2012&country=FRANCE&product=Balances.
7. Bureau of Labor Statistics. Employment situation, Table A-15, "Alternative measures of labor utilization". http://www.bls.gov/news.release/empsit.toc.htm. Accessed 8 Feb 2014.
8. Global footprint network. (2015). http://www.footprintnetwork.org. Accessed July 17, 2015.
9. Lewis, M. (2011). *The big short*. New York: W.W. Norton.
10. Living Planet Report. (2014). WWF in collaboration with Global Footprint Network, Water Footprint Network, and Zoological Society of London.
11. McKibben, B. (1995). *Hope, human and wild: True stories of living lightly on the earth*. Boston: Little, Brown and Co.
12. Wackernagel, M. & Rees, W. E. (1997). Perceptual and structural barriers to investing in natural capital: Economics from an ecological footprint perspective. *Ecological Economics, 20*, 3–24.

Part II
The Long-Run Model

Here we use the pieces laid out in Part I to build a model of how the economy evolves in the long run. It starts with a production function describing how the economy combines labor, capital, technology, and resources to create output. This is divided up to various purposes based on the economy's expenditure functions for consumption, investment, exports, imports, and government spending.

Putting this all together, we analyze equilibrium and how it is affected by changes in expenditure functions, labor supply, capital stock, technology, or resource availability. This tool is also used to think through how growth happens in the long run, in a situation where resource availability is not a concern.

By design, this part of the book does not explain business cycles. It assumes that the labor market is always in equilibrium and that the economy is always operating at the level it should be, given the inputs available to it. The departure from that ideal state is left for Part III.

Also, this part of the book assumes that more resources can be easily made available as the economy's demand for them develops. Part IV revisits both the long-run model of this next part and the business-cycle material of Part III under conditions when resource constraints are actually a problem.

Chapter 4
Labor, Resources, and the Production Function

Abstract This chapter introduces a more-or-less "classical" production function, a widely used tool for analyzing economic behavior in the long run. The version presented here is conventional in its derivation of labor demand. However, it is atypical in that, following the logic of Chaps. 1 and 2, it includes resources along with the usual productive factors of labor, capital, and technology. These are introduced via resource supply curves which Chap. 6 will then feed into the supply side of the labor market. The chapter introduces the Cobb-Douglas specification for the production function and ends with the derivation of the per-worker form.

4.1 Overview

The starting point for the classical view of the macroeconomy is the idea of the production function; many Keynesian models employ it as well. There is often a tension in economic analysis between simplifying the world to make it easier to understand and adding in details to make the model more closely reflect reality. The aggregate production function laid out here is at the simplification end of the spectrum, which certainly has its shortcomings but also allows us to see some underlying trends that would be obscured by more detail.

Though they use them differently, the labor demand and labor supply functions are also common to the classical and Keynesian models, and so are introduced here along with the production function. Labor demand is derived from the production function, while labor supply is determined by various demographic and social factors.

This book departs from the standard approach by including resources as a factor of production, and so resource markets, with their supply curves and relationships between use and price, are also explained at this point.

4.2 The Production Function

To think of the production function in intuitive terms, you could imagine an automobile factory which takes a bunch of inputs (metal, rubber, glass, electricity, etc.), brings them into a factory (a form of capital), and uses labor to produce cars:

K. Seeley, *Macroeconomics in Ecological Context*, Studies in Ecological Economics 5, DOI 10.1007/978-3-319-51757-5_4

$$(\text{Number of cars}) = f(\text{labor, number and type of factories, material inputs}). \quad (4.1)$$

That is, the number of cars the company can produce is a function of the labor used, the number and type of factories the company owns, and the material inputs consumed. The notation $f(\cdot)$ implies a kind of mathematical relationship: tell me how much you have of each of these factors of production, and I'll tell you how many cars you can produce.

For the whole economy, we make a couple of simplifications. First, we take all the factories in the economy, together with all the railroads, highways, office buildings, etc.—all the durable inputs to production—and lump them together as "**capital**," denoted ***K***.

Second, we group all resources into two types: "**exhaustibles**," denoted ***E***, and "**renewables**," denoted ***B*** (for "biological," since the description of renewables used in constructing their supply curve is more appropriate for biological renewable resources such as fish, trees, and crops than for non-biological ones such as wind power and solar power). These two groups can then be combined into a single measure of "**resources**," ***R*** (the division of R into B and E will be specified later in the explanation of the model).

A third assumption was slipped in already in the example of the car factory: all workers are lumped together as a homogeneous thing called "labor." If you think about the real economy this may feel odd: an oil-pipe fitter wouldn't be very useful teaching an economics class, and an economics professor wouldn't be very useful working on an oil rig. But macroeconomics is, in part, about the big picture, and it simplifies that picture a lot to just talk about "**labor**," so that's what we'll do, and we'll denote it as ***N***.

Along with labor, capital, and resources, there is technology, and just as we forced each of those other concepts into a single number, we'll take the myriad technologies employed in many different parts of the economy and summarize all of them in a single term for "**technology**," denoted by ***A***.

All of that leads to the economy's aggregate production function. You take aggregate capital (K), aggregate resources (R), and aggregate labor (N) and put them together using the prevailing technology (A)[1] to get the economy's output (Y):

$$Y = F(K, N, R, A).$$

Over time the economy creates new capital (that's what investment is doing) and technology evolves, presumably improving (that's also a benefit of investment), but in the short run, capital and technology are fixed. We have a certain number of factories, roads, etc., and right now that's all we have. And we have certain ways we know of how to do things, and we don't (yet) know any better ones.

[1]The reason for using these symbols rather than others is explained in the appendix on "Why K? Why N? …".

Labor, on the other hand, is what's known as a "variable input." I can rush out and hire new workers a lot faster than I can build a new factory. If business is slow, I can easily fire some workers, reducing N, while there's not much point in destroying capital or forgetting how to do things, so K and A stay the same. For a given amount of capital and a given level of technology, the more workers I have, the more I can produce—up to a point.

Resources would also seem to be a variable input, just like labor. My machinery and my technology are what they are right now, but the quantity of resources used is a decision made in the present, not inherited from the past. However, as will be developed further below, the model imposes a useful simplification, which is that at any given time, the quantity of resources used is in a fixed relationship to the quantity of labor. The idea is that a given capital stock and technology determine the quantity of resources that goes with a typical employee, and that as technology and capital change, the labor-resource ratio changes as well.

As a concrete example, recall the comparison of a stagecoach driver and a train crew from Chap. 2. The locomotive allows the train crew to move far more people a greater distance per labor hour than can be accomplished with the stagecoach. It's also true that the train allows—or requires—far more energy to be used per labor hour than does the stagecoach. And to a reasonable first approximation, the productivity of labor and the use of resources per labor hour are fixed in the short term by the technology and the capital stock. In the early nineteenth century the railroad is not an option and the resources used are predominantly renewable: a mostly-wooden stagecoach, pulled by horses that are fed solar-grown oats. In the mid twentieth century the stagecoach isn't an option, both because it can't compete with the railroad and because the capital stock of vehicles and horses doesn't exist, and the resources used are predominantly exhaustible: a metal locomotive, powered by coal or diesel, pulling cars made out of metal and wood.

This (temporarily) fixed relationship between labor and resources can be captured with the term ρ, where $R = \rho \cdot N$. So resources still matter for production, but R is no longer an independent factor—at any given time, if you know the quantity of N, you know the quantity of R. What *is* independent is ρ. It changes over time, but at any given time it is fixed and is unaffected by the level of N.

Note that the meaning of "technology" has now changed. At the beginning of the chapter, it was *all* of technology—anything that wasn't captured in "labor" and "capital." But the resource-intensity of labor is also an aspect of technology. The ability to use lots of resources at once—your economy's resource-intensity of labor—is a function of your technology and the capital in which it is embedded.

So instead of A as our catch-all for "technology," we have the **resource-intensity of labor** ($\boldsymbol{\rho}$), and we have this other this other thing: given how much labor and capital you're using, and given what quantity of resources each worker uses in his or her work, how much output are you able to produce? In other words, this other part of technology is something like "**input efficiency**," and to distinguish it from our earlier term for "technology," we'll use the letter **Z** for it.[2]

Now we can rewrite the production function as

$$Y = F(K, Z, \rho, N).$$

To review the aspects of technology, ρ is the ability to get more done by using more resources per worker, while Z is the ability to get more done without increasing any of your inputs, including resources.

4.2.1 *Diminishing Marginal Product*

The marginal product of labor is the increase in output from an additional unit of labor, holding other things constant (in this case, "other things" are capital, input efficiency, and resources per worker)—in more common language, if I hire one more worker, how much more stuff will I be able to produce?

If you think about getting things done in the real world, it's not immediately clear how this "marginal product" should behave. You can imagine a situation where one person can't work very effectively and adding a second worker more than doubles your output. You can also imagine a situation where you've already got a pretty good set of workers and an additional pair of hands would just get in the way.

But on the macro scale it's convenient to assume diminishing marginal product. Your first worker takes you from zero to something—a big jump. Your second worker takes you from that "something" to more, but not by as much. Your third worker provides still more output, but the increase isn't as much as the increase from the second one. And so on.

4.2.2 *Output, Value, and GDP*

We started with the concrete example of producing cars, then abstracted up to aggregate capital, aggregate labor, and aggregate resources being used to produce our aggregate output. But what's *that*? It's all our final goods and services: the car you bought this year, the clean-room installed by a computer-chip manufacturer, some lumber sold to Japan, etc. In other words, it's our GDP (see Sect. 3.1). The production function tells us how we combine labor, resources, and capital to churn out our Gross Domestic Product.

[2]A precursor of this approach is Moroney [3]. Wils [6] has a different way of breaking out the general technological parameter A into more specific components.

Recall from Sect. 3.1.2 that the GDP is a measure of all the value-adding activity performed in an economy in a given year (or quarter of a year), and that adding value requires the reduction of one or more gradients. The necessary role of gradients is reflected in the production function by the presence of either R or ρ.

The conventional production function is simply $Y = f(A, K, N)$, ignoring the role of resources, while our model fixes that. Both approaches, however, are vulnerable on the subject of value added.

When we combine labor and capital (and resources) to make cars, we're talking about a strictly physical relationship, defined by our technology, our capital, the skill of our labor, and the quality of our resources. But when we combine those same things to get value added, another factor comes in, which is the relative prices of the different productive factors we use and the relative importance of resources in the different kinds of production that are hidden under the shroud of "aggregate output." These prices arise from the interaction among availability, usefulness given our current capital stock and technology, and people's preferences among the different things that can be made.

This price-setting process is a knot of physical and social factors that are very difficult to disentangle, and its impacts on the creation of value—and thus on GDP—have not been much explored, though it is touched on somewhat in [1] and developed further in [4] and [5].

The upshot is that changing resource availability affects GDP in two ways. One is that it changes how easy or hard it is to simply get stuff done. The other is that it changes the relative prices of various inputs and thereby changes the way in which the economy translates "getting stuff done" into "adding value." This may be an important phenomenon, particularly if we face a future of tighter resource constraints. It's also a very subtle phenomenon which this book's model is not built to address. On the other hand, more conventional models that ignore resources aren't designed to address it either. For your purposes now, just remember that it's something to keep in mind.

4.2.3 *Graphical Presentation*

If we graph output as a function of labor (remember, capital and technology are fixed quantities in the short run), we get a curve that slopes upward (each additional worker adds to output), but it does so more and more slowly (each additional worker adds less to output than the previous one hired). If N_1 people are employed, output will be Y_1; if N_2 people are employed, output will be Y_2, and the same for N_3 and Y_3. When labor increased from N_2 to N_3, output went up (from Y_2 to Y_3), but not by as much as when labor increased from N_1 to N_2 (see Fig. 4.1).

This is the visual representation of the phenomenon of diminishing marginal product of labor. That phenomenon, whether shown algebraically or graphically, is key to the demand for labor.

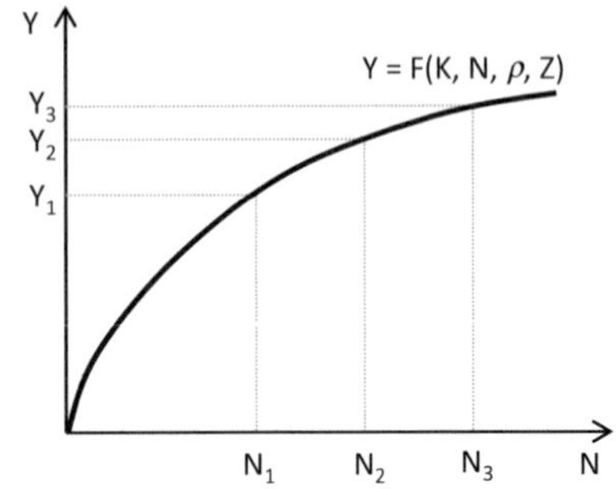

Fig. 4.1 The production function, with diminishing marginal product of labor

4.3 Labor Demand

At the risk of stating the obvious, firms hire workers in order to make profits. So how many workers should your firm hire? First the intuition: the lower the wage, the more people you can afford to hire; if wages go up, you're reluctant to bring people in and may even let some people go.

The key to the more technical explanation is the marginal product of labor. Every time you hire another worker, your output goes up by the **marginal product of labor** (call this **MPN**). If you sell that output at a **price *P***, then your revenues go up by MPN $\times$ P (the marginal product times the price). This is sometimes called the "**marginal value product**," or **MVP**.

But the labor doesn't come for free: each time you hire another worker, you have to pay out another unit of the **nominal wage**, or ***W***. Each firm (including yours) is assumed to be relatively small. The relevant implication of that is that you can't affect the wage. In the aggregate, you and other employers have an impact on the wage by your hiring decisions, but as an individual firm you don't, so you treat W as given and make your profit-maximizing choice in response to that wage level.

When you have no workers, the additional output from hiring one worker is large, so MPN $\times$ P is large, and presumably bigger than W. If you hire a worker, your revenue goes up by MPN $\times$ P, while your costs only go up by W. You should hire that worker.

As you hire more workers, MPN $\times$ P starts coming down (because of the diminishing marginal product of labor); eventually, you'll get to the point where

$$\text{MPN} \times P = W. \tag{4.2}$$

Once you get there, you shouldn't hire anyone else. If you do, you'll find that MPN $\times$ P is less than W, so your revenue will go up by less than your costs.

Now rearrange Eq. 4.2, dividing both sides by P:

$$\text{MPN} = W/P. \tag{4.3}$$

Translating this into English, it says: Look for the amount of labor where the marginal product of labor equals the real wage. (There's a convention in macroeconomics of using capital W to denote the nominal wage and lower-case w for the real wage, which is the nominal wage corrected for changes in the price level.)

Now we pretty much have a labor-demand function. In running your business, you don't get to choose the nominal wage, W. (You can try to pay less, but in a competitive labor market you'll have trouble getting people to work for you.) And you can't choose the level of prices in the economy, P. So the real wage is something you have to just accept at whatever it is.

What you *can* choose is the level of MPN, and you do this by choosing the number of people you have working for you. If you want a high MPN, hire very few workers; if you want a low one, hire lots of people. So you choose the number of workers that makes Eq. 4.3 true for your company. As firms throughout the economy follow this simple rule, we find that Eq. 4.2 is true for the economy as a whole.

So **labor demand**, denoted N^D, is a function of the real wage. Specifically, the lower the real wage is, the lower the level of MNP you're trying to reach, so the more people you hire.

And this is the same thing indicated by the intuition at the beginning of this section: when wages are lower, firms want to hire more people.

In algebraic notation, we can write

$$N^D = h(W/P),$$

where the real wage has a negative effect on the amount of labor hired.

Graphically, we get a shape that slopes downward (like any self-respecting demand curve), as shown in Fig. 4.2.

If the real wage is high—like at $(W/P)_2$—then only N_2 workers will be hired. If the wage drops to $(W/P)_1$, then employment will increase to N_1.

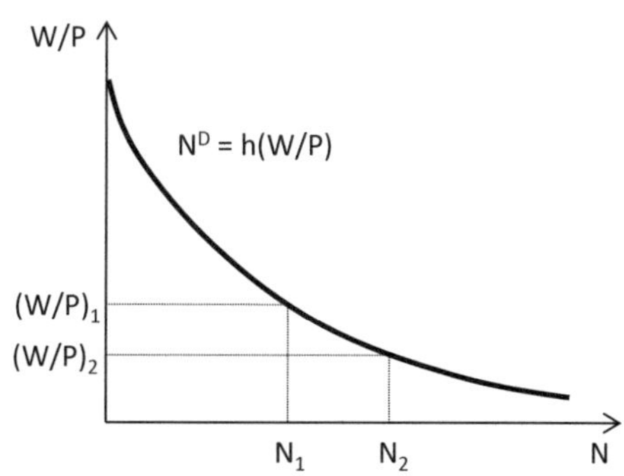

Fig. 4.2 The demand for labor

4.4 Labor Supply

In the real world, people's motivation for work is a complex thing. Given a choice of two jobs, you might choose the one with the lower wage if you liked that boss's management style better, or if it was work that you believed was in a good cause. Labor markets tend to compensate somewhat for risky work—coal miners make more than other workers whose jobs require similar levels of skill and physical exertion. And compensation involves a lot more than just the wage: depending on the job, there's some mix of vacation time, health insurance, flex time, stock options, etc.

But just as it does in many other respects, macroeconomics simplifies away from all of that. In looking at people's decisions about work, it doesn't say that those things don't matter, it simply focuses on the role played by wages. Or rather, it uses the wage as a stand-in for overall compensation.

And here the intuition is pretty simple. When you work, you give up leisure, so, all else being equal, you'd like to work as little as possible. But of course, when you work you gain income, which allows you to buy many of the good material things in life besides leisure. If the wage is \$5 /h, you don't get that much for each hour of leisure you give up; at \$15 /h, you get a lot more stuff for each sacrificed hour of leisure. So the higher the wage, the more leisure you're willing to give up. This means that the supply of labor is an upward-sloping shape.

At the same time, it doesn't make sense for the supply curve to go up at the same rate, regardless of how much you're already working. There are only 24 h in a day and you have to sleep and eat sometime. Also, the more hours you're working, the less time you have to enjoy all the stuff that you're buying. So at low wages, an increase in the wage causes a large increase in how much people want to work; at a higher wage, the same wage increase only causes a small increase in quantity of labor supplied.

Algebraically we can write the labor supply as

$$N^S = g(W/P), \tag{4.4}$$

where g is a function that makes N^S go up as W/P goes up. Figure 4.3 shows that relationship graphically.

4.5 Resource Markets

As with labor, we need to develop the logic of supply and demand for resources used in the production function. These two sides of each resource market come from very different places. The supply is the outcome of the interaction among several factors:

- Geology (for exhaustibles) or ecosystems (for biological renewables);
- Extraction or harvest in the past;

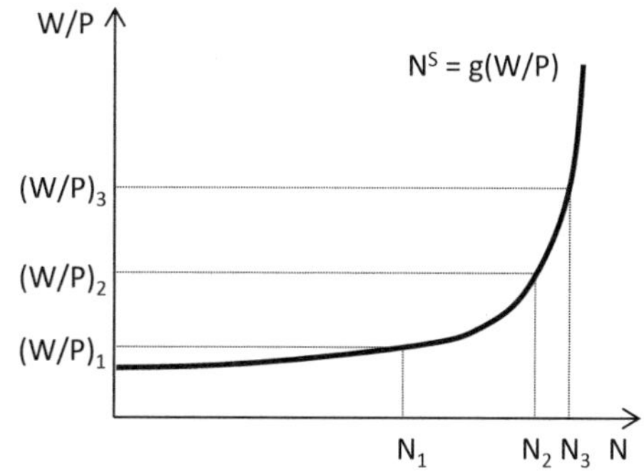

Fig. 4.3 The supply of labor

- Damage from pollution in the past (for biological renewables); and
- The current state of technology embodied in the current capital stock for extraction or harvest.

Demand, following on what was assumed earlier about the relationship between labor input and resource use, is directly related to the demand for labor.[3]

4.5.1 Resource Supply

Imagine a forest containing potentially useful trees. If appropriately managed, the forest can continue providing the resource of wood indefinitely: the total quantity that can be harvested over time is not meaningfully bounded. However, that's not the quantity that is relevant for economic production in any given period (a year, or a quarter). Rather, what matters is the quantity that can be harvested and put to economic use during that period, and that quantity presumably has some maximum. You may not have enough lumberjacks and saws to go get more trees. You may not have the railroad capacity to bring more trees to market. Part of the forest may be effectively inaccessible given current technology.

The concept of a maximum harvestable quantity in the current period leads to the kind of supply curve depicted in Fig. 4.4. The price of renewable resources is denoted P^B and $B_{\max(1)}$ is the maximum that can be harvested in period 1. The graph illustrates the simplified reality that increasing quantities are available at increasing prices, up to the quantity $B_{\max(1)}$.

Over time, two different types of forces act to move the renewables supply curve. On the increasing side, new harvesting technologies (such as feller-bunchers in the logging industry) make harvesting cheaper, moving the supply curve down and to

[3]Note that this approach to non-renewables is different from the standard economic models of foresight in the use of an exhaustible resource, such as the Hotelling Rule and the Hartwick Rule. It is closer—but not identical—to the geology-driven model of M. King Hubbert. All three will be discussed in Chap. 19.

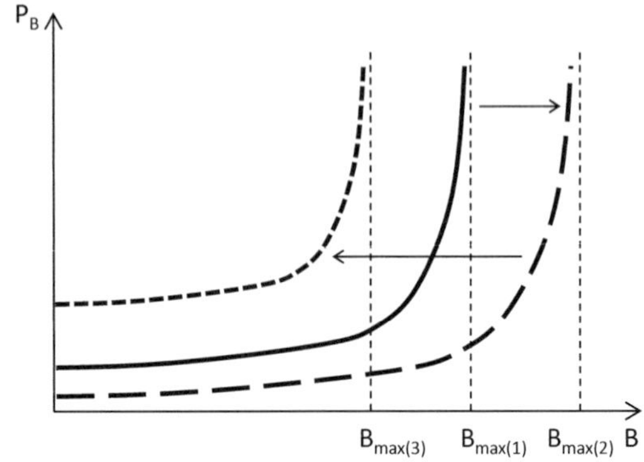

Fig. 4.4 Supply curves for renewable resources

the right. Other new technologies such as the railroad or the steam ship give access to stocks that were previously inaccessible, again pushing the supply curve to the right, and possibly down as well. Even with a given technology, increases in capital can also shift the curve to the right, as the construction of additional miles of railroads or roads for logging makes available larger quantities of timber.

Working against these effects of innovation and investment, there are the forces of harvest and ecosystem damage. All else being equal, the more trees or fish you harvest this year, the fewer there will be out there next year, moving B_{max} to the left. If human harvest is small enough this won't be significant, but as harvest expands it starts to matter. Similarly, all else being equal, the more pollution added to a waterway, the fewer fish there are, and the further left B_{max} moves.

At least for a time, these negative effects of harvest and pollution can be overcome by the positive effects of investment and innovation. If trees near your city are cut down faster than they grow back, you can still increase your current wood supply by building railroads to more distant timber stands; as fish near your city are killed off by your effluent, you can still increase your catch by building more and bigger boats that are able to go further out to sea. But if harvest and/or damage are sufficiently large, there must come a point where the maximum harvest is decreased.

Figure 4.4 illustrates a sequence of three different renewables supply curves, starting with the solid line, moving to the right as investment and innovation dominate and increase the currently available supply and shifting the maximum from $B_{max(1)}$ to $B_{max(2)}$, then moving back to the left as pollution and past harvest become stronger forces, reducing the maximum available down to $B_{max(3)}$.[4]

[4]Note that this discussion ignores questions of scarcity rent, an item that should in principle be included in the selling decisions of people who own renewable resources such as forests. I make this simplification for two reasons. First, some renewables such as marine fish are generally poorly regulated, so that no actor is in a position to include a scarcity rent in his or her calculations. Second, the scarcity-rent idea is questionable in the context of exhaustible resources (Chap. 19 will address this further) and for simplicity I have similarly omitted scarcity rent from renewables.

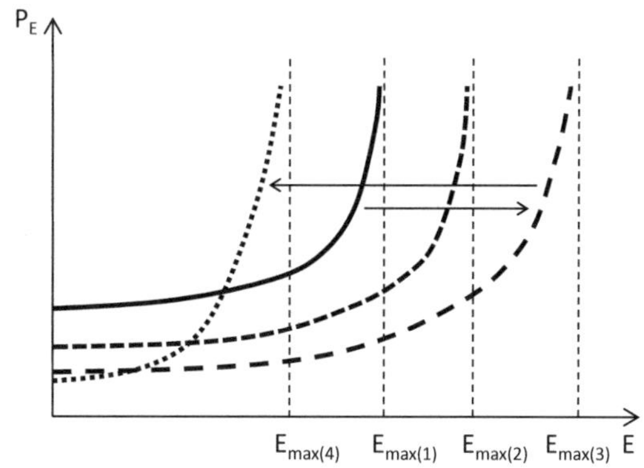

Fig. 4.5 Supply curves for exhaustible resources

The obvious difference between renewable and exhaustible resources is that, regardless of how well the extraction of exhaustibles is managed, there is by definition some maximum total amount that can ever be extracted. However, as with renewables, the immediately relevant question isn't the total available over time, but the amount that can be brought into the economy this period, and at what price. And it turns out that the dynamics—the way the supply evolves over time—are very similar to what we find with renewables.

As long as supplies in the ground are relatively abundant, more can be brought to market through investment: opening new mines, extending old mines, drilling new wells. Innovation can also expand the supply by helping locate previously unknown deposits or providing access to known but previously unreachable deposits (as with deep-sea oil drilling). But at some point, past extraction must leave so little in the ground (or so little that is easily accessible) that the supply curve has to move left and/or upward.

Figure 4.5 illustrates the market for exhaustible resources. The initial supply curve is the solid line. Over time, new discoveries, new extraction technologies, and new capital increase the amount available to the economy, moving the supply curve to the dashed line and then to the long-dashed line. Eventually, however, these factors cannot overcome the depletion of the resource, and the supply curve shifts back to the left, to the curve made of small dots and hemmed in by $E_{max(1)}$.

4.5.2 Resource Use

In Sect. 4.2 above on the production function, we simplified the relationship between labor and resources into one that evolved over time, but was a fixed ratio in the short

It remains as a research topic whether that simplification can be as well justified here as in the exhaustibles case.

run, determined by the state of technology and the stock of capital. And the portion of those resources that come from the exhaustible side has the same traits of being fixed in the short term but changing over time.

The exhaustibles share is some number between 0 and 1, being closer to 0 for stagecoaches and closer to 1 for coal-fired steam locomotives. If we denote the **exhaustibles share** by the Greek letter η ("eta"), we can modify our specification of resource use from Sect. 4.2 to show the use of exhaustibles and renewables specifically. The quantity of exhaustibles will be:

$$E = \eta \cdot R = \eta \cdot \rho \cdot N.$$

And since all resource use in this model is either exhaustible or renewable, use of renewables is the residual left by use of exhaustibles:

$$B = R - E = (1 - \eta) \cdot R = (1 - \eta) \cdot \rho \cdot N.$$

In Chap. 6 we will use these equations to combine resource use and labor supply in a single system. They will also allow us to derive resource demand from labor demand.

4.5.3 *The Biosphere's Absorptive Capacity*

There's another interaction between the economy and the environment that can be thought of as a "resource," and that's the biosphere's ability to absorb the wastes we produce in the course of our economic activity. But it's a resource with some important differences from the ones we've been looking at.

When you provide transportation using horses, there's a renewable input in the form of the crops you feed the horses. There's also the unavoidable reality of the horse manure. When you provide transportation with a coal-powered steam engine or a gasoline-powered car, there's an exhaustible input in the form of the fossil fuel you're burning, but there's also the unavoidable reality of the CO_2 you're releasing.

The biosphere has some capacity to absorb the manure without being harmed; if it's properly spread out, it can even be a benefit. Similarly, the biosphere can absorb small amounts of CO_2 without meaningfully changing the atmospheric composition of that gas; it can absorb larger amounts without causing undesirable changes in climate. And similar stories can be told about pretty much everything we think of as "waste," with each type having different quantities that can be "dealt with" (for some kinds of pollution that amount is very small).

And so when we engage in economic activity we are "using" some of the biosphere's absorptive capacity, just as we are using some amount of renewable and/or exhaustible resources. But as mentioned above, there are two ways that absorptive capacity differs from "normal" resources, and the first is that we aren't charged for the use of this resource. If you want to use some fish, or timber, or coal, etc., somebody has to do some work to harvest or extract it. And before that, somebody had to have done some work to build the machines used in harvest or extraction. And if it's not fish on the open ocean or a large lake, somebody probably owns the land on or under which the resource is found, and they'll want some payment for allowing you to harvest or extract the resource. In other words, the economy forces the person using the resource to pay for it. This is the framework in which Figs. 4.4 and 4.5 make sense and it's key to the equilibrium solution that will be defined in Chap. 6, where the prices of the resources feed back into the decision about how much labor to use. When we push up against the biological or geological impossibility of having more, high prices push back and force us to somehow moderate our use.

Absorptive capacity is different. Generally speaking, nobody owns the rivers into which excess manure might wash, or the atmosphere into which our CO_2 rises, so there isn't anyone to charge us for such use. And there's no labor cost either. In the case of a horse-drawn stagecoach we need the labor of the driver to control the vehicle, and the labor of everyone who provided the food for the horses. But we don't need any extra labor to cause the horses to produce manure; it happens automatically as a byproduct of providing the service of transportation. Similarly, we have to pay for the fuel that goes in our cars, but we don't pay extra to have CO_2 come out. In fact, while the production of waste is generally free for the waste producer, the thing that has a cost is the *limitation* of waste. So the first difference from other resources is that an economy doesn't automatically provide a price signal for absorptive capacity.

The second difference concerns limits. As explained at the end of Sect. 2.4, when you've cut all the trees, you can't cut any more. But even when you've far exceeded the biosphere's capacity to absorb waste and you've committed your planet to a future that resembles Venus, you can still emit pollution.

With normal resources, we are forced to stop using them when they die. With absorptive capacity, we are forced to stop using them when *we* die.

We'll revisit this issue in Part IV.

4.6 The Cobb-Douglas Function

The production function given above was entirely general, telling you nothing more than that you combine labor, capital, and resources to get output. Sometimes it's useful to put more structure on the relationship among the inputs—that is, you want to specify the functional form. A conventional way of doing that is with what's known as a Cobb-Douglas function.

First a note about how input efficiency is described in macroeconomics. Capital and labor, though they're abstractions, have a pretty clear quantitative sense: more labor means hiring more people; more capital means having more machines.

Resource intensity of labor and exhaustibles share of resource use are also measurable in principle. But how do you put a number on better input efficiency? The key is that better input efficiency allows you to produce more with the same amount of capital, labor, and resources as before. That means that when we put it into a production function, we can actually just use a number for Z, the level of input efficiency, and a more advanced technology reflected in higher input efficiency will be a bigger value of Z, which will in turn lead to a more productive economy. We then put labor, capital, input efficiency, and resource intensity of labor into the Cobb-Douglas function.[5]

We combine labor and input efficiency by defining input efficiency as labor's "effectiveness" and then treating $Z \cdot N$ as a single term. That leaves in addition the level of the capital stock and the quantity of resources. Each term is raised to an exponent, so the Cobb-Douglas function can be written as

$$Y = K^{\alpha} \cdot (Z \cdot N)^{\delta} \cdot R^{\gamma}. \tag{4.5}$$

The exponents α, δ, and γ are all numbers between 0 and 1, usually chosen such that

$$\alpha + \delta + \gamma = 1.$$

They represent each input's relative contribution to output. If, say, δ is bigger than α, it means that a given increase in labor will have a bigger effect than the same percentage size increase in capital.[6]

This function has a number of desirable properties, including diminishing marginal product of capital, diminishing marginal product of labor, and constant returns to scale.

Diminishing marginal product of capital (MPK) is analogous to diminishing marginal product of labor: if you hold labor and resources constant and keep increasing capital in even increments, you'll get more output, but in ever smaller increments. You can confirm this in a crude empirical fashion by choosing any fixed levels of Z, N, ρ, α, δ, and γ, then plugging in ever-larger amounts of K in even increments (for instance, 10, 20, 30, etc.) and see how Y grows by ever-smaller amounts. You can also see diminishing MPK with a little calculus, shown in the "Treatment in calculus and algebra" appendix at the end of this chapter.

[5] Note that in most macroeconomic models, the concept of resource-intensity of labor is missing, and so what we're describing here as "input efficiency" is usually referred to as "technology."

[6] Because the three exponents are assumed to add up to 1, we could actually eliminate one of them. For instance, we could define $\delta = 1 - \alpha - \gamma$ and then get rid of δ. However, it will sometimes be convenient to be able to refer directly to all three, so we won't make that substitution except when it helps with some algebra.

Diminishing marginal product of labor was explained above in general terms. The algebraic demonstration of it for the Cobb-Douglas function is entirely analogous to the demonstration of diminishing MPK and is also given in the calculus-and-algebra appendix.

Constant returns to scale (CRS) is the idea that if you double your labor and capital inputs, you also double the output. This contrasts to diminishing returns to scale (double the inputs and get less than double the output) and increasing returns to scale (double the inputs and get more than double the output). CRS is not generally a true description of the world, but it is convenient; among other things, the per-worker form of output discussed below in Sect. 4.7 is only possible with a CRS production function. A rigorous demonstration of the CRS property of the Cobb-Douglas function is in the calculus-and-algebra appendix.

4.7 The Per-Worker Production Function

Since a society's prosperity is determined more by its output per worker than by its total output, it's useful to look at production in per-worker terms, and the Cobb-Douglas function specified above is particularly convenient for that.

First, define output per worker as y, and capital per worker as k. That's the same as saying

$$\begin{aligned} y &= Y/N \\ k &= K/N. \end{aligned} \tag{4.6}$$

Carry this through to the definition of Y given above in Eq. 4.5:

$$Y/N = (K^\alpha \cdot (Z \cdot N)^\delta \cdot R^\gamma)/N.$$

Now replace R using the fact that $R = \rho \cdot N$:

$$Y/N = (K^\alpha \cdot (Z \cdot N)^\delta \cdot (\rho N)^\delta)/N.$$

The numerator on the right-hand side has two terms with N and we can combine them using the rules of exponents:

$$Y/N = (K^\alpha Z^\delta \rho^\gamma N^{(\delta+\gamma)})/N.$$

Now we can neatly divide out the N, noting that dividing by N is like multiplying by N^{-1} and again applying the rules of exponents:

$$Y/N = K^\alpha Z^\delta \rho^\gamma N^{(\delta+\gamma-1)}.$$

Then we can draw on the assumption that $\alpha+\delta+\gamma = 1$ to note that $\delta+\gamma-1 = -\alpha$:

$$Y/N = K^{\alpha}Z^{\delta}\rho^{\gamma}N^{-\alpha}.$$

Finally, with some regrouping and noting again that $N^{-\alpha} = 1/N^{\alpha}$, we have:

$$\begin{aligned} Y/N &= K^{\alpha} \cdot N^{-\alpha} \cdot Z^{\delta} \cdot \rho^{\gamma} \\ &= K^{\alpha}/N^{\alpha} \cdot Z^{\delta} \cdot \rho^{\gamma} \\ &= (K/N)^{\alpha} \cdot Z^{\delta} \cdot \rho^{\gamma} \\ y &= k^{\alpha} \cdot Z^{\delta} \cdot \rho^{\gamma}. \end{aligned} \tag{4.7}$$

So it turns out that output per worker can be expressed in terms of technology, resource intensity of labor, and capital *per worker*, without having to know the actual quantity of the labor input. This will be convenient in Chap. 7's discussion of long-run growth. Remember, however, that it depends on the assumption of constant returns to scale embodied in $\alpha + \delta + \gamma = 1$.

Appendix: Summary of Terminology

K	capital
R	resources ($E + B$)
E	exhaustible resources
B	renewable resource
η	share of resources provided by exhaustibles ($E = \eta \times R$)
ρ	resource intensity (quantity of resource used per unit of labor; part of technology)
N	labor
A	overall technology level
Z	input efficiency (part of technology)
MPN	marginal product of labor
MPK	marginal product of capital
P	price level of output
P_B	price of renewable resources
P_E	price of exhaustible resources
P_R	composite price of resources ($= \eta P_E + (1 - \eta)P_B$) (this will come up in Chap. 6)

MVP	marginal value product (MPN × P)
W	nominal wage
w	real wage ($= W/P$)

Appendix: Why *K*? Why *N*? Why *A*? Why *Z*?

It might seem more straightforward to refer to capital as "*C*" and labor as "*L*". Unfortunately, we'll want those worthy letters for other roles later. *C* will be taken for "consumption" and *L* for the demand for money (sometimes also referred to as the demand for liquidity, so it's not completely bizarre to use *L* for it). *K* makes some sense for "capital" because at least it sounds right, and anyway, it was Marx who made the word really famous, and in German it's "das Kapital." If you want to make some sense of *N* for labor, you can imagine it stands for the "number" of workers.

The use of *A* for technology is purely arbitrary and conventional. Some specifications of the production function, such as in [2], use *E* to represent the "effectiveness" of labor, which is the logic behind combining that *E* (or our *Z*) with *N* before applying the exponent in the Cobb-Douglas function. But we're holding *E* in reserve to stand for "exhaustible" resources when we bring those back in.

The use of *Z* for input efficiency is, of course, particular to this text. It was chosen because it's available and because it's at the opposite end of the alphabet from *A*.

Appendix: Treatment in Calculus and Algebra

This appendix fleshes out some algebraic details of the Cobb-Douglas function, with a particular focus on diminishing marginal product of capital, diminishing marginal product of labor, and constant returns to scale.

Diminishing MPK and MPN

Diminishing marginal product of capital (MPK) can be shown algebraically with a little calculus. First, MPK is the first derivative of the production function with respect to *K* (this means that everything in the expression is treated as a constant except for *K*):

$$\text{MPK} = \partial Y/\partial K = \alpha K^{\alpha-1}(Z \cdot N)^{\delta} \cdot R^{\gamma}.$$

(The strange symbol ∂ is called "del", and the expression $\partial Y/\partial K$ simply means "the partial derivative of Y with respect to K—in other words, what is the rate at which Y changes as K changes by an infinitessimally small amount.)

"Diminishing MPK" is a claim that, as more and more capital is used with fixed amounts of other inputs, the MPK goes down. In other words, as K gets bigger, MPK gets smaller. In algebraic terms, this is a claim that the second derivative of Y with respect to K is negative. (The second derivative is the derivative of the first derivative.) With the Cobb-Douglas function, this is necessarily true. To start, take the second derivative:

$$\partial \text{MPK}/\partial K = \partial^2 Y/\partial K^2 = \alpha(\alpha - 1)K^{\alpha-2}(Z \cdot N)^{\delta} \cdot R^{\gamma}.$$

The notation $\partial^2 Y/\partial K^2$ denotes the second derivative of Y with respect to K

Now look at the parts. Since Z, K, R, and N are all positive numbers, it must be true that

$$K^{\alpha-2}(Z \cdot N)^{\delta} \cdot R^{\gamma} > 0.$$

And with α between 0 and 1, we know that α is positive while $\alpha - 1$ is negative. So we know that for any Cobb-Douglas function with α between 0 and 1, MPK gets smaller as K gets bigger.

Diminishing marginal product of labor is exactly analogous to diminishing marginal product of capital: MPN is the first derivative of the production function, only this time with respect to labor rather than with respect to capital. And the second derivative with respect to labor tells you how MPN changes as N increases; as with MPK, a negative second derivative tells you that MPN goes down when N goes up.

Start from the form of the production function in which R has been replaced by ρN and the N terms have been grouped:

$$Y = K^{\alpha} Z^{\delta} \rho^{\gamma} N^{(\delta+\gamma)}.$$

The first partial derivative of the production function with respect to N is then

$$\begin{aligned} \partial Y/\partial N &= (\delta + \gamma)K^{\alpha} Z^{\delta} \rho^{\gamma} N^{(\delta+\gamma-1)} \\ &= (1-\alpha)K^{\alpha} Z^{\delta} \rho^{\delta} N^{-\alpha} = \text{MPN} \end{aligned} \tag{4.8}$$

and the second derivative of the production function with respect to N is:

$$\partial \text{MPN}/\partial N = \partial^2 Y/\partial N^2 = -\alpha(1-\alpha)K^{\alpha} Z^{\delta} \rho^{\gamma} N^{-\alpha-1}.$$

By the same reasoning as with MPK, we know that $K^{\alpha} Z^{\delta} \rho^{\gamma} N^{-\alpha-1}$ is positive, and that $-\alpha(1-\alpha)$ is negative, so the whole thing must be negative.

Constant Returns to Scale

The idea of constant returns to scale is that you could double *all three* of labor, capital, and resources, or triple them, or multiply them by 1.5, or by any factor, and the output will go up by that same multiple. It doesn't matter what you multiply K and N and R by, so long as you multiply them all by the same thing. If your production function has constant returns to scale, output will go up by that same multiple.

The way to demonstrate this algebraically with the Cobb-Douglas function (or to test for it in any other function) is to multiply the inputs by a completely general term (call it t), and see whether that same t shows up in output. (Because resources are themselves a function of the labor input, we apply the t factor only to capital and labor.)

We start with arbitrary levels of inputs K_1 and N_1, and then we look at a future where those have all increased by some common multiple, t. That means that $K_2 = t \cdot K_1$ and $N_2 = t \cdot N_1$. Then $Y_1 = F(K_1, N_1)$ and $Y_2 = F(K_2, N_2)$, and we want to see whether $Y_2 = t \cdot Y_1$.

With the Cobb-Douglas form we get:

$$\begin{aligned} Y_2 &= {K_2}^{\alpha}(ZN_2)^{\delta}(\rho N_2)^{\gamma} \\ &= (tK_1)^{\alpha}(ZtN_1)^{\delta}(\rho tN_1)^{\gamma} \\ &= t^{\alpha}{K_1}^{\alpha}Z^{\delta}t^{\delta}{N_1}^{\delta}\rho^{\gamma}t^{\gamma}{N_1}^{\gamma} \\ &= t^{\alpha}t^{\delta}t^{\gamma}{K_1}^{\alpha}Z^{\delta}{N_1}^{\delta}\rho^{\gamma}{N_1}^{\gamma} \\ &= t^{(\alpha+\delta+\gamma)}{K_2}^{\alpha}(ZN_1)^{\delta}(\rho N_1)^{\gamma} \\ &= tY_1, \end{aligned} \tag{4.9}$$

which is what we set out to prove: when you multiply all the inputs by t, the output goes up by a factor of t as well.

If you followed that, you may have noticed the role of the exponents. There were terms of t^{α}, t^{δ}, and t^{γ}, and when you multiply those together, you get t^1, also known as t. This suggests some slight variants to the Cobb-Douglas form. The exponents on K, ZN, and R could add up to more than 1, in which case there would be increasing returns to scale (doubling the inputs more than doubling the output); or the exponents could add up to less than one (doubling the inputs increases the output by less than double).

Problems

Problem 4.1 The text explained renewables in terms of biologically-based resources. Consider now the supply curve for a non-biological renewable resource.

(a) What determines the maximum amount you can obtain in a given period (e.g., a year or a quarter)?
(b) Does obtaining more now affect the amount that will be available in the future?
(c) What shortcoming(s) might non-biological renewable resources have as substitutes for large amounts of fossil fuel consumption?

Problem 4.2 These questions relate to the per-worker form of the production function discussed in Sect. 4.7. In each case, explain the logic behind your answer.

(a) What happens to output per worker if there is an increase in capital per worker?
(b) What happens to output per worker if there is an increase in input efficiency (Z)?
(c) What happens to output per worker if there is an increase in resource-intensity of labor (ρ)?
(d) Why does the per-worker form of the production function talk about increased capital *per worker*, but can speak directly of an increase in input efficiency or an increase in resource-intensity of labor?

Problem 4.3 The calculus-and-algebra appendix explains that the marginal product of labor in a Cobb-Douglas function is:

$$MPN = (\delta + \gamma)K^{\alpha}Z^{\delta}\rho^{\gamma}N^{(\delta+\gamma-1)}$$

(see Eq. 4.8).
Use the values in Table 4.1.

(a) What is the real wage?
(b) Given the choices of 67, 72, 77, 82, 87, 92, which is closest to the equilibrium level of labor? Explain.

Table 4.1 Values for Problem 4.3

$K =$	100
$Z =$	25
$\rho =$	10
$\alpha =$	0.3
$\delta =$	0.3
$\gamma =$	0.4
$W =$	10
$P =$	2

(c) If capital changes from $K = 100$ to $K = 107$, which level of N (from the same list of choices as above in part b) is closest to the equilibrium level of labor? Explain.

(d) If capital stays at its new level of $K = 107$ and the nominal wage falls from $W = 10$ to $W = 9.65$, which of those same options for N is closest to the equilibrium level?

References

1. Baumol, W. J. (1967). Macroeconomics of unbalanced growth: The anatomy of urban crisis. *American Economic Review, 57*(3),415–426.
2. Bradford deLong, J. (2002). *Macroeconomics*. Boston: McGraw-Hill Irwin.
3. Moroney, J. R. (1992). Energy, capital and technological change in the United States. *Resources and Energy, 14*, 363–380.
4. Seeley, K. (2009). Creation of value and the recession of 2007—?, June 2009. Presented at the U.S. Society for Ecological Economics conference, Washington, DC.
5. Seeley, K. (2014). Shifting values: Efficiency and debt service in a no-growth economy, March 2014. Presented at the Eastern Economic Association conference, Boston.
6. Wils, A. (2001). The effects of three categories of technological innovation on the use and price of nonrenewable resources. *Ecological Economics, 37*, 457–472.

Chapter 5
The Composition of Output

Abstract This chapter develops a set of functions that describe in a stylized way the components of output: consumption, investment, government expenditure, gross exports, and imports.

5.1 Introduction

Chapter 4 gives an explanation for how output is produced, but the point of producing stuff is for it to be bought and used. The different ways of buying final goods and services add up to aggregate demand, that total that is being spent on buying output. In a classical, long-run perspective, we assume that output is determined on the supply side, as will be done in Chap. 6, so aggregate demand doesn't determine the quantity of output. But the individual expenditure functions within aggregate demand do determine how that output is divided up, so even in the long-run model they are informative.[1]

5.2 Components of Aggregate Demand

Aggregate demand comes from four places:

C *consumption expenditure*: This is cars, medical care, food, gas, rent, etc.—things bought by private households for their own use.

I *investment*: This term covers firms' creation of physical capital, whether buying new equipment or upgrading existing machinery. In the Keynesian framework we'll have to distinguish between intended and unintended investment (see the Appendix in this chapter on "Unintended investment"), but for now, we'll just deal with investment in total.

G *government expenditure*: Examples of government expenditure are when government pays senators, judges, police officers, teachers, etc., or buys an airplane

[1]The specific forms of the expenditure functions given here follow [1].

K. Seeley, *Macroeconomics in Ecological Context*, Studies in Ecological Economics 5, DOI 10.1007/978-3-319-51757-5_5

for the military or copier paper for a government office, or builds a road, or pays a private company to run a prison, etc. The term "*G*" does *not* include what are known as "transfers," programs such as food stamps or unemployment insurance. In those cases, the payment from the government isn't in return for a person selling the government their services or some goods, but simply because the law defines the person as eligible for certain benefits. These transfers will show up in aggregate demand when the people who receive them turn around and spend them.

NX net exports: When you buy a French wine, that money becomes part of the aggregate demand in France's economy and is subtracted from the aggregate demand in ours. When a Parisian buys a ticket to *Star Wars, Episode 42*, the portion of the ticket price that makes its way back to California becomes part of the aggregate demand in our economy and is subtracted from the aggregate demand in France. Net exports (exports minus imports) thus capture the net addition to our aggregate demand from all foreign-trade activity. If imports are larger than exports, then *NX* is negative.

Aggregate demand is summed up by the equation:

$$AD = C + I + G + NX.$$

5.3 Consumption

The consumption function is based on three ideas: first, an important determinant is "disposable income," which simply means the income that's left after you've paid taxes. We can call that Y_D and represent it as $Y_D = (1 - t)Y$, where t is the tax rate.

The second factor is the tendency for consumption to change with disposable income, but not one-for-one. That is, if your income goes up by \$100, your consumption expenditure will change as well, but by something less than \$100—maybe \$80, maybe \$60, or some other number less than \$100.

Third, though consumption changes by less than disposable income, it doesn't stay a fixed portion of disposable income as consumption and income change. In other words, if consumption goes up by \$80 for every \$100 of new disposable income, the total amount isn't 80% of disposable income.

Combining these three ideas, a simple specification of the consumption function is

$$C = C_0 + C_Y \cdot Y.$$

C_Y is the "marginal propensity to consume" (MPC): with every additional dollar (marginal dollar) of disposable income, how much do people tend to increase their consumption? This will be a number between 0 and 1.

C_0 is "autonomous consumption," the part of consumption expenditure that's independent of disposable income. Algebraically, it also looks like the level of consumption that would happen if income were zero. But this is the *aggregate* consumption function, the level of consumption expenditure for the economy as a whole, and income for the economy as a whole is never zero.

Changes in people's mood or confidence about the future could be reflected in either C_0 or C_Y. Increased confidence would cause in increase in one or both of those parameters.

Also, over the long run, C_0 generally grows as the economy grows. If it didn't, it would be a smaller and smaller fraction of Y and the consumption function would move in the direction of being $C = C_Y(1 - t)Y$.

This view of consumption is sometimes called the "Keynesian" consumption function, but it can also be used in the classical model.

(For the major alternatives to the Keynesian view see the appendix on "Alternative consumption functions.")

5.4 Investment

Investment is modeled as responding to the real interest rate. Every potential investment has an expected rate of return; perhaps you predict that a new car factory will give you profits equivalent to earning 8% on your money, while you predict opening a restaurant will make profits equivalent to a 5% return on your money. If you can borrow money at a 2% interest rate, both investments make sense. If instead the interest rate is 4%, the restaurant isn't worth doing, once you figure in risk: you *expect* to make 5%, but it could be 6% or 3%, and you're not confident enough of your estimate of 5% to be willing to borrow money at 4% in order to finance it. The car factory, however, still looks good. But when you have to pay 7% to borrow money, perhaps the car factory also stops being worth doing.

The bottom line is that at higher real interest rates, fewer potential investment projects are worth doing, and therefore the quantity of investment goes down as the real interest rate goes up.

But investment responds to more than just interest rates. New technologies can spur investment as firms see profit opportunities in the installation of the new equipment. For example, robots for assembly lines raise all sorts of possibilities for profitable manufacturing, but first you need to make an investment expenditure to buy and install the robots.

Or a new technology can increase the demand for goods that are currently not produced in large quantity, so that there are now profits to be made in expanding production capacity of those goods. The growth of the car industry in the early twentieth century kept raising the profitability of pumping petroleum out of the ground and turning it into gasoline.

Also, the moods of investors can change, so that their perception of risk or profitability shifts *en masse*. This effect can go in either direction, as investors either grow more confident or succumb to group skepticism or pessimism. Changes in regulations or tax law can also change the expected return to a given investment activity. In any of these cases, the amount of investment that happens at any given interest rate changes.

The simplest way of capturing these two basic parts of investment behavior is with a function sort of like the consumption function:

$$I = I_0 - I_r \cdot r.$$

The term I_r is simply the coefficient of the interest rate, with the subscript r differentiating it from I_0. It represents how sensitive investment expenditure is to the interest rate; if a change in r causes a large change in I, then that gets reflected in I_r being a relatively big number. To reflect the intuition that higher real interest rates mean less investment, $I_r \cdot r$ is subtracted from I_0 rather than being added to it. I_0 is "autonomous investment," just as C_0 in the consumption function is autonomous consumption. The term I_0 captures all those factors other than the interest rate that affect willingness to invest: expectations of the future state of the economy; regulations and taxes; new technologies; etc.

5.5 Government Expenditure

The level of government expenditure, G, is set through a political process rather than through market forces. In this regard it is like t, the tax rate: it has quite significant economic effects, but it does not have economic determinants that are worth pursuing in this context. As a result, in most macroeconomic models G is simply taken as given.

5.6 Net Exports

Net exports are simply gross exports minus imports, and we'll take these two parts separately.

$$\text{Net Exports} = \text{Gross exports} - \text{Imports}$$

Gross exports (GX) are affected by two factors. First, just as consumption by Americans is affected by our level of disposable income, consumption of our stuff by foreigners is determined by their income. But instead of talking about foreigners' *disposable* incomes (income minus taxes), we just talk about their *gross* incomes, Y^f, where the superscript f distinguishes foreigners' incomes from our own income, Y. There are two reasons for this simplification. First, it's simpler not to have to consider foreign levels of taxation. Second, exports go not only to consumption by foreigners but also to investment activity (for instance, if a foreign company buys American computers or software) and to government expenditure (as when foreign governments buy American weapons).

The other major influence is the real exchange rate, ε, which captures the quantity of American goods and services we have to give up to get foreign-made goods and services. At a lower value of ε, we don't have to give up as much stuff to get a particular quantity of foreign stuff, which is the same as saying that foreigners have to give up more stuff to get a particular quantity of American stuff. If that's true, they won't buy as much from us, so a lower value of ε results in a lower value of gross exports.

These two assumptions about export behavior are captured in the function:

$$GX = GX_Y \cdot Y^f + GX_\varepsilon \cdot \varepsilon.$$

As with investment, the subscripts distinguish the two coefficients, with GX_Y being the coefficient on foreigners' income and GX_ε being the coefficient on the real exchange rate. Both of them are greater than zero: more income in foreigners' hands means higher exports by us, and a higher real exchange rate similarly means that we export more.

Imports (IM) would seem to be influenced by the real exchange rate as well, but we leave that out of the import function. This is partly for simplicity, but also because of the double-edged nature of exchange rates. When the real exchange rate goes down, the *quantity* of our imports does increase, but the prices of those imports, in dollar terms, have gone down, and we're interested in the dollars spent on imports rather than on the quantity of stuff imported. And while these two forces are unlikely to exactly balance, it's close enough so that it's not worth complicating things by throwing ε into the mix.

What does affect imports is our income, Y. As was true of the role of foreigners' income in our exports, we put our total income in the import function, rather than disposable income, and for the same reason: imports go not only toward our consumption but toward investment (for instance, a firm might buy machinery from Germany) and toward government expenditure (for example, when U.S. military bases overseas buy goods and services from surrounding communities). So the import function is a very simple one:

$$IM = IM_Y \cdot Y.$$

The coefficient IM_Y is the "marginal propensity to import," much like C_Y is the marginal propensity to consume.

Similarly, GX_Y can be thought of as foreigners' marginal propensity to import. Empirically, for the last few decades our marginal propensity to import has been higher than other countries' marginal propensity to import, so that if everyone's income goes up by the same amount, our imports go up by more than our exports.

The net export function is then:

$$\begin{aligned} NX &= GX - IM \\ &= GX_Y \cdot Y^f + GX_\varepsilon \cdot \varepsilon - IM_Y \cdot Y. \end{aligned}$$

Since all three coefficients are positive, net exports go up with foreigners' incomes and with the real exchange rate, and go down with our income.

5.7 Real Exchange Rates

The real exchange rate is affected by the demand for dollars relative to the demand for other currencies. And a major influence on that demand is the difference in real interest rates between the U.S. and elsewhere.

Higher interest rates here than elsewhere lead to strong demand for dollars: if owning American stocks or American factories earns you 5% real interest a year, and owning Japanese or European assets only earns you 2% or 3% a year, you're going to want to own American assets. So a positive difference between our real interest rate and other countries' rates leads to strong demand for dollars. Use r^f to denote the foreign interest rate, the rate earned in other countries. Then we're saying that if $(r - r^f) > 0$, there will be high demand for dollars.

This strong demand translates in turn into a low real exchange rate—that is, you don't need many dollars to buy other currencies because people with other currencies are so willing to buy dollars. This leads to a negative relationship between the interest-rate gap described above and the real exchange rate.

The only remaining piece, as with investment and consumption, is a constant term to reflect "other factors" besides differences in interest rates: confidence in how the economy is run, expectations of future shifts in exchange rates, etc. Putting it all together, we can specify the real exchange rate as:

$$\varepsilon = \varepsilon_0 - \varepsilon_r \cdot (r - r^f).$$

For example, increased confidence in the U.S. economy would decrease ε_0: because of the increased demand for dollars, the real exchange rate would go down, representing a stronger dollar. (Recall the explanation in Sect. 3.7 that a lower value of ε represents your currency being stronger.)

Appendix: Summary of Terminology

AD	Aggregate Demand ($C + I + G + NX$)
C	Consumption ($C_0 + C_Y \cdot Y_D$)
C_0	Autonomous consumption
C_Y	MPC (marginal propensity to consume)
I	Investment ($I_0 - I_r \cdot r$)
I_0	Autonomous investment
I_r	Interest-rate sensitivity of investment
r	Real interest rate
r^f	Foreign interest rate
ε	Real exchange rate ($\varepsilon_0 - \varepsilon_r \cdot (r - r^f)$)
ε_0	Long-run equilibrium real exchange rate
ε_r	Interest-rate sensitivity of exchange rate
G	Government Expenditure
NX	Net Exports ($GX - IM = GX_Y \cdot Y^f + GX_\varepsilon \cdot \varepsilon - IM_Y \cdot Y$)
GX	Gross Exports ($GX_Y \cdot Y^f + GX_\varepsilon \cdot \varepsilon$)
GX_Y	Foreign-income sensitivity of gross exports
GX_ε	Exchange-rate sensitivity of gross exports
IM	Imports ($IM_Y \cdot Y$)
IM_Y	Marginal propensity to import
MPC	Marginal propensity to consume
T	Tax ($t \cdot Y$)
t	Tax rate
Y	Income
Y_D	Disposable Income ($Y - T$)
Y^f	Foreign income

Appendix: Unintended Investment

"Unintended investment" is basically unplanned changes in inventory. Let's say you planned to produce 100,000 cars this month and 100,000 next month; you planned to sell 95,000 cars this month and put 5,000 in inventory, expecting to sell 105,000 next month. Additions to inventory are technically counted as part of investment, so those 5,000 you plan to put in inventory are part of intended investment. Now it turns out you only sold 92,000 cars instead of 95,000, so your addition to inventory was 8,000 instead of 5,000. The extra 3,000 into inventory was unintended, but any addition to inventory is still counted as investment, hence the 3,000 represent an unintended investment.

From the perspective of your individual company, your failure to sell as many cars as you expected may have been due to people buying other things rather than cars. But for the economy as a whole, unintended additions to inventory must mean less total spending than firms expected in aggregate, which amounts to more total saving. Thus the inclusion of unintended investment helps make the national accounts balance out. But intended and unintended investment have very different effects in terms of aggregate demand.

Intended investment shows up in firms spending money, and thus an increase in intended investment is a cause of increased aggregate demand. An increase in *un*intended investment is a *result* of people *not* spending money and, far from causing an increase in aggregate demand, it acts as a signal to firms to scale back production, because they already have more goods on hand to sell than they expected to.

Appendix: Alternative Consumption Functions

The Keynesian consumption function dominated macroeconomics for many years and it's still useful for getting a rough handle on multiplier effects, but most modern theory gives at least some credence to some version of what is known as "consumption smoothing," primarily the "permanent income hypothesis" and the "life-cycle model."

Both of these point out that people should respond differently to a change in income, depending on whether they expect the change to be a short-term event or to last a long time. Compare the situation where your company has an exceptionally good year and you get a $5,000 bonus (after taxes), vs. a situation where you are promoted within the company and get a $5,000 raise (after taxes). The naïve Keynesian consumption function says that in either case your spending goes up by $C_Y \cdot \$5,000$; if $C_Y = 0.8$ as in the example above, then your spending goes up by $4,000.

But does this really make sense? In the case of the bonus, your spending goes up by $4,000 this year above what you were doing originally, but then next year it has to plummet pretty drastically—at most, you have $\$1,000 +$ interest left over from the $5,000. You *might* do that. But you're far more likely to increase your spending by $4,000 in the case of the promotion or raise, knowing that you can spend an extra $4,000 the next year as well, and the year after that.

The idea of "permanent income" (see [2]) is that you save large amounts of unexpected windfalls, in order to have savings to cover unexpected hits in income, keeping your consumption not entirely smooth, but smoother than it would be if you simply spent a fixed portion of every new dollar that came into your wallet and cut your spending in a similar fashion when your income falls.

The life-cycle hypothesis (developed in [3]) says that you base your consumption not on what you're earning right now, but on your best guess of what your typical income will be, averaged over the course of your life. This is consistent with students spending more than they earn (borrowing to cover the difference), financially successful middle-aged people spending less than they earn (using the savings to pay back their student debts and to build up a retirement fund), and older people again spending more than they earn (drawing down the savings the built up in their middle years). On the other hand, it's hard to predict your income over your entire career.

Problems

Problem 5.1 Assume the following parameter values:

Autonomous consumption = \$200
MPC = 0.75
Income = \$2,024
Tax rate = 20%

(a) According to the consumption function given in Sect. 5.3, what is the level of consumption?
(b) If income increases to \$2,080 what is the new level of consumption?
(c) If income is returned to \$2,024 but taxes are cut to 18%, what is the new level of consumption?

Problem 5.2 Use the investment function in Sect. 5.4 to calculate the levels of investment for these two sets of parameters:

(a) $I_0 = \$300, I_r = \$1,200, r = 5\%$
(b) $I_0 = \$350, I_r = \$1,190, r = 4.5\%$

Problem 5.3 Looking at the two sets of parameters in problem 5.2, if there were an innovation that promised great increases in future productivity, would it make more sense for the investment function to change from b. to a., or from a. to b.? Explain.

Problem 5.4 Under the following parameters, calculate net exports. To find that quantity, you will first need to calculate the real exchange rate, gross exports, and imports.

Foreign income = \$3,000
Foreign interest rate = 5%
Domestic interest rate = 4%
Domestic income = \$2,100
$IM_Y = 0.1$
$GX_Y = 0.02$
$GX_\varepsilon = \$1$
$\varepsilon_0 = 110$
$\varepsilon_r = 700$
$\varepsilon =$
Imports =
Gross exports =
Net exports =

Problem 5.5 How do your answers to problem 5.4 change if domestic income drops to $2,000 and the domestic interest rate rises to 6%?

References

1. Bradford deLong, J. (2002). *Macroeconomics*. Boston: McGraw-Hill/Irwin.
2. Friedman, M. (1956). *A theory of the consumption function*. Princeton: Princeton University Press.
3. Modigliani, F., & Brumberg, R. (1954). Utility analysis and the consumption function: An interpretation of cross-section data. In K. K. Kurihara (Ed.), *Post keynesian economics*. New Brunswick: Rutgers University Press.

Chapter 6
The Long-Run Model (The Classical World)

Abstract This chapter ties together the pieces from Chap. 4 to show how the equilibrium level of output is determined, and then how the output and the expenditure functions from Chap. 5 together tell us how much of each type of expenditure there is, as well as determining the equilibrium interest rate. Also, this is where the information about resource supply from Chap. 4 gets incorporated into the labor market in a way that allows the conditions of resource supply to help determine equilibrium in the labor market. The concept of "potential output" is introduced and identified with the equilibrium output level of the model here.

6.1 Overview

We now have all the pieces to put together the model of the long run.

1. Input efficiency, capital, and resource intensity of labor determine the production function and labor demand.
2. Population, demographics (the age and gender structure of the population), preferences, and social customs determine simple labor supply.
3. Resource supplies modify simple labor supply, leading to resource-inclusive labor supply.
4. Supply and demand in the labor market determine the equilibrium quantity of labor.
5. The equilibrium quantity of labor put back into the production function tells us the equilibrium output.
6. The various expenditure functions from Chap. 5 tell us saving and investment, both as functions of the interest rate.
7. Saving and investment are combined in a "loanable funds" market, where equilibrium tells us the actual quantity of saving and investment, as well as the interest rate.
8. The interest rate allows us to figure out the components of demand that we still hadn't been able to solve.

Once you have equilibrium, you can use the model to answer economic questions. If people consume less, what happens to the economy? If investors get

K. Seeley, *Macroeconomics in Ecological Context*, Studies in Ecological Economics 5, DOI 10.1007/978-3-319-51757-5_6

more optimistic about the future, what happens? If there's a major innovation, what happens? The method is always the same in its general structure:

1. Find equilibrium.
2. Change some aspect of the model to reflect your question.
3. See how equilibrium has changed.

Notice that the solution proceeds from the production function to the expenditure functions, with no influence back the other way; if you know technology, capital, resource-intensity of labor, labor supply, and resource supply then you know equilibrium employment and output. The willingness to consume, or the desire to invest, or foreigners' interest in buying our stuff—those are all things that certainly matter in this model, but they only determine *how that output is divided.* They have no impact on the level of output itself.

What's presented here is to some extent a caricature of more subtle thinking about macroeconomics that existed before Keynes [5]. Nonetheless, as a background it helps clarify some of the ideas in Keynesianism, and even in this caricatured form it provides some useful insight concerning long-run trends in the economy.

The Keynesian model will also use the same building blocks of production function and expenditure functions. What distinguish the classical model are the assumptions that:

1. **prices are entirely flexible;** and
2. **the economy actually operates at its equilibrium.**

The stuff we care about—the level of output and employment—is determined entirely on the supply side. This leads to a view of the world in which there's little role for government in "managing" the economy; macroeconomic "policy," to the extent it can be said to exist, is for government to limit itself to those things that only it can do (national defense is a typical example) and to fund these necessary activities using the least obtrusive tax structure possible. The Keynesian, short-run model will relax the assumption about the labor market always being in equilibrium, and as a result, changes in the expenditure functions will actually alter output. That includes government expenditure and the effects of taxation and interest rates, which opens up room for fiscal and monetary policy, which will be addressed in Part III.

6.2 Labor-Market Equilibrium

As in any other market, equilibrium is defined by the intersection of labor demand and labor supply. This equilibrium determines the wage that labor gets paid and the number of people who have jobs. If the wage were any higher, lots of people would want to work, but not that many firms would want to hire. If the wage were lower, firms would want to hire, but there wouldn't be as many people willing to work at such low wages. In setting up the labor market we will also incorporate the

Fig. 6.1 Labor market equilibrium

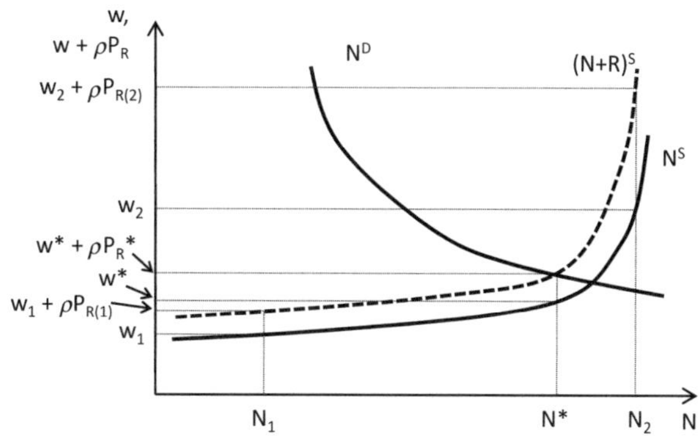

resource-supply situation (as described in Chap. 4, so that equilibrium in the labor market simultaneously takes account of resources and tells us quantities and prices for resources as well.

Recall the labor demand as specified in Chap. 4 (Fig. 4.2 of that chapter). For any given quantity of labor, it translated the marginal value product (the marginal product of labor, times the price of the output) into a wage that employers would be willing to pay if they were using that quantity of labor. The idea was that the marginal value product is the benefit to the employer from hiring one more worker, and the employer would keep hiring until the amount it had to pay just balanced the marginal benefit it got.

But remember that every time you hire a worker, the resource-intensity of labor tells you what quantity of resources you also have to buy. So the marginal value product MPN $\times$ P has to support not only the wage, but also the quantity of associated resources, at the price those resources are currently fetching.

In Fig. 6.1, imagine that, for some arbitrary reason, we're employing a quantity of labor N_1. We've inherited particular values of ρ and η (recall from Chap. 4 that ρ represents the amount of resource used per worker, and η represents the share of that resource that comes from exhaustible source), so the labor quantity N_1 can be translated into particular quantities of exhaustible resources E_1 and renewable resources B_1. We've also inherited supply curves for exhaustible and renewable resources, so that the quantities E_1 and B_1 translate in turn into particular resource prices, $P_{E(1)}$ and $P_{B(1)}$. The final link in this chain turns these two resource prices into a composite resource price $P_{R(1)}$. Our overall resource price is just a weighted average of the exhaustibles price and the renewables price. Since we know we're getting a share η of our resources from exhaustibles, that's also the weight to apply to the exhaustibles price, leaving $(1 - \eta)$ as the weight on the renewables price:

$$P_{R(1)} = \eta \cdot P_{E(1)} + (1 - \eta) \cdot P_{B(1)}.$$

We now have the full marginal cost that has to be covered when the economy uses N_1 units of labor; If we use lower-case w to signify the real wage ($w = W/P$), we can say the marginal cost of the labor itself is w_1, and the marginal cost of the associated resources that must also be bought is $\rho \cdot P_{R(1)}$ (since each unit of labor requires ρ units of resources, using another unit of labor requires buying an additional ρ units of resources, at the price $P_{R(1)}$), so the full, resource-inclusive marginal cost of labor is $w_2 + \rho \cdot P_{R(1)}$.

At some larger level of labor N_2 there would in turn be larger resource levels E_2 and B_2, leading to higher resource prices $P_{E(2)}$ and $P_{B(2)}$, with composite resource price $P_{R(2)}$. So in that instance the resource-inclusive marginal cost of labor is $w_2 + \rho \cdot P_{R(2)}$.

Every level of N similarly has an associated wage level, resource price, and resource-inclusive marginal cost. So we can draw a labor market with a simple labor supply curve that translates quantities of labor into wages (label this N^S) and a resource-inclusive labor supply curve that at each level represents the wage plus the resource price, adjusted by ρ; this curve can be labeled $(N+R)^S$.

If we now combine the labor demand curve and the resource-inclusive labor supply, equilibrium follows directly. In Fig. 6.1, at labor input N_1, the marginal value product is higher than the required wage plus associated marginal resource costs, so the economy can benefit by employing more labor. At N_2, the marginal value product is below the resource-inclusive labor cost, so the economy is employing labor that does not produce as much as its full marginal cost. At N^*, the marginal value product just covers the full marginal labor cost, so there's no incentive to either increase or decrease the labor input. This is illustrated in Fig. 6.1, where N^* is linked with w^* and $w^* + P_R^*$.

6.3 Equilibrium Output

Equilibrium output follows directly from the equilibrium in the labor market. Capital and technology are unchanged in the short run, so we know the levels of K, Z, and ρ. When you combine those with the N^* that comes out of the labor market, you get equilibrium output, Y^*. This is illustrated in Fig. 6.2.

Fig. 6.2 Equilibrium output

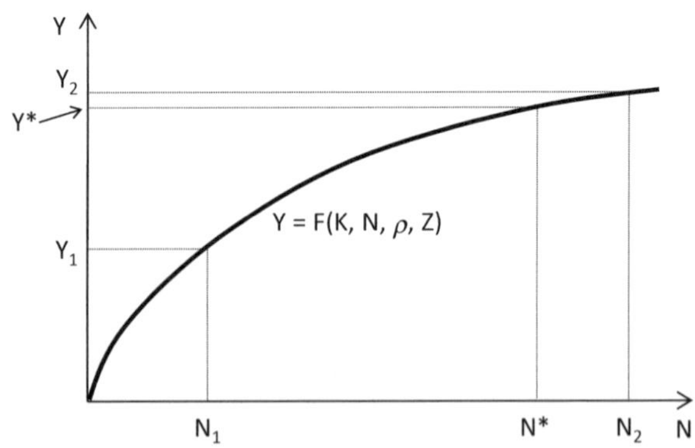

6.4 Markets Work Well

A key component of the classical world is the idea that markets work nearly perfectly. In terms of the present model, that shows up in two relevant ways: the real wage will adjust to changes in labor-market conditions, and everything that is produced will be sold.

6.4.1 *The Real Wage Will Adjust*

Remember the technical definition of unemployment: it's not simply that you don't have a job, it's that you're willing to work at the prevailing wage but nobody will hire you. In the classical framework, this suggests disequilibrium. If the wage is $10 /h, it must be true that anyone not working is simply not willing to work for less than $10. If they were, there would be an employer willing to offer them, say, $9.50 to replace someone currently working for $10.

So if, for some reason, labor demand were to shift to the left (employers have less interest in hiring at any given wage level), the wage would drop—from w_1 to w_2 in Fig. 6.3—and employment would drop—from N_1 to N_2—but there would be no unemployment: the people between N_1 and N_2 who are no longer employed are simply unwilling to work for anything less than w_1. The market adjusts rapidly to this new equilibrium.

6.4.2 *What's Made Is Sold*

The classical economists made the important observation that everything produced belongs to someone, and that therefore all output was also income. And if people would either spend their income or lend it to someone else to spend, then it would

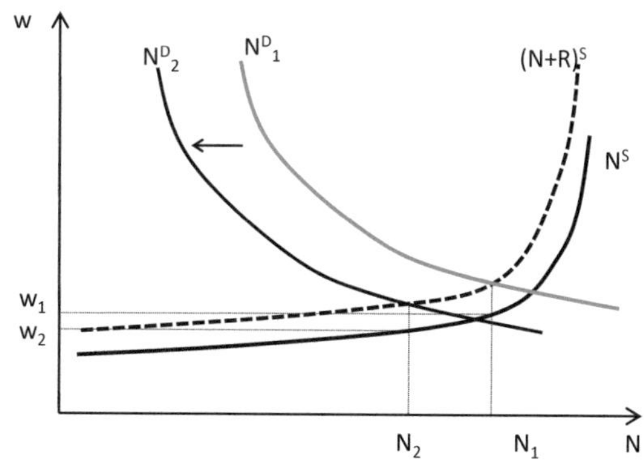

Fig. 6.3 Changing employment level and wages

seem to be impossible that there should ever be too little spending for economy's productive capacity. This idea is often known as "Say's Law," after the French economist Jean-Baptiste Say.

Part III works through details of why this idea is mistaken, despite its intuitive appeal. But if we think of the classical model of this chapter as a description of the long run, we can define the long run as a span of time big enough to ignore effects caused by fluctuations in demand and maintain the assumption that what's made is sold. So while aggregate demand is central to the short-run model, it plays no role in determining the economy's level of output or employment in the long-run model. These crucial variables are determined strictly on the supply side.

We now consider what *does* change output and employment in the classical vision.

6.5 What Changes Output

In the classical model, the only things that can change output are *real* factors: a change in capital, a change in technology, or a change in labor supply.

An increase in capital, as shown in Fig. 6.4, provides a straightforward illustration of how the model works.

The increase in capital moves the production function up, as shown in the upper part of Fig. 6.4: with more capital, any given quantity of labor produces more output than before. This also increases the marginal product of labor at each level of labor input—if you add new machines or factories to your capital stock, the next worker you hire will add more to output than before. The increase in marginal product of labor increases the demand for labor: if an additional worker can produce more than before, you want more workers and your profit-maximizing choice includes paying them more. The lower part of Fig. 6.4 shows this increase in labor demand. The new labor-market equilibrium has more employment—N_2 instead of N_1—and a higher wage—w_2 instead of w_1.

Now return to the upper diagram. With employment N_1 and the old level of capital, the economy produced output Y_1; employment level N_2 and the new level of capital leads to output Y_2.

Increased capital leads to higher wages and higher employment, and the increased labor and increased capital lead synergistically to higher output. It's a beautiful world.

Turning to technology, remember that as discussed in Chap. 2 in general, and in terms of the model in Chap. 4, technological change has two fundamental forms:

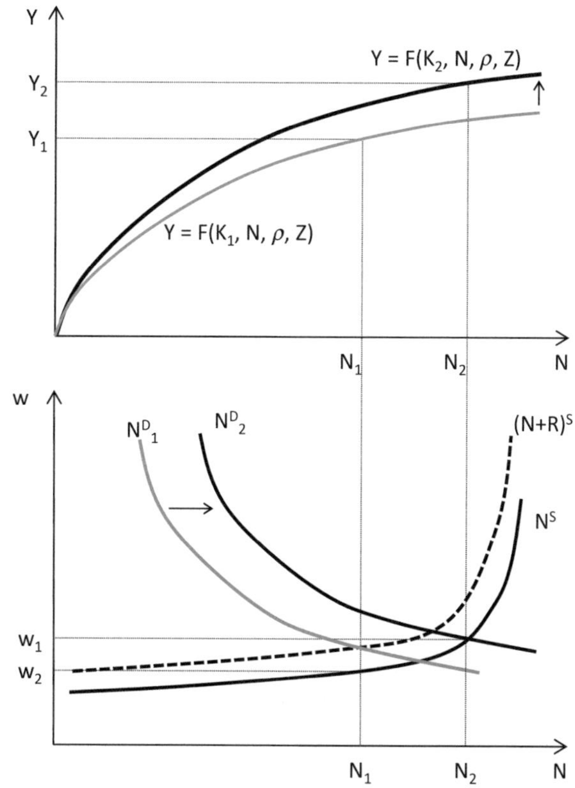

Fig. 6.4 An increase in capital stock in the classical system

- A change in the efficiency of turning inputs into outputs, captured by changes in the parameter Z;
- A change in the amount of resources used by each worker, captured by changes in the parameter ρ.[1]

These will have similar, though not identical, effects.

In the case of an increase in Z, things work out qualitatively the same as in Fig. 6.4 with an increase in K, because Z and K enter the production function in the same way. The production function shifts up as better technology makes labor more productive. That same effect moves labor demand to the right, so the equilibrium quantity of N is higher and labor is paid a higher wage. This greater amount of labor is put back into the raised production function, resulting in a significantly increased equilibrium level of output.

[1]Technological change can also involve changes in the exhaustibles share η, but for our current purposes that is secondary.

Improved technological efficiency leads to higher wages and higher employment, and the increased labor and increased efficiency lead synergistically to higher output. Once again, it's a beautiful world.

The resource intensity of labor acts in a slightly different way. In terms of the production function, an increase in ρ is again qualitatively the same as an increase in Z or K: the production function shifts up and the labor demand curve shifts rightward. But that's not all that is affected by the increase in ρ; the gap between simple labor supply N^S and resource-inclusive labor supply $(N+R)^S$ is defined by $\rho \cdot P_R$ or the resource intensity times the resource price. If ρ increases, there are two things that happen to that gap. Since ρ itself is bigger, that directly increases the gap. At the same time, the higher ρ is pushing the economy further out along the resource supply curves, so that any given level of N is associated with a larger quantity of resource use and a higher resource price. So while the increase in ρ is moving labor *demand* to the right, tending to push up both employment and wages (and resource use), it is simultaneously moving the *resource-inclusive* labor *supply* to the left, which tends to reduce employment and wages.

The net effect of these two opposing forces is not immediately clear: an increase in resource intensity could in principle result in higher employment and wages, or lower. Specifically, if resource prices are already high, then an increase in ρ will cause $\rho \cdot P_R$ to increase a lot; the same thing will happen if the increase in ρ pushes up P_R significantly. Either of these scenarios represents a large leftward move of the resource-inclusive labor supply curve, and the possibility that the net change in employment and wages is negative. Figure 6.5 illustrates that scenario.

It follows that if resource prices are low, and if they *stay* low even when resource intensity of labor increases, then resource-inclusive labor supply doesn't move very far left, and the net effect of a higher ρ is likely to be *higher* employment and wages. This is shown in Fig. 6.6.

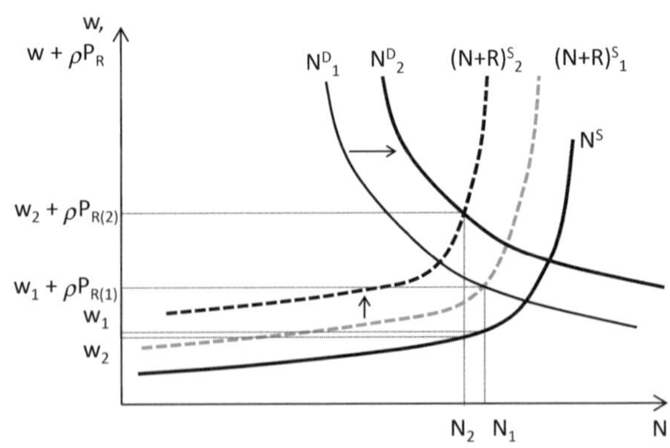

Fig. 6.5 Increased ρ leading to decreased employment

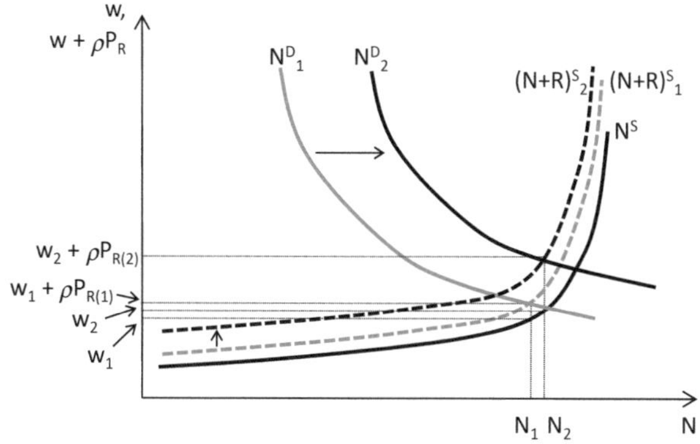

Fig. 6.6 Increased ρ leading to increased employment

So much for general possibilities. Which one is more likely? Think back to Chap. 2—the blockbuster innovations of the Industrial Revolution and modern economic growth were things that massively increased the resource-intensity of labor: railroads, steamships, the assembly line, the internal combustion engine, aviation. This period has also been marked by historically unprecedented increases in employment and wages. On that heuristic evidence, it seems that the predominant situation for the last 200 years has been one of low resource prices, resulting in the happy scenario of Fig. 6.6 rather than the unhappy one of Fig. 6.5. The behavior of the economy when that's no longer true is the subject of Part IV of the book.

***When resource prices are low*, increased resource-intensity of labor leads to higher wages and higher employment, and the increased labor and increased use of resources lead synergistically to higher output. Once again, it's a beautiful world—at least so far.**

The other major influence on output is the labor supply. If the workforce grows or if workers simply become more willing to work, the labor supply will shift to the right, as shown in Fig. 6.7.

Because there has been neither increased capital nor improved technology, the curves for the marginal product of labor and the demand for labor are unchanged. Also, the gap between the simple labor supply curve and the resource-inclusive labor supply curve is unchanged. The increased labor supply therefore leads to higher employment—N_2 instead of N_1—at a *lower* wage than before. The increased employment does lead to more output, but not by much, since there's been no change in the production function itself, only in the level of labor input.

Note one of the implications of these various scenarios for increased employment and output. In the last one, when the labor supply itself has increased, we can

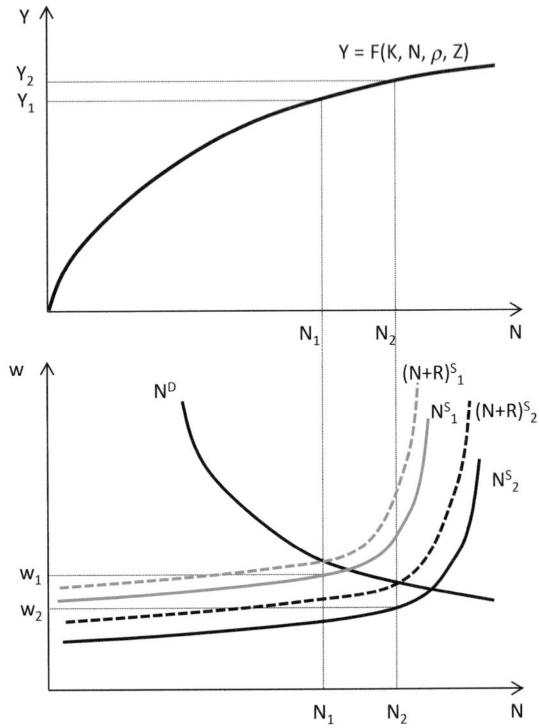

Fig. 6.7 An increased labor supply in the classical system

tell that output hasn't gone up by as much as the labor force—that's reflected in the lower wage. In the others, in contrast, when capital or efficiency or resource intensity has gone up (and resource prices have stayed low), the increase in output outpaces the increase in employment, as reflected in the higher wage. An economy that increases its labor pool without increasing its capital stock or improving its technology is an economy that is getting poorer in terms of output per hour worked; if the increased labor pool is from more workers, it's getting poorer measured as output per worker; and if the increased labor pool is proportional to an increasing population, the society is getting poorer on a per-capita basis, even if total output is going up.

6.6 Real-Nominal Divide

In the classical model there's a strict division between *real* quantities and *nominal* values. Real quantities are the amounts of goods and services produced (Y), the level of employment (N), the real wage w, the real interest rate (r); nominal values are the price level (P), the nominal wage (W), and the nominal interest rate (i). In this model, the real quantities are determined entirely on the supply side: tell me your society's quantity of capital, its level of technology, the size of the labor force and its willingness to work, and I'll tell you your economy's output and employment. Changes in aggregate demand only affect prices. In contrast, in the Keynesian models that follow in Part III, output, employment, and prices are all determined by the interaction of aggregate supply and aggregate demand, so that it is not enough to know merely the conditions of production: you have to know the conditions of demand as well.

6.7 Money and Prices

The classical view of prices is based on the quantity theory of money: the quantity of money determines the level of aggregate demand, which in turn determines the price level, but has no effect on anything real.[2]

The basis of this theory is the equation of exchange. We already know the variables P (the price level) and Y (the amount of output). Then nominal output is PY. ("Nominal output" is explained in the appendix, "What is 'nominal output'?".)

Two new variables are M, the stock of money, and V, the velocity of money. The velocity simply tells you how many times a given unit of money changes hands over a period of time (usually a year). Suppose you get paid on January 2—that's one transaction. A month later you spend a dollar of that money at a restaurant—there's another transaction. The restaurant gives the dollar to a farmer, who pays a babysitter, who gives the buck to a gas station, which uses it to buy more gas, etc. If an average dollar changes hands 20 times in a year, then the transactions velocity is 20.

Not all of these purchases are counted in the GDP. Your restaurant bill, the babysitter's pay, and the babysitter's purchase at the gas station are all "final goods and services," and therefore part of GDP. When the restaurant pays the farmer and the gas station buys gas to sell to its customers, those are intermediate goods, not expenditures on final demand, meaning that they are not part of GDP. So we can distinguish between "transactions velocity" V_T, which is based on every changing of hands (i.e., every transaction), and "income velocity" V, which counts only those transactions that are part of GDP.

We then have the equation of exchange:

$$MV \equiv PY. \tag{6.1}$$

The funny equals sign "$\equiv$" is an identity, something that doesn't just happen to be true, but must be true by definition. In this case, the identity says that the amount of spending on components of the GDP (MV) is necessarily equal to the nominal GDP (PY).

[2] A modern explication of the theory is in [3].

After those preliminaries, we're ready to say something about the price level in the classical model. Make the simplifying assumption that velocity is constant. Now what happens if the government increases M, the stock of money? With a constant V, the amount of money spent (MV) must go up. Because of the identity above, that means that nominal GDP must go up. But real GDP, or Y, doesn't budge. It's determined on the "real" side of the economy, by the labor force and by the quantity and quality of the economy's capital stock. Increasing the amount of money in the economy doesn't affect any of these real determinants, so it can't change Y. If Y doesn't grow but PY does, then it follows that P must have increased.

Now let's relax that assumption of constant velocity and again consider an increase in money supply M. It's still true that Y hasn't changed for the same reasons as in the preceding paragraph. But it doesn't have to be true that P went up. What if P was unchanged, so that PY was also unchanged? Then we know that MV must be unchanged, and since our scenario is that M is bigger, it follows that V must be smaller. An increase in the money supply is compatible with stable prices *if the income velocity of money falls*. But there's still no effect on real GDP.

In the classical world, an increase in the money supply has no effect on the real economy (output and employment), but it does drive up prices, unless velocity falls enough to offset the increased money supply.

There's more money chasing the same amount of stuff as before, so the general level of prices must increase, unless the money stops chasing as hard.

6.8 Interest Rates

Interest rates in the classical model are the key equilibrating factor, the term that ensures that everything made will be sold, or that output will equal expenditure. And the way that the long-run model thinks about them is with a simple version of a loanable funds market.

Start with a simple economy that has no government and no foreign sector. Remembering that output equals income, all output in this economy must go to one of two places: it can be consumed or saved:

$$Y \equiv C + S.$$

What about expenditure? There are only two things in this economy to spend money on: consumption or investment:

$$EX \equiv C + I.$$

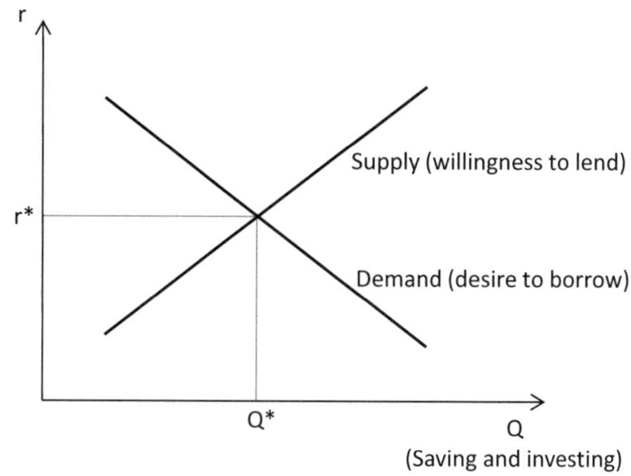

Fig. 6.8 The loanable funds market

Equilibrium is that condition of the economy wherein all income is spent, or put another way, output equals expenditure:

$$EX \equiv C + I \equiv C + S \equiv Y.$$

If we focus on the central pairing and drop the C from each side of this equation, we get:

$$I \equiv S; \tag{6.2}$$

the economy will be in equilibrium as long as investment equals saving.

In our loanable funds market, the demand side is shaped by the desire of firms to undertake investment expenditure and the supply side is determined by the willingness of various entities in the economy to save.[3] Investment gets less attractive as the interest rate goes up, so demand is downward sloping. Saving, on the other hand, gets more attractive as the interest rate goes up, since you get a bigger return on your savings, so supply is upward sloping (Fig. 6.8).

Just as in any other market, equilibrium will occur at the "price" (i.e., the interest rate) where the quantity supplied equals the quantity demanded—or in this case, where the quantity of saving equals the quantity of investment.

Now that we have the basic principle of equilibrium, we have to put some detail back into the idea of saving, and review the nature of investment behavior.

Saving is in essence spending less than one's income, and we can think of domestic saving (saving by entities within the economy) and international saving (saving by entities outside the economy). The domestic saving can in turn be split

[3]We assume that investment either requires firms to borrow, forcing them to pay the interest rate, or will prevent them from lending the money spent on investment, thereby foregoing earning the interest rate.

into private saving, carried out by households, and public saving, carried out by the government. For each of these entities that can save, we define the entity's income and its expenditure, and then its saving is simply the difference between them.

Private savers receive the economy's output, Y, as income. From that, they must pay taxes, T (or tY), giving them disposable income of $Y_D = Y - T = (1 - t)Y$. Spending by the private sector, other than investment, is consumption, C. So **private saving** is $Y_D - C$, or

$$S_P = Y - T - C = (1 - t)Y - C.$$

The entity that carries out **public saving** is the government. Its income is T, and its expenditure is G, so public saving is simply

$$S_G = T - G.$$

Combining private and public saving into **domestic saving**, S_D, we have

$$\begin{aligned} S_D &= S_P + S_G \\ &= (Y - T - C) + (T - G) \\ &= Y - C - G. \end{aligned} \tag{6.3}$$

In other words, the saving done within an economy with which it can support private investment, if it is not drawing on international sources, is its income minus whatever it spends on consumption and government activities.

International saving is developed along the same lines. From the perspective of one's own economy, foreigners' "income" is what they earn by selling stuff to you—in other words, your own imports from them. Foreigners' "expenditure" is what they spend buying things from you—in other words, your exports to them. Then international saving—the income of foreign entities that exceeds their expenditure—is simply your own imports minus your own exports:

$$S_I = IM - GX.$$

Note that net exports (NX) are gross exports minus imports, so we can also write

$$S_I = -NX.$$

The next step is to determine how these items are affected by the interest rate, drawing upon the expenditure functions in Chap. 5 and the production function from earlier in this chapter. Starting with private saving, the components are Y, C, and T. Output is determined by conditions of production; consumption is determined by output, the tax rate, and parameters of the consumption function; taxes are determined by the tax rate and output; and the tax rate is determined by the government. So none of these items is influenced by the interest rate, and private saving can be depicted as a vertical line when it is graphed against interest.

Public saving is even simpler: taxes, as mentioned above, are a product of output and the tax rate chosen by the government, and government expenditure is directly chosen by the government. As with private saving, there is no influence of the interest rate on public saving, and it too can be depicted as a vertical line when graphed against the interest rate.

The sensitivity of saving to the interest rate comes in through the gross-exports side of international saving. Imports are the product of the import rate and income, so again there is no responsiveness to interest rates. Gross exports, however, are determined by foreign income and the real exchange rate, and the real exchange rate is itself a function of the interest rate. It turns out that gross exports go down when the domestic interest rate goes up (the proof of that is left as an exercise). Since international saving is $S_I = -NX = IM - GX$, it follows that when gross exports are down, international saving is up; in turn, that means that when domestic interest rates are up, international saving is up.

So much for the supply side of this loanable funds market, i.e., saving. As specified in Chap. 5, the demand for investment depends on two things: entrepreneurs' predictions of the future profitability of various possible investments, and the interest rate. The lower the interest rate, the less profitable an investment has to be in order for it to make sense. The demand for loanable funds (money that an entrepreneur would spend building capital) is therefore downward sloping.

We thus have an upward-sloping supply of loanable funds, with its position determined by people's saving activity and the sensitivity of international saving to the interest rate (through the effect on the exchange rate which in turn affects the level of gross exports) and a downward-sloping demand for loanable funds, driven by entrepreneurs' investment behavior, as illustrated in Fig. 6.9.

The distance from the vertical axis to the solid vertical line is the quantity of public saving. (Note that public saving can easily be negative, which is the case when the government runs a deficit; that would be shown by drawing this line to the *left* of the vertical axis.) The distance from the heavy solid line to the heavy dashed line is private saving. (Again, this can be negative, though less commonly than with public saving. If it is negative, then the heavy dashed line will be to the left of the heavy solid line.) The distance from the vertical axis to the heavy dashed line is total domestic saving (public plus private). The distance from the heavy dashed line to the sloping, dotted-dashed line is international saving. Total saving is the distance from the vertical axis to the dotted-dashed line.

The equilibrium interest rate r^* is determined by the intersection of investment demand (the demand for loanable funds) and total saving (the supply of loanable funds). The interest rate in turn determines the actual quantity of saving and the actual quantity of investment. In this way, the interest rate r^* ensures that the economy as a whole is in equilibrium.

Note that, while the quantities of public and private saving are known without reference to the interest rate, the actual quantity of international saving depends on

Fig. 6.9 The loanable funds market (with positive international saving—a trade deficit)

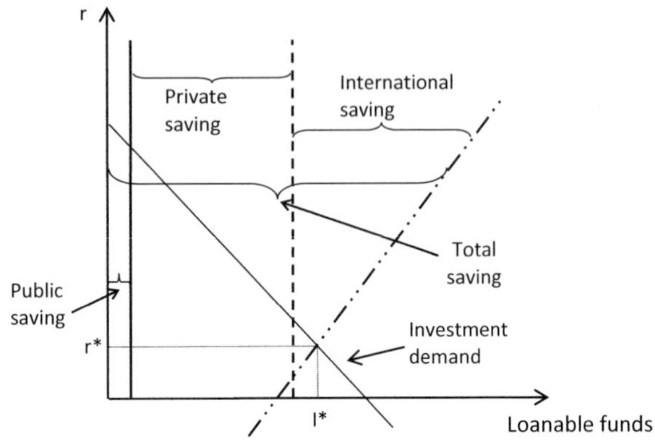

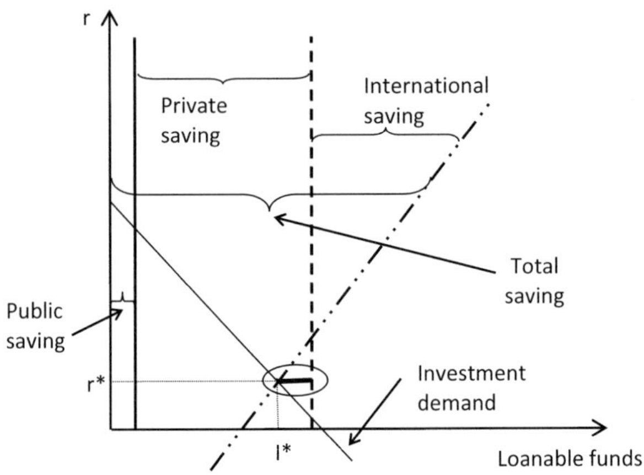

Fig. 6.10 The loanable funds market (with negative international saving—a trade surplus)

the interest rate. With the curves positioned as they are in Fig. 6.9, at a high interest rate, the quantity of international saving will be large and positive—the country will be running a large trade deficit. At a moderate interest rate, international saving will be still positive, but small. At a very low interest rate, international saving can be negative, corresponding to a trade surplus.

Figure 6.10 shows the curves in different positions, such that at a similar interest rate as in Fig. 6.9, international saving is indeed negative. The circled heavy line at the interest level r^* represents the actual quantity of international saving, and since it is measured from the domestic saving line *leftward* to the international saving line, the quantity of international saving is negative.

Despite the reassurance of Say's Law (see Sect. 6.4.2), a venerable concern in macroeconomics is that people might spend "too little": if they try to save too much, producers will find they can't sell everything they've made, so they cut back on production and the economy experiences a recession. This is related to an idea

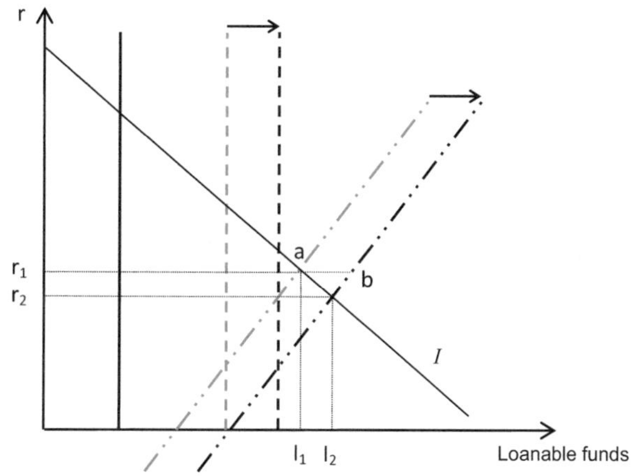

Fig. 6.11 The loanable funds market showing the response to an increased desire to save

known as the "paradox of thrift,", where everyone is trying to save money, so they all cut back on their spending, so nobody can earn as much as they would like to in order to meet their savings goals.[4]

In the classical model, this doesn't happen—indeed, it *can't* happen. The increased desire to save is the same as having the supply of domestic saving move to the right (at any given interest rate, people want to save more money than before). Figure 6.11 shows why that's not a problem. The rightward shift in the quantity of domestic saving moves the total supply of loanable funds rightward by an equal amount. As a result, the equilibrium interest rate falls from r_1 to r_2. At the lower interest rate, the real exchange rate is reduced, so gross exports increase, thus decreasing international saving. If people wanted to save an extra \$40 million, perhaps the weaker real exchange rate has reduced the trade deficit by \$15 million—foreigners have stepped up to buy part of the output that domestic consumers are no longer purchasing. At the same time, businesses considering investments find that spending on new capital has gotten more attractive at the new, lower interest rates, so instead of spending only \$100 million on capital, they spend \$125 million. Thus investment expenditure makes up the rest of the expenditure that went missing when domestic savings increased.

The lower interest rate both reduces the amount of increased total saving and increases the amount of investment. The new equilibrium interest rate is where these two forces balance out, and the economy as a whole remains in equilibrium without any change in output.

In Fig. 6.11, the horizontal distance from *a* to *b* shows how much people would want to increase their saving if the interest rate were to stay at r_1. The distance from I_1 to I_2 shows how much saving and investment actually increase as the interest rate drops to r_2.

[4]See [6] for an interesting discussion.

What about deficit spending by the government? Let's say the economy is in a recession (though as discussed below, it's not clear in this model how we got there) and someone advocates increased government spending or decreased taxes as a way of solving the problem.

In the terms of the model, this person is advocating some combination of increasing G and decreasing T. Since public saving is $S_G = T - G$, it's clear that either of these actions would decrease public saving. In the graphical representation, that moves the public saving line to the left, bringing with it the domestic saving line and the total saving line. With less total saving, the interest rate goes up, but nothing has happened to the level of output or employment. We have more consumption (if taxes were cut) and/or more government expenditure (if government expenditure was increased), but those changes are fully offset by a combination of less investment and more international saving (i.e., less gross exports). So an attempt to revive the economy through a government deficit merely results in reduced investment (a phenomenon known as "crowding out") and an increased trade deficit. All in all, a pretty pointless policy.

In this model, the level of employment and the level of output are determined by labor supply and the components of the production function. Changes in the expenditure functions (including t and G) change how that output is used, and they may alter the interest rate, but they don't change the level of output itself.

6.9 Policy Implications

The discussion of interest rates and deficit spending may leave one wondering whether there is any role at all for policy in the classical model. There is, and that is to keep taxes low.

In the classical world, taxes tend to be distortionary: they change people's behavior, and the assumption is that the untaxed behavior is optimal, so the behavior under taxation is less desirable.

The clearest case of this is in the labor market, where an income tax provides a disincentive to work. If an employer offers \$15/hr, you're more willing to take that offer if you get to keep \$13 of that than if you only get to take home \$10. So a higher income tax shifts the labor-supply curve to the left. If you reverse the motion in Fig. 6.7 above, you can see that this shift results in less employment and therefore less output. And all else being equal, less output means less saving, and therefore less investment, providing less capital to make the economy grow. So the classical model gives a pretty clear argument for how excessive taxation can hurt an economy in the long run. (The effect on wages is explained in the appendix on "Taxes and the effect on wages".)

So should we just have no taxes? No. At the beginning of the discussion of interest rates, we pretended we had an economy with no government, which implies no taxes, which sounds great. But if you look around the real world, you find that places without effective governments—sometimes referred to as "failed states"—

tend to be quite poor. Places with too much government, like the former Soviet Union, also tend to be fairly poor. The richest countries in the world—the U.S., Canada, western Europe, Japan—all have large but not huge levels of government.

It turns out that government plays a pretty crucial role in the economy. At the most basic economic level, it makes property rights meaningful. But it also undertakes useful collective action—from national defense to public health—that the economy would be worse off without.

Given that taxes are distortionary, but that some level of government activity is necessary for a healthy economy, the implicit guidance of the classical model is:

1. Have government, but limit it to those things which it truly does better than the private sector (there are, of course, large disagreements about which things those are);
2. Whatever level of government you decide is necessary, fund it with the least distortionary taxes you can;
3. Don't bother with deficit financing to get out of a recession—you'll crowd out private investment, thus hurting the economy in the long run, without improving the economy in the short run.

6.9.1 The Problem of Recession

The classical model has some important virtues in understanding long-term growth (which is the subject of Chap. 7), but it has a major shortcoming, and that is its inability to explain recession.

In a recession, output falls and there is, apparently, a significant level of involuntary unemployment—people willing to work at the prevailing wage but not finding jobs.

There are only two ways the classical model can explain a drop in output: either a downward shift in the production function, or a leftward shift in the labor supply curve.[5]

What could cause the production function to shift down? If technology suddenly got worse, that would do it. There are historical instances of technological regress, but they involve large historical events, such as the fall of the Roman Empire, and have effects lasting centuries. They're not a credible explanation for recessions like the one that started in December, 2007, and officially ended in June, 2009, or even for a major modern depression such as the Great Depression of the 1930s.

A decrease in the capital stock would also shift the production function down, but again, this doesn't fit the historical record. Modern recessions and depressions are marked by capital sitting idle, not by capital being destroyed. In an economy more directly based on natural resources, such as a primarily agricultural one, bad

[5]This is addressed further in the discussion of "real business-cycle" models in Chap. 18.

weather could have the same effect as a loss of capital, but yet again, this does not fit the modern experience of recessions. We do have one fairly strong natural-resource dependence in our economy, and that's oil. A sudden decrease in the availability of oil would have effects on the economy, which we'll explore in Part IV, but that can't account for all the recessions we've had.

What about a leftward shift in the labor supply? One cause of that would be a large decrease in the population. There are insights from applying this approach to great plagues of the past, such as the Black Death of the fourteenth century (the supply of labor went down, and wages went up), but it hardly fits the modern experience. The remaining possibility is that people suddenly get less interested in working, so you have to pay them more to get off their shiftless butts. The first problem with this explanation is that it's ad hoc—there's no clear reason why people's preference between labor and leisure should suddenly shift. The second problem is that, while it does reproduce the observed effects of decreased employment and decreased output, it doesn't explain *involuntary* unemployment. Yes, the model shows fewer people working, but it also says that this is entirely by choice.

So while the classical model gives some insight into long-run issues, it comes up short in explaining the business cycle. Part III is devoted to fixing that.

6.10 Growth, the Long-Run Model, and Potential Output

Chapter 7 goes into more detail on how an economy increases its output over time: more capital, a larger labor force, better technology, more resources—these all add up to increased output. The long-run model takes those elements and gives one particular explanation for how much labor is applied to the capital and technology you have.

One way to think of "potential" output is as the level of output the long-run model says you *should* have, given your capital stock, technology, resource situation, and labor force. It's possible for actual output to be less than potential, if you have workers sitting around unemployed. It's even possible for output to be more than potential, if you've got unsustainably high numbers of people working. But potential output is the equilibrium level of output determined by the long-run, classical model that has been the subject of this chapter. Buried under all the ups and downs of the business cycle, the level of potential output is there in a sort of Platonic purity, the "true" level of economic output, obscured by the temporary swings of boom and bust.

One big catch with potential output is that it's not something you can observe directly. Rather, it's based on best guesses as to what constitutes a "normal" or healthy rate of unemployment, and a "normal" rate of capital utilization. You can observe the capital stock and the labor force. You can estimate the level of technology from econometric analyses of the economy using a production function, whether a Cobb-Douglas type or some other. Then you plug into that production function the "normal" rates of employment and capital utilization and see what level of output your production function tells you *would have* occurred. That's your potential output. The actual technique is somewhat more sophisticated, and not entirely settled (see [2, 1, 4]. But the basic idea is as described here.

So while the *concept* of potential output is simply the equilibrium of the long-run model, the actual *measurement* of it is an estimate based on guessed values plugged into an estimated production function. But then again, potential output is the Platonic ideal of the economy's performance, and it's in the nature of Platonic forms that we can't actually see them.

Appendix: What Is "Nominal Output"?

Nominal output is the value of output, measured using current prices. This is in contrast to real output, which is output measured using fixed prices of some particular period.

Let Y_1 represent some level of output of goods and services. To add up cars, oranges, dental services, etc., we need to use some set of prices, and let's say the total comes to \$1 million. Since the price level is an arbitrary thing, let's say that initial level P_1 is equal to 1. Then $P_1 \cdot Y_1 = 1 \cdot \$1,000,000 = \$1,000,000$.

What happens if the economy now produces twice as much of everything? Then $Y_2 = \$2,000,000$. If the price level is still at 1, we have nominal output of $P_1 \cdot Y_2 = 1 \cdot \$2,000,000 = \$2,000,000$. Nominal output has doubled, but so has real output.

On the other hand, what if everything gets twice as expensive ($P_2 = 2 \cdot P_1 = 2$), but we don't produce any more than we used to? Then nominal output is $P_2 \cdot Y_1 = 2 \cdot \$1,000,000 = \$2,000,000$. In nominal terms (how many dollars were spent on it), our economy is twice as big as it used to be, but in real terms we're no better off.

Appendix: Taxes and the Effect on Wages

Look again at Fig. 6.7. If you add an income tax, that's like shifting the labor supply curve leftward, because the amount the employer is willing to pay has to cover not only the wage the worker demands, but also the taxes. If we run Fig. 6.7 "backwards" (going from N_2^S to N_1^S), you might notice that this would seem to drive the real wage *up*, from w_2 to w_1. And it does—but that's the before-tax wage. With fewer people working, the marginal product of labor is higher, so employers are willing to pay more. But the increased tax must more than offset this gain, or else workers would be willing to work more, not less. So in this model a higher income tax raises the gross wage but decreases the net wage (that is, what you're left with after taxes, your disposable income).

Problems

Problem 6.1 What are the assumptions that distinguish the long-run (classical) model from the Keynesian perspective?

Problem 6.2 Make a diagram in the style of Fig. 6.11 to illustrate the effect of a decrease in taxation. Consider the effect of taxation not only on the government's balance, but also on any other elements of the loanable-funds market that are affected by the tax cut.

Problem 6.3 Explain the effect of increasing η in a situation where exhaustible resources are easier to come by than renewables. Use a diagram of the resource-inclusive labor market (e.g., Fig. 6.3) to illustrate your answer.

Problem 6.4 Using the expenditure functions from Chap. 5, show that gross exports depend on the domestic interest rate, and that when the domestic interest rate is higher, the level of gross exports is lower.

Problem 6.5 The consumption function as given in Chap. 5 is not sensitive to the interest rate, but one could make an argument that in fact people's consumption behavior *does* respond to the interest rate.

(a) If consumption is modeled as being sensitive to the interest rate, should it increase or decrease as the interest rate goes up?
(b) Based on your answer to (a), should private saving increase or decrease as the interest rate goes up?
(c) Based on your answer to (b), redraw Fig. 6.9 to reflect a consumption function that is sensitive to the interest rate.
Now modify that diagram to show an increase in investment demand.
(d) What has happened to private saving as a result of the increase in investment demand?
(e) Based on your answer to (d), what has happened to consumption as a result of the increase in investment demand?

Problem 6.6 Why does the classical model have trouble explaining recession?

Problem 6.7 Consider an economy with the following parameters:

Production:	$Z = 38, K = 4,000, N = 157, \alpha = 0.3, \delta = 0.35, \gamma = 0.35,$ $\rho = 3$
Government:	$G = 400, t = 20\%$
Consumption:	$C_0 = 200, C_Y = 0.75$
Imports:	$I\!M_Y = 0.1$
Exchange rate:	$\varepsilon_0 = 110, \varepsilon_r = 700, r^f = 5\%$
Gross exports:	$G\!X_Y = 0.02, Y^f = 3,000, G\!X_\varepsilon = 1$
Investment:	$I_0 = 400, I_r = 2,000$

(a) Solve the model. All dollar quantities can be rounded to no decimal places. The interest rate should be shown to two decimal places (e.g., 3.45%, or 0.0345).

$Y =$
$R =$
$T =$
$C =$
S_P (private saving) =
S_G (public saving) =
$IM =$
$r =$
$GX =$
$NX =$
$I =$

(b) Change the tax rate to 15%. Solve the model. (You can save yourself time by noting which calculations are unchanged from part a. and reusing those answers rather than repeating the calculation.)

$Y =$
$R =$
$T =$
$C =$
S_P (private saving) =
S_G (public saving) =
$IM =$
$r =$
$GX =$
$NX =$
$I =$

(c) What has the tax cut done to investment? Why? (In other words, what was the chain by which government policy affected investment?)
(d) What has the change in government policy done to the trade balance? Why? (In other words, what was the chain by which government policy affected the trade balance?)
(e) Based on your results here, are tax cuts good for the economy?
(f) Although it's not reflected in the numbers you've worked through here, what limitation would you put on your conclusion from Problem 6.7e?

Problem 6.8 Assume the following values for the labor market and resource situation:

N	1,451
η	0.35
P_B	0.8
P_E	0.2
ρ	7
w	12.80

(a) Use the information provided to determine the composite resource price P_R.
(b) Calculate the full marginal cost of employing 1,451 units of labor, i.e., the increased cost of wages and resources associated with increasing employment by 1 when you're at $N = 1,451$.
(c) If η increases to 0.7, what is the new composite resource price?
(d) With that higher η of 0.7, what is the new full marginal cost of employing 1,451 units of labor?
(e) Based on your answer to Problem 6.8d, how would you expect the labor-market equilibrium to change? That is, should the new N be smaller or larger than 1,451? Explain.

References

1. Basu, S., & Fernald, J. G. (2009). What do we know (and not know) about potential output? *Federal Reserve Bank Of St. Louis Review, 91*, 187–213
2. Cahn, C., & Saint-Guilhem, A. (2009). Issues on potential growth measurement and comparison: How *Structural* is the production function approach? *Federal Reserve Bank Of St. Louis Review, 91*, 221–240.
3. Friedman, M. (Ed.) (1956). *Studies in the quantity theory of money*. Chicago: University of Chicago Press.
4. Gordon, R. J. (2014). A new method of estimating potential real GDP growth: Implications for the labor market and the debt/GDP ratio. NBER working paper 20423.
5. Keynes, J. M. (1936/1973). *The general theory of employment, interest, and money*. London: Macmillan.
6. Nash, R. T., & Gramm, W. P. (1969). A neglected early statement of the paradox of thrift. *History of Political Economy, 1*, 395–400 (1969)

Chapter 7
Growth with Abundant Resources

Abstract An examination of the different factors that can contribute to growth: increased capital, abundant resource supplies, a larger labor force, and innovation, though the effect of different types of innovation will depend on the ease with which resource supplies can be expanded. A distinction is made between the things that physically have to happen for growth to occur and the social arrangements that make those physical outcomes more likely. The question of convergence between rich countries and poor is considered by means of the diminishing marginal product of capital. The end of the chapter introduces "conditional equivalence," describing what has to be true for the conventional model and this book's model to provide the same view of growth. An appendix goes through the algebra of the steady state.

7.1 Introduction

Adjusted for inflation, America's GDP has risen from $1,056 billion in 1929 to $15,767 billion in 2013 (in chained 2009 dollars)—increasing by almost 15 times over those 84 years, which included the Great Depression (data from [7]). The population was growing over that time as well, but even in per-capita terms the country's GDP grew by a factor of more than three between 1950 and 2007, from $12,990 to $42,887 (data from [4]). Such increases in material well-being obviously suggest sustained economic growth.

When GDP is converted at purchasing-power parity (PPP), US per-capita GDP in 2007 was more than 11 times that of India, and more than 100 times that of the Democratic Republic of the Congo. While the US's increase in GDP indicates sustained GDP growth, these differences in material well-being between countries suggest that different countries have experienced different growth rates over time (in the case of the Congo, their GDP per capita actually dropped between 1950 and 2000, even as ours grew) (data again from [4]).

Why does that matter? Remember from Chap. 3 that GDP, though flawed, still gives us some useful information. The differences in quality of life between France and the US don't have much to do with differences in GDP per capita, but when comparing any rich country to any poor one, the differences in quality of life are large, and they are at least in part related to differences in GDP per capita. A poor

K. Seeley, *Macroeconomics in Ecological Context*, Studies in Ecological Economics 5, DOI 10.1007/978-3-319-51757-5_7

country's inability to provide adequate levels of safe drinking water or schooling or medical care is simultaneously a cause of continued poverty and a result of current inability to afford such measures.

This points to the importance of understanding what causes an economy to grow, or keeps it from doing so. Even if one questions the benefit of further growth in a society that's already rich,[1] it's still good to understand how growth happens.

7.2 Capital and Investment

One of the things that is most striking in comparing rich and poor countries is the difference in the amount of capital that the average worker makes use of. Farmers in the US and western Europe drive tractors and huge combine harvesters while many farmers in poor countries use draft animals for plowing—if they're lucky. Each rich-country farmer can work far more land and therefore produce more food. The same phenomenon applies throughout the economy. A single construction worker with a back-hoe can accomplish as much as a large crew of people with shovels and wheelbarrows. It's thus a reasonable assumption that a high capital-labor ratio is a precondition for a materially prosperous economy, and an increasing capital-labor ratio is necessary for increasing prosperity.

Investment is the creation of capital, so it plays a crucial role in economic growth, but investment doesn't automatically turn into increased capital per worker. Investment gets split three ways. First, it must make up for depreciation, which is when capital needs maintenance, wears out and must be replaced, or becomes obsolete. Second, if the labor force is growing, some investment is used just to provide the new workers with the economy's current average level of capital. What's left after accounting for those two factors is all that's available for increasing your capital-labor ratio. A high depreciation rate or fast population growth makes it harder just to stay in place, never mind increasing your capital-labor ratio.

These factors are explored in more detail in the appendix on "Growth and the steady state."

7.3 Resources

Along with the greater capital stock per worker in rich countries, there are large differences in the use of resources between rich and poor.

[1]There is an entire "degrowth" movement devoted to the exploration of this idea; for example, see [8].

As described in Chap. 3, "resources" are such a heterogeneous category that it's hard to come up with a single measure, but a plausible one is the idea of a country's "ecological footprint." This measure takes an economy's consumption of crops, lumber, and fish, and translates them into the acreage of productive ground or water necessary to produce those quantities of consumption. It adds in built-up land that is used for cities, roads, factories, and the like. And it takes the economy's emissions of CO_2 and translates them into a number of acres that would have to be devoted to growing crops to capture that carbon if the country were to be "carbon neutral" (emitting no more carbon than it soaked up).

If you take these in their parts, the footprints for cropland, grazing land, forests, and fishing grounds add up to a rough measure of the economy's use of renewable resources, the carbon footprint is a strong proxy for the economy's use of fossil fuels, and a decent proxy for its use of exhaustible resources in general, while the built-up footprint gives an idea of a country's relative capital stock (though it can't say anything about the quality of that capital stock). When you add all the parts together into the total footprint, you have a plausible measure of an economy's overall use of resources.

Table 7.1 gives average footprint data for three groupings of countries by income level ("High," "Middle," "Low"), as well as a selection of individual countries with their levels of per-capita GDP.

The links between income (i.e., per-capita GDP) and resource use are obvious in the table. Note in particular that the while the rich use more of everything than the poor, the difference is smallest in built-up area, next smallest in use of renewable resources, and largest in consumption of fossil fuels.

Notice also that, by this measure, poor countries rely more on renewable resources than on fossil fuel, and rich countries, though they use more of both than do poor countries, also rely more on fossil fuels than they do on renewable resources. We'll revisit the role of resources in Sect. 7.6.

Table 7.1 Sample of ecological footprints and GDP-per-capita levels for 2005 (Footprint data from [6]; GDP data from [5])

Country or group	Total	Built-up area	Renewables	CO_2	GDP per capita
High income	6.4	0.13	2.21	4.04	
Middle income	2.2	0.08	1.11	1.00	
Low income	1.0	0.05	0.70	0.26	
United States	9.4	0.10	2.81	6.51	41,890
Germany	4.2	0.21	1.70	2.31	29,461
Mexico	3.4	0.08	1.39	1.30	10,751
China	2.1	0.07	0.90	1.13	6,757
Bangladesh	0.6	0.04	0.41	0.04	2,053

7.4 Labor Force

All else being equal, a large population will produce more than a small one. More specifically, a larger *labor force* will produce more than a smaller *labor force*. So one way for an economy to grow is for the population to increase with a constant share of the population working. This by itself, however, won't increase GDP *per capita*, which is usually of more interest than the total GDP.

Another way to grow is to have a larger portion participating in the labor force. The US has actually experienced this phenomenon, with a sharp increase in labor-force participation by women since the 1940s (from the low-30% range to near 60%) while men's participation has fallen, but less dramatically (from near 90% in 1948 to the mid-70% range). This by itself *will* increase output per capita, though not output per worker. (To the extent that the increase in women's labor-force participation reflects greater opportunities for people to arrange their lives the way they want, it's arguably a good thing; to the extent that it reflects families' perceived need for a second income, it may be less desirable.) An increase in labor-force participation will increase output per capita (because there's more labor per capita), but may not increase society's well-being, because there is less time for leisure or useful non-market activities (like child-rearing, volunteering, political involvement, and other social interactions).

As discussed in Sect. 7.2, a growing labor force needs a growing capital stock just to maintain the level of capital per worker; an *increase* in capital per worker thus requires an even higher level of investment.

7.5 Diminishing Returns to Capital

We know that more capital allows for more output, but what's the quantitative nature of that relationship? The standard assumption is that the production process exhibits diminishing marginal product of capital (or MPK, "K" standing for capital). Going from no capital to a little increases output a lot; adding the same amount of capital again increases output further, but not by as much; a third increase of capital results in an even smaller increase in output.

(Note that the Cobb-Douglas production function exhibits this property, as illustrated in the calculus-and-algebra appendix of Chap. 4.)

Combined with depreciation, this has important implications for growth. The easiest way to model depreciation is as a constant percentage of the capital stock—say, every year, something like 5% of your existing capital stock wears away. So as the capital-labor ratio doubles, the amount of depreciation that needs to be covered also doubles, but diminishing MPK means that the amount of output goes up by less than double. This implies that an ever-larger portion of output goes toward covering depreciation. With a given level of technology and a fixed savings rate (implying a fixed level of investment as a portion of output), the economy will plateau out to a steady state in terms of the capital-labor ratio, and thus in terms of material well-being. The only way around this form of stagnation is through improved technology.

7.6 Innovation

Americans in the early twenty-first century not only have more capital per capita, but also more sophisticated capital, as a result of continuous innovation over time. As explained above, if the economy really is characterized by diminishing returns to capital, then innovation is the only way for output per worker to keep increasing.

Innovation may be the result of insights gained naturally in the course of working with a particular manufacturing process or industry. It may also come from research and development (R&D), which is a specific kind of investment activity, where productive capacity (the time of the researchers and whatever physical inputs the R&D process requires) are devoted not to the production of goods and services for consumption, but rather to the creation of new knowledge.

Remember also from Chap. 2 that the normal usage of the word "innovation" in economics lumps together two different kinds of change with very different implications. One kind can be thought of as "input efficiency," getting a greater amount of output out of unchanged amounts of *all* inputs, including resources; we've described this in the model as an increase in the parameter Z. The other kind of innovation is the discovery of new supplies of resources and new ways of using resources; the discovery of new supplies is an increase in the resource supply curves described in Chap. 4, while the construction of capital that uses those resources is an increase in ρ, the resource intensity of labor.

Note an important difference between both kinds of technological change (Z and ρ) and the savings rate. If you increase the savings rate, you will increase the economy's long-run steady-state level of capital per worker, and thus increase the long-run steady-state level of output per worker, all else being equal. And, in transitioning to that new steady-state level, the economy will exhibit an increase in growth of output per capita. However, once it reaches the new steady-state, it settles down to the level of growth determined by the rate of technological change. If you want to *permanently* boost the growth rate via higher saving, you need to keep raising the savings rate. And of course the savings rate mathematically can't be greater than 100%, and in practical terms can hardly be more than 50%. So increased saving can't be a driver of continually high growth.

This leads to a couple of important facts about the role of innovation in economic growth. First the purely good news. Efficiency gains (increases in Z) are not like capital: they're not subject to depreciation, and they tend to spread across the whole economy, regardless of the labor force (as opposed to machinery, which gets spread thin as your labor force grows). This has the effect that, while growth from increased capital stock alone is ultimately self-defeating, growth from improved efficiency is, in principle, open-ended.

Then the mixed news. Increases in resource-intensity of labor are, like efficiency, not subject to depreciation. However, while you can't "run out" of efficiency, you *can* encounter resource scarcity, in which case a high level of ρ will not be a great benefit to your economy. Also, as your labor force grows you'll need a greater quantity of resources themselves, even if the level of resources per worker is unchanged. The larger your per-worker resource requirement, the bigger a problem this is. Referring back to the framework of Sect. 7.3, rich countries exhibit a high level of resource use per capita, which indicates that they combine a large value of ρ with access to ample resource supplies.

7.7 Convergence

Another implication of diminishing MPK is that poor countries should catch up to, or "converge" with, the rich countries. A poor country has a lower capital-labor ratio, which means, if diminishing MPK is true, that the MPK in a poor country is higher than in a rich one: a unit of capital created in a poor country will increase output by more than if that same unit were invested in a rich country. This in turn means that the returns to investment (the creation of capital) should be higher in poor countries, creating an incentive for high investment there. With lots of investment in poor countries, and that investment having a high marginal product, poor economies should grow faster than rich ones, and thus should converge on their rich counterparts.

Recent decades have seen instances of high GDP growth in some poor countries, most notably China, India, and Brazil. But the pattern is far from universal; possible reasons will be discussed below in Sects. 7.9 and 7.10. But first we'll take a digression to look at what's going on in the model from Chaps. 4 through 6 when growth happens.

7.8 Mechanics of Growth

The preceding sections give some stereotypical characteristics of growth:

- Increased capital
- Increased labor force
- Increased resource use
- Improved technology

In terms of the model, those are increases in K, N^S, R, Z, and ρ. Let's see how those play out and work together.

The increase in N^S is a rightward shift in the simple labor supply. Increases in K, Z, and ρ all contribute to a rightward shift in labor demand (because they all shift the production function upward, thus increasing the marginal product of labor). Those two shifts by themselves suggest an increase in the equilibrium level of employment, and if a greater quantity of labor is used in an improved production function, the result is more GDP. If the increase in the production function is large enough, then there will be more GDP *per capita*. This will show up in the labor market as the demand curve moving right by more than the simple labor supply curve moving right, resulting in higher wages (higher wages are how higher *per capita* GDP affects the individual, in principle).

But there's a wildcard here, because ρ doesn't only shift labor demand to the right; it also shifts resource-augmented labor supply to the *left* (recall Figs. 6.5 and 6.6). If the leftward shift is large enough, employment would go *down* rather than up. So which is it?

In Chap. 6 we observed that, "*When resource prices are low*, increased resource intensity of labor leads to higher wages and higher employment, and the increased labor and increased use of resources lead synergistically to higher output." The key thing that makes an increase in ρ good for employment rather than damaging is low resource prices (and *falling* resource prices are even better).

And what does it take to keep resource prices low even as resource use increases? A large enough rightward shift in the resource supply curve will do the trick.

So we can recharacterize growth in the model. Rather than happening through increases in K, N^S, R, Z, and ρ, it happens through some combination of those things *and* a substantial rightward shift in the resource supply curve, R^S.

7.9 Institutions

If high investment, not-too-high population growth, abundant resources, and starting from relative poverty were enough to make an economy grow, then the countries of the Soviet bloc should have been stars of economic growth. And in the early part of the Soviet period that may well have been true, as backward Russia experienced a crash program of industrial expansion and the spread of electrification. But from the 1960s through the 1980s the Soviet Union and its satellites showed disappointing results, given the large portion of their output devoted to investment. And since the fall of Soviet-bloc communism in 1989–1991, some former communist countries have made serious strides toward catching up with western Europe, while others remain relatively stagnant. Along with many Third World countries that have shown unimpressive growth, they illustrate the importance of institutions.

The word "institutions" covers a very broad range of social arrangements, everything from the formal structures of government and corporate organization to customs supported by nothing more than tradition and wide acceptance. They are often intangible, but they have a large effect on how well an economy functions (see, e.g., [1]). What kinds of institutions tend to promote growth?

First, a society's economic incentives must make it worthwhile to innovate. The USSR produced many brilliant scientists, and when the regime chose to focus on some particular area, such as tanks during World War II or fighter jets in the Cold

War, they were able to come up with technologically respectable ways of doing things. But on an economy-wide scale the countries of the Soviet bloc weren't good at coming up with new production technologies.

Second, there have to be incentives for applying known technology. Not only did the Soviet-bloc countries fail to innovate on their own, they were also poor at making use of new technologies developed elsewhere. They should have been able to reverse-engineer computers developed in the West and Japan, but didn't.

Third, whatever capital and technology you have at your disposal, you need incentives to use it and your labor supply well. In a market economy, economic rewards more or less flow toward those who do things that are economically efficient. In the Soviet bloc, economic rewards flowed toward those who fulfilled the commands of the political leadership, regardless of how economically useful those commands were.

In poor countries throughout the world, a host of problems hold back economic activity:

- insecure property rights limit people's incentives to invest;
- corrupt regimes reward political and social connections rather than economic contributions;
- misguided development efforts (and corruption) mean that what investment there is doesn't always go toward the most useful ends;
- social divisions, ethnic tensions, and even civil war impede economic activity and misdirect what activity there is toward conflict rather than productive efforts.

In short, without good institutions, the more tangible components of economic growth are less likely to occur, and to the extent that they do occur, they may not be used well. The importance of good institutions is one reason for the failure of convergence in many countries.

7.10 Diminishing MPK Revisited

Economists like to see diminishing marginal returns and so we've built a theory of growth that assumes diminishing marginal product of capital, and we've chosen a functional representation of the economy (the Cobb-Douglas function) that embodies that assumption. But the assumption does not necessarily reflect reality all that well.

Consider the act of building a factory in a developed country (that is, one where there's already a lot of capital). The "convergence" story says that, because there's already so much capital, the marginal product of capital is low. The same investment in a country lacking capital would produce much greater returns. But think about some of the implications of the already-developed country having lots of capital. It means there are other factories nearby that can efficiently manufacture the inputs you need, leading to an abundant supply of those goods and a lower price than otherwise. And there is also another set of factories nearby that can make efficient use of your output, which amounts to high demand for your products (which will in turn be reflected in relatively high prices for your output, and high returns to capital). And this developed country will have a good transportation system to bring inputs to your factory and carry the outputs away. In other words, making good use of one piece of capital (your factory) depends on the existence of lots of other pieces of capital.

The idea of diminishing MPK makes sense if all of your capital is the same thing: the first factory of a given type you build is quite useful; the second one increases your production, but not by as much; the third factory causes an even smaller increase. But capital isn't lots of *one* thing, it's lots of a lot of *different* things, all more or less working together; each piece is a complement to other pieces. Given that reality, diminishing MPK may be true in some situations but not necessarily everywhere all the time.

There's also complementarity of human capital. A skilled doctor may in principal be more useful in a country where doctors are scarce than in a rich one that is amply supplied with hospitals and medical personnel. And to an extent that's true in fact, not merely in principal. Adding one doctor where there are none might mean reducing some basic illnesses that are easy to treat but that have debilitating effects if left untreated; this reduction in illness will in turn produce large social benefits. But the doctor's skills may not be that productive if she is not supported by adequate nurses, doesn't have access to sanitary conditions, and can't get hold of adequate supplies of medicine. Simple theory says that the marginal productivity of a skilled person should be higher where there are few other skilled people. More sophisticated theory suggests that harnessing the benefits of those skills depends on having other skilled people around. Many skilled people will naturally migrate to where they are most effective, which means they will migrate to places that are already rich, leaving behind a reduced pool of human capital in their home countries (this is often referred to as a "brain drain"). And those skilled people who stay at home will be in circumstances that make them less productive than if they migrated.

The complementarity of both physical and human capital creates a dynamic under which rich countries grow faster than poor ones, and the lack of convergence is not a surprise.

7.11 The Value of Growth

The discussion of GDP in Chap. 3 suggested some broad conclusions about the desirability of a growing GDP: if your country is growing from poor to rich, you're probably having a real and positive effect on people's material standard of living. If you're growing from rich to richer, the connection to quality of life may be much less clear.

Even in a fast-growing poor country, conclusions about quality of life may be more complicated if the high growth comes with widespread and serious pollution and disruptive social change. But even so, it may be a tradeoff most people are willing to make—China in the last 30 years has seen exactly this mix, and many people seem to prefer it to what came before.

Even in the case of rich countries, however, there are powerful arguments in favor of growth.

7.11.1 Employment

One attribute of growth is clear to most lay observers, and that is the connection between growth and employment. Technological progress tends to make labor more productive. If labor gets more productive, then GDP *per capita* had better keep up, or else we won't need as much labor. And while we could, in theory, keep the same number of people employed and just have them work 20 h a week, there are economic, institutional, and cultural factors that tend to work against such an outcome. So then our only alternative to ever-increasing unemployment is ever-increasing GDP *per capita*.

7.11.2 Political Stability

Probably the most famous case of a bad political outcome from an economic event is the link between Germany getting socked by the Great Depression and then Hitler gaining a plurality in the 1933 elections. Less well known, but not surprisingly, the U.S. experienced political turbulence during the 1930s; in retrospect, Roosevelt made it look easy to sustain democracy, but people at the time were fairly nervous. Europe today flirts with political extremism as some parts of the continent continue to be affected by the financial crisis of 2008.

Simply put, growth may make people more willing to display the tolerance that a democracy needs in order to function.[2]

7.11.3 The Functioning of the Money System

Growth may also be important for the way the monetary system operates at present. This will be discussed in more detail later in the book, but briefly here: money usually comes into existence through loans; loans require the payment of interest; in aggregate, the payment of interest is only possible if there is growth, so stagnation brings with it very serious monetary problems (see [9]).

[2]This case is made extensively in [3].

7.11.4 *Questioning the Value of Growth*

Aside from potential environmental problems, there's another, more subtle argument against growth in countries that have already achieved what may generally be termed a "comfortable" standard of living. The argument begins with the observation that continual growth requires continual increases in consumption. The next step is to question the standard economic assumption about non-satiation. That is, economists routinely assert that people inherently always want more than they have; the counter-argument claims that people aren't so simple, and that in fact once we have a decent standard of living, we have to be actively convinced to want more. And to convince us to want more, it's necessary to alter our values: instead of enjoying our modest but comfortable goods in the company of friends and family, our values get refocused on the ever-greater acquisition of material goods. And since we are social animals, this change in values leaves us fundamentally unsatisfied. We're worse off, and yet that very dissatisfaction is exactly what is needed to convince us to buy even more goods: Here, buy this—it will fill that empty place in your soul.[3]

In this line of argument, it's not so much that growth itself is undesirable, as that growth isn't possible without an undesirable change in values. It strikes me as an important perspective to consider, while noting that it finds very little acceptance among economists.

7.12 Conditional Equivalence

This book has been laying out a particular model of the macroeconomy, one where resources are assumed to matter and resource-supply curves are fully integrated into the set of tools we have for understanding the economy. In this model, shifts in resource supply have clear macroeconomic effects in the model, and changes in resource availability are part of the story of growth that this chapter has told.

Pretty much every other macroeconomics textbook doesn't tell that story. Instead of output being a function of K, Z, N, ρ and R^S, it's merely a function of K, A, and N (capital, technology, and labor). If resources are so important, if the economy *is* analogous to an ecosystem and *is* truly subject to the laws of thermodynamics and the realities of obtaining and using resources, why doesn't everybody use a resource-based model?

Think about the mechanics of growth in the conventional model:

- Saving provides the means for investment.
- Human curiosity and experience with production lead to innovation.
- Investment and innovation result in larger amounts of improved capital.

[3] Bowles [2] provides an interesting exploration of the malleability of preferences and the effects of promoting one kind rather than another.

- This in turn leads to more output.
- The increased level of output allows there to be more savings, and the cycle continues.

This book doesn't disagree with that story; it just asks you to look a little closer at what's happening with investment and innovation.

Some of investment and innovation is new means and new ways of *using* resources. But some of it is new ways of *obtaining* resources—in other words, ways of increasing resource supply. A logging railroad is an investment that increases the supply of lumber. An oil rig is an investment that increases the supply of oil. Seismic techniques for finding oil, and deepwater-drilling techniques for extracting it, are innovations that increase the supply of oil.

Resource supply curves are not simply facts of nature. They are shaped by the interaction between the possibilities that nature creates and the techniques and equipment we have developed and built in order to take advantage of those possibilities.

So consider a world where innovations and investments aimed at making resources available pretty regularly succeed in shifting the resource supply curve rightward. Now revisit the growth cycle described above:

- Saving provides the means for investment.
- Human curiosity and experience with production lead to innovation.
- Investment and innovation result in larger amounts of improved capital.
- *Some of that increased and improved capital leads to an increased supply of resources.*
- *Some of the increased and improved capital is allowing us to make use of more resources.*
- *Increased availability of resources supports increased use of resources.*
- *Increased resource use*, in an enlarged and improved capital stock, leads to more output
- The increased level of output allows there to be more savings, and the cycle continues.

It's easy enough to simplify this second story down to the first one. Investment and innovation lead to growth. What difference does it make whether that's the whole story, or whether they work partly by increasing the supply of resources?

Look again at the assumption made before walking through the growth cycle in a model that includes resources: "a world where innovations and investments aimed at making resources available pretty regularly succeed in shifting the resource supply curve rightward."

That has been the experience of the last 500 years, and particularly the last 250 years, since the beginning of the age of coal. It has not always been true in the past. And we have no guarantee that it *will* always be true in the future. Let's look at that growth cycle again, but now in a world where resource supply is stagnant, or even shrinks, *despite innovation and investment aimed at shifting it to the right*:

- Saving provides the means for investment

- Human curiosity and experience with production lead to innovation
- Investment and innovation result in larger amounts of improved capital
- *Resource supply fails to expand, and maybe even contracts*
- *Decreased availability of resources means decreased use, and this in turn stymies growth, in spite of increased and improved capital—unless that improved capital is able to more than overcome the decrease in resource use*
- *The stagnant or diminishing level of output cuts into society's ability to save, and the cycle is broken.*

This is obviously a very different story. So sometimes the resource-based model and the conventional model tell you the same thing; sometimes they tell you drastically different things. The **condition** under which they tell you the same thing is when innovation and investment aimed at increasing resource availability regularly succeed. When that's true, the models are the same; when it's not, they go their separate ways.

That's **conditional equivalence**: this book's model is *equivalent* to the standard model, *under the condition* that human activity is successful at increasing resource supply.

Appendix: Growth and the Steady State

Given particular parameters for growth, what level of output will the economy reach over time? In other words, what is the "steady state" toward which it is heading? It turns out we can solve for the level of capital per worker in the steady state, and that in turn implies a particular level of steady-state output per worker.

We start with the observation that next year's capital is this year's capital, plus whatever we build over the course of this year, minus whatever depreciates over the course of the year.

If we use a subscript t for this year and $t + 1$ for next year, we can write:

$$K_{t+1} = K_t + \text{investment} - \text{depreciation}.$$

Then we just have to get more specific about investment and depreciation.

Make a couple of simplifying assumptions: first, that investment equals saving, and that we save a constant portion of each year's GDP. If that portion is s, we can write:

$$(\text{Investment})_t = sY_t.$$

We can then make a similar simplifying assumption about depreciation, namely, that a constant portion of capital wears out in any given year. If that portion is d, then we can write:

$$(\text{Depreciation})_t = dK_t.$$

Now we can describe the evolution of capital in algebraic terms:

$$K_{t+1} = K_t + sY_t - dK_t.$$

Having done that, we bring K_t over to the left-hand side, and divide both sides by N_t, the labor force:

$$\frac{K_{t+1} - K_t}{N_t} = s\frac{Y_t}{N_t} - d\frac{K_t}{N_t}.$$

To simplify the notation, remember from Sect. 4.7 that $Y/N = y$, or output per worker, and $K/N = k$, capital per worker:

$$\frac{K_{t+1}}{N_t} - k_t = sy_t - dk_t.$$

Note that the first fraction can't quite be gotten rid of the way the other fractions could, because the subscripts on K and N aren't the same; *next year's* capital stock divided by *this year's* work force isn't a meaningful quantity. But it would be nice to be able to do something about that fraction, which will require getting a term N_{t+1} under there. We can do that by multiplying by $\frac{N_{t+1}}{N_{t+1}}$ and rearranging:

$$\frac{K_{t+1}}{N_{t+1}}\frac{N_{t+1}}{N_t} - k_t = sy_t - dk_t.$$

We need to put some meaning to this new fraction that has appeared, $\frac{N_{t+1}}{N_t}$. If you look at the terms, it's next year's labor force divided by this year's labor force. If we say that the labor force is growing at the rate n, then we can rewrite $\frac{N_{t+1}}{N_t}$ as $(1+n)$ and put this into our equation (also noting that $K_{t+1}/N_{t+1} = k_{t+1}$):

$$k_{t+1}(1+n) - k_t = sy_t - dk_t.$$

Now we isolate the k_{t+1} term:

$$k_{t+1}(1+n) = sy_t + (1-d)k_t,$$

and divide both sides by $(1+n)$:

$$k_{t+1} = \frac{sy_t + (1-d)k_t}{(1+n)}.$$

The next step is to subtract k_t from both sides:

$$k_{t+1} - k_t = \frac{sy_t + (1-d)k_t}{(1+n)} - k_t,$$

and bring k_t into the numerator on the right by multiplying it by $(1+n)/(1+n)$:

$$k_{t+1} - k_t = \frac{sy_t + (1-d)k_t - (1+n)k_t}{(1+n)}.$$

On the right, we have a $(+1k_t)$ and a $(-1k_t)$, so we can consolidate:

$$k_{t+1} - k_t = \frac{sy_t - dk_t - nk_t}{(1+n)}.$$

What we have on the left is the growth of capital per worker (next year's level, minus this year's level). To turn it into a growth *rate* in percentage terms, we have to divide by k_t, this year's level, so of course we have to do the same to the right-hand side as well:

$$\frac{k_{t+1} - k_t}{k_t} = \frac{s\frac{y_t}{k_t} - d - n}{(1+n)}. \tag{7.1}$$

Now, it would be nice to be able to do something with that y_t/k_t term on the right-hand side, and it turns out we can. Remember (Sect. 4.7) that the per-worker form of the Cobb-Douglas function is

$$y_t = k_t{}^{\alpha} Z^{\delta} \rho^{\gamma},$$

and if we divide both sides of that by k_t we get

$$\frac{y_t}{k_t} = k_t{}^{\alpha-1} Z^{\delta} \rho^{\gamma}. \tag{7.2}$$

So if we take this expression in Eq. 7.2 and substitute it into Eq. 7.1, we get:

$$\frac{k_{t+1} - k_t}{k_t} = \frac{sk_t{}^{\alpha-1} Z^{\delta} \rho^{\gamma} - d - n}{(1+n)}. \tag{7.3}$$

Now, believe it or not, we're almost there.

The steady state is defined by things not changing. Among the things that have to not change in the steady state is the level of capital per worker. In other words, we can define the steady state as the situation when the left-hand side of Eq. 7.3 is zero (we can also move the $k_t{}^{\alpha-1}$ around within its part of the right-hand side):

$$0 = \frac{sZ^{\delta} \rho^{\gamma} k_t{}^{\alpha-1} - d - n}{(1+n)}.$$

Our goal now is to solve for k_t, in order to be able to define steady-state capital per worker in terms of the other items in the equation. Except that now we'll call it

$\overline{k}$ (pronounced "k-bar") instead of k_t, because the time subscript suggests something that's changing from one period to the next, and the whole point of this exercise is that we're looking for a value that's fixed; the bar over the k will denote that fixed, steady-state level of k.

The first step is to multiply through by $(1 + n)$, so it disappears from the denominator on the right; it doesn't show up on the left, since it's getting multiplied by zero:

$$0 = sZ^{\delta}\rho^{\gamma}\overline{k}^{\alpha-1} - d - n.$$

Next we can move the things that are just added on (d and n), and also turn the equation around for notational convenience:

$$sZ^{\delta}\rho^{\gamma}\overline{k}^{(\alpha-1)} = d + n.$$

Now we divide both sides by all the stuff that $\overline{k}$ is getting multiplied by:

$$\overline{k}^{(\alpha-1)} = \frac{d+n}{sZ^{\delta}\rho^{\gamma}}.$$

If we take the exponent on $\overline{k}$ and turn it around (so it becomes $[1 - \alpha]$), that's the same as taking the inverse of the left-hand side of the equation (in other words, 1 divided by $\overline{k}^{(\alpha-1)}$, which means we have to flip over the right-hand side as well:

$$\overline{k}^{(1-\alpha)} = \frac{sZ^{\delta}\rho^{\gamma}}{d+n}.$$

And now we are actually, really, truly, almost there—we just need to get rid of the exponent on $\overline{k}$. If you raise both sides to the $1/(1 - \alpha)$, that shows up as an exponent on the right, while it cancels out the exponent on the left:

$$\overline{k} = \left(\frac{sZ^{\delta}\rho^{\gamma}}{d+n}\right)^{\frac{1}{(1-\alpha)}}. \tag{7.4}$$

A few pages later, and we've done it: we have an expression for capital-per-worker in the steady state, expressed as a function of the level of efficiency, resource intensity of labor, the savings rate, the depreciation rate, and the growth rate.

If you plug that back into the per-worker form of output, you get the level of output per worker in the steady sate, as a function of the same factors that determine steady-state capital per worker.

Problems

Problem 7.1 The table below shows eight fictitious countries (creatively named "A" through "H"). Each country is given with its CO_2 footprint per capita, its renewables footprint per capita, and its GDP per capita. For each country, say whether it fits the expected pattern in terms of the relationship between resource use and GDP per capita. If your answer is that it doesn't fit, explain specifically how it's "out of line."

Country	CO_2 footprint	Renewables footprint	GDP per capita
A	0.5	1.1	1,000
B	2.8	6.9	3,000
C	7.0	3.2	2,500
D	0.8	2.5	39,000
E	1.5	0.5	1,500
F	2.1	0.9	38,000
G	8.0	3.3	42,000
H	4.1	5.8	35,000

Problem 7.2 Identify a social institution. Say whether it tends to foster economic growth or hinder it. Your answer should operate through one of the more tangible factors of economic growth (e.g., saving, investment, innovation, access to resources, population growth).

Problem 7.3 The table below gives another four (fantastically creatively named) imaginary countries, this time "J" through "K". The data show population (in thousands) and GDP (in billions) for each country in two different periods (1 and 2).

For each country calculate GDP per capita in each of the two periods, as well as the *percent* change in GDP from period 1 to period 2, and the *percent* change in GDP per capita from period 1 to period 2.

Country	Pop_1	Pop_2	GDP_1	GDP_2	GDP/ cap_1	GDP/ cap_2	ΔGDP	ΔGDP/ cap
J	1,542	1,628	45	65				
K	2,563	2,000	84	80				
L	32,832	49,036	120	135				
M	11,561	10,493	85	79				

Problem 7.4 Equation 7.4 of the appendix defines steady-state capital per worker $\bar{k}$ as a function of various influences, including s, Z, ρ, n, and d. For each of these influences:

(a) Say what the letter represents.
(b) Give a *mathematical* explanation of how that factor influences $\bar{k}$. For example, "A larger value of s makes $\bar{k}$ get" (and here you have to say "larger" or "smaller") "because ...", and your explanation should be based simply on the equation for steady-state capital per worker.

(c) Provide the economic logic behind the impact you identified in the previous part of the question. That is, why does it "make sense" that the relationship should be what you said it was in that part of the question?

Problem 7.5 Explain the circumstances under which the resource-inclusive growth model of this book leads to a different conclusion than a model that neglects the role of resources.

References

1. Acemoglu, D., Johnson, S., & Robinson, J. A. (2001). The colonial origins of comparative development: An empirical investigation. *The American Economic Review, 91*(5), 1369–1401.
2. Bowles, S. (1998). Endogenous preferences: The cultural consequences of markets and other economic institutions. *Journal of Economic Literature, 36*(1), 75–111.
3. Friedman, B. M. (2006). *The moral consequences of economic growth*. New York: Vintage.
4. Heston, A., Summers, R., & Aten, B. (2009). Penn world table version 6.3. http://pwt.econ.upenn.edu/php_site/pwt63/pwt63_form.php. Downloaded March 14, 2010; data series is rgdpch, "Real GDP per capita (Constant prices: chain series)".
5. Human development report 2007/2008. (2008). http://hdr.undp.org/en/media/HDR_20072008_Tables.zip, Table 1, downloaded on June 8, 2009.
6. National footprint accounts 2008 edition. (2009). http://www.footprintnetwork.org/download.php?id=509 at http://www.footprintnetwork.org/en/index.php/GFN/, downloaded June 8, 2009.
7. National Income and Product Accounts, Table 1.1.6, "Real Gross Domestic Product, chained dollars". (2009). http://www.bea.gov/national/nipaweb/SelectTable.asp, downloaded February 22, 2014.
8. Research & degrowth. http://www.degrowth.org/.
9. Tverberg, G. (2010). Delusions of finance: Where we are headed. "The oil drum" blog, http://www.theoildrum.com/node/6191. Accessed August 7, 2015.

Part III
Business Cycles

Part I of the book introduced the physical nature of the economy, as a structure for obtaining resources from the world around us, transforming them to suit our needs, and distributing them among the economy's various entities. That was an unconventional approach, but in Chap. 3 it also reviewed the basic terms used in standard macroeconomic analysis (and used here as well).

Coming out of Part II, we've got the long-run model, or the classical model, a useful tool for understanding long-run growth. We know that investment and innovation lead to more and better capital, raising the production function and increasing the marginal product of labor. If they're also successful at leading to an increased resource supply, then all the curves of the labor-market move to the right more or less together, so we have increasing employment, quite possibly also with increasing wages, and increasing output.

But as discussed at the end of Chap. 6, the model has one great flaw, which is that it can't explain the business cycle. It's a model of an economy that is at its long-run equilibrium, and the thing that's at the very core of the model is a labor market that has balanced the marginal product of labor and the cost of employing people. The path of output and employment that we actually observe is hard to explain just in terms of what the long-run model has to offer.

The first important difference is that money plays a central role. In Part II we had a price level and money and velocity and a difference between nominal wages and real wages. But money didn't actually *do* anything. Firms looked at the real marginal product of labor and the real wage, and acted accordingly. It was assumed that people were paid in money wages and then used that money to buy things, but in principle they could have been acting in a barter economy.

Money is the key to escaping from another trap that the long-run model contains. Notice that everything that is produced belongs to someone: in other words, all output is income. The long-run model then closes the loop by saying that all income is spent, and that all spending comes from income. One of the things about money is that it allows us to break that second part of the loop. It's still true that output becomes income. But when people receive their income as money, they don't have to spend it all, and the part they don't spend doesn't have to be lent out. And when systems of credit exist, there can be a certain amount of spending beyond income.

In addition to adding a real role for money, Part III makes use of the long-run equilibrium from Part II as "potential output"—the state the economy would "like" to be in, the state it would be in if it were at its long-run equilibrium. In the end, people's preferences and the physical ability to produce stuff plausibly shape how much the economy is capable of doing, and the long-run model addresses that. The short-run model of this section explains how the actual output of the economy can diverge from its potential output. And it turns out that the key to that ability to diverge is having a money system.

The first three chapters of Part III cover money: Chap. 8 explains the role of money in big-picture terms, as part of the change in the organization of human societies over millennia. Chapter 9 uses a parable to get into the nature of money itself. And Chap. 10 builds on Chap. 9 to explain the functioning of banks and the creation of money.

Chapter 11 uses the understanding of money to explain the idea of the multiplier, which then feeds into the workings of monetary and fiscal policy in Chaps. 12 and 13. These are tied together in the IS-LM framework of Chaps. 14 and 15. The next chapter gives two different ways of thinking about aggregate supply and aggregate demand, and Chap. 17 uses the framework of Part III to evaluate the impact of recent macroeconomic policy.

And now our first stop on the money tour: money as part of the natural world—a "natural history" of money.

Chapter 8
A Natural History of Money

Abstract Money is an essentially social phenomenon. In its details it is uniquely human, but it is enmeshed with the economy's physical processes and in its functioning it bears a limited resemblance to mechanisms of social coordination that exist in other species. We begin with examples from those other species, covering both production for current use and behaviors that are functionally forms of investment. We then sketch different forms of coordination structures that humans use, leading to the coordinating role of money. The consideration of investment leads to the role of credit and its relationship to money.

8.1 Introduction

Economists sometimes explain the phenomenon of savings in terms of Robinson Crusoe, the lone human stranded on an island. He grows some corn, and what he harvests is his income. The corn he eats is his consumption. The corn he holds aside is his savings, which he uses to "fund" next year's production by planting the unused seeds. But that's not really economics, because an economy is an inherently social entity—after all, economics is grouped with the *social* sciences. And if you're going to have people engaging in economic activity with each other, you're going to have to solve some basic questions:

- Who is going to undertake each of the economy's tasks?
- How will the economy's physical resources be allocated among the various kinds of production?
- How will the resulting output be distributed?
  - How much for investment?
    - And what kinds of capital should that investment build?
  - What isn't invested is consumed—who gets how much of that?

K. Seeley, *Macroeconomics in Ecological Context*, Studies in Ecological Economics 5, DOI 10.1007/978-3-319-51757-5_8

8.2 In the Animal Kingdom

Humans are not alone in undertaking complex tasks that require coordination among different individuals. What does separate us is the means we use to achieve that coordination. Money and credit have an important place among the tools we've evolved to accomplish what other species do through more genetically-determined behaviors. Because of the similarity in the underlying tasks, understanding money is easier if we first step back and look at other species' problems, taking ants, beavers, and termites as our examples.

8.2.1 Coordinating Current Production

An ant colony is made up of various castes that perform distinct roles. The queen produces all of the eggs for the colony's multiplication. Workers play different roles, from those that tend the eggs to others that go out foraging and bring back food for the colony. Worker ants that do a particular kind of work are physically specialized for their tasks and make up what is called a "caste." For instance, soldiers are specialized for their military task by having stronger mandibles than other members of the colony. All of these different groups are necessary for the colony's prosperity. An individual ant has no chance of survival, and even an entire caste is unlikely to last long without the rest of its colony.[1]

What the ants face is a problem of coordinating current production. The work that needs to be done is of various types and it needs to be divided up among the colony's members. The ants' solution for this is a set of evolutionarily determined behaviors. Conditions in the colony and the feeding of the larvae interact with the larvae's genes to determine what caste those larvae will grow to be part of. Once in their castes, the individual ants respond to conditions around them and to chemical signals emanating from other ants, and their responses are generally pre-programmed.

The aggregate effect of that rule-following mechanism is the seemingly purposive behavior of the colony: seeking and gathering food; defending the nest; caring for eggs and larvae.[2] And the genetically coded behaviors of the individual ants ensure that each ant plays its role in its caste, each caste plays its role in the colony, and the colony in turn provides for the ants of which it is composed.

---

[1] An engaging treatment of many aspects of ant life is in [6].

[2] Some essays in [5] play with the idea of an ant colony as a single thinking entity engaged in purposeful behavior.

8.2.2 *Building the Future*

As described above, an ant colony solves a problem of current production: food has to be provided, the colony needs to be defended, and offspring need to be reared. But other actions are aimed not at producing stuff now, but at improving or increasing production in the future.

A beaver family puts great effort into damming a stream to make a pond. Time spent building the dam is time not spent gathering food, but the pond creates conditions under which it will be easier to gather food and provide safety at some later time.

In other words, if the beavers were human, we would say that the dam and the pond behind it are the beavers' physical capital, and the building of the dam is an investment expenditure. Food and safety are the "consumption goods and services" of the beaver "economy" and dam construction is an action that is not itself the production of consumption goods, but that makes it easier to produce consumption goods later. Where ants are programmed to respond to chemical signals, it may be that evolution has selected beavers that respond to the sound of rushing water by gathering sticks and mud to try and stop it.[3] That is, they don't consciously build a pond, with the "intention" of later providing themselves with food and safety. Rather, evolution has bred into them a behavioral response which supports their survival because it leads them to behave *as if* they were engaged in investment. At any rate, the result is the archetypal metaphor in nature for an engineer (adopted by the Massachusetts Institute of Technology as its mascot).

Like the beaver, some species of termites in Africa and South America build what can be called physical capital, but rather than ponds, they build mounds. These structures stand several feet high and are brilliantly engineered with patterns of passages to ensure ventilation, temperature control, and regulation of moisture in the nest (see [16]).

Not only are the termite mounds arguably more subtle pieces of engineering than what beavers accomplish, their construction requires the solution of a more complicated coordination problem. A beaver dam is the product of one mating pair, and so it's conceivable that an individual beaver could "comprehend" the whole of the work (though the sources cited above suggest more autonomic behavior). A termite mound is the creation of a vast number of individual termites, each one of which can only have played a minute role in the project. There are thousands upon thousands of individual workers, with nobody in any position to be in charge of construction, and yet they build a marvel of engineering, for the future good of the whole. As with the productive activity of the ants, coordination is achieved as the aggregate effect of individuals following simple rules. The payoffs are likewise built into the animals through the genetic evolution of behavioral rules that lead to a useful aggregate effect.

[3]Per [13], though [18] questions that finding.

Ants solve a problem of coordinating current production. Termites solve a problem of coordinating investment for future production.[4]

8.3 The Human Problem

Humans face problems that are fundamentally similar to those of ants, termites, and beavers. At a minimum, even the members of a homesteader family have to coordinate their day-to-day economic activity with the others in their nuclear family, and the more typical situation is that people subsist within a clan or some larger grouping.

Coordination within these groups has to happen both when we provide for current consumption and when we undertake investment. We'll proceed by way of a stylized historical survey of how humans have gotten this done and how money and credit came into the picture.

8.3.1 Non-monetary Means of Coordination

If you go back far enough, the way people solved the problem of coordinating their activities was to rely on cultural norms: "It's just what we do." One such norm is the convention that a successful hunter shares his bounty with others, in the expectation that others will do likewise when they have a good day. The successful one isn't selling his extra meat and storing up purchasing power to be used later. All he's doing is maintaining his standing in a society where that's simply how things are done. The anthropologist David Graeber [4] calls this "baseline communism."

There's evolution at work here, because societies that develop "good" cultural norms will thrive, and the people in them will thrive, while people in societies with less helpful rules will be at a disadvantage. So behavioral norms that usually help people will tend to be more common than destructive norms. This is a bit like the coordination of an ant colony, where the individual ants follow simple rules, and the interactions of those rules create a structure that almost seems to have a sense of purpose. Except that in humans it's not genetically determined. The mental capacity to have such norms is a product of our genes, but the norms themselves are culture.[5]

This kind of structure has at least a couple of advantages. The norms include not merely how people interact with each other, but how they use the world around them,

[4]Ants do this too, of course, when they build their nests, but I'm particularly taken with the engineering of the termite mound and its ability to deal with a relatively harsh climate.

[5]The dividing line between genes and culture is not necessarily as clear as this sentence portrays it; see [11].

and these "technological" norms evolve the same way the interpersonal ones do: if your society has well-adapted ways of using the world, you've got an advantage over someone with clumsier ways of making a living.

The result can be great subtlety in the use of the environment, as anthropologists learn when they spend time with traditional peoples.[6] Another advantage is a form of robustness in the face of varying conditions. Species with genetically-driven behaviors often have genes to respond to some degree of fluctuation in their environment, but a culture can store a greater variety of patterns, and so it can deal with greater variability in the conditions in which it lives—as long as the variation is generally within parameters that the culture has experienced and somehow recorded in its habits. As a hunter-gatherer or a primitive farmer, you're probably skilled at dealing with the normal swings of wet years and dry, but you may be wiped out by a drought that's deeper and longer than anything in your cultural memory. Your group perishes or migrates before your culture finds a way of adapting.[7] Still, cultural norms are a powerful way of coordinating people's behavior, and they worked for tens of thousands of years.

But they have their downsides too, one of which is that a norm-governed society has limited dynamism. It's not that such cultures are static; in fact, evolution has to be at work there somewhere, since even the most traditional society must have somehow come to be, rather than having existed since the beginning of the world, but there's a fundamental tension between a traditional society and the drive for rapid change. What makes norms work is their stability; otherwise, they're not norms.

After societies built on norms like baseline communism, we move into the hierarchical economy, where the community is organized such that some people command and others obey. An example would be the priest-bureaucrats of ancient Mesopotamia, who commanded the labor of others in order to build temples, granaries, monumental irrigation works, and the like [17]. Closer to us in time, but still a good long time ago, are the manorial lords of medieval Europe. By social contract, a lord could direct a portion of his peasants' labor to the lord's purposes, and/or claim a portion of the peasants' harvest. The lord didn't pay for the labor or the food; those things were supplied as a matter of social relationship between the lord and the peasant. For the peasants, life was primarily a local subsistence economy, combined with the required provision of food and labor. But for the lord, there was the possibility of coordinated activity on a larger scale than what a few households could manage.[8]

[6] Numerous examples are in [14].

[7] Examples are in [12] and [8].

[8] Pieces of this are in [2], in the context of evolving legal standards around feudal arrangements.

In Mesopotamia, the irrigation works that the hierarchy created arguably had an element of being a social good. They may have resulted from and supported a despotic system, but they also increased the total food-producing capacity of the region.[9] In the case of medieval Europe, the ability of the lords to command resources looks more pathological. The castles built with peasant labor served primarily to reinforce the position of the lords as a whole having command over the peasantry and to defend individual lords from each other, without ever getting around to serving the general welfare.[10] The other great product of this system was churches and cathedrals, and your view of their usefulness to society will depend on your view of the nature of religion, the role of religion in society, and your aesthetic judgments.

8.3.2 Enter Money

I've described these ancient and medieval economies as "hierarchical" economies, governed by social conventions regarding who got to order whom around, but this structure coexisted with money. The usual treatment in economics textbooks is that societies started with barter, and that people therefore were burdened with the obvious difficulty of the "double-coincidence of wants": you have to find someone who has the thing you want and wants the thing you have. Eventually someone comes up with the clever idea of using some commodity like silver, gold, or even seashells as stand-ins for the things traded, allowing Jane to buy from Bill, who buys from Ramanan, who buys from Ester, and back to Jane. In this telling, the next clever step was that people realized they could create pieces of paper that represented particular amounts of gold and then use those papers instead of the gold itself—as long as they did actually have the gold somewhere. From paper money we progressed to mere ledgers, records of who owed how much to whom, and in recent decades we've transferred those ledgers to computer memory, so that money becomes nothing more substantial than electrons governed by keystrokes.

This is a widely-told story and it sounds plausible, but there's not a lot of evidence behind it. Anthropological research, as opposed to economics textbooks, suggests a very different sequence of development [4, 1]. Money certainly can replace barter, but that *can't* be the step by which we moved from primitive societies using barter to modern societies using money, because in baseline communism, *people don't use barter*. Where money exists in these societies, it's not used for day-to-day transactions, but to rearrange social relationships, such as marriage or adoption, or to repair social relationships, as with atonement for murder. It's what Graeber [4] calls a "social currency."

---

[9]The famous treatment of this is [17].

[10]Tuchman [15] provides an evocative treatment of the lack of social benefit in this arrangement.

Instead of arising as a replacement for barter, money starts as a unit of account, a way for temple priests and tax collectors to keep track of who owes how much, who has deposited how many measures of grain in the storehouses of the temple. It *starts* as entries in ledgers. The conventional story sees this keeping of accounts as a much later development, something we figured out after we'd progressed from barter, to metal coins, then on to paper money, but there is archaeological evidence that money grows out of credit, rather than credt being an advanced stage in the evolution of money [1, p. 5].

Because once we know who has what laid up in the temple storehouses, we can start trading on it. I can purchase from you a donkey in exchange for a transfer of ownership of some of my stored grain. It would be absurd for me to actually bring you the grain, since you would merely bring it right back to the temple. What changes hands is simply a record of ownership, and if I can use that record to pay you, then you can use it to pay someone else. When money is based on ledger entries that record ownership of practical things like grain, it ceases to be a social currency; it is no longer merely a means of rearranging weighty social relations, but instead becomes something useful for day-to-day transactions. So we start with records of ownership, and then we can use those records of ownership as money (paper money if our society has the technology for paper). And metal coins come last of all, as a physical representation of a social arrangement that already exists.

And the ledgers that support this virtual money don't have to be about grain stored at the temple; they can instead be any reliable record of a credible promise. In medieval England, merchants recorded debts with a "tally stick," a piece of wood that was notched in a way that denoted payment owed in exchange for goods sold. The stick would be split, with one piece indicating how much the holder was owed, while the other piece confirmed the validity of that claim. These were apparently a common instrument of commerce in their time [7]. They "were not primarily used to settle bi-personal debts but circulated as means of payment." [1, p. 6]. If a debtor is considered a good risk, the record of his debt may then circulate as money; other people will accept it from the lender as payment, because they are confident that the original debtor will honor it. Which leads us to the connection between trust and money.

David Graeber has written, "the value of a unit of currency is not the measure of the value of an object, but the measure of ones trust in other human beings" (quoted from [4] in [3]), which is close to true but not quite right. The strength of a currency isn't the measure of our trust in other human beings *in general*. Rather, it measures how much we trust them in one particular regard: we accept money in exchange for something directly useful, because we trust that other human beings will do exactly the same thing. Beyond that, money makes it possible for us to interact with other people without trusting them worth a damn. In baseline communism, I share with you because I know you and trust you. In hierarchical society I give to you because it's my obligation, or I take from you because it's my right. In a market society, I need not know anything about you other than that you've put cash on the table. If I trust the money, I no longer need to trust you. This is a key feature of money for its role in coordinating human economic activity.

Adam Smith's parable of the invisible hand is a vision of decentralized coordination. Nobody needs to see the big picture and give orders; nobody needs to be in charge at all. The ants in their nest mindlessly follow the right chemical signals, and the result is a functioning, living entity. And the butcher, the baker, the candlestick maker all do nothing more than follow the scent of money, yet end up creating an economy, complete with a rational division of labor. If there's a shortage of bakeries, wages for the few existing bakers will rise; more people will be drawn into the trade; wages will even out; society's desires will have been met without any formal command having been issued.

Money is one solution to the problem of coordinating current production. The wider the area over which some particular form of money is trusted, the more people can be included in the process.

But there's not just current production to think about. There are also activities to enable future production—i.e., investment. And to address investment, we need to think about credit.

8.3.3 *Taking on Credit*

Credit and money are natural partners. The tally sticks described above were introduced to the discussion as a form of money, but they are also a form of credit. The merchant sells you something of value now, in exchange for another notch on your stick; he gives you something now, in exchange for your promise to provide him something of value in the future. And that's the essence of credit. I grant you control of something valuable in the present—some labor, some food, some steel—and you promise to hand over to me something of value in the future.

In the case of the tally sticks, the debts were incurred to pay for present consumption, so they're almost like a formalization of the I-share-with-you, you-share-with-me practices of the norm-governed society. They allow a somewhat enlarged sphere of operations, but they're still basically about transferring items of current consumption. The more interesting stuff happens when we bring real investment into the mix.

As discussed in earlier chapters, investment is the creation of real capital. That is, it's a rearrangement of the ways that energy and matter can flow through the economy, so as to be more valuable to people. When I build a railroad, I make it possible for coal to be run through a locomotive, so as to improve society's ability to move people and goods around.

Carrying out the investment—building the railroad—requires command of things of real value in the present. I need to convince laborers to work for me; I need to convince steel producers and locomotive builders to hand over to me some of their output; you can extend the example with details of your own. Once the railroad is built, its ability to move people and goods will create value; people in the future will pay to use my road, which means that I will acquire claims on things of value in the future.

So: you grant me control over things of value in the present; I use that control to create a railroad (or some other piece of capital that creates value); I promise you value in the future.

This promise of mine is not itself money; as a claim on value, it's far too large a chunk to be used in everyday dealings. But it *is* an asset, a thing of value worth acquiring.[11] If I have promised to pay you a certain sum of money every year for 30 years, that promise has a value in the present. In fact, someone just might pay you for it: Here, take this money now, and give me that railroad builder's promise of money paid in the future.

In this natural history of money, the important thing about these kinds of assets and their relationship to money, is that they allow for the same kind of flexible decentralization of investment expenditure that money makes possible for everyday trade. If a financial asset is backed by a real investment—like my promise to pay you out of the revenues of my railroad—it gets its value, ultimately, from people's perception of the worth of the investment behind it. If people think a railroad would be a useful thing, they're likely to trust my promise, so the asset (my promise) has high value. They're willing to accept my promise in exchange for control of things in the present, and so I get to build my railroad.

If you propose a canal and promise to pay your lenders out of your revenues, you may find fewer people willing to credit your promise. In 1825 the Erie Canal was a breakthrough, but once we got to the age of railroads, canals were a much harder sell. Say you're proposing a canal from Busytown to Workville, but I'm also proposing a railroad. Once my tracks are in operation, your canal will be less useful; your future customers won't pay much to use it; your promise to pay your lenders in the future is less credible than mine—not because you yourself are untrustworthy, but because your project has thinner prospects of success. And so it is harder for you to acquire control of the inputs you need to build your canal than it is for me to get what I need to build my railroad.

Decades later, highways and airports will come along, and railroads will have trouble acquiring purchasing power to support some of their old role in the shipment of goods. If they focus on heavy goods traveling long distances with no time pressure—like coal from Wyoming's Powder River basin destined for the power plants of the Southeast—their promises will be valued.[12] If they try to compete with airplanes and cars at moving people across the country, their promises will be considered worthless.

And so investment gets coordinated by credit markets and financial assets the same way that everyday trade is coordinated by money. When horses and oxen are the best ways of hauling goods, a canal is a real improvement. Railroads make canals (mostly) obsolete, and they in their turn are rendered (partly) obsolete by cars and planes. And the miracle of credit, the miracle of financial assets backed by real investments, is that this progression will happen of its own accord. The people who

[11] Assets are explained in Chap. 10.

[12] An engaging account of this specific transaction is in [9] and [10].

undertake to build the railroad have to have *some* vision of how their project fits into the economy as it is, and they will oversee the work of building it. But nobody needs to see the entire picture; nobody needs to give orders for the economy as a whole; at the level of the economy itself, nobody needs to be in charge at all.

Money makes us into ants operating a colony. With credit, we become termites building a mound.

Problems

Problem 8.1 Think of a purchase you've made—it doesn't matter whether the means of payment was cash, check, credit card, debit card, bank withdrawal, or even Bitcoin.

(a) Write down as many steps as you can figure out, guess at, or research, starting from your purchase and working back in the direction of raw materials out in the world. Distinguish among purchases of final goods, purchases of intermediate goods, and investment expenditures.
(b) From your list compiled in the previous question, choose one investment expenditure and one purchase of an intermediate good. Explain how money and credit are playing their coordinating roles in the economy.

Problem 8.2 What is a resemblance between the function of money in a human economy and the behaviors of other animals?

Problem 8.3 What is a difference between the function of money in a human economy and the behaviors of other animals?

Problem 8.4 What is a resemblance between the function of credit in a human economy and the life cycles of other animals?

References

1. Bezemer, D. J. (2015). Banks as social accountants: Credit and crisis through an accounting lens. Munich Personal RePEc Archive, paper no. 15766 (2009). http://mpra.ub.uni-muenchen.de/15766/1/MPRA_paper_15766.pdf. Accessed August 4, 2015.
2. Chibnall, M. (1986). *Anglo-Norman England* (pp. 1066–1166). New York: Blackwell.
3. Goodreads. Debt quotes. https://www.goodreads.com/work/quotes/6811142-debt-the-first-5-000-years. Accessed July 31, 2014.
4. Graeber, D. (2011). *Debt: The first 5,000 years.* Brooklyn: Melville House.
5. Hofstadter, D. R. (1981). *The mind's I: Fantasies and reflections on self and soul.* New York: Basic Books.
6. H olldobler, B., & Wilson, E. O. (1994). *Journey to the ants: A story of scientific exploration.* Cambridge: Belknap Press.
7. Innes, A. M. (1913). What is money? *The Banking Law Journal.* https://www.community-exchange.org/docs/what%20is%20money.htm. Accessed August 4, 2015.

8. Kolbert, E. (2005). Climate of man – II. *The New Yorker* (pp. 64–73), May 2, 2005.
9. McPhee, J. (2005). Coal train, Part I. *The New Yorker* (pp. 72–83), October 3 2005.
10. McPhee, J. (2005). Coal train, Part II. *The New Yorker* (pp. 62–71), October 10, 2005.
11. Ostrom, E. (2000). Collective action and the evolution of social norms. *Journal of economic perspectives, 14*(3), 137–158.
12. Redman, C. L. (1999). *Human impact on ancient environments*. Tucson: University of Arizona Press.
13. Richard, P. B. (1983). Mechanisms and adaptation in the constructive behaviour of the beaver (c. fiber l.). *Acta Zoologica Fennica, 174*, 105–108.
14. Scott, J. C. (1998). *Seeing like a state: How certain schemes to improve the human condition have failed*. New Haven: Yale University Press.
15. Tuchman, B. W. (1978). *A distant mirror: The calamitous 14th century*. New York: Knopf.
16. Turner, S. Termite research. http://www.esf.edu/efb/turner/termitepages/termiteMain.html. Accessed July 31, 2014.
17. Wittfogel, K. A. (1957). *Oriental despotism; a comparative study of total power*. New Haven: Yale University Press.
18. Żurowski, W. (1992). Building activity of beavers. *Acta Thereologica, 37*(4), 403–411.

Chapter 9
What Money Is

Abstract Chapter 8 gave a very general overview of money's role in an economy in the context of how other social animals organize joint activity (and how we humans organize our activity in ways other than with money). This chapter uses a parable about the construction of a mill to lay out with more substance what money is and how it works. The context is a physical economy in which money doesn't yet exist. The parable shows how a set of social arrangements around an investment project can lead to the existence of money. Money itself is tied to debt and credit. Extensions of the main story lead to observations about the relationship between saving and investment, and about the government's role in the monetary system. Appendices discuss: value and money's roles and attributes; saving not tied to other people's obligations; and the connection between money and precious metals.

9.1 The Money Mystery

Money is one of the most perplexing, contradictory things around. It's the subject of contradictory sayings: "Money is the root of all evil." "Money makes the world go 'round." (Wait, maybe those aren't contradictory ...) We use money on a daily basis and take its existence for granted, yet when we stop to think about what it is and how it works, we often find ourselves confused.

This chapter shows you that money is simple, but also that it's magical. It can be called into being out of thin air. And yet this conjured thing can bring about changes in the real, physical world.

The first requirement is to get past the story of barter. As described in Sect. 8.3.2, a common story about money is that began as a way of surmounting the inconvenience of barter, but the archeological evidence actually suggests that money has a different genesis [1]. Perhaps the intuitive attraction of the barter story is that it begins with trade. Two people have different things, and each wants some of what the other has. The obvious solution is some form of exchange. Eventually they realize that barter is awkward, so they invent money.

Following the lead of Graeber [3] and Bezemer [1], we don't have to start with an exchange of things—we can start with debt instead. And surprisingly, this story doesn't even need two goods. All we need is one good, and the ability to make a promise, and we can get to money.

K. Seeley, *Macroeconomics in Ecological Context*, Studies in Ecological Economics 5, DOI 10.1007/978-3-319-51757-5_9

This isn't meant to be an account of how money actually started; it's a parable to help understand what money is and how it works.

9.2 The Physical Economy

Imagine an agricultural economy. We're going to simplify all the way down to where there's only one thing produced, and we'll call it "food." And we'll define one unit of food as the amount that a household needs in a year. Because this is the economy's only good, your standard of living is defined by access to food. You can eat more than 1 unit, maybe 1.5 units, but at some point, the extra enjoyment from the increased food is not worth the extra work required to produce the extra food.

It's a purely physical economy, with no money, no banks. And for that matter, no saving: the food is perishable, so what you don't eat this year is gone, making it pointless to save.

9.2.1 The Investment Project

Now we introduce an investment project: I want to build a watermill to grind grain.

This can actually increase the community's production of food. We're currently grinding grain using mills powered by donkeys. We need to feed those donkeys, so a portion of the crops we grow is devoted to feeding our "machines" instead of feeding us. Once the watermill is built, we can either reduce our number of donkeys or redirect their labor to cultivating more land. Either way, the new mill will allow the community to produce more food.

In other words,

The mill is a piece of capital that will lead to economy-wide economic growth.

In addition to benefiting the community, the mill will benefit me personally. It will be far bigger than I would need just to grind my own grain. Since it will allow other farmers to get rid of their donkeys and produce more food, they'll be willing to pay me to grind their grain rather than doing it themselves. And they don't need money to pay me, because they can pay me in food: if I grind 10 sacks of grain for my neighbor, she'll let me keep one of them. Let's say it's a big enough operation that my revenue will be comfortably more than 1 unit of food a year—at least 2.5 units, but maybe more.

9.3 Getting it Built

Building the mill will take a year using the labor of 10 people, including me. While we're busy building, we won't be able to produce food, which means that I'll have to find some way to provide food for all of us for the year. But remember that food is not really storable, which means that I can't solve the problem by putting aside half a unit of food for 20 years until I've got 10 units stored up to pay my builders. I've got to convince people who are producing food now to hand over some so that I can feed (pay) my builders.

Let's say there are (at least) 10 farmers in this village who are good farmers, and you're one of them. Right now, you good farmers are each producing 1.5 units of food, and also eating 1.5 units. But you've got enough land, equipment, skill, and labor power that you could produce 2 units each—you just don't bother, because you'd have no use for the extra food. Still, given that you can produce 2 units, and you only *need* to eat 1, each of you is capable of providing me with 1 unit of food to feed my builders. But since there's no such thing as money in this economy, how do I pay for this?

I can make a promise to each of you:

- Give me 1 unit of food this year.
- Then next year, and the year after that, and every year for 10 years, I'll give you 0.15 units of food.

You may recognize this as essentially no different from a mortgage, where you make an agreement with a bank:

- Give me $150,000 right now.
- Then next month and every month after that for the next 15 years, I'll give you $1,445.

(Both of those examples happen to represent an annual interest rate of 8.14%.)

So you farmers agree to this deal. To hold up your end of the bargain and actually hand over 1 unit, you have to do two things.

1. Work harder and increase your output to 2 units; and
2. Cut back your consumption to only 1 unit.

The unit of food I get from each of you is the result of your activity of saving. The part that comes from consuming less sounds more like our intuitive notion of saving; saving means "not spending." But the other part is equally saving: working more but not consuming the increased output.

Each farmer has to open up a space between output and consumption. Creating that space is the farmer's act of saving. But what are the farmer's savings, the things he or she can draw on in the future? It's not the food that they grew and didn't eat—remember, if you put that aside, it would just rot, and in this parable you handed it over to me, and my laborers and I ate it. Rather, the savings are nothing other than my promise.

Let's pause for a moment to look at the effects of this investment project.

1. *Real output has gone up in the present.* The ten of us engaged in construction aren't growing food, so that represents a decrease in the village's food production, but we're working just as hard building the mill instead. Presumably the nine other builders I'm paying aren't the super-productive ones who were growing 1.5 units before; I should hire the less competent farmers who were only growing 1 unit (as long as they're not also incompetent as construction workers). I hired them, because I'd only have to provide 1 unit of food to entice them to work for me, and apparently I think that's what they're worth, since that's what I'm paying them. So there's no change in the value of what they produce, it's just that their output is now a mill instead of a quantity of food. On the other hand, if we look at the "good" farmers who accepted my promise and provided me with food, they were producing 15 units in total, and now they're producing 20, so the economy as a whole has seen an increase of output worth 5 units of food.
2. *Real output will increase in the future.* As explained in Sect. 9.2.1, the mill will allow everyone to produce more food.
3. *The debt is sustainable.* I've promised to hand over 0.15 units every year, to each of 10 farmers, or 1.5 units a year. But my income will be at least 2.5 units a year, and I only need 1 to live on, so I'm "solvent": my debt obligations are no more than the revenues I expect to have available for meeting them.

All of this happens as the result of my entrepreneurialism, the farmers' ability to produce more and willingness to consume less, and a promise. Let's take the next step, toward money.

9.4 Beyond Promises

My promise works (as long as you accept it), but it's somewhat clunky. It's an individualized thing, attached to a particular farmer. When *you*, a farmer by the name of Dear Reader, show up at my mill a year from now, I'll give *you* 0.15 units of food. But if some Joe Schmoe shows up, I owe him nothing. You could in theory take your copy of my promise and transfer it to Joe Schmoe, but what would you sell it for? There's no money, so it would have to be another version of what you and I did (Joe Schmoe gives you food now, you give Joe a promise of food later—only it's not a promise *you* made, it's a promise I made, to *you*). And selling just part of it rather than the whole thing might be laborious.

But what if I replace the promise with a set of tokens?

Let's make each token worth 0.01 units of food, and also give it a "maturity" date. If we start in 1950, then 15 tokens become valid in 1951, another 15 in 1952, etc., with the last 15 becoming valid in 1960. It's the same deal we agreed to above, but it's more convenient. If you show up at my mill in 1953 and give me one of these tokens with a 1953 "maturity" date, I'll give you 0.01 units of food. You could also show up at my mill with a token that matured in 1952 but that you had decided to hold onto rather than using right away.

And it doesn't even have to be you. *Anyone* who shows up at my mill can get 0.01 units of food, so long as they hand over a "mature" token that I originally gave to one of the farmers. But this has big implications.

Because now other people have a motive to accept these tokens from you and give you something real: they're confident they can take the tokens to my mill and get something real for them (0.01 units of food for each token). So a "mature" token should be accepted in the village at face value; a person who gets it can take it to my mill right away if they want. An "immature" token, one whose maturity date is a couple of years further into the future, will still have value, but it should trade at a discount: people are confident they'll eventually be able to bring me the token and get food, but they can't do that just yet.

Look at what's happened now. These tokens are of no *direct* use to anybody, their only value is only as a representation of my promise, yet they are circulating around. People are accepting tokens in exchange for something real, something with a physical use. **The tokens have become money.**

9.5 Money, Debt, Saving, Borrowing, Investment

The tokens have value because somebody (in this story it happens to be me) has made a credible promise to redeem them for real goods (either now or at some defined point in the future). That credible promise is my debt, my obligation. In other words:

Money is generally linked to the existence of debt.

What happens when you (or someone else) *does* bring me a "mature" token? When you and Joe Schmoe traded, you gave Joe a token, and he gave you food; that was the end of the trade. When Joe brings me the token, he gives me the token, I give him food, I reduce the amount of food I owe by 0.01 units, *and I take the token Joe paid me with and remove it from circulation*. When you and Joe traded, you got food, he got a token. When Joe and I trade, he gets food, I get a token, *and I get my debt reduced*. I don't *have* to remove the token from circulation; I could turn around and spend it, using it to buy something from someone else. But if I do that I will have incurred a new debt. The token represents a claim on me, an obligation for me to provide food to the token's holder. When it's in my hands, it's not circulating as money, nor do I owe anything to anybody on its account. As long as it is in anyone's hands but mine, it is functioning as money but it also represents my debt. Which leads to our next observation:

The money only exists so long as my debt exists.

What about saving? It turns out that it would be impossible for you to *have savings* without my borrowing. The food rots, so you could engage in *saving activity* by consuming less than you produce, but you wouldn't end up with savings—you'd end up with a rotten mess. I made a credible promise to *provide* food in the future, and that gave you the ability to claim some food in the future, even if you aren't producing any at the time. That's something you can't do on your own.

Your ability to save depends on my willingness to take on an obligation for some future action.

Debt-based money is the representation of *somebody's* debt, and saving (the accumulation of claims on stuff that will be produced in the future) is made possible here through *somebody* assuming debt (an obligation to hand over some of what gets produced in the future). (The appendix on "Savings without obligation" toward the end of this chapter will discuss other ways of saving.)

And investment? It turns out my investment would have been impossible without your saving. I needed food for my builders and me, and for that food to be available, I needed you to work harder and consume less—I needed you to engage in saving.

But my investment would have been equally impossible without my borrowing, without my creating money out of thin air. And isn't that what it was? I *did* create money, and it was based on nothing more than my credible promise that I would obtain food in the future and hand it over.

The borrowing was necessary because of the relationship between the investment and the 10 person-years' worth of labor required to carry it out. I could perhaps have built the mill myself, devoting two thirds of my time each year to producing food and a third of my time to construction; it would have taken me (at least!) 30 years to complete it, if it were possible at all. My borrowing and your saving and lending allowed it to get done in a year.

Borrowing and lending and money creation allow us as a society to direct far more resources to investment than otherwise, and thus to grow faster.

9.5.1 Magic Money

So let's see what all happened here.

- I had no prior saved wealth.
- I had no "money" on hand.
- The whole economy had no money in it at all.
- There was no prior trade of any sort.
- Gold played no part in this story.

What we *did* have was:

- My knowledge of how to build the mill.
- My willingness to arrange and supervise the building of the mill.
- Your belief in my promise to hand you real goods in the future. (This includes your belief that I'll be *able* to do it, and your belief that I *will actually* do it.)

  Those requirements are actually pretty significant, but that is "all it takes."

9.6 Different Responses to Expenditure

So the farmers and I worked out a deal where they gave me the 10 units of food I needed, and I gave them tokens worth 10 units of food. (We know that the tokens are worth that much, because I did in fact get 10 units of food in return for them.) We could say that I made an **expenditure** of 10 units (we don't yet have a name for this currency that has come into existence).

Before that, the level of expenditure in the economy was zero. There was production and consumption—people were growing food and consuming it—but nobody was buying anything from anybody else. So my action amounted to 10 units of increased expenditure. That's the money side.

On the physical side, in response to my expenditure you farmers:

- Increased your output by a total of five units of actual food
- Decreased your consumption by a total of five units of actual food
- Handed me a total of 10 units of actual food.

Increased expenditure of 10 has led to increased output—increased real economic activity—of 5.

There's a term for your decrease in consumption, which is "crowding out." In addition to causing you to work harder, my expenditure has pushed aside some of your consumption—though note that it was an entirely voluntary action on your part: I had no way of forcing you to accept my offer that I would give you tokens in exchange for you giving me food.

What if you wanted to take my offer but didn't want to cut your consumption below 1.5? How could you still provide me with the one unit of food that I wanted to buy?

You might think about increasing your production all the way to 2.5. That way you can give me 1 unit and still have 1.5 for your own consumption. But we assumed in the first part that the most you could produce was 2, so keeping your consumption at 1.5 by increasing production to 2.5 isn't an option. At the same time, we also saw in the first part that the tokens I gave you are like money. So you have another way of upholding your end of the bargain:

- Find some other farmer—call her Jill Hill—willing to sell you half a unit of food.
- Give Jill half your tokens.
- Increase your production to 2.
- Keep your consumption at 1.5.
- Combine your "extra" half unit with the half unit you bought from Jill and hand me a whole unit, as you agreed.

Now let's assume that all 10 farmers who took my tokens do the same thing. Each of them keeps consumption at 1.5, increases production to 2, and finds some *other* farmer (not one of the original 10) to buy half a unit from. We've brought 10 new farmers into the picture, and let's assume each of them makes the same production and consumption decisions as the first 10. They accept the half-unit worth of tokens and keep them; they increase output to 2; they keep consumption at 1.5; and they hand over half a unit of food. Have a look at what's happened to the economy.

Instead of 10 farmers each building up savings of 1 unit, we have 20 farmers each building up savings of 0.5 units, so the total amount of savings is still 10. But instead of 10 farmers increasing output from 1.5 to 2, we have 20 farmers doing that, so output has increased by 10, instead of by 5 as in the original example. There's more than one way to skin a cat.

And it makes a lot of sense that the total amount of savings hasn't changed. Remember that, in this story, your ability to save is the flip side of my willingness to assume debt.

If you're going to be able to get stuff in the future without producing income in the future, someone has to be obligated (or willing) to give you something in the future. In this story, that "someone" is me, and since my willingness hasn't changed—I'm still borrowing to buy 10 units of food—you farmers can't acquire savings of more than 10 units in total.

But you can't have less, either. Problem 9.2 asks you to trace the chain of events when people take the tokens but nobody wants to actually do any saving. The upshot is that

My ability to borrow depends on other people's willingness to save.

There may be more than one way to skin a cat. But the cat has to get skinned.

9.7 Physical Saving vs. Financial Savings

Part II explained interest rates and the level of investment through a model of a loanable-funds market. The mill parable leads to a different perspective that will be important in the course of this part of the book. The differences are tied to the difference between physical actions and monetary amounts, and the difference between the supply-determined output of the long-run model and a more demand-driven approach.

We can summarize the economy of the mill parable before the mill as:

$$\text{Output} = \text{Food (which is consumption)}$$

During the mill's construction this changes to:

$$\begin{aligned}\text{Output} = {} & \text{Food (which is consumption)} \\ & + \text{Construction of the mill (investment activity)}\end{aligned} \tag{9.1}$$

All the food was consumed, whether by the farmers who grew it or by the builders whom I employed (and fed). The mill, of course, is not a thing that can be consumed, but it was part of output. When you have output that you're not consuming, you are by definition engaged in saving, so we can change the representation of the economy to:

$$\begin{aligned}\text{Output} = {} & \text{Consumption} \\ & + \text{Saving (which is not-consumption).}\end{aligned} \tag{9.2}$$

Combining Eqs. 9.1 and 9.2 we can simplify to

$$\text{Investment} \equiv \text{Saving} \tag{9.3}$$

which is the investment-saving identity.

The algebraic expression and the term may look familiar, since they showed up as Eq. 6.2 in Chap. 6. But because they appeared in the context of the long-run model, they may tend to reinforce two unfortunate misconceptions: first, that output is a fined amount, and second, that there is a fixed quantity of money.

Independent of its setting in a particular model, the identity of investment and saving, and the expression of both in money terms, leads to a confusion as to the usefulness of savings as a quantity of money or a stock of purchasing power, compared to the necessary act of saving, in the sense of putting aside some of your current income.

Starting with this second issue, we can work our way back to the question of output and money not being fixed amounts.

9.7.1 Money as a Means, Not an End

For example, in the mill parable money was useful as a way of embodying the agreement between me and the farmers who provided me with food, and my payment to them left them with a quantity of savings. But what I needed was not any *quantity of savings* stored up, but the farmers' *act of saving*. I could have had $100 million stashed somewhere, and it would have been irrelevant if people hadn't been willing to sell me food. And if farmers were going to sell me food, they were going to have to consume less than they produced—they were going to have to engage in the activity of saving. In other words, my $100 million, my quantity of savings, would only be useful if it convinced people to engage in the activity of saving.

Conversely, if I can somehow convince the farmers to give me food, to undertake the activity of saving, then I can carry out my investment, regardless of how little a quantity of savings I may have socked away. The investment-saving identity introduced above is not fundamentally about money. It usually gets expressed in money terms, but underneath, it's an identity between investment activity and the activity of saving, the act of consuming some amount less than current output.[1]

A further twist on the mill story, a macabre one this time, will sharpen the distinction between saving activity and accumulations of money.

Suppose you accept my offer. You take my tokens, you give me the food I need for my workers, and you look forward to enjoying the benefits of your thrift. The mill gets built, the food you gave me is all used up and then—Calamity! A spring flood sweeps away the mill, and me with it. Your savings are destroyed: you still have my tokens, of course, but they're worthless, because everybody knows I'm not in a position to honor them. In contrast, your saving activity is unaffected: it happened in the past, so nothing in the present can cause it to unhappen. When it happened, it was balanced by my investment activity, as required by the investment-saving identity. The flood can only destroy your savings, the value of the quantity of money you stored up after engaging in the act of saving even if there's no longer any trace of my mill, just as there's no trace of value in your money savings.

---

[1]Part of the confusion here is that, for an individual, having $100 million saved up actually is useful. You could go and spend 10, or 50, or all 100 of those millions, and in an economy with a GDP of $14 trillion, you would certainly find someone to respond to your money by making something to sell you. But the economy as a whole can't live off of money savings accumulated in the past. Money saved in the past only helps the economy as a whole in the present if it was used in the past to create capital that allows the economy to produce desired goods and services in the present.

9.7.2 Flexible Saving and Output

The mill parable also highlights that neither the level of output nor the saving curve is fixed in advance, as they are in the loanable-funds market of Part II. The willingness to save can change in response to people's willingness to borrow, their willingness to undertake real investment. The mill parable started with no savings stored up, and no saving activity; everything produced was consumed. What made my mill project possible was not that 10 or 20 farmers suddenly thought, "I'd like to consume less than I produce this year, in exchange for the ability to consume more than I produce in future years. I wonder if that nice fellow over by the creek would like to promise us food in the future in exchange for food in the present so that he can build a mill." It went completely the other way. I conceived the notion of the mill, and the farmers responded. It's true that I depended on their willingness to accept my offer, or else I would have been up a creek, not just next to one. But it was my desire to create the mill that not only provided them with their tokens (their quantity of savings), but called into being their physical activity of saving. And my investment activity, and the farmers' response to it, caused output to go up, not just in the future as a result of the mill's contribution to productivity, but in the present because of the activity of building it.

The investment-saving identity must hold, but not because investment is limited by the level of saving activity that people have already decided to engage in, much less the quantity of savings that they already own. Rather, investment is only limited by the extent of saving activity that people can be induced to choose.

What's more, without the borrower, your saving activity would be pointless. I said above in Sect. 9.6 that, "Your ability to save is the flip side of my willingness to acquire debt." That is, your ability to acquire claims on future output depends on my willingness to give you those claims. But then, without someone willing to provide you with claims on future output, without the ability to accumulate a quantity of savings, why would you bother to engage in saving activity? Why consume less than you produce today, if it won't lead to any future benefit?

This question of flexibility in savings—and in output—is key for one of the hot-potato questions in macroeconomics, which is whether government spending can lead to an overall increase in economic activity and employment. Without a government in the mill story, we can't really answer that yet. But we can address one common objection, the idea that "the money has to come from somewhere," so that any increased spending by the government must by mathematical necessity be offset by decreased spending somewhere else.

It's true that money has to come from somewhere, but one of the places it can come from is thin air. We'll see later whether government can pull off this same trick.

9.8 Comparing Money Stories

We now have two types of stories about money. In one, money is accepted because it represents some specific person's promise. Going back to Chap. 8, there are the tally sticks on which medieval merchants recorded debts, and which themselves could be used as a means of payment. There are the statements of ownership of grain in temple storehouses in Mesopotamia, statements that could change hands to buy things without the grain itself moving an inch. There are the tokens in the mill parable that has been a recurring feature of this chapter.

In the other kind of story, money is a completely arbitrary social convention. You accept these things as money because you know that I will do the same, and I accept them because I know that someone else will, and so on. But nobody has taken upon themselves an *obligation* to accept them. We have an infinite regress, floating free from any specific promise by any specific entity.

Is there any reason we should prefer a story of money as a debt or a promise, over an idea of money as a pure social convention? After all, what matters to you as a user of money in your everyday life is that others will accept it the same as you do. Why they accept it isn't important. It turns out there are two reasons to go with a debt story: evidence, and origins.

First, we have plenty of evidence (e.g. [1]) that records of debt do serve as money, such as the examples above. It's not that debt accounts for all money. There's the case of the "social currencies" used in some societies to establish and repair social relationships (arrange a marriage, atone for a murder). These might be shells or giant stone wheels—things that are neither useful in themselves nor representations of any particular person's obligation. They are pure social convention: this thing is money because we all agree that it is money. There are gold and silver, which at various times in various places have attained a status of being money in and of themselves. But *promises also serve as money*. The story of the mill is a simplified parable to lay bare the underlying mechanism, but the idea behind it is real.

Second, there's the problem of origins of a system where money is only a convention, without a promise behind it. Once it's up and running, it works, but how does it get started? Somebody has to be the first one to accept a thing as money, and to do that they need to believe that others will also accept it, and that's a reasonable thing for them to believe because . . . ? And there's no good answer to that.

If money starts as debt or as transferable records of ownership of some real thing, the problem of origins goes away. Your reason for starting to accept money is as clear as the individual promise behind it. If you trust the promise, or if you trust the temple priests to acknowledge the statement of ownership, then the thing you're using as money is not an arbitrary social convention. It is inherently a claim on something real. That's not changed by the fact that you can use it to buy, in principle, anything, not just the thing that it directly gives you a right to. The promise or the statement of ownership is merely the backing, the reality that gives other people the confidence to accept money as money, for whatever purpose they may conceive.

So the debt story has a lot to recommend it. And we can add a useful twist on it by bringing in a state or a government.

9.9 State Money

For good or ill, governments need some way of commanding resources, such as soldiers to fight a war, food to sustain the soldiers, and arms for them to use. One way to do that is taxes in kind,, which are essentially direct compulsion: "Bill, join my army. Jenny, give me food for Bill. Chris, make a sword for Bill."

It's simpler, of course, to collect taxes in the form of money, then use that money to hire your soldiers and buy supplies for them. But taxes are just another form of compulsion: "You must hand over this much money." However, money taxes open up a possibility that doesn't exist with taxes in kind.

The state can impose a tax, and it can simultaneously specify that your tax obligation is to be discharged in *these things*—these coins with the king's profile on them, these dollars, whatever the state chooses. *Now* there's a clear motive for other people to accept the money as payment. You have to pay taxes, and this money stuff is what you need in order to pay them. And even if you yourself don't owe any taxes, other people do, and their tax-driven willingness to accept the state's money gives you a good reason to accept it yourself. This is the kernel of the view of money that goes by the name of "chartalism."[2]

The state has played a nice turn on the principle of debt-backed money. In the parable of the mill, the tokens that I issued had value because they represented my credible promise to provide something of value to anyone who handed one over to me. State money is different. The government hasn't taken on an obligation to hand you something valuable when you bring in its coins. Instead, it has imposed an obligation *upon you*, but promised that you will be released from that obligation if you bring in its tokens.

This has some advantages over the use of voluntary, private debts as the backing of money. For those private arrangements to work, enough people have to have reason to believe that the creditor, the one making the promise, will have both the ability and the will to honor his/her promise. Governments typically don't have that kind of credibility problem. Do you think the government will impose taxes? Do you think the government will insist that people actually pay those taxes using the government's form of money? If you answered "yes" to both those questions, then you have every reason to believe that other people will accept the government's form of money.

---

[2]A useful discussion of chartalism is in [5].

There's also the question of geographic reach. The usefulness of a private loan as money is limited by the area over which the borrower can be known well enough for people to trust his promise. A government's credibility reaches into every corner of the territory over which it exercises effective control, everywhere that it can actually collect taxes.

9.10 Exchange Value and the Roles and Attributes of Money

At this point we leave behind the parable of the mill to think about money in more general terms, starting with the idea of exchange value then proceeding to money's roles and attributes.

9.10.1 Exchange Value

In understanding money, it helps to distinguish between "**direct use value**" and "**exchange value**."

For our purposes, let's say that a thing has "direct use value" for you if you want the thing in itself, for yourself. A chair to sit in, a meal to eat, an item of clothing to wear, an evening at the theater—all those things have use value.

Note that this is slightly different from the existing term "use value," which simply describes something that is useful. So in addition to the items listed above, steel would have use value in the standard terminology because you can use it to make anything from a car to a kitchen pot or a gardening tool. The concept of "direct use value" excludes the steel. Yes, it can be used to make things that people want, but they don't want the steel itself *except to transform it into something else*. The steel itself has no direct use value for anyone.

Something has "exchange value" if there is someone who is willing to give something up in order to get it—in other words, if someone is willing to *exchange* something for it.

Most of the time, a thing will have exchange value because of direct use value. This can be immediate: everything on my list of direct-use-value items above also has exchange value (people pay for them because they like them). It can be indirect as well: steel has exchange value (people are willing to pay money to get it) without having direct use value (untransformed steel isn't much good to you in your daily life), but the willingness to pay for it is driven by the useful things that the steel can be made into: a car company is willing to pay for steel because they can make a car from it, and you'll pay for the car because it has direct use value for you.

However, you can have exchange value without any connection to direct use value. This is what happens in a bubble, when people buy a thing not because they want it, nor because they can turn it into something else that another person will want, but simply because they think someone else will buy it for a higher price later.

And that later buyer is motivated by the hope that *another* person will buy it for a still higher price. This is what happened in the housing market in the U.S. and several other countries in the 2000s.[3]

And you can have direct use value without exchange value, because direct use value by itself is not enough to make me willing to pay for something. It has to also be true that I can't get the item without paying for it, or I can't get it as easily without paying for it. That is, there has to be an element of excludability. Access to city streets provides direct use value, but it's impractical to exclude people from such access pending payment, so city streets have direct use value without having exchange value.

The very fact that something has exchange value means that it can also be to some extent a claim on exchange value. A stack of lumber has exchange value because people will give up something to get the lumber. But that means that the lumber is itself a claim on the exchange value of whatever it is that people would give up for it. It may be linked to something with direct use value, but as the appendix on gold and silver discusses, it need not be. It doesn't even have to be linked to anything useful at all. It requires nothing more than a credible promise. Viewed through the lens of value,

The essence of money is that it is a pure claim on exchange value.

Now that we know what money *is*, we turn to look at what it *does* (its roles), and what makes something fit play those roles (its attributes).

9.10.2 The Roles of Money

Medium of exchange: Money is the thing we use by default in any transaction; we exchange everything for money, and money for everything.

Unit of account: Another important function of money is that it is the unit of account, the way of expressing the value of everything else in common terms.

This is actually different from saying that money is the medium of exchange, used for actually buying and selling all things, because the unit-of-account function can come into play even if we're not directly using money. Let's say you have sandwiches and I have packs of cards, and we're interested in making a trade. If there's no unit of account, we look first to our own preferences (How much do I like that sandwich? How much do I like playing cards?), and then to our best *guess* of what someone else might be willing to give up for a sandwich, or a pack of cards. But if sandwiches and cards have known prices in dollars

[3] A classic treatment of bubbles is [4].

(or cigarettes, or whatever else we're using as money), then we can trade on that basis. If a sandwich is worth two cigarettes and a pack of cards is worth four, then we should be happy to trade two sandwiches for one pack of cards, even if no cigarettes change hands.

A store of exchange value: This one is usually written as "store of value," without specifying that what's involved is specifically exchange value. Let's say I raise some chickens and sell them; I give up the use value of the chickens for the exchange value of the money. I could turn around and use the money to buy something, but I don't have to. I can hold onto it, or put it under my mattress, or deposit it in a bank. I can store up exchange value, and then at a later time take my exchange value out of storage and go buy stuff with it—turn my exchange value back into some sort of direct use value.

What I can't do is store *direct use value*. I can store things that *have* direct use value, or things that could be transformed into other things that have direct use value: wheat, land, oil, paint, metal, and so on. But storing use value itself in some abstracted form would be a bit like storing time. The thing that money can store is exchange value.

9.10.3 The Attributes of Money

There's a conventional list of attributes that make something a good candidate as money. In examining them, I will refer repeatedly to the chicken of our initial barter transaction in Sect. 9.10.2.

Storable: You don't want the money to melt away in your pocket between the time you receive and when you want to spend it. Precious metal performs well on storability. Paper money does too, with the exception of its vulnerability to fire.

Chickens are sort of storable, but they have to be fed, and they don't live up to the saying that "money doesn't stink."

Transportable: It should be easy to move your money from one place to another. Silver and gold give you a pretty good amount of purchasing power before their weight becomes problematic. Paper money is even more transportable than metal, and we can make paper money with as large a denomination as we find useful: \$1, \$50, ... \$1,000,000.

Transporting one chicken is a nuisance; transporting more than a few is a real burden.

Hard to produce: There has to be some aspect of scarcity about money. The reason I give you, say, a chicken, a real thing, in exchange for money, is that, (1) I want to have money for purchases of my own; and (2) I can't get my hands on money without giving up something of value—an object that I own, or my time. What if we were to use colorful autumn leaves as currency, in October, in New England? If I needed money, I could just stoop down and pick up as much as I wanted. But then I wouldn't be able to buy anything with it, because nobody would accept it from me: why should someone go to all the work of raising a chicken to get money when they can just stoop down and pick up as much as they want?

Or think about it this way: exchange value requires some degree of scarcity, and money is pure exchange value. If you make money obtainable with no effort, you destroy its exchange value.

Precious metals pass the test of being hard to produce, because they require a mine with ores of gold or silver, and the labor to pull out the ore and extract the desired metal from it.

With paper money there's very little inherent difficulty in producing it, so governments *make* it hard to reproduce their currency, with fancy engraving, watermarks, little strips of metal embedded in the paper, and so on. And then they define criminal penalties for trying to overcome those hurdles and they go after anyone who does it.

As for chickens, anyone who starts with a male and a female chicken can produce more. Not for nothing, though, since the parents and the chicks have to be fed, but the process may nonetheless be easier than is ideal for something that is being used as money.

Easily divisible: Let's say you get your salary every two weeks, and you get $2,000. If you received your salary as a single, very valuable coin, you'd find it very inconvenient when you went to the sweet shop and wanted to buy a mini donut for $0.50. Paper money is, in principle, infinitely divisible; just as we could create a piece of paper money with as large a value as we find useful, we could also create one with as little value as is worth doing, though obviously we generally use coins for the smallest amounts.

The difficulty—or point—of giving half a chicken as change is left as an exercise for the reader.

Widely accepted: Remember that the important thing about money is that it stands for exchange value in general, not for any particular thing. You accept it and give *someone else* a real thing because of your confidence that someone else will in turn accept it and give *you* a real thing. That confidence can only last so long as it is regularly reinforced; it doesn't take too many instances of people turning down your money before you decide that it's not actually money.

At one level it doesn't matter *why* a particular form of money enjoys wide and dependable acceptance, as long as people *do* accept the money, but there are actually good reasons for such acceptance to get off the ground. Chapter 8 told about receipts for grain stored at temples in Mesopotamia. And this chapter explained the role of the government and its taxing power in giving credibility to government-issued money.

On the inevitable issue of chickens-as-money, would you accept a chicken as payment for your time? And I mean regularly, not just once or twice, as a lark.

Appendix: Savings Without Obligation

The mill parable focuses on the link between savings and debt, between your ability to have savings and my willingness to carry debt. But more generally, there can be savings without that particular type of specific obligation, involving instead ownership of productive assets.

The essence of having savings stored up is that they give you the ability to obtain things without producing anything, or to obtain things of more value than you are currently producing. If you are currently producing things worth $40,000, that's the most you can consume—unless you can borrow, or unless you have savings.

One way to do that is the way the mill parable illustrates. You handed me something useful in the past, so I have to hand you something useful now, without you *doing* anything useful now. But what about the ownership of the mill?

We assumed in the parable that it would clear 2.5 units of food a year, enough for me to have a unit to eat and 1.5 units to pay my annual debt service to my lenders. But that debt obligation only lasts 10 years. After that, I'm earning 2.5 units a year with no further obligation. Well, I do have to operate the mill, since the food doesn't grind itself, but I could hire someone to do that. I could pay someone 1 unit of food to operate the mill, then have 1.5 left as my income.

There's no *obligation* in this income stream from mill ownership. If people stop bringing their grain to be ground, the mill will produce zero. I will have to fire my employee, and my own income will drop to zero. When I borrowed to build the mill I issued coins that represented an obligation: bring this to me in the future, and I will give you food. Owning the mill is good, but it doesn't provide me with anything analogous in terms of other people's obligation to provide me with real goods in the future.

But as long as people *do* continue to use the mill, the ownership of it allows me to consume more than I produce. (I'm leaving out the issues of overseeing the employee and seeing to maintenance.) The mill is the savings I have, it's just in a different form from the coins I put into the farmers' hands earlier in the story.

The other way I can benefit from the mill, besides collecting the annual profit, is to sell it. Someone may be interested in giving up a lot of purchasing power now in return for ownership of the mill and the annual profit that it brings (and that they hope it will continue to bring). If such a buyer exists, I can give up the future profits of the mill in exchange for a large sum of purchasing power now.

In a modern economy a bond is like the coins in the mill parable: you give me a specific amount of money now, and I give you a specific amount of money at specific times in the future. The bond represents savings that you have because it also represents an obligation that I have.

In contrast, ownership of a share of stock is analogous to ownership of the mill, in that nobody has a future *obligation* to the saver. *If* the company is profitable, then you the saver own some of that profit, and it should come to you as some combination of dividends paid to shareholders and in increased market price of the shares. But if the company's customers stop showing up, you'll discover that nobody owes you anything.

Appendix: Gold and Silver

There's a common thought that gold is the essence of money; sometimes this is expanded to include silver. A striking statement of this view is the speech of Francisco d'Anconia from Ayn Rand's book *Atlas Shrugged*:

> Whenever destroyers appear among men, they start by destroying money, for money is men's protection and the base of a moral existence. Destroyers seize gold and leave to its owners a counterfeit pile of paper. This kills all objective standards and delivers men into the arbitrary power of an arbitrary setter of values. Gold was an objective value, an equivalent of wealth produced. Paper is a mortgage on wealth that does not exist, backed by a gun aimed at those who are expected to produce it.[4]

Most people probably wouldn't state it as vehemently as Rand, but may hold to some version of it: real money is precious metal, and paper money is only real or legitimate to the extent that it represents a legally enforceable claim on a specific quantity of precious metal.

In contrast, note that this chapter has developed the concept and functions of money without reference to gold (except to note that there was no reference to gold). There's a good reason for that, which is that I think gold fetishism is wrong.

More than that, the obsession with gold fails a simple test. Note that nothing stops people from setting up a gold-backed currency of their own. If people really did prefer using such a currency, they would move away from "worthless" paper money (except for enough to pay their taxes), and the all-knowing market would show the superiority of "real" money.

Third, there was only a relatively brief window when most of what was then the rich world operated on a gold standard. There were particular conditions that made it viable in the period before World War I, and then different conditions that made it a detriment in the post-war period. Once the Great Depression started, the faster a country left the gold standard, the faster it recovered.[5]

Money is a claim on exchange value. Gold and silver are metals that many humans value above any "practical" use they have. That means that in some situations they can be used as claims on exchange value, as money. But gold and silver are not inherently money, and money is not equivalent to gold and silver.

What about the more distant historical experience where, as mentioned in Sect. 9.8, gold and silver have sometimes "attained a status of being money in and of themselves." Recall from Sect. 9.9 the role of effective taxation in supporting

---

[4]Reprinted in [6].

[5]See [2].

the value of a state-issued money. When people were trading long distances, beyond the range of their own sovereign's ability to tax (and to regulate economic affairs in general), they sometimes used precious metals as something acceptable "internationally."[6] And when invaders looted cities, they would often strip the churches or temples of gold and silver decoration; the attackers placed no artistic value on what they stole, but they knew that if they melted it down they could get it accepted far and wide. So there is something peculiar about the role of gold and silver.

But that "something" should not be confused with the idea that precious metals *are* money, or that any other form of money is only "honest" or "true" if it represents a claim on some specific amount of gold or silver. To see the fallacy here, consider the case of silver and gold coins, stamped with the king's likeness.

If the metal itself is the essence of the money, then what's the point of stamping the king's face all over it? It's a lot of work for nothing. Well, not really for nothing, because precious-metal coins typically traded at greater value than the equal quantity of unstamped metal. The king could use a single one of his silver coins to buy unstamped silver weighing as much as two of his coins. So his face on the coin was worth something after all. But why?

One answer is that the monarch's stamp was a way of "vouching for" the weight and purity of the coin. In this explanation, the metal is still the thing that is the real carrier of the coin's value; the royal imagery merely saves you the time of precisely weighing and chemically testing every coin that you're offered. This sounds plausible, but ...

It turns out that a funny thing happened at the border of the kingdom. Coins that had literally been "worth more than their weight in gold," suddenly weren't. If the king's face were there only as authentication of the coin's metal content, that shouldn't have happened. People on the other side of the border weren't part of the kingdom, but they should have had some sense of the king's honesty. What was different about these "foreigners" was that they had no legal obligations to some other country's king. Since he couldn't force them to pay tax in his coin, they had no reason to accept his coins for anything more than their underlying value. (Well, they had a little reason, for when they did engage in trade across the border.)

Lastly, ask yourself whether you've ever accepted payment in regular ol' U.S. dollars, whether for work or in return for an object you were selling. Did you feel you were getting cheated by being paid in a currency that wasn't backed by precious metal? Did it cross your mind that you might be unable to find anybody else willing to accept the "fake money" you'd been paid with, because it wasn't backed by gold? Probably not, and it's no wonder. You've lived your whole life in an economy where the money wasn't backed by gold, and yet it's extremely unlikely that you've ever encountered a situation where someone refused payment in "mere" dollars and wanted gold instead.

Money is as money does, and U.S. currency, whether paper bills or entries in bank accounts, acts in all ways like money, even though it is "no more" than promises

---

[6]The rest of this example follows Graeber [3].

of debt or valid payment of tax obligations so there's something question-begging about insisting that it's not "real" money. Money itself may be magical, but there's nothing magical about precious metals that makes them money in some essential way that other things aren't.

Problems

Problem 9.1 Consider two scenarios. In both of them, there is the desire to undertake an investment activity of $1,000. The difference is that in World *A* the investor owns $1,000 worth of savings, but there is no current saving. In World *B* there is no stock of savings, but there is a willingness to engage in saving worth $1,000. In which world is the investment actally possible? Explain how that would happen, and what would prevent investment in the other world.

Problem 9.2 Look at a different scenario from Problem 9.1. Each of you 10 original farmers agrees to my deal, but none of you wants to work harder, nor do you want to consume less. "No problem," you say, "I'll just take all the tokens I received and go buy a whole unit of food from someone else." So you go to Jill Hill and give her all your tokens. She's just like you, Dear Reader—she doesn't feel like working harder or consuming less, so she takes the tokens from you and goes off and finds another farmer.

Carry this idea to its logical conclusion: what happens when there are no more farmers for the person holding the money to go and try to buy the food from? What happens to the money? What happens to the price of food? What happens to my ability to undertake my investment project?

Problem 9.3 Section 9.4 suggested that a token that matured in 1952 could be brought into the mill in 1953 and treated just the same as a token that had matured in 1953.

(a) Can you see a potential problem with that idea, and a reason to limit redemption only to tokens that mature in the current year?
(b) In the real world, our money doesn't have maturity dates at all. Why is this generally not a problem?

References

1. Bezemer, D. J. (2009). Banks as social accountants: Credit and crisis through an accounting lens. Munich Personal RePEc Archive, paper No. 15766. http://mpra.ub.uni-muenchen.de/15766/1/MPRA_paper_15766.pdf. Accessed Aug 4, 2015.
2. Eichengreen, B. & Sachs, J. (1985). Exchange rates and economic recovery in the 1930s. *The Journal of Economic History, 45*, 925–946.
3. Graeber, D. (2011). *Debt: The first 5000 years*. Brooklyn: Melville House.

4. Kindleberger, C. P. (1989). *Manias, panics, and crashes: A history of financial crises*. New York: Basic Books.
5. Tcherneva, P. R. (2006). Chartalism and the tax-driven approach to money. In P. Arestis & M. Sawyer (Eds.), *Handbook of Alternative Monetary Economics* (pp. 69–86). Cheltenham: Edward Elgar.
6. The Daily Paul. (2010). Francisco d. Anconia's (Ayn Rand's) money speech in 'Atlas Shrugged'. http://www.dailypaul.com/133313/francisco-d-anconias-ayn-rands-money-speech-in-atlas-shrugged. Accessed Feb 24, 2014.

Chapter 10
Banking

Abstract The mill parable of Chap. 9 was a device to get at the essence of money as a credible promise. But to understand how money works more realistically, we have to look at how banks work. We start with how a checking account functions, which leads us to the bank balance sheet. The balance sheet in turn sets up how money is actually created by banks (as opposed to how it's created by entrepreneurs building water mills in fictional villages growing homogenous food). The balance sheet raises the issue of banks' need for credibility and how they establish that. The role of the central bank grows out of this need for credibility, and ranges from regulation of banks to acting as a lender of last resort for them. The chapter ends with a brief discussion of fractional-reserve banking.

10.1 Introduction

Chapter 8 provided a very general view of the role money plats, in the context of the evolution of societies. The mill parable of Chap. 9 was meant to get more at how money emerges in relation to credible promises. The actual workings of money in a modern economy, however, are tied in with banks and with a country's central bank, so a treatment of money must extend to these institutions.

The key to understanding a bank's operations is its balance sheet, which is at the core of this chapter. As a prelude, we start with a bank's role in clearing the checks written by its depositors. The balance sheet is then built up from a relatively intuitive situation involving cash to the greater abstraction of reserve balances.

The questions of illiquidity and insolvency lead to the importance of credibility and the central bank's role in stabilizing the system.

10.2 Checking Transactions

An important role for a bank is as a clearing house for payments, keeping track of who has how much purchasing power and how much of that purchasing power has been transferred to whom. The money-creating role of banks grows from their

K. Seeley, *Macroeconomics in Ecological Context*, Studies in Ecological Economics 5, DOI 10.1007/978-3-319-51757-5_10

lending practices, which are tied in with their clearing-house function, so we'll start with the simple mechanics of checking transactions.

Imagine four people—Grant, Schultz, Lin, and Nehru—who have checking accounts at two different banks: HisBank and HerBank. The four people start off with the following balances in their accounts.

HisBank		HerBank	
Grant's account	$2,000	Schultz's account	$1,500
Lin's account	$1,200	Nehru's account	$3,000

Grant writes Schultz a check for $200, and Schultz deposits it in her account. HerBank increases Schultz's balance to reflect the new situation:

HisBank		HerBank	
Grant's account	$2,000	Schultz's account	**$1,700**
Lin's account	$1,200	Nehru's account	$3,000

At the same time, Nehru writes Lin a check for $250, and Lin deposits this in his account, so HisBank increases Lin's balance by $250:

HisBank		HerBank	
Grant's account	$2,000	Schultz's account	$1,700
Lin's account	**$1,450**	Nehru's account	$3,000

Now HerBank and HisBank get together. HerBank says, "Your customer Grant wrote a check for $200 to my customer Schultz. We've increased Schultz's balance; now you owe us $200." And HisBank says, "Your customer Nehru wrote a check for $250 to my customer Lin. We've increased Lin's balance; now you owe us $250."

Once they combine these claims, all that's left is that HisBank owes HerBank $50. HisBank reduces Grant's balance by $200, to reflect the check that Grant wrote, and HerBank reduces Nehru's account by $250, because of the check that Nehru wrote:

HisBank		HerBank	
Grant's account	**$1,800**	Schultz's account	$1,700
Lin's account	$1,450	Nehru's account	**$2,750**

The net result of all of this is that we had $450 worth of transactions, but only $50 ever moved from one bank to the other. The rest was just offsetting adjustments to this or that account at one bank or the other.

If we step back to view a bank balance sheet as a whole, the same kind of principle is at work, just with more categories and with different effects.

10.3 The Bank Balance Sheet

The two big categories of a bank balance sheet are:

- Liabilities and equity
- Assets

Liabilities Liabilities are things the bank owes to other people or to other entities. The largest component of this is usually their customers' accounts: if you have $2,000 in a bank account, that represents your ability to come into the bank and ask for some or all of it, or to spend some by writing a check. In other words, the bank owes it either to you or to whomever brings in a check you've written to them.

Assets Assets are things the bank owns. If you bring in $1,000 in cash and deposit it in your account, your account balance goes up by $1,000 (the bank's liabilities just increased) but the bank now owns the cash you brought in (the bank's assets also went up by $1,000).

Another important item among a bank's assets is outstanding loans. Say you ask the bank to lend you $500, and they give it to you. Presumably you promised to pay them back, with interest (maybe the interest is $50, so the total you've promised to pay back is $550). From your perspective, that promise is a liability: you owe the bank $550. From the bank's perspective, that same promise is an asset: they own your obligation to pay them in the future.

A third type of asset is reserves at the central bank. We'll explain them in more detail in Sect. 10.4, but the basic idea is that, if you're a bank, you have an account at your country's central bank, and your central bank reserves are the balance in that account.

The last type to mention here is financial assets: bonds and stocks and other things that represents ways of holding wealth. One type of these financial assets is government bonds, which are debts of the government (in the U.S. they're called Treasury bonds). These will be important in discussing monetary policy in Chap. 12.

Equity Equity is the value of owning the bank, what's left after you subtract the liabilities from the assets. This will be clearer in the context of the example developed in Sect. 10.3.1.

Table 10.1 "OurBank" balance sheet, Day 1

Item	Assets	Liabilities and equity
Founding capital (the money you put in)	$500	
Equity		$500
Totals	$500	$500

Table 10.2 "OurBank" balance sheet, Day 2

Item	Assets	Liabilities and equity
Founding money plus the cash that grant deposited	$1,500	
Grant's account balance		$1,000
Equity		$500
Totals	$1,500	$1,500

10.3.1 Balancing Your Balance Sheet

As the name suggests, your balance sheet has to balance. What that means is that your liabilities and equity have to add up to the same amount as your assets. To illustrate how that works through various types of transactions, we'll use a very simplified bank balance sheet worked up from scratch.

You and some friends want to start a bank, and you've got $500. So you set up a legal structure, call it "OurBank," and you give OurBank the $500. That's the bank's first asset.

It doesn't yet have any liabilities—it doesn't owe anybody anything. But you and your friends own it. And how much is that worth? Well, OurBank has $500 sitting in the vault and nothing else, so $500 would be a pretty reasonable guess for its value.[1] That's your equity (Table 10.1).

And now you get yourselves an actual depositor. Grant walks in with $1,000 in cash, opens up an account, and deposits his cash in it. The cash is now yours, so it's an asset to OurBank. But Grant now has an account with a balance of $1,000, and that's a liability to the bank. Here's the revised balance sheet (Table 10.2).

10.3.2 Loans Two Ways

Now Lin comes into the bank and wants a loan of $400, and you think he's a good risk. One way to provide the loan is to take $400 of the bank's cash and hand it to Lin. That will reduce your assets by $400. On the other hand, Lin has promised to pay the money back, with interest. Let's say he's promised to pay $450. That promise is a new asset. When you combine those changes, the asset side of the

[1] For simplicity, we're setting aside the value of the vault itself, and the building the vault is in, etc.

Table 10.3 "OurBank" balance sheet, Day 3

Item	Assets	Liabilities and equity
Cash, minus the $400 lent to Lin	$1,100	
Grant's account balance		$1,000
Lin's promise to pay in the future	$450	
Equity		$550
Totals	$1,550	$1,550

Table 10.4 "OurBank" balance sheet, Day 4

Item	Assets	Liabilities and equity
Cash, minus the $400 lent to Lin	$1,100	
Grant's account balance		$1,000
Lin's promise to pay in the future	$450	
Schultz's account	($600)	
Schultz's promise to pay	$660	
Equity		$550
Totals	$1,610	$1,610

balance sheet has gone up by $50, so the liabilities-and-equity side has to go up as well. You haven't picked up any new liabilities, so the extra $50 must be an increase in your equity—an increase in the value of owning the bank (Table 10.3).

But there's another way of making a loan. You don't have to actually hand someone cash in order to make them a loan. You can just as well create a checking account in their name and say that there's money in it. Say Schultz comes in and requests a $600 loan; she promises to repay $660 later (the $600 principal, plus $60 in interest).

Rather than taking $600 cash out of your vault and giving it to Schultz, you create an account for her, and simply declare that it has $600 she can spend. This gets counted as a negative asset (we'll see below why that makes sense). And you also list Schultz's promise to pay $660, which is a positive asset. Taken together, your assets have gone up by another $60, and as before, there's no way to balance that out other than by a corresponding increase in equity (Table 10.4).

Notice what your bank just did with both of these loans: **it created money.**[2] In the case of the cash loan to Lin, it helps to know that cash sitting in a bank's vault is not part of the money supply. Banks don't spend money, they provide it to other people to spend. So when the $400 was sitting in OurBank's vault, it effectively wasn't money, but only became money when it was brought out of the vault and handed to Lin.

That may seem like an odd distinction, but follow the money a couple of steps further. Presumably Lin is going to spend the $400—that's why he borrowed it. Say

[2] An interesting recent explanation of this process is from the Bank of England, at [1].

he spends it all buying something from you. You take the $400 and bring it to your own bank to deposit it. Just as in Table 10.2, the cash now belongs to your bank and goes into their vault, where it stops being money. But your checking or savings account at your bank goes up by $400, and your account at your bank *is* money, because it represents an amount that you're able to spend.

The situation with the loan to Schultz is similar, though perhaps simpler, because there isn't the strangeness of cash being money when it's in your hands and the very same pieces of paper ceasing to be money when they pass into the vault of a bank.

In this case, you didn't take anything out of your vault. You still have the same $1,100 sitting there, but Schultz now has $600 she can spend. Of course, that $600 is sitting there on your balance sheet as a negative asset, because of what will happen when Schultz spends the money you created for her.

Say she writes a check to Grant for $100. Grant has an account at HisBank, so he brings the check there and deposits it, and HisBank increases Grant's balance by $100. At the end of the day, HisBank brings the check to OurBank and says, "Your customer Schultz wrote this check to our customer Grant. Give us $100." And what if Schultz wrote six $100 checks, so suddenly you owe $600 to other banks? Now your cash is looking rather depleted.

But remember what happened in the checking-account balance at the beginning of the chapter. Suppose that while you were making a loan to Schultz, HisBank was making a loan to Winston, and HerBank was making a loan to Nehru. And while Schultz was writing his checks, Winston and Nehru were doing the same thing, and some of those checks were written to some depositors of yours.

This means that HerBank shows up with Schultz's check and says, "Pay us $100," and you say, "Well here's a check that your customer Nehru wrote, for $80. Here's $20, and we're even." So when you make the loan, you figure that Schultz is going to spend that money before she pays it back, and you're going to be liable for those checks she writes—there will be claims against your bank. But you also assume that other customers of yours will be getting paid for things, and they'll bring those checks in and you'll then have claims against other banks. And just as with the cash that you handed to Lin, when Schultz spends the $600 you created to give her the loan, the -$600 asset on your balance sheet gets converted into $600 worth of deposits on the "liabilities" side of various banks' balance sheets.

10.4 Reserves

We've been telling the story as if the bank's only positive asset, other than people's promises to pay, were the cash in its vault. But cash actually makes up a very small portion of a bank's balance sheet. Most of what acts like cash is actually the bank's Federal Reserve balance.

You often see a bank that has "national" in its name, and other banks are also "national" banks, even without the name. In either case, what makes something a national bank is that it has an account with the Federal Reserve.[3] Recall the discussion of "state money" in Sect. 9.9. Something is "state money" if the government (the state) imposes a tax and declares that particular kind of money is what people have to use to pay their taxes. Thus "state money" is money that is backed, ultimately, by the credibility of the government. The bank's balance with the Federal Reserve is the bank's claim on "state money."

There are now two kinds of reserves. Reserves are anything a bank can use to settle up with other banks at the end of the day. Currency and Federal Reserve balances count equally as reserves. If OurBank owes HerBank $20 at the end of the day, they can send HerBank a $20 bill, but they can also contact the Federal Reserve and say, "Reduce our balance at the Federal Reserve by $20 and increase HerBank's balance by $20." Either way, OurBank now has $20 less, and HerBank has $20 more.

We can redraw the OurBank balance sheet to show very little currency and a much larger Federal Reserve balance (see Table 10.5). The currency and Federal Reserve balance are added together to get Total reserves.

The last thing to observe about reserves is that they generally don't earn interest. If I lend you $400, I expect to get back something like, perhaps, $440. If I hold $400 as currency, it will always be $400. And if I have $400 in Federal Reserve balances, it will always be $400.[4]

Because of this, banking is partly the art of managing your assets between reserves and loans. I need to have some reserves around so that I can settle up with

Table 10.5 "OurBank" balance sheet, day 5

Item	Assets	Liabilities and equity
Currency	*$50*	
Federal Reserve balances	*$1,050*	
Total reserves	$1,100	
Grant's account balance		$1,000
Lin's promise to pay in the future	$450	
Schultz's account	($600)	
Schultz's promise to pay	$660	
Equity		$610
Totals	$1,610	$1,610

[3]This is the U.S. structure in particular and will be covered in more detail in Chap. 12. Other countries have similar systems with minor differences.

[4]During the financial crisis following the market meltdown of 2008, the Federal Reserve has sometimes paid positive interest on reserves, ostensibly as a way of keeping the banks healthy. There have been proposals that it should actually do the opposite, *charge* interest (or pay negative interest) as a way of encouraging banks to make more loans rather than sitting on their reserves.

other banks.[5] But in general, I'd rather have my assets in the form of loans—my borrowers' promises to pay—since those earn interest.

10.5 Illiquidity vs. Insolvency

Illiquidity and insolvency are both bad things that can happen to a bank, but insolvency is much worse.

Insolvency is when your assets are less than your liabilities. In other words, you're bankrupt. We'll explore below how that can happen.

In the case of illiquidity, your assets are greater than your liabilities, so you're solvent, but you're being asked to pay something right now, and you don't have the reserves to do that.

Let's walk through four more transactions to see how this all works. We'll start from a situation where OurBank has been up and running for a while (see Table 10.6), so you have lots of depositors and lots of borrowers, and it makes sense to consolidate them on your balance sheet.

Note that the line for "Borrowers' accounts" is a lot smaller than the line for "Borrowers' promises to pay." Go back to the loan you made to Schultz. You lent her $600 and she promised to pay $660. Maybe the terms of the loan were that she would pay that off two years from now. In the meantime, she's gone and spent most of the $600 she borrowed—after all, the reason she wanted the loan was to be able to buy something now and come up with the income for it later. If Schultz has written $500 worth of checks, you've already settled those out with other banks, and in the course of doing that, you've reduced Schultz's account by $500. That is, your negative asset from having lent Schultz $600 is now only a negative asset of $100.

Table 10.6 "OurBank" balance sheet, Day 100

Item	Assets	Liabilities and equity
Currency	*$20*	
Federal Reserve balances	*$600*	
Total reserves	$620	
Depositor's accounts		$5,100
Borrowers' accounts	($400)	
Borrowers' promises to pay	$5,400	
Equity		$520
Totals	$5,620	$5,620

[5]In the U.S., a bank that is part of the Federal Reserve system has a reserve requirement: there's a minimum amount of reserves it has to have, defined in relation to the total deposits on their balance sheets. In Canada, on the other hand, there is no minimum requirement; it is left to the banks to determine the quantity of reserves they need in order to function reliably.

Table 10.7 "OurBank" balance sheet, Day 101

Item	Assets	Liabilities and equity
Currency	*$20*	
Federal Reserve balances	*$700*	
Total reserves	$720	
Depositor's accounts		$5,200
Borrowers' accounts	($400)	
Borrowers' promises to pay	$5,400	
Equity		$520
Totals	$5,720	$5,720

Table 10.8 "OurBank" balance sheet, Day 102

Item	Assets	Liabilities and equity
Currency	*$0*	
Federal Reserve balances	*$0*	
Total reserves	$0	
Excess claims on reserves		$580
Depositor's accounts		$3,900
Borrowers' accounts	($400)	
Borrowers' promises to pay	$5,400	
Equity		$520
Totals	$5,000	$5,000

If we extend this to a bunch of borrowers, you probably have a bunch of loans on your books where the promise to pay is still mostly there, but the negative asset has mostly been spent down, because the borrowers wrote checks, you cleared them with other banks, and reduced the borrowers' balances.

Next let's look at a day that works out well for OurBank (Table 10.7). A bunch of our depositors wrote checks totaling $1,000, so when other banks show up, we owe $1,000. At the same time, other depositors of ours received checks written by customers of other banks, and those checks totaled $1,100. All of us banks settle up at the end of the day, and OurBank comes out $100 ahead. Our balance at the Federal Reserve has been increased by $100, and the total of our depositors' accounts has also been increased by $100.

The next day doesn't go so well for us (Table 10.8). Some of our depositors write checks totaling $1,500, so that's what we owe other banks. Other depositors receive checks totaling $200, so that's what other banks owe us. When we balance up with other banks, we owe $1,300, but our reserves are only $720. We are **illiquid**.

Our depositors' balances are reduced to $3,900 ($1,500 out, partly offset by $200 back in).

Our reserves are wiped out: we transfer all our currency and all our Federal Reserve balances to other banks, and we still owe another $580, which shows up in the row of "Excess claims on reserves."

We're still solvent: we have all those borrowers' promises to pay, and so far as anyone knows, those borrowers actually *will* pay, and when they do, our reserves will go back up. The problem is that our agreements with them specify when they have to pay, and they don't have to pay *yet*. Maybe they're obligated to pay in a month, or a year, or a few years, but that doesn't help us right now, because the other banks don't want our customers' promises to pay. They want reserves, and we're out of those.

In Sect. 10.7 below on central banks, we'll get into how to respond to this situation.

For now, let's say we get through this horrible day, and the next day everything turns around. Our depositors bring in $1,300, so we wipe out our excess claims on reserves and restore the reserves themselves. Our balance sheet goes back to looking just like it did on day 101 in Table 10.7.

But things can get worse.

When you make a loan, there's always a chance that the borrower could default (stop paying back a loan). In the mill parable of the previous chapter, the mill could be swept away, making it impossible for the miller to repay. In the real world, a home-buyer may lose her job, so she defaults on her mortgage. A business could lose customers, or make a bad business decision, and so stop earning profits and default on its loans.

If 5% of our loans go bad, that means we have to "write off" $270 worth of borrowers' promises. We thought we had $5,400 coming in eventually, but now we realize that we'll only ever see $5,130.

We rewrite our balance sheet to reflect the new reality (Table 10.9). The loss of assets has to be balanced by *something* on the other side of the ledger. We still owe our depositors $5,200, so we can't reduce that. What happens is that the equity is reduced: when a bank makes a loan, and then the borrower defaults, the value of owning the bank goes down.

But we're still solvent: Our assets are still greater than our liabilities.

This is the flip side of how you make money in banking. You *make* money by creating money out of thin air and charging interest. And you *lose* money in banking

Table 10.9 "OurBank" balance sheet, Day 104

Item	Assets	Liabilities and equity
Currency	*$20*	
Federal Reserve balances	*$700*	
Total reserves	$720	
Depositor's accounts		$5,200
Borrowers' accounts	($400)	
Borrowers' promises to pay	$5,130	
Equity		$250
Totals	$5,450	$5,450

Table 10.10 "OurBank" balance sheet, Day 105

Item	Assets	Liabilities and equity
Currency	*$20*	
Federal Reserve balances	*$700*	
Total reserves	$720	
Depositor's accounts		$5,200
Borrowers' accounts	($400)	
Borrowers' promises to pay	$4,830	
Equity		$0
Totals	$5,150	$5,200

by having those loans go bad. And you lose your shirt in banking by having so many loans go bad that you're insolvent, which is the next step to look at.

Day 105 (Table 10.10) is even worse than Day 104: another $300 in loans goes bad. We write off that as well, so our borrowers' promises are down to $4,830. Our assets now only come to $5,150. We wipe out all our equity, but that's not enough: we still owe our depositors $5,200.

We are **insolvent**. In Sect. 10.7 on central banks, we'll see what to do about that, along with what to do about illiquidity. (The bottom line in the "Assets" column is underlined to draw attention to the fact that it is less than the bottom line in "Liabilities and equity".)

10.6 Tools for Credibility

If Grant is a depositor at this bank, the scenario on Day 105 is pretty unsettling. Is OurBank going to fold? If it does, what happens to his deposits there? Will he be able to get his money out? If people think a bank is unsound, they're unlikely to deposit their money there in the first place, so a bank can't even do business if people don't think it will be able to stay solvent. A bank needs credibility in order to function.

As the mill parable of Chap. 9 illustrated, any record of a promise can serve as money, and the history of Mesopotamian temple records shows that any tradable record of ownership can also serve as money. These *ad hoc* forms of money are real, but they can also vanish relatively easily, since they depend on a single promisor or owner.

One way of thinking about what banks do is that they formalize the process laid out in the mill parable. In that story, money was created when the farmers gave me food in return for the tokens that promised them food in the future. They extended credit to me, and the value of the resulting money depended on the strength of people's belief that I'd pay.

Analogously, banks create money when they extend credit to their borrowers. However, unlike in the mill parable, we don't have to trust the borrowers directly. We can trust the bank: we can believe in the bank's ability to figure out which people asking for loans are unlikely to pay back, and not lend to them. So the first element of a bank's credibility is our trust in its judgment.

The next defense is the bank's capital. If we go back to the beginning of the story of OurBank, a group of friends put up $500 actual money and started a bank. That $500 was the bank's capital. The point of running a bank is to not have to spend that; what you want is that the claims that you have on other banks exceed the claims that other banks have on you, so that your reserves increase. Or you want the claims in each direction to be roughly equal. If things run against you, you'll have to dip into your capital, the money that you put up to start the bank in the first place. You don't want to have to do that, but the fact that you *can* do it improves the credibility of your bank.

When a bank creates money out of thin air by extending credit, it's making a promise: it's promising anyone who does business with the bank that when its borrowers' checks come in for settlement, it will be able to meet those claims. It hopes to meet those claims with other claims that it has, but its capital acts as a backstop to its promises.

10.6.1 Bank Runs and Deposit Insurance

There's a special kind of bank problem represented by the mismatch between deposits and reserves.

Look back above at the change from Day 101 to Day 102. When we have a bank account, we talk about having "money in the bank," but if we picture currency notes sitting in the bank vault, equal in value to our account balance, we're wrong. The bank doesn't hold onto our money, it lends it out to earn interest. And it doesn't just lend out the money we brought in, it also creates new money and lends *that* out, thus taking on additional obligations, on top of what it already owes us.

If one average individual comes into the bank and wants to close her account and withdraw all her money, that's no big deal. But if too many people want to withdraw their money at the same time, as with the Day 102 balance sheet in Table 10.8, we've got a problem.

Let's go back earlier on that same fateful Day 102 in Table 10.8. The $1,300 withdrawal doesn't happen all at once. Let's say a normal day sees swings of $100 or $200: some days deposits are coming in, and the bank's reserves go up by $100 or $200; other days, there are more withdrawals, so the reserves fall by $100 or $200.

But this morning at 10:00, you learn that withdrawals are already $200 ahead. By noon, they're $400 ahead. The bank started the day with $720 in reserves. If another $320 gets withdrawn, the bank will be out of reserves. Any depositor who tries to withdraw after that will find that the bank is illiquid, and the depositor will be disappointed. Being unable to pay, the bank will have to close. In other words, if more and more people come in wanting to withdraw, the bank's illiquidity can cause the bank to fail.

So at noon, you see that your bank is down $400. If you wait to see what happens, the bank may become illiquid, and then go bankrupt, and you will have lost all the money you have in your account there.

It's obviously stupid for you to wait it out, so you head down to the bank to get withdraw your own $80 before the bank collapses. But you're not the only one smart enough to figure this out. A lot of the bank's other customers are also heading down there, trying to make sure that they get their money out while they still can.

Depositors converge on the bank, hoping to withdraw $2,000. This is a **bank run**, or **a run on the bank**. The bank's reserves are $320. The bank satisfies the first four or so depositors, then it's out of money. The bank fails, and everyone else loses their deposits.

Let's consider a different outcome. In this alternative, most depositors weren't paying any attention to the bank's fate, so they didn't know that at noon the bank was down to $320 in reserves. Not knowing what the situation was, they didn't converge on the bank to withdraw their money. And at noon the withdrawals stopped, and at 1:00 pm some deposits came in, and at 2:00 pm some more, and by the time the day ended, the bank was only down $150 in reserves. A normal day.

So what happened on that day with the bank run? The bank's solvency was never in doubt—the problem wasn't loans going bad, so assets were never in danger of falling below liabilities. Instead, because depositors got worried about the accessibility of their money, a whole bunch of them came to withdraw their deposits. A perfectly healthy bank was suddenly faced with illiquidity and then forced to shut down. Most of the depositors lost their money. And the whole thing was brought on by depositors' attempts to *protect* their money.

This is obviously an absurd outcome. Fortunately, there's a pretty simple solution to prevent it, called deposit insurance. In the U.S. it's carried out by the Federal Deposit Insurance Corporation (FDIC).

When you insure your house against fire, you pay a certain amount of money every year (your insurance premium), based on the value of your house. Then if your house burns down, the insurance company gives you money to replace it.

With deposit insurance, a bank pays insurance premiums to FDIC. The size of the premiums is based on the quantity of deposits the bank has on its books. If the bank fails, the depositors don't lose their money; instead, the FDIC "makes them whole"—that is, the insurer gives depositors the amount of money they lost when the bank failed.[6]

---

[6]This is only good up to a certain limit. As of August, 2014, the FDIC "insured limit" is $250,000 per depositor per bank. If you have an account balance of less than $250,000, you'll get all your money back. If you have an account of more than $250,000, you'll get $250,000 back. If you want to protect more than $250,000, you can have accounts at more than one bank.

Deposit insurance is a pretty neat invention. Fire insurance on your house doesn't make your house less likely to burn down, and accident insurance on your car doesn't make you any less likely to have an accident. But deposit insurance makes people relax about losing their savings, so they don't get involved in a run on the bank, so they don't cause a basically healthy bank to collapse for no good reason.

Deposit insurance makes the problem it insures against less likely to happen.[7]

10.7 Central Banks

The core function of a central bank is to act as a backstop to the country's other banks. The key to this role is the central bank's position as gatekeeper controlling access to "state money."

Remember that a large part of a bank's reserves are its balances at one of the country's 12 Federal Reserve Banks.[8] The essence of those balances is that they are claims on state money.

That can mean currency. If you're a bank and you find that you have a lot of depositors coming in and making withdrawals specifically of currency, you can turn your other reserves into currency. You just tell the Federal Reserve (or "the Fed") that you need, say, \$100 in currency. They reduce your balance with them by \$100 and send you the currency you requested.

But your Fed balance also represents claims on state money in another way, and that is through the payment of taxes.

Let's say Nehru has a tax bill of \$200. She'll probably just write a check for that amount to the IRS. The IRS will then bring the check to HerBank, which will look at Nehru's account. If she has more than \$200 in her account, they reduce her balance by \$200, and then they ask the Fed to transfer \$200 of HerBank's Fed balances to the IRS's account at the Fed. The IRS notes the transfer, and acknowledges that Nehru has paid her tax bill.

HerBank's Fed balances were valid in payment of taxes—in other words, they were recognized claims on state money.[9]

---

[7]There is a caveat to this point, which is that if a bank knows that it's insured, it also knows it can take greater risks in its efforts to earn higher interest earnings. In theory, without insurance a bank has to worry about risky loans, because if depositors see it making too many risky loans, they won't want to be depositors anymore, and the bank will fail. In practice, many households may not be good judges of how much risk a bank is running—the people who work at the bank are supposedly experts at judging such risks, whereas almost all of the depositors are experts at something else, but not at assessing risks. And on top of that, when a bank is part of FDIC, they don't just pay insurance premiums, they also submit to regulation of what kinds of loans they can make, so as to limit the riskiness of their portfolios.

[8]The following discussion will focus on the U.S. system with the Federal Reserve. The details are different in other countries, but the core functions and operations are similar.

[9]This relationship between taxes and money is at the core of "Chartalism"; see, e.g., [2].

10.7.1 Lender of Last Resort

What does it mean for the central bank to be the "backstop" for other banks? Look back at the balance sheet for Day 102 up above in Table 10.8, the day OurBank stumbled into illiquidity. Remember that the bank was still *solvent*—so far as anyone knew, all of its loans were still good, all of its borrowers were still going to pay what they owed. Its only problem was that people wanted to withdraw more on that day than the bank had in reserves.

What are the options here? The simplest one is that the bank closes. It said it would give depositors their money whenever they asked for it. Now they're asking for it, and it can't give it to them. It has failed in its obligations to its depositors, so it goes out of business.

As explained in Sect. 10.6.1, this is not a sensible outcome. A bunch of depositors have lost their money, and the combined skills represented by the bank's staff have been broken up and rendered less productive. And it's not that OurBank did anything wrong; its loans were still good. All that happened was bad luck in terms of too many withdrawals happening at once; to break up a bank over that would be a waste.

Even worse, there can be ripple effects at other banks. Say Grant owes Nehru some money, and Nehru has a loan from HerBank. But Grant got wiped out when OurBank had a liquidity problem, so he can't pay Nehru what he owes. Suddenly Nehru finds that she can't pay what *she* owes on her loan from HerBank, so she defaults, and HerBank writes off Nehru's loan—it accepts that it won't be getting that money back from her. And if enough of HerBank's borrowers have the same thing happen to them, suddenly HerBank is facing a risk of insolvency, all because of a bad solution to a liquidity problem at OurBank.

If there's some way to avoid the failure of OurBank, that would be a good outcome.

And there is! The first thing the bank can do is try to borrow reserves from other banks. It can show them its books: Look how many good loans we have, look at how high our repayment rate is. If OurBank can convince other banks that it's solvent, they might be willing to lend OurBank some reserves. After all, banks exist to make loans (and charge interest on them). If the risk looks low enough, some bank may be willing to step in.

But what if there's no willing bank?

Who knows why OurBank is experiencing a run? Maybe there's actually some problem hidden on its books. Or maybe whatever's causing people to withdraw money from OurBank is about to make them start withdrawing money from HisBank. The result of that would be that HisBank wouldn't want to lend out its reserves, in case it suddenly finds a bunch of *its* depositors making withdrawals.

So what now? You turn to the Fed, that's what.

The Federal Reserve is the "lender of last resort" for a bank: after a bank has tried borrowing from anyone else it can think of, and not had any luck, it turns to the Fed. And the Fed can always lend to a bank. One thing it can do is take reserves from some other part of its operation and add them to OurBank's balance. "There, you have a bunch more reserves. Go satisfy your depositors and their desire to make withdrawals. We see that you're solvent, so we trust that things will turn around, your situation will return to normal, and you'll be able to repay us (with interest, of course)."

And so OurBank is able to keep operating, we avoid a pointless bankruptcy, and the economy is spared the ripple effect of damaging other banks.

Part of what enables the Fed to play this role is that it is the custodian of the national currency. Remember in the story from Sect. 10.3.1 of OurBank's creation that the founders started with some bank capital, some already-existing money to act as their reserves. Their ownership of that money gave confidence to the bank's potential customers: trust us—we have all this money that we can use to settle accounts.

The analogous thing for a central bank is its control of state money. As discussed above, "state money" is money that is backed by the state's ability to impose and collect taxes. State money will thus last as long as the state itself—or rather, it will last as long as the state has the ability to levy and collect taxes and stand by its promises to repay whatever it has borrowed. And the central bank is the custodian of that state money. So they're in a position to say, "Trust us—we have access to the ultimate social agreement to pay."

On the other hand, if a bank is insolvent, it probably needs to be shut down. The equity is wiped out (the banks' shareholders lose their money), the defaulted loans are written off, the remaining loans are sold to other banks (they pay money now for the expectation of receiving the borrowers' loan payments in the future) and deposit insurance makes whole the depositors.

So: Lend to illiquid banks to keep them afloat, and arrange for the shutdown of insolvent banks.

So far so good. The trick is in differentiating between illiquidity and insolvency. In the examples above, it was perfectly clear because we assumed that we knew when OurBank's loans were good and when they were bad. Reality can be much more complicated.

Perhaps Nehru has been having a harder and harder time financially. She's heading toward default on her loans, but it might be that HerBank doesn't know that until the day the payments stop arriving. In reality, the worth of Nehru's loan had been declining for a while, as the odds of Nehru's full repayment kept shrinking. But the bank wouldn't have known and would have counted her loan at face value, making it appear that the bank had more assets than it really did.

Also, banks have balance sheets that are much more complicated than the illustrative ones shown here, and they have other types of assets. Perhaps HisBank's assets include some mortgage-backed securities (MBS). These are financial instruments that give the owner a piece of many people's mortgage payments. When housing prices started falling badly in 2007 and unemployment started rising in 2008, many people stopped paying their mortgages. Not surprisingly, this diminished the value of owning MBS. But by how much? And for how long? If 2009 brings higher housing prices and lower unemployment, then an MBS regains its value and HisBank's balance sheet looks better again. But if prices stay down and unemployment stays up, then MBS remains in a world of financial hurt.

The lender-of-last-resort role is simple in theory, and it's an important tool for a central bank to prevent a problem in the banking sector from becoming a problem for the economy as a whole. But fulfilling the lender-of-last-resort role can be very tricky in practice.

10.7.2 Capital and Reserve Requirements

Another pair of tools is capital requirements and reserve requirements.

As the above examples illustrate, it's very valuable for a bank to have access to the services of the central bank. On a day-to-day basis, it eases the bank's interactions with other banks, since they can settle accounts through simple transfers of Fed balances. And if it gets into trouble, it has the Fed's lender-of-last-resort role to help it out.

So the central bank is in a position to make some demands in return for access to its services.

The first such demand is a capital requirement: If you want to run a bank that has access to the central bank, you must have a certain minimum amount of capital, a minimum amount of the owners' wealth that is at risk in the bank. As discussed above, this kind of (financial) capital serves to shore up the bank's credibility.

It should also encourage the bank to make better decisions. If the owners of OurBank have almost none of their own money in the bank, then they may be inclined to be overly risky. If their loans don't work out, the worst that can happen is that they lose their jobs; they didn't lose much of their own wealth. But if they're required to have a decent portion of money in the bank, then they have an incentive to be careful to avoid the bank going under and them losing their capital.

The second typical requirement is a reserve requirement. As mentioned in footnote 5, these aren't universal: the U.S. has them, but Canada doesn't.

In principle, a reserve requirement provides an extra element of security, since it means that a bank that wants to have access to the services of the Federal Reserve can't cut things too close as far as having enough reserves on hand to deal with the kinds of contingencies the bank should reasonably expect it might encounter.

In normal times, reserve requirements in the U.S. have tended to be binding—that is, banks hold the amount of reserves the Fed requires them to have, and not a lot more. Since the financial meltdown of 2008, the Fed has shored up the banking sector by adding lots of reserves to bank balance sheets, while at the same time banks have gotten much more cautious, much less willing to lend. The result is that, as of August, 2014, banks are sitting on reserves far in excess of what the Fed requires them to hold.

10.7.3 Monetary Policy

The other role of the central bank—and the one that gets most of the attention—is that it intentionally influences the size of the money supply and banks' willingness to make loans. This is what's known as "monetary policy," and it gets its own treatment a couple of chapters from now in Chap. 12. Hopefully when we get there, the functioning of monetary policy will make more sense to you, now that you've had a tour through the basics of how the banking system works.

10.8 Fractional Reserve Banking

The type of banking illustrated in Tables 10.6 through 10.10 is known as "fractional reserve banking," because the bank's reserves are only a fraction of its customers' deposits.

If you look on the web, diatribes against fractional reserve banking are a dime a dozen (check back in a few years—maybe they'll be a quarter a dozen). Some of these are based on the idea that the only "real" money is gold, or things that are directly claims on gold. But as Chap. 9 explained, the essence of money is simply some sort of promise. If people arrange it to be a promise of a claim on gold, that's fine, but it doesn't *have to* be gold; it can be whatever promise people are willing to accept.

Banks aren't "tricking" you by operating with fractional reserves. When you open an account with a fractional-reserve bank, the only thing they promise you is that your "money units" will be there when you come back for them, with interest if it's an interest-bearing account. And they generally keep their promise. The Federal Reserve helps them keep their promise, and the FDIC helps protect you from loss when a bank *does* go under. Whatever it is that's in our bank accounts, it certainly *acts* like real money.

Another major attack is that a fractional-reserve system drives business cycles, first creating a boom, and then exacerbating the bust that inevitably follows. The banking system is certainly capable of contributing to that problem, but the central bank has the tools to mitigate it—whether it chooses to *use* those tools is another question, but it has the tools.

Problems

All of the problems start from Table 10.11 below, showing a bank balance sheet. To answer each question, modify the numbers in Table 10.11 to reflect the scenario in the question.

Table 10.11 Starting balance sheet for Chap. 10 problems

Item	Assets	Liabilities and equity
Currency	*$570*	
Federal Reserve balances	*$8,350*	
Total reserves	$8,920	
Other financial assets	$2,345	
Depositor's accounts		$31,470
Borrowers' accounts	($736)	
Borrowers' promises to pay	$24,790	
Equity		
Totals	$35,319	$35,319

Start each new question from the original Table 10.11—that is, don't answer Problem 10.2 and then use the *modified* Table 10.11 as your starting point for Problem 10.3.

In some cases a legitimate answer might be that the scenario described in a given problem represents no change from Table 10.11.

Problem 10.1 Based on the numbers in the table, how much is this bank's equity, and where in the table does it belong?

Problem 10.2 Show a cash loan of $65 (the bank hands the borrower $65 in cash), with a promise to pay worth $80.

Problem 10.3 Show a $400 loan made through the extension of credit (the bank creates an account for the borrower with $400 in it), with a promise to pay of $550.

Problem 10.4 Show the bank receiving a cash deposit of $120.

Problem 10.5 Show the bank receiving a deposit by check (on another bank) of $450.

Problem 10.6 Show the bank receiving a deposit by check (written by another depositor at this bank) for $320.

Problem 10.7 Show the bank receiving a deposit by check for $245. The check writer is someone who has received a loan from the bank, the check is written against their "borrower's account," and the person they wrote the check to is a depositor at the bank who has brought the check in to deposit it.

Problem 10.8 Show the bank being presented with a check written by one of its depositors, for $780, payable to a customer of another bank.

Problem 10.9 Show the bank "settling up": one of its customers has written a check to a customer of another bank, for $395, and a customer of that other bank has written a check to a customer of the first bank, for $360.

Problem 10.10 Show the bank acknowledging that a loan worth $1,200 has gone bad (the borrower will not actually be paying back the loan).

Problem 10.11 Show a customer withdrawing $45 in currency.

Problem 10.12 Show a borrower bringing in a check for $100, in repayment of a loan; the check was written by a depositor at another bank.

Problem 10.13 Show a borrower bringing in a check for $200, in repayment of a loan; the check was written by a depositor at the same bank shown in Table 10.11.

Problem 10.14 Of the preceding transactions, which ones show either the creation of some money or the disappearance of some money?

References

1. McLeay, M., Radia, A. & Thomas, R. (2014). Money creation in the modern economy. *Quarterly Bulletin, Q1*, 1–14.
2. Tcherneva, P. R. (2006). Chartalism and the tax-driven approach to money. In P. Arestis & M. Sawyer (Eds.), *Handbook of alternative monetary economics* (pp. 69–86). Cheltenham: Edward Elgar.

Chapter 11
Expenditure Multipliers

Abstract We extend the mill parable of Chap. 9 to develop some intuition about how expenditure multipliers work, as well as conditions under which thy're more or less likely to be relevant. This covers both physical inability and simple unwillingness to increase output. We then derive the conventional Keynesian multipliers for changes in expenditure and taxation. The informal version from the mill parable is used to introduce some limitations of multiplier analysis.

11.1 Mills and Multipliers

Sometimes people find the idea of an expenditure multiplier to be highly counterintuitive. In a struggling economy, it seems like everyone is short of money. If people spend money they don't have, how can that be good for the economy? To get some intuition on that, let's go back to the mill story, but instead of focusing on how money is related to debt as we did there, we'll focus on the effects of expenditure.

Section 9.6 on "Different responses to expenditure" looked at some of the actions a farmer could take when presented with the miller's offer of food now for a promise of food later. We're going to revisit that to see the different ways that expenditure (the miller buying food to feed workers building the mill) can affect total output in the economy. To make sense of it we have to distinguish among income, revenue, and expenditure.

Take a farmer who was growing 1.5 units of food before the mill project. Remember that there was no money in this economy, so they couldn't have had any revenue. That also means they didn't have any expenditure. But they had output of 1.5 units of food, which was also their income, the amount they were able to consume, if they so chose.

Then the miller came along and bought one unit of food. The farmer increased output to 2 units, decreased consumption to one unit, and sold one unit to the miller. The farmer's revenue has gone up from 0 to 1 (the revenue is measured in how much food the "money" buys, and we know the farmer's revenue was 1, because she sold 1 unit of food). Since the farmer's production of food has increased from 1.5 to 2, it's also true that her income has gone up from 1.5 to 2. Consumption has fallen by 0.5, from 1.5 to 1. And she still has no expenditure.

K. Seeley, *Macroeconomics in Ecological Context*, Studies in Ecological Economics 5, DOI 10.1007/978-3-319-51757-5_11

But a farmer could make a different choice. She could take the money for a whole unit of food, but only increase her output to 1.6 and only decrease her consumption to 1.4. She's able to provide 0.2 units by her own act of saving, so she'll have to turn around and buy 0.8 units from someone else.

It's common to observe that, in macroeconomics, income equals output. We often use the symbol Y to designate an economy's GDP, which is its output, and which is also its income, because for the economy as a whole, your ability to have stuff is linked to your ability to do stuff.

The same holds true in the mill parable. Each farmer's income is the food he or she grows—their output. And each builder working on the mill has an income (the food with which they're paid) because their work on the mill is an output that their employer values. Income equals production, or output.

To extend this example and illustrate the multiplier concept, we start by adding a little specificity to the original story. We had "normal" farmers who are capable of growing the 1 unit of food that a household needs in a year, and "good" farmers who are capable of producing 2 units, but only bother producing (and eating) 1.5. Now let's say specifically there are 20 of the good farmers and 80 of the normal farmers.

In order to keep the numbers simple, let's consider just one unit of expenditure. In Chap. 9, I needed to obtain 10 units of food to feed myself and the nine other people who would spend the year building a mill instead of growing food. Now I've got some smaller investment expenditure, so I just need to feed myself for the year. Other than that, we have the same conditions as in the original story: I'm able to make a credible promise of repayment (giving you food in the future, in exchange for you giving me food now); I give you tokens that represent my promise, and because the community at large believes my promise, the tokens can function as money.

For the next modification to the story we have to clarify the differences among expenditure, revenue, and income.

In the initial situation, before the mill (or the smaller investment imagined here), nobody buys or sells anything, because there's only one good produced (and consumed): "food." So if we measure "income" by money coming in, of course everybody's income is zero. But if people had no income, then they would in fact be starving. It makes more sense to say the normal farmers have an income of 1 unit, and the good farmers have an income of 1.5, and everybody consumes their whole income. That also implies that saving is zero.

The "Initial" column of Table 11.1, part a., illustrates the overall situation. A "seller" is one of the good farmers who could potentially sell food. The output, or income, of an individual seller is denoted y and their consumption is c. The row I tracks the investment, which doesn't exist in the initial scenario, so that's zero. Total output is 80 normal farmers producing 1 unit each, and 20 good farmers producing 1.5 units each, for 110, and the consumption is also 110.

Now we introduce my small investment, and in our small economy there is now an expenditure of 1: I'm buying 1 unit of food. You're one of the good farmers, so I go to you, and you agree to sell me a unit, so *my expenditure* of 1 becomes *your revenue* of 1. As we saw in Chap. 9, you have a couple of ways of holding up your end of the bargain.

Table 11.1 Varying responses to one unit of increased expenditure

Part (**a**)									
Scenario	Initial	A	B	C	D	E	F	G	H
Exp	0	1	1	1	1	1	1	1	1
y	1.5	2	2	1.5	1.7	1.7	1.9	2	2
c	1.5	1	1.5	1	1.5	1.6	1.7	1.9	1.8
I	0	1	1	1	1	1	1	1	1
Farmers selling	0	1	2	2	5	10			
Total food	110	109.5	110	109	110	111			
Y	110	110.5	111	110	111	112			
Total C	110	109.5	110	109	110	111			
Saving	0	1	1	1	1	1	1	1	1

Part (**b**)									
Scenario	Initial	A	B	C	D	E	F	G	H
Δ[Exp]	NA	1	1	1	1	1	1	1	1
Δy	NA	0.5	0.5	0	0.2	0.2			
Δc	NA	−0.5	0	−0.5	0	0.1			
ΔY	NA	0.5	1	0	1	2			
μ	NA	0.5	1	0	1	2			
$\Delta c/\Delta y$	NA	−1	0	NA	0	0.5			
$1-\Delta c/\Delta y$	NA	2	1	NA	1	0.5			
$1/(1-\Delta c/\Delta y)$	NA	0.5	1	NA	1	2			

The first is to increase your output from 1.5 to 2, and also reduce your consumption from 1.5 to 1. Your change in revenue was 1 (you had zero before), but your change in income was only 0.5 (you were producing 1.5 and you increased to 2). These alterations are reflected in column "A" of part a of Table 11.1, and the change from the initial scenario is in column A of part b in the same table. The "seller" in this case doesn't represent any random good farmer, but only you, the one who is actually selling some food.

Let y and c be the output and consumption of one of the sellers, while Y and C are total output and consumption in the valley as a whole. Then Δc, ΔY, ΔC, and ΔY are changes in those quantities, while Δ[Exp] is the change in expenditure.

Total food is down to 109.5, because you increased by 0.5, but I stopped farming entirely, which took away 1 unit. But output includes whatever it is I'm producing instead of food, which we value at 1 (since that's what it's costing me to produce it), so total output is 110.5. We increased the purchase of final goods in the economy by 1 (or expressed in symbols, Δ[Exp] = 1) and output went up by 0.5 (which is expressed as Δ [Total Y] = 0.5).

Let's turn to the second way you can sell me a unit of food. If you don't want to reduce your consumption, you can make an arrangement with Farmer Bob:

- You'll each take half the money
- You'll each increase output to 2

- You'll each keep consumption at 1.5
- He'll deliver his "extra" 0.5 food to you, and you'll combine that with your 0.5 and give me the 1 unit that I paid you for.

Now you and Farmer Bob are both "sellers." The other 18 good farmers plod along, growing 1.5 and eating the same amount. Our new situation is in column B of Table 11.1a, b. Now with the same expenditure increase of 1, we have an output increase of 1, instead of the 0.5 that we got in Scenario A. (Remember that the extra unit of food that you and Bob produced is offset by the loss of 1 unit from my giving up farming, and then we add back in the 1 unit of output that my investment represents.)

On to scenario C. This time, rather than being unwilling to reduce your consumption, you're unwilling to increase your output. Farmer Bob feels the same way. You make a slightly different arrangement with him:

- You'll each take half the money
- You'll each keep output at 1.5
- You'll each reduce consumption to 1
- He'll deliver his "extra" 0.5 food to you, and you'll combine that with your 0.5 and give me the 1 unit that I paid you for.

While you and Bob keep your output unchanged, I reduce my food output by 1, and instead have my investment output of 1, so food output is down 1 overall, and total output stays at 110.

In scenario D, you're willing to work harder, but not a *lot* harder: you'll increase your output to 1.7, and leave your consumption at 1.5. You find Farmer Bob and another three good farmers who feel likewise, so now five of you are splitting up the revenue you got from me. The results are in the "D" columns of Table 11.1.

Scenario E relaxes the constraint we had in Chap. 9, where 1.5 units was the most anyone can eat. Before you were growing and eating 1.5, end of story. But now I'm offering you the possibility of accumulating savings—remember, you acquire my tokens by engaging in the act of saving, and any tokens that you hold onto represent the savings that you have). And let's say that in response to that prospect you decide to live it up a little now. You're willing to increase your output (which is your income) to 1.7, but you'll also raise your consumption to 1.6. Now you've only got 0.1 units available for me, so if everyone's like you, you'll have to put together a group of 10: you, Farmer Bob, and eight others.

- You'll each take one tenth of the money
- You'll each raise output to 1.7
- You'll each raise consumption to 1.6
- The other 9 will all deliver their "extra" 0.1 food to you, and you'll combine that with your 0.1 and give me the 1 unit that I paid you for.

The 10 of you collectively have increased food output by 2, so once we subtract the food I'm no longer growing, total food has risen to 111.

Columns F, G, and H are left partly blank to be completed as an exercise. But even with those three scenarios being incomplete, we have enough examples to extract the general principles behind them that determine the multiplier.

11.1.1 Multipliers

First, look at the row of Table 11.1, part b, labeled "μ", which gives the multiplier. We want to know how much total output went up when we increased expenditure by 1 unit. To find that, we divide ΔY by Δ[Exp]. In the scenarios of Table 11.1, Δ[Exp] is just 1, so the division is pretty easy, but the idea would work with any Δ[Exp]. We're simply interested in the ratio of the change in output to the change in expenditure that caused it. In the completed examples we can see that the multiplier ranges from $\mu = 0$ to $\mu = 2$ (some additional values should be revealed if you complete Problem 11.6). Remembering that increased income isn't the same as increased revenue,[1] we can link changes in consumption and income to the multiplier in a simple formula:

$$\mu = \frac{\Delta y}{\Delta y - \Delta c} \tag{11.1}$$

If people take the increased revenue but don't increase output ($\Delta y = 0$) then the multiplier is 0. And for a given level of increased output, a bigger increase in people's consumption leads to a bigger multiplier.

We can rearrange this first form of the multiplier by dividing numerator and denominator by Δy:

$$\mu = \frac{1}{1 - \frac{\Delta c}{\Delta y}} \tag{11.2}$$

This highlights the role played by the ratio of increased consumption to increased output.

Remember that what the economy needs to accomplish in each scenario is to free up a unit of food for me to eat while I'm busy not farming. On the one hand, if an individual seller is willing to work harder (Δy is bigger), we don't need as many sellers. On the other hand, if an individual seller wants to keep more of that extra output for themselves to eat, we need more sellers. The net effect is that what matters is neither the individual seller's increase in output, nor the individual seller's increase in consumption, but rather the consumption increase as a portion of the output increase.

[1]Keep in mind that a farmer's "income" here is how much food she produces, not her revenue. Let's say she accepts tokens in payment of food but she doesn't increase her output nor does she decrease her consumption, opting instead to use the tokens to buy the extra food from someone *else*. (This is the situation of Problem 9.2.) Her income in that case is unchanged ($\Delta y = 0$). Her revenue has increased, but her expenditure has increased an equal amount.

Note that this formula works even when the increase in consumption is zero (Scenarios B and D), or even negative (Scenario A). What about Scenario C?

Mathematically, our multiplier formula doesn't work, because $\Delta y = 0$ (the individual sellers don't change their output), and that's the denominator of $\Delta c/\Delta y$, so $\Delta c/\Delta y$ is undefined. Empirically, looking at our table, we can see that $\mu = 0$.[2] Intuitively, the multiplier is zero because there's nothing to multiply. The response to my increased expenditure is not to increase output, but to cut back consumption in order to make food available for me. So my expenditure doesn't lead to any new output; instead, it merely rearranges who gets what, which is what the long-run model of Part II says will happen.

This connection leads us to the concept of crowding out.

11.1.2 Crowding Out

The long-run model of Part II leads to conclusions that are very different from what this little mill exercise suggests. In the long-run model, more spending on one thing means less of something else:

- If you increase consumption, you cut into domestic saving, pushing up the interest rate and thus driving down investment and gross exports.
- If you increase government expenditure, or if you decrease taxes without cutting government expenditure, you again cut into domestic saving.
- If you increase investment, you don't cut into domestic saving, but you do push up the interest rate; international saving has to increase, which is accomplished by gross exports going down.

The same thing is behind all these results: namely, the level of output in the long-run model *is not affected by expenditure*. And that's true by assumption. If you know K, Z, R^s, N^s, and ρ, then you can figure out N^* and Y^*. If output is known before you even look at expenditure, then of course more of one kind of expenditure (say, consumption) must mean less of others (like investment).

In the mill parable, as adapted and extended in this chapter, things are very different. In scenario E above there's a multiplier of 2: one extra unit of expenditure causes output to increase by 2 units. Far from crowding out, my extra unit of investment expenditure has caused other people's consumption expenditure to go *up*.

---

[2]If you're familiar with the concept of limits, you can approach the problem that way. What happens as Δy gets smaller and smaller, heading towards zero? That is, what's the limit of μ as $\Delta y \to 0$? The term Δc in this case is negative, which means that $\Delta c/\Delta y$ becomes a larger and larger negative number, approaching $-\infty$. That implies that $1 - \Delta c/\Delta y$ becomes an ever larger positive number, approaching ∞, and the multiplier in turn is approaching $1/\infty$, which is the same as approaching 0. You can also revert to Eq. 11.1, where there's no problem with $\Delta y = 0$ and we can directly calculate that $\mu = 0$.

But there can still be crowding out. In scenarios A and C, consumption went down by varying amounts in response to my expenditure. Scenario C is like the long-run model, in that total output didn't go up at all. Scenario A is more "moderate": when I spent my 1, output went up by 0.5, so consumption only had to go down by 0.5, rather than by 1. But either way, the logic is the same as in the long-run model. I need a unit of food for my project. If that unit is going to be made available, and people aren't going to produce more to make that happen, then the only other way to accomplish the goal is for some people to reduce their consumption. On the other hand, if output goes up by more than what I need, then there doesn't have to be crowding out at all.

11.2 Logical Limits to the Multiplier

We've tweaked the mill parable to illustrate the logic by which more spending by me can mean *more* for you, not less. So if spending is good, does that mean that more spending is better? If 1 unit stimulated our economy, how about 2? Or 4?

We can see the problem with this idea through a further modification to the story.

We started the chapter with an investment project that cost 1 unit of food, and scenarios A through E worked out different possible consequences. What happens if we have a more expensive investment, one that costs 2 units of food? I want to focus on two of the scenarios: D and E.

In scenario D, each seller is making 0.2 units available for the investment, so we needed five of them; now we need 10. The behavior of the individual seller is the same as above, but with twice as many of them, we see output going up to 112 instead of to 111. The multiplier still works: $\mu = 1$, and an expenditure increase of 2 has led to an output increase of 2.

In Scenario E2, since each seller only provides 0.1 units for the investment, we need 20 sellers. So we get $\mu = 2$, and expenditure of 2 leads to extra output of 4, and extra consumption of 2.

But now we've reached a limit, as we can see by increasing expenditure all the way up to 4. In Scenario D4 things work out as before. We have 20 sellers, and output goes up to 114.

The problem comes in E4. Each seller is only providing 0.1 units of food to the investment project, so to make 4 units of food available, there would have to be 40 sellers. But the setup of the problem was that there are only 20 good farmers who would be in a position to sell. In other words, we've run up against the economy's capacity to produce more. That's why several items in column E4 of Table 11.2 have been replaced with question marks.

I've pulled four regular farmers out of growing food to building my machine, so there are 76 left producing 1 unit each. And I've got all 20 "good" farmers growing 1.7 each, so there are 110 units of food in total. But those 20 good farmers also want to eat 1.6 each. I need 4 units of food, and only 2 are available, so my investment project can't happen.

Table 11.2 Varying responses to greater levels of increased expenditure

Part (**a**)					
Scenario	Initial	D2	E2	D4	E4
Exp	0	2	2	2	2
y	1.5	1.7	1.7	1.7	1.7
c	1.5	1.5	1.6	1.5	1.6
I	0	2	2	4	?
Farmers selling	0	10	20	20	?
Total food	110	110	112	110	110
Y	110	112	114	114	?
Total C	110	110	112	110	108
Saving	0	2	2	4	?
Part (**b**)					
Scenario	Initial	D2	E2	D4	E4
Δ[Exp]	NA	2	2	4	4
Δy	NA	0.2	0.2	0.2	0.2
Δc	NA	0	0.1	0	0.1
ΔY	NA	2	4	4	?
μ	NA	1	2	1	?
$\Delta c/\Delta y$	NA	0	0.5	0	?
$1 - \Delta c/\Delta y$	NA	1	0.5	1	?
$1/(1 - \Delta c/\Delta y)$	NA	1	2	1	?

Will the sellers change their behavior? Will the investor just be out of luck? One way to think of it is that the investor goes and spends a certain amount of money, expecting to walk away with 4 units of food, but she only gets 2—in other words, there's been inflation. Or she could be determined to get 4 units, so she keeps increasing her spending until she convinces the sellers to consume less of their increased output, or to grow more than 1.7 and give her what she wants—again, that would mean there had been inflation.

Either way, these outcomes are exactly the point of this section. The multiplier formula given earlier works *so long as the economic agents are willing and able to respond to increased expenditure by increasing output.*

If an expenditure of 1 unit is good, and an expenditure of 2 units is better, why not spend 10, or 20, or 100? Won't that make us all fabulously wealthy? Obviously not.

This is a key point in understanding multipliers. The long-run model of Part II is misleading in its conviction that expenditure doesn't matter. But expenditure isn't a magical balm for an economy, and the expenditure multiplier isn't a magic wand that automatically spreads expenditure around everywhere. Rather:

Expenditure *influences* how much of current productive ability gets used. But it can't instantly conjure new productive ability into existence, nor can it force individuals to put available productive capacity to work if they don't see that as being a good idea.

11.3 The Standard Keynesian Multipliers

We made our extended detour back into the mill parable both to develop a feel for how the multiplier works and to see the limits of what it can actually do. It's now time to look at the traditional expenditure multipliers based on the expenditure functions from Chap. 5. After working those out, we'll revisit the mill-parable multiplier to see how its lessons apply.

11.3.1 The Aggregate Expenditure Function

Start by looking at the total amount of expenditure on domestic production, called "aggregate expenditure" and denoted "EX". The pieces of this are consumption expenditure, private investment expenditure, government expenditure, expenditure by foreigners on our gross exports, minus our expenditures on our imports. In other words,

$$\mathrm{EX} = C + I + G + GX - IM$$

Our interest in this expression is in how aggregate expenditure depends on income, or Y, so we rewrite it fleshing out those components of expenditure that depend on Y:

$$\mathrm{EX} = C_0 + C_Y(1-t)Y + I + G + GX + IM_Y \cdot Y$$

This implies that when income goes up by ΔY:

- EX increases by $C_Y(1-t)\Delta Y$ as some income is respent;
- EX decreases by $IM_Y \cdot \Delta Y$ as imports go up;
- There's a net expenditure increase of $[C_Y(1-t) - IM_Y] \cdot \Delta Y$

So in response to an increase in income, expenditure is up, and in the Keynesian model that means that income is up, by that same $[C_Y(1-t) - IM_Y] \cdot \Delta Y$. Of that, the same portion $(C_Y(1-t) - IM_Y)$ will be respent, which will amount to $[C_Y(1-t) - IM_Y] \cdot [C_Y(1-t) - IM_Y] \cdot \Delta Y$ or $[C_Y(1-t) - IM_Y]^2 \cdot \Delta Y$. If you keep going and add up all these pieces, you end up with a total increase of

$$\frac{\Delta Y}{1 - [C_Y(1-t) - IM_Y]} \tag{11.3}$$

To look at a numerical example, assume values of $C_Y = 0.8$, $IM_Y = 0.1$, and $t = 0.2$. Then if, say, government expenditure goes up by \$100, that expenditure is somebody's income, so Y has gone up by \$100, and we see that consumption will go up by \$64 while imports will increase by \$10, for a net increase in aggregate expenditure of \$54. That new expenditure is in turn somebody's income, so 54% of *that* will be respent, or \$29.16, which is in turn new income, of which 54% will be respent, or \$15.75, and so on.

The total increase in Y is

$$\$100 + \$54 + \$29.16 + \$15.75 + \$8.50 + \$4.59 + \ldots$$

all of which adds up to \$217.39. Checking that with the formula from expression 11.3, we have

$$\begin{aligned}\frac{100}{1-[0.8(1-0.2)-0.1]} &= \frac{100}{1-[0.64-0.1]}\\ &= \frac{100}{1-0.54}\\ &= 100/0.46\\ &= 217.39\end{aligned} \tag{11.4}$$

11.3.2 Algebraic Treatment

To be more systematic about this, recall that output is made up of consumption, investment, government expenditure, gross exports, and imports: $Y = C + I + G + GX - IM$. And that looks like it should be equal to aggregate expenditure: $\mathrm{EX} = C(Y) + I + G + GX - IM(Y)$. We define equilibrium as the value of Y such that Y and EX *are* equal:

$$Y = C(Y) + I + G + GX - IM(Y).$$

We can then flesh out the functions $C(Y)$ and $IM(Y)$ and solve for Y:

$$\begin{aligned}Y &= C_0 + C_Y \cdot (1-t) \cdot Y + I + G + GX - IM_Y \cdot Y\\ &= C_Y \cdot (1-t) \cdot Y - IM_Y \cdot Y + C_0 + I + G + GX\\ Y - C_Y \cdot (1-t) \cdot Y + IM_Y \cdot Y &= C_0 + I + G + GX\\ Y \cdot \big(1 - [C_Y \cdot (1-t) - IM_Y]\big) &= C_0 + I + G + GX\end{aligned}$$

$$Y = \frac{C_0 + I + G + \mathit{GX}}{1 - [C_Y \cdot (1 - t) - \mathit{IM}_Y]} \tag{11.5}$$

Equation 11.5 shows equilibrium output as a function of the parameters or values of the various expenditure functions. We can simplify it by using two abbreviations. First, the items in the numerator are elements of "autonomous" expenditure—that is, expenditure which is not functionally dependent on Y. Denoting these autonomous expenditures as $\mathscr{A}$, we have

$$\mathscr{A} = C_0 + I + G + \mathit{GX}.$$

Second, define the marginal propensity to expend on domestic output, or the MPE for short. This is the increase in consumption caused by an increase in income, reduced by the increase in imports that comes with an increase in income. In other words,

$$\text{MPE} = C_Y \cdot (1 - t) - \mathit{IM}_Y.$$

With these shorthands, we can rewrite Eq. 11.5 as

$$Y = \mathscr{A}/(1 - \text{MPE}). \tag{11.6}$$

Equation 11.6 is the basis for the expenditure multipliers. Returning to the example in Eq. 11.4, an extra \$100 leads to a change in Y of

$$\Delta Y = \Delta G/(1 - \text{MPE}) = \$100/(1 - \text{MPE}) = \$217.39. \tag{11.7}$$

The rate of increase—how much Y goes up for a dollar increase in G—is

$$\Delta Y/\Delta G = 1/(1 - \text{MPE}) \tag{11.8}$$

The right-hand side of Eq. 11.8 is in fact the expenditure multiplier not only for government expenditure, but for all the other components of autonomous expenditure $\mathscr{A}$ (C_0, I, GX):

$$\mu_E = \frac{1}{1 - \text{MPE}} \tag{11.9}$$

11.3.3 The Tax Multiplier

Getting the tax multiplier is a little trickier than the expenditure multiplier, because we'd like to know the effect of, say, cutting taxes by \$100, but we've defined taxes in terms of the tax rate t rather than the number of dollars collected T. It's true that $T = t \cdot Y$, and so it's tempting to think that the change in the tax amount should just be the change in the rate times income, or $\Delta T = \Delta t \cdot Y$. The problem is that when you change t you also change Y, so to be more accurate we have to say that the relationship is only approximate:

$$\Delta T \cong \Delta t \cdot Y. \tag{11.10}$$

That approximate relationship will be one component in our derivation of the tax multiplier. We also need to get a handle on how much Y changes in response to a change in t, or $\Delta Y/\Delta t$. We can approximate that by taking the derivative of Y with respect to t, which doesn't tell us exactly what would happen if we dropped t, say from 20% to 18%, but it does tell us the rate at which Y changes right as we start changing t from its initial value. Differentiating Eq. 11.5 with respect to t gives us

$$dY/dt = -C_Y \cdot \mathscr{A}/(1 - \text{MPE})^2. \tag{11.11}$$

(If you know calculus, you might try to replicate the derivation of this.)

Now we're ready to work out the tax multiplier, the amount that Y changes for a change in T, or $\Delta Y/\Delta T$. Along the way we'll use the approximation from expression 11.10 and the observation that $\Delta Y/\Delta t \cong dY/dt$.

$$\begin{aligned}
\Delta Y/\Delta T &\cong \Delta Y/(\Delta t \cdot Y) \\
&= (\Delta Y/\Delta t)/Y \\
&\cong (dY/dt)/Y \\
&= \left(-C_Y \mathscr{A}/(1 - \text{MPE})^2\right) / \left(\mathscr{A}/(1 - \text{MPE})\right) \\
&= -C_Y/(1 - \text{MPE}) \\
\mu_T &= -C_Y/(1 - \text{MPE}) \qquad (11.12)
\end{aligned}$$

There are three things to notice about μ_T. First, it has the same denominator as the expenditure multiplier μ_E.

Second, it's negative, because of its numerator; if you cut taxes (so that the change in the amount of tax collected is a negative number) that leaves people with more after-tax income to spend, so expenditure and output should go up, which is what the multiplier tells you when you multiply a negative tax change times a negative tax multiplier.

Third, the tax multiplier has a smaller magnitude than the expenditure multiplier because $C_Y < 1$. So a \$100 tax cut should have somewhat less effect than a \$100 increase in government expenditure. There's some sense to that relationship. When the government spends \$100, that's already an extra \$100 of expenditure, and then some of that gets respent (\$54 in the earlier example), and some of *that* gets respent, and so on. If you take a \$100 tax cut, that's not itself a form of expenditure. It increases what's in people's pockets, but they only spend some of it (say, \$54), so the initial \$100 isn't part of the expenditure.

This leads to the balanced-budget multiplier. If I increase government expenditure by \$100 but also increase taxes by \$100 to keep the budget balanced (or to keep it from moving further into the red), how will GDP be affected?

The increase in G will raise GDP by $\$100/(1-\text{MPE})$. The increase in T will lower GDP by $\$100/(1-\text{MPE})$. So the net gain is $\$100 \cdot (1-C_Y)/(1-\text{MPE})$. Remembering that the tax multiplier is approximate, we can conclude that the balanced-budget multiplier is (approximately):

$$\mu_{BB} = \frac{1-C_Y}{1-\text{MPE}} \tag{11.13}$$

11.3.4 Sanity

The Keynesian multipliers provide a quick and easy way of estimating how changes in spending or taxes should affect an economy, but as Sect. 11.2 argued they need to be used with a sense of proportion.

Suppose you have an economy where GDP is \$300,000, and the parameters of your expenditure functions translate into a balanced-budget multiplier of $\mu_{BB} = 0.33$. What should happen to your economy if you raise G by \$100 and also raise T by \$100? Your income should rise by $\$100 \cdot 0.33 = \$33$.

What about an extra \$100,000 in G and T? The naïve answer is that Y will go up by \$33,000. But in reality it can't be that easy to boost GDP by 11%. Think about that extra \$100,000 in tax revenues. That represents a tax hike as big as 33% of current GDP, on top of whatever taxes were already being collected. Is the economy really going to respond well to that sort of change?

Remember the form of the multiplier from Sect. 11.1.1 (Eq. 11.2):

$$\mu = \frac{1}{1-\frac{\Delta c}{\Delta y}} \tag{11.14}$$

Note that $\Delta c/\Delta y$ is essentially the marginal propensity to consume (how your consumption will change for every extra dollar of income), and that in the self-contained economy of the mill parable, where there are no imports or exports, the marginal propensity to consume is essentially the same as the marginal propensity to expend on domestic production. Then we have:

$$\mu = \frac{1}{1-\frac{\Delta c}{\Delta y}} = \frac{1}{1-MPC} \cong \frac{1}{1-\text{MPE}} \tag{11.15}$$

In other words, the Keynesian expenditure multiplier is directly related to the multiplier from the world of the mill parable. That earlier version includes a term specifically about increased output in response to expenditure, which means it can help us understand the limitations of the tool. These limitations show up in the differences between increases in nominal output and increases in real output.

11.3.5 Nominal vs. Real

The standard Keynesian multipliers say that increased expenditure is somebody's increased revenue, and that's true. They also implicitly assume that increased revenue gets turned into increased output.

But what if that second step doesn't actually hold?

One response to that question is to reinterpret the standard multipliers as boundary cases that hold when increased revenue translates one-for-one into increased real output. The actual effect is reduced by a couple of factors.

One of those is the possibility of physical difficulty in increasing real output. Perhaps there's no available labor. Perhaps your physical capital is already heavily utilized. Maybe you can't get your hands on increased flows of resources.

It's possible that psychological factors could play a role as well. A business agreeing to expand output will likely have to incur expenses in advance of receiving the revenue. Uncertainty, for instance about customers' ability to actually pay when the time comes, could limit the translation of revenue into output.

As with the case of the multiplier from the mill parable, if expenditure goes up without a corresponding increase in output, then there should be an increase in prices, which points to the need to distinguish nominal effects from real ones. We've worked out the multipliers in terms of real output Y, but it would be more accurate to do it in terms of nominal output PY. New expenditure doesn't have to turn into new real output, but it is nonetheless someone's revenue. Chapter 16 on aggregate supply and aggregate demand will build on this distinction, with aggregate expenditure being in nominal terms while aggregate demand deals with real quantities.

Problems

Problem 11.1 Start with the parameters from Table 11.3:

(a) Calculate the MPE, i.e., the marginal propensity to expend (on domestic production).
(b) Calculate autonomous expenditure (the quantity denoted in the chapter as $\mathscr{A}$).
(c) Calculate the equilibrium level of output Y for the values given in Table 11.3.
(d) Starting from your answer for Y, calculate the values of C, IM, NX, T, S_P (private saving), S_G (public saving), and I.

Table 11.3 Parameters for Problem 11.1

G:	260
I:	200
GX:	90
C_0:	100
C_Y:	0.7
IM_Y:	0.15
t:	25%

(e) Now assume a recession causes I to fall to 150, while everything else in Table 11.3 remains unchanged. What is the new value of Y?
(f) Calculate the same components of Y as in Question 11.1d, but with the new value of Y from Question 11.1e.

Problem 11.2 Calculate two values of the expenditure multiplier μ_E, first with MPE = 0.7, then with MPE = 0.6. How does a larger MPE affect the expenditure multiplier? Why does that make sense?

Problem 11.3 Assume $C_Y = 0.8$, $t = 0.2$, and $IM_Y = 0.1$.

(a) Calculate the MPE.
(b) Calculate μ_E and μ_T.
(c) Increase C_Y to 0.9 and calculate the new MPE.
(d) With the new value of $C_Y = 0.9$, calculate the new values of μ_E and μ_T.
(e) How does an increase in C_Y change μ_E? Why does that make sense?
(f) How does an increase in C_Y change μ_T? Why does that make sense?
(g) How does an increase in C_Y change the relative sizes of μ_T and μ_E? Why does that make sense?

Problem 11.4 Start with $C_Y = 0.8$, $t = 0.25$, and $IM_Y = 0.1$.

(a) Calculate MPE.
(b) Change IM_Y to 0.15 and recalculate MPE.
(c) How does an increase in IM_Y change MPE? Why does that make sense?

Problem 11.5 Table 11.4 shows a part of an economy with a contractor (BuildCo), a steel company (SteelCo), an ore-mining operation (OreCo), and an energy supplier (EnergyCo). The three companies SteelCo, OreCo, and EnergyCo only sell their products to the other companies in this table, while BuildCo sells its services to the rest of the economy. Also, BuildCo's output will often be a piece of capital, which means that the revenue BuildCo earns is someone else's investment expenditure—in other words, what BuildCo sells is part of final demand.

The table shows BuildCo with revenues of 50,000. It spends 5,000 on energy (which then shows up as part of EnergyCo's revenue) and 20,000 on steel (see SteelCo's revenues). It spends 20,000 on wages (see "Labor") and has profits of 5,000. The "Value added" is the sum of the lines for "Labor" and "Profits". The columns for the other firms work similarly.

Table 11.4 Starting figures for Problem 11.5

	BuildCo	SteelCo	OreCo	EnergyCo	GDP
Revenue	50,000	20,000	5,000	13,000	
Energy expenditure	5,000	5,000	3,000	0	
Steel expenditure	20,000	0	0	0	
Ore expenditure	0	5,000	0	0	
Labor	20,000	8,000	1,500	10,000	
Profits	5,000	2,000	500	3,000	
Value added	25,000	10,000	2,000	13,000	
GDP by final demand	50,000	0	0	0	50,000
GDP by value-added	25,000	10,000	2,000	13,000	50,000

Table 11.5 Altered figures for Problem 11.5

	BuildCo	SteelCo	OreCo	EnergyCo	GDP
Revenue	60,000	24,000	6,000	?	
Energy expenditure	6,000	6,000	3,600	0	
Steel expenditure	24,000	0	0	0	
Ore expenditure	0	?	0	0	
Labor	24,000	9,600	?	12,000	
Profits	6,000	2,400	600	?	
Value added	?	12,000	2,400	15,600	
GDP by final demand	60,000	0	0	0	?
GDP by value-added	30,000	12,000	2,400	15,600	?

Since BuildCo is the only company here whose output is part of final demand, the line for "GDP by final demand" is the same 50,000 as BuildCo's revenue.. "GDP by value-added" reaches the same total, but shows each firms's individual contribution toward creating the total value of the things BuildCo sells.

Table 11.5 shows an altered situation where the government has paid BuildCo an additional 10,000 to build a new bridge.

(a) Fill in the spaces in the table that have question marks, using the relationships among the parts to figure out what the missing values must be.
(b) In this example, how much did GDP go up because of the government's increased expenditure?
(c) What differences between the two tables suggest further increases in GDP in the near future? What does that have to do with multipliers?
(d) What happens if OreCo is incapable of increasing its output beyong the 5,000 worth of ore it's selling in Table 11.4?

Problem 11.6 Extend the patterns of Scenarios A through E to fill in the empty cells of Table 11.1.

Problem 11.7 Work out the consequences in Scenario G if I increase my expenditure by 4 (that is, if I try to buy 4 units of food, rather than zero).

Chapter 12
Monetary Policy

Abstract We look first at the aims of monetary policy in terms of balancing the control of inflation with limiting excessive unemployment. The next consideration is the interaction between the money supply and economic activity. Turning to the actual mechanics of monetary policy, we address the issue of how the money supply is measured, including the various definitions of money. The specific tools discussed include not merely the traditional emphasis on open-market operations, but also the emergency measures and quantitative easing that have turned out to be important in the post-2007 era. The appendix provides an example of an open-market operation.

12.1 The Aims of Monetary Policy

The mill parable of Chap. 9 illustrated how the creation of money can influence *real* economic activity: the mill builder created some money, which enabled him to carry out the project of building the mill, something that would have been difficult or impossible without the social coordination enabled by using money.

At the same time, the discussion of multipliers showed how more spending doesn't necessarily have to lead to more output (Sects. 11.3.4 and 11.3.5). If producers are unable or unwilling to increase output, then more spending will lead to higher prices, but not to more output (and without increasing output, it's hard to increase employment).

So we have some basic facts about changes in the economy's quantity of money. Providing the economy with more money might lead to more spending, and this spending can either increase output (and thus employment), or it can push up prices, or it can do some combination of those things.[1]

The basic goal of monetary policy is to see to it that the economy has enough money to support a rate of growth and employment that policy makers think is "good," while not causing there to be so much money that inflation becomes a serious problem.

[1]This range of possible outcomes is the focus of Chap. 16.

K. Seeley, *Macroeconomics in Ecological Context*, Studies in Ecological Economics 5, DOI 10.1007/978-3-319-51757-5_12

If you think the economy is "underperfoming" and unemployment is too high, encourage there to be more money. If you're worried about inflation taking off, pull back.

That's monetary policy in a nutshell. The rest of this chapter is simply about how that is actually done.

12.2 Who Makes Monetary Policy

Monetary policy is carried out by a country's central bank, such as the Federal Reserve System in the U.S., the Bank of England in the United Kingdom, and the European Central Bank for the eurozone, the group of countries who use the euro as their currency.

Current practice is for central banks to be somewhat independent of a country's government. The idea is that elected governments (or even dictatorships that don't want their public to be mad at them) will face pressure to stimulate the economy too much, resulting in high inflation. An independent central bank will—in theory—pursue what's best for the economy as a whole.

In the U.S. the Federal Reserve System is overseen by a Board of Governors whose members are appointed by the president, subject to confirmation by the Senate. That gives a degree of political influence, but governors are appointed for single terms of 14 years, so they have time to take a long view, and the impossibility of reappointment provides some insulation from presidents' and senators' views once they're on the job. The chairman and vice chairman, also appointed by the president and confirmed by the Senate, have terms of only four years and *can* be reappointed (Alan Greenspan served as chairman from 1987 to 2006), so the elected officials have more influence there, but the chairman (or chairwoman), while influential, only has one vote on the board.

Within the Federal Reserve, the Federal Open Market Committee (see below in Sect. 12.5.1) is made up of the seven Federal Reserve governors, plus five of the presidents of the twelve regional Federal Reserve banks (the president of the Federal Reserve Bank of New York is always among the five, due to New York's out-sized importance in the country's financial system). The presidents of the regional Federal Reserve Banks are chosen by a subset of their directors, subject to the approval of the Board of Governors in Washington, and some of the directors are chosen by the private banks that are members of a given district. The result is that policy in the FOMC is under a subtle mix of public and private influences.

In the eurozone, the running of the European Central Bank (ECB) is an even more complicated affair, partly as a result of the bank's unusual position. It is the central bank for the eurozone, which includes most but not all the member countries of the European Union (of the EU members that aren't in the eurozone, the United Kingdom is the most significant in the global economy). In the U.S. there is a single national government carrying out fiscal policy and a single national currency overseen by the Federal Reserve. The eurozone has a single currency (the euro) and a single central bank, but as of January, 2017, there are 19 national governments, each with their own fiscal policy (within limits prescribed by the euro system) and their own political calculations and economic goals and challenges. The EU itself, including the non-eurozone members, is largely an economic entity with some common political bodies—not quite a United States of Europe, but a group of countries more closely tied to each other than the U.S. is to anyone.

The operation of the ECB is, therefore, not only a mix of public and private as in the U.S., but also a balancing of different countries' national interests. The potential difficulties created by such a system are most visible in the crisis surrounding debts of the Greek government, which has been a contentious issue in the eurozone since 2009.

12.3 The Money Supply

We've spent four chapters now approaching money through the back door, as it were, starting with stories to try to understand its deep role in the economy (the coordinating mechanism tying together the decentralized actions of people all over the economy) and the basic nature of money (a system of promises).

Now we're ready to look at the actual data and see what they reveal. In the mill parable, I controlled all the aspects of the story, so we could easily calculate how much money there was: it was whatever amount the story said had been created. Out in the real world, what should we measure if we actually want to figure out how much money there is in the economy and how that changes over time?

12.3.1 Definitions of Money

In practice, measurable definitions of money are built up out of the various things that people use as means of payment.

- To the average person the most obvious component is currency (paper bills, coins). The part of it that counts is what is held by the public, i.e., not in a Federal Reserve Bank or the vault of a depository institution (see the example of a cash loan in Sect. 10.3.2).
- Your checking account also acts as money: it's an account on which you can write checks or pay with a debit card.
- And your savings account is pretty close to that: in the old days, you could walk into your bank and withdraw as much of it as you wanted, and in the new days many savings accounts let you walk up to an ATM and pull out currency.

- Next, there are "money-market mutual funds," accounts that lend your money on short term to businesses (in the "money market") and give you the ability to write checks on it.
- For completeness, we can throw in travelers checks, though they're a tiny amount compared to the other items.

If we add up these terms, we get what is known as "money of zero maturity," or MZM (see [9, p. 19]). This odd-sounding name doesn't mean that the money hasn't yet learned how to behave, but refers to "maturity" in the financial sense. This may be clearer if you compare it to how a bond works.

When you buy a bond, you're lending someone money, which they can spend right away. They're obligated to pay you back, but only at some time in the future. Let's say in May, 2012 you buy a $1,000, 3-year bond paying 5%. In other words, you paid about $864, and in May, 2015, the borrower will pay you $1,000 (that works out to your $864 earning 5% per year for three years). We say that your bond "matures" in three years. Of course it's worth something even before then: at any time, I (or someone else) may decide I like the prospect of being paid in May, 2015, so I might offer to pay you for the bond; if you accept, the borrower now owes *me* $1,000 in May, 2015, instead of owing *you*.

But I'm under no obligation to offer you the face value of the bond—I can pay you whatever price you and I agree on. If it's May, 2014, the "fair" value would be about $952. That would give you your 5% annual return for the two years you owned the bond, and it would give me a 5% return for the remaining year until maturity. But I could offer $920, or $900, and if you accept, then the bond is mine. And why would you accept less than the face value? Because you need the money back sooner than May, 2015. The bond is only definitively worth $1,000 at that point—that's when its "maturity" has fallen to zero. Before then, its maturity is some positive amount of time: 3 years, 2 years, a few months. At zero maturity, it's worth $1,000; at any positive maturity, it's worth whatever someone's willing to pay for it, and so it trades at an uncertain price.

Money, in contrast, has a very certain price, because $1 of money is always worth exactly $1. The point of the MZM measure is that everything in it is usable as purchasing power on a one-for-one basis. Other assets, like bonds, have to be converted into money before they can be used to buy everyday things, and the conversion to money takes place at unpredictable prices.

So we'll generally use MZM as our measure of "money," but there are other terms you may encounter, primarily M1, M2, and M3 (though M3 has been discontinued by the Federal Reserve, so it's getting ever less likely that you'll see it). As you go up from M1 through M3, you're getting a broader definition of money; that is, you're including more and more things. But none of them is exactly MZM. Either they leave something out (M2 leaves out large money-market accounts, and M1 leaves out *all* of them), or they include something that doesn't have zero maturity (such as time deposits—better known as "certificates of deposit," where you give your money to a bank for a fixed period of time, and you pay a penalty if you want your money back earlier than that fixed time).

The other term that's useful here is the "monetary base." When we introduced state-based money in Chap. 9, the central idea was that state money is money that has value because the state accepts it in payment of taxes. The monetary base is made up of money that meets that condition:

- Currency outstanding
  - This means currency held by individuals or companies, plus currency sitting in the vaults of banks that aren't Federal Reserve Banks. Of course, it's generally impractical to pay your taxes with coins and dollar bills, but I imagine if you found the right office you could do it.
- Banks' reserve balances at the Federal Reserve.

These two forms of money that make up the monetary base are direct claims on a very specific thing: the ability to satisfy your tax obligations. The rest of the money supply—all the money that banks create when they make loans—is claims on the monetary base.

The monetary base is important for monetary policy, because it is the part of the money supply that the Federal Reserve controls directly.

12.4 The Relationship Between the Money Supply and Economic Activity

Chapter 6 presented the equation of exchange:

$$M \cdot V \equiv P \cdot Y, \tag{12.1}$$

a statement that *must* be true, just by virtue of how the terms are defined: the quantity of money, multiplied by the number of times each dollar gets spent in a year, must be equal to the price level times real GDP (which is to say, nominal GDP). Back in Chap. 6 we had two assumptions built in that allowed us to draw a particular conclusion about the effect of changes in the money supply. The first assumption was that Y was fixed; remember, this was the long-run model, where *real* GDP was determined strictly by the physical productivity and available quantities of real factors of production (labor, capital, technology, and resources). The second, introduced almost in passing, was that V was also fixed.

If both those assumptions are true, then it must also be that the only possible effect of changing M would be a change in P. Put another way, if you increase the money supply, you can't have any effect on the *real* economy; all you will do is push up the price level (cause more inflation). But both those assumptions are faulty, at least in the short run.

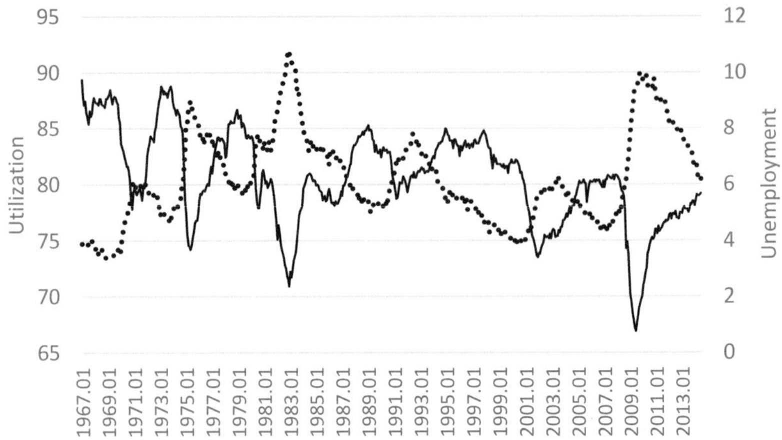

Fig. 12.1 Total capacity utilization (From Federal Reserve Board of Governors), and the Civilian Employment-population ratio (From Bureau of Labor Statistics)

First, business cycles are poorly explained by fluctuations in the *availability* of factors of production. Figure 12.1 illustrates fluctuations in the portion of physical capital actually being utilized and the portion of the workforce actually being employed. When we have a recession, it's generally not that we have a shortage of productive inputs; rather, it's that we aren't making use of the ones we have. That in turn suggests that Y is not determined strictly on the supply side. (Chapter 18 will discuss the real business cycle theory, which argues that recessions result from rational, optimal supply responses to changed technological conditions, which is related to what is being discussed here.)

Second, velocity is not constant, as Fig. 12.2 shows. Rearranging Eq. 12.1, we see that $V \equiv \frac{M}{PY}$, or in words, velocity is the supply of money, divided by nominal GDP. Figure 12.2 shows the velocity of MZM, M1, and M2 from 1959 into 2014. While M2's velocity is fairly steady, M1 and MZM show large changes over time, and even M2 can vary its velocity by over 5% from one quarter to the next.

So we need to consider a range of possible outcomes in addition to the link between increased money and higher prices. If the money supply increases, but velocity and the price level don't change as much, then we *will* in fact see an increase in real GDP. And if the money supply increases but real GDP doesn't change, that doesn't necessarily mean we'll get inflation, because the velocity of money could decrease.

And we don't have to limit ourselves to causality running *from* money to effects on real GDP. In the mill parable, the creation of money allowed an investment to happen—it allowed me to mobilize the resources I needed in order to create the mill. But the creation of money was completely tied up with the investment itself: I didn't create the money "on speculation," as it were, assuming that someone would find a good use for it. I had a specific, credible idea for an investment, an action that

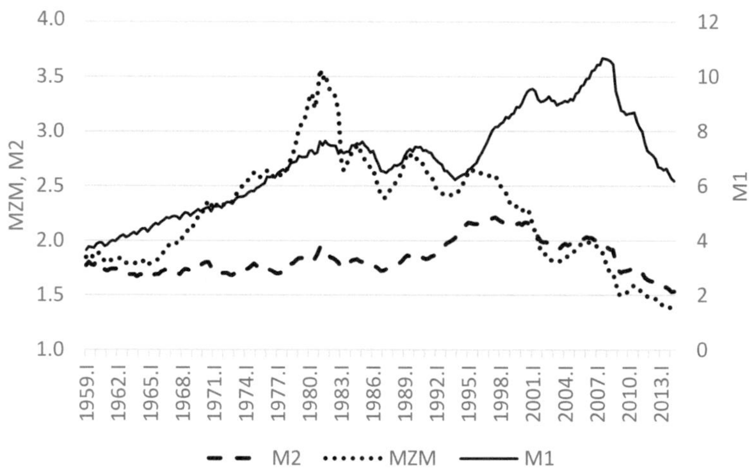

Fig. 12.2 Income velocity of MZM, M1, and M2. Velocities calculated based on nominal GDP (From Bureau of Economic Analysis) and monetary aggregates (From the Federal Reserve Bank of St. Louis)

my neighbors believed would lead to greater wealth in the future. That belief was the real "backing" of the money I created.

In fact, in the actual economy, not just the made-up world of a parable, we see something similar. Remember from Chap. 10 that banks create money, and that the way they do that is by making loans—not loans at random, but loans to specific people and firms, for specific plans that have been laid out for the bank.

What this means is that it's possible for the causality to run either way. Rather than a change in the money supply causing a change in real GDP, it can also be that new investment plans (if banks decide to fund them by creating money) simultaneously cause a change in the GDP and a change in the money supply. This is related to what is known as the theory of "endogenous" money, which holds that banks decide how much to lend, thereby creating money in a process "endogenous" to the economy, and the Federal Reserve creates the reserves needed to accommodate the lending (see [15]).

A more conventional approach focuses on a kind of multiplier based on the relationship between the monetary base and the money supply: the central bank acts "exogenously" by increasing the monetary base (by increasing reserves), and banks respond by making more loans so as to keep the old reserve ratio. This process is certainly possible, but note that even if the Fed *is* acting exogenously rather than responding to and accommodating banks' lending decisions, it can't *force* its alterations of the base to be translated into changes in the money supply (except when banks are already at their minimum required reserves and the central bank reduces those reserves further). The money supply is thus jointly determined by the central bank and by the lending decisions of banks, and those lending decisions are affecting the economy's performance and responding to it at the same time.

12.5 Tools for Influencing the Money Supply

Central banks have various tools for affecting the supply of money in an economy. For many years, the only one worth studying at an introductory level was "open-market operations," but events since 2008 have highlighted the importance of the other ways that a country's monetary authority can try to influence the economy.

12.5.1 Open-Market Operations

The most routine tool in a central bank's toolbox is what are known as "open-market operations." The goal is to change the quantities of reserves that commercial banks have on their books, which in turn should change how willing those banks are to make loans.

If the Federal Reserve wants to increase bank reserves, it lets it be known that it wants to buy some Treasury bonds (that's the "open market" part). Some entities agree to sell some Treasury bonds that they own (the "entity" could be a bank, or it could be a non-bank company or a private individual). The Fed pays for the bonds by paying the seller. If the seller is a bank, then ownership of the bond is transferred to the Fed, and the check is transferred directly to the bank's reserves (there's an increase in the bank's balance at the Fed). If the seller is something other than the bank, the chain has an extra step: the seller takes the check to his or her bank and deposits it. The bank then brings the check to the Fed (since that's who issued it), and the Fed increases the bank's reserves by the amount of the check. (The appendix walks you through an example of an open-market transaction, complete with balance sheets.)

Either way, the net result of the Fed buying Treasury bonds in open-market operations is that bank reserves are increased. The key is that the Fed can pay for things by creating monetary base. When the bond seller brings the Fed's payment to the bank, the Fed increases that bank's reserves (part of the monetary base) without having had to decrease some other amount of money somewhere else.

And it can run the exact same operation in the other direction if it wants to decrease reserves: it finds someone willing to buy a Treasury bond from it; when the buyer pays, the Fed takes that payment and brings it to the appropriate bank; in order to clear the payment, the bank's reserves are reduced by the same amount, which in turn lowers the monetary base.

What does this have to do with banks' willingness to lend? Remember that in the U.S. banks have reserve requirements: their reserves have to be at least as large as a defined portion of the deposits on their books. If a bank ends the day short on reserves, it has to cover that shortage somehow, and the most common way to do it is to borrow reserves from other banks.

You can see from Fig. 12.3 that banks generally keep little more in reserves than they are required to. In December, 1999 there's a spike in required reserves, which

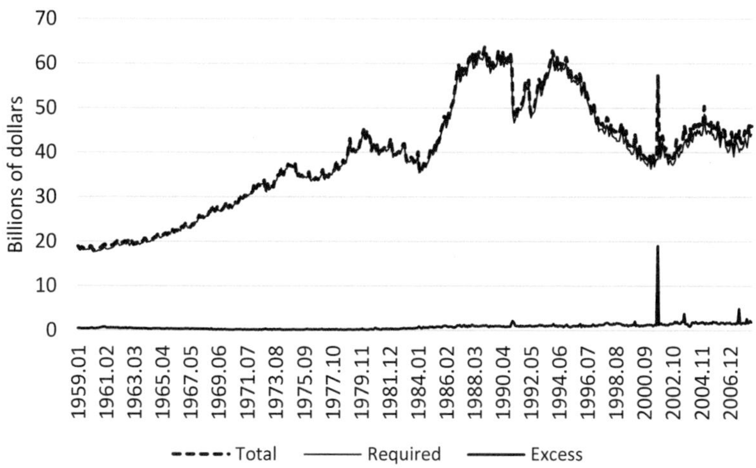

Fig. 12.3 Reserves, required reserves, and excess reserves, through July, 2008. Total and Required from Federal Reserve Board of Governors; Excess from Federal Reserve Bank of St. Louis

was the Federal Reserve making sure banks were ready for Y2K (the concern that there would be computer glitches as the year-count went from 1999 to 2000). And in September, 2001 there was a spike in excess reserves, as the Fed flooded the banking system with extra reserves to keep things stable in the wake of the attacks of September 11, 2001. But otherwise, required reserves grow (in spurts) along with the economy, and excess reserves are kept to a minimum.

The interest rate at which banks lend reserves to each other is called the Federal Funds rate (since it's the interest rate on balances, or "funds," held at the Federal Reserve). The Federal Reserve doesn't directly tell banks what rate to use—they can lend and borrow at whatever interest rate both sides of a deal agree to. But the Federal Reserve *can* for all practical purposes set the rate. The more reserves there are in the banking system, the less need banks will have to borrow reserves from other banks. With less need for borrowing, the interest rate on that borrowing should be lower.

The execution of open-market operations makes use of this relationship. The Federal Open Market Committee (FOMC) sets a "target" for the Fed Funds rate—maybe 5%, maybe 2.75%, maybe 0.25%; the FOMC can choose whatever rate it thinks will be best for achieving its policy goals. Bond traders at the Fed then carry out open-market operations to whatever extent necessary to see that the Fed Funds rate that banks are setting for each other is the level that the FOMC has specified.

If the bond traders see the interest rate getting too high, they know the system needs more reserves in order to bring the rate down, so they buy some bonds, causing banks' reserve balances to go up. If the traders see the rate going too low, they sell some bonds, bringing reserves down.

And as Fig. 12.4 shows, they do their job pretty well. If you stand back so that you can't see the wiggles, the "target" Fed Funds rate is pretty clearly visible, and the

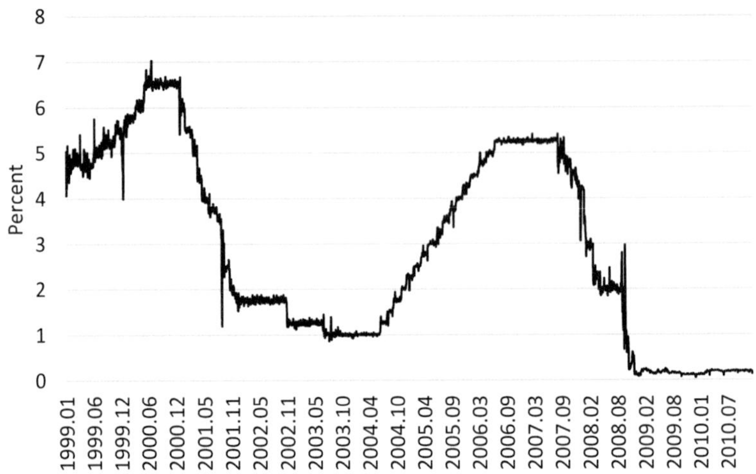

Fig. 12.4 The effective Federal Funds rate (From Federal Reserve Board of Governors)

wiggles show the deviations around that. They're almost all insignificantly small. The big "errors"—when the open-market desk couldn't keep the rate so close to the target—come around Y2K (New Year's 2000), September 11th, 2001, and the Lehman Brothers bankruptcy in September, 2008.

But what does this have to do with banks' willingness to lend to the general public?

When a bank makes a loan, it has to weigh two factors. On the positive side, there's the interest to be earned on the loan (with some allowance being made for the chance that the borrower won't repay). On the negative side, the loan will require the bank to acquire more reserves, or it will push it closer to the reserve requirement, increasing the chance that it will need to borrow in the Fed Funds market.

If the Fed Funds rate is low, then it won't cost the bank much to borrow the extra reserves it needs. As the Fed Funds rate rises, it becomes more and more costly to obtain those funds, and so a bank should become more hesitant to make a loan.

By carrying out open-market operations and changing banks' costs of borrowing reserves from each other, the Fed should be able to influence banks' willingness to make loans, and thereby influence the level of economic activity.

12.5.2 The Discount Rate

I said above that the Federal Funds rate is an interest rate that banks charge each other when one bank borrows reserves from another. The discount rate is different. It's the rate that the Federal Reserve charges member banks when they borrow from what's called the "discount window" of the Federal Reserve itself. Since the Federal

Reserve is the lender, it can set the interest rate directly. (This is in contrast to the Federal Funds rate, where banks set the rate to whatever they can agree on among themselves, but the Federal Reserve influences it through open-market operations.)

It used to be that the discount rate was set a little bit below the target for the Fed Funds rate. It would seem that this would cause banks to only borrow from the Fed's discount window—why pay some other bank 3% interest when you can borrow from the Fed and only pay 2.5%? The solution was to discourage banks from going to the discount window by means of reviewing a potential borrower's request to see if it was for an appropriate purpose and that other "reasonably available sources of funds [had] been exhausted" [11, p. 315]. In the early 2000s the procedure was switched, with the discount rate now being set about 0.5% to 1% *above* the Fed Funds target. That way it acts as a backstop: if banks can borrow cheaply from each other, they will, but if something causes banks' willingness to borrow to shoot up, or their willingness to lend to collapse, the discount rate keeps the Fed Funds rate from skyrocketing.

12.5.3 Reserve Requirements

In many countries the central bank imposes a reserve requirement: in order for a bank to have access to the services of the central bank, it must maintain some minimum quantity of reserves. In the U.S. these requirements are defined as a percentage of "net transaction accounts" (roughly speaking, the amount of checking-account balances at a bank, modified by other payments the bank reasonably expects to receive).

If the money supply is (approximately) the sum of everybody's checking-account balances, then you can see the relationship between reserves and the money supply. If the reserve requirement is 10%, then a bank with reserves of $400 million can have checking accounts worth $4 billion. If it already has $4 billion of checking accounts on its books, then it can't make additional loans (and thus create additional transaction deposits) unless it gets hold of more reserves.

This leads in turn to how reserve requirements can be used as a tool of monetary policy. If the central bank wants to increase the money supply, it can lower the reserve requirement. In the case above, if the central bank lowers the reserve requirement from 10% to 8%, the same $400 million in reserves can now support $5 billion in transaction accounts instead of $4 billion ($400 million is 8% of $5 billion). Raising reserve requirements obviously has the opposite effect.

There is an asymmetry here: If banks have only their required reserves, or not much more, then raising the reserve requirement will clearly force banks to reduce their lending in order to stay in compliance. On the other hand, reducing reserve requirements *allows* banks to make more loans, but doesn't *require* them to.

Changes in reserve requirements are a less common tool than open-market operations. The key purpose of reserves is not to affect the money supply, but to provide safety in the banking system: adequate reserves are supposed to ensure that a few days of unusual claims on a bank don't bring a solvent bank to the point of being unable to pay. Given that primary role, when the central bank is setting reserve requirements it should principally consider what it thinks is necessary to keep the banking system functioning, rather than what effect it wants to have on the money supply.

Note that not every country has reserve requirements—Canada, for instance, manages without them. Canadian banks still have reserves, but they choose their level based on their own assessment of what they need in order to operate reliably and profitably. It's clearly a viable system in principle, since Canadian banks came through the financial crisis of 2008 better than U.S. banks, but it does mean that the central bank in such a system can't use reserve requirements as a policy tool.

12.5.4 Emergency Measures

September, 2008 was a very scary time in the world of finance. The long-established financial firm Lehman Brothers went bankrupt in the middle of the month, and it was unclear to what extent the entire financial system was a house of cards.

In the earlier part of the 2000s, housing prices had risen in what many people considered to be a bubble. Bank balance sheets included significant amounts of MBS (mortgage-backed securities)—financial assets whose value was based on homeowners continuing to pay what they owed on their mortgages. But with house prices falling, unemployment starting to rise, and high energy prices hitting household budgets, mortgage default rates started rising.

In principle it was clear that the value of MBS was falling, but there was an additional wrinkle. The MBS themselves were very complicated instruments, involving repeated recombinations of obligations to pay, so it was hard to figure out how much any individual bank was actually affected.

There were two intertwined fears. The first was that many banks would be found to be insolvent once the true value of all the MBS was worked out. The other was that even solvent banks would be severely damaged as the insolvent banks failed to fulfill financial obligations they had to the solvent ones.

The Fed had already started expanding its set of tools in late 2007 with something called the Term Auction Facility, which was a new way of increasing the cash on banks' balance sheets. In March 2008 they added the Term Securities Lending Facility as a way of adding treasury securities to bank balance sheets. In Fig. 12.5, this is the period where the dotted "Other assets" area is increasing while the gray "US Treasury securities" area shrinks, and the total keeps rising at its usual, modest rate. The Fed was in essence carrying out a trade with banks: it was buying "other assets"—presumably relatively risky ones—from the banks, and using Treasury securities to pay for them. This improved the balance sheets of private banks, because they no longer had so many risky items on them.

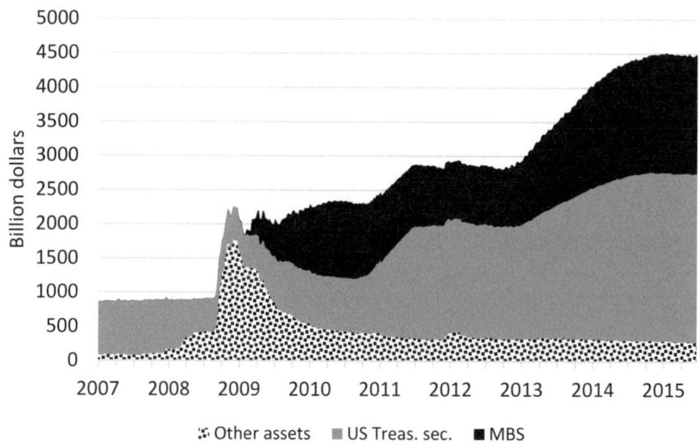

Fig. 12.5 Assets on the Federal Reserve balance sheet, simplified. Federal Reserve Board of Governors, Table H.4.1

After the Lehman Brothers collapse, the Fed massively expanded its actions, buying far more "other assets," but this time it didn't pay for them by giving banks Treasury securities—you can see in Fig. 12.5 that the dotted area expands and the gray area rises right with it. The Fed was paying for the assets by creating reserves and giving them to the banks (in other words, increasing the banks' balances with the Federal Reserve).[2]

The emergency measures were very controversial at the time: the Fed was engaging in creation of monetary base on a massive scale and handing "free money" to banks. The justification was that, without such drastic measures, the banking system would have collapsed, and a bad downturn would have turned into a catastrophic depression.

12.5.5 *Quantitative Easing*

By March, 2009, the worst of the crisis was past—people were no longer worried about a general collapse of the banking system—but unemployment was still rising and the stock market was still falling. And the Federal Reserve's Open Market

[2]At the same time, Congress passed and President Bush signed the Troubled Assets Relief Program, or TARP, in which the government allocated money for the Treasury to buy "troubled assets"—that is, things like MBS which were becoming unsellable. Like the Fed's emergency measures, it was meant to stabilize the banking system and consisted essentially of giving the banks money. But rather than being funded through the creation of money like some of the Fed programs, it was funded by government purchasing power, based on tax revenues and debt, and so it was part of fiscal policy.

Committee had already dropped the discount rate essentially to zero.[3] In other words, they had adopted a "zero interest-rate policy," or "ZIRP," which also meant they had run into the zero lower bound, or "ZLB."

The zero lower bound represents the fact that, in practice, the Federal Reserve can't force the nominal Federal Funds rate below zero. The most it can do is provide such a large quantity of reserves that banks are willing to lend to each other essentially for free; there's no amount that would cause banks to pay one another to lend rather than to borrow. So if the Fed Funds rate is already at zero and the Open Market Committee feels that's not enough stimulus, there's nothing more they can do with that tool and they have to turn to other options.

The tool they adopted in 2009 was something called "quantitative easing," which happened in three rounds. The first one entailed spending up to $1.75 trillion buying MBS and federal agency debt [2].[4] The first round ended in March 2010, and can be seen in Fig. 12.5 with the expansion of the solid black area.

QE 2 started in November, 2010 and ran through June, 2011, involving the purchase of $600 billion in US Treasury securities [3]. This shows up as the expansion of the gray area around the middle of Fig. 12.5.

QE 3 was announced in September, 2012, and this time it would be open-ended: the Fed would buy $40 billion a month of MBS until there was a large enough improvement in the labor market [5]. This was on top of a program begun in September, 2011, under which every month the Fed sold about $45 billion worth of its holdings of U.S. Treasury bonds that had maturities of less than three years and used the sale proceeds to buy other bonds with maturities from six to 30 years [4]. The purpose of this was to keep down not just the short-term interest rates more easily affected by the Federal Funds rate, but to put direct downward pressure on longer-term rates as well. That's potentially important, since many purchases are funded with longer loans. At the beginning of 2013, the Fed continued the purchase of longer-term Treasury securities at $45 billion a month, without selling shorter-term securities, so that all in all it was spending $85 billion a month [6].

Starting in December, 2013, the Fed began "tapering" QE 3, pulling back its purchases by $10 billion every meeting (i.e., every six weeks). Purchases ended in October, 2014 [7], but as of June, 2015, the bank was holding onto the assets that had been bought in the course of the program [8].

Taken all together, there was a radical expansion of the Federal Reserve's balance sheet. During the week of September 17th, 2008, its balance sheet showed assets of just under a trillion dollars, and it had been growing smoothly at about 5% per year since 2002. Just two months later the number was over $2 trillion, and the various emergency measures would push it up to nearly $4.5 trillion by September, 2014. From September, 2008 to September, 2014, the growth rate averaged about 30% per year.

---

[3] "[a] target range for the federal funds rate of 0 to 1/4 percent" [1].

[4] "Federal agency debt" is debt of agencies that were chartered by the federal government to buy existing mortgages and thus make it easier for banks to provide mortgages.

We'll look at the effect of these actions in Chap. 17, but for now we can ask, Where did the money go? And the simplest answer is that it went onto bank balance sheets and stayed there, without being loaned out. "Excess reserves"—the amount of reserves that banks hold beyond what Federal Reserve regulations require of them—were about \$2.3 billion at the beginning of September, 2008. Two months later they had shot up to \$600 billion. By June, 2014, they were at \$2.6 trillion. From September, 2008, to September, 2014, the Federal Reserve increased its assets by \$3.4 trillion; at the same time banks increased their excess reserves by \$2.6 trillion. Problem 12.2 explores this further.

12.6 Monetary Targeting, Inflation Targeting, Taylor Rules, Nominal GDP Targeting

Section 12.1 gave very general guidance as to what a central is trying to accomplish: supporting decent growth while not provoking inflation. But that's not the only way of conceiving of the role of a monetary authority.

Milton Friedman and others advocated monetary policy that simply had the money supply grow at a steady rate. Say you thought the long-run growth rate of the economy was 2.5%; then you could have the money supply grow at 4.5% and, over the long run, inflation would have to be about 2%. After all, remember Eq. 6.1, stating that $MV \equiv PY$. If M is growing steadily, then over the long run the growth of P would just be the growth of M minus the long-run growth of Y.

The hope was that, if economic actors could predict the long-run level of inflation, that would improve business conditions. Also, the knowledge that the monetary authority wouldn't be trying (in a possibly misguided way) to smooth out recessions would further increase predictability, thus making it easier for the economy to get out of recessions on its own.

There were two problems with this idea, however. First, it depended on the idea that V was relatively constant, and as Fig. 12.2 shows, that wasn't true. Second, there are multiple ways of defining "money", and while you could in principle pick any one of them, they behave in different ways, so the implementation of your rule would depend on which version of money you chose to target.[5]

An alternative to monetary targeting is inflation targeting, a self-explanatory policy: the monetary authority chooses a cap they'd like inflation to stay under, or a range that they'd like it to fall in. Then they look at recent inflation and forecast

[5]Mishkin [12] documents the relative success of monetary targeting in Germany, but notes that it included the flexibility of being long-run targeting, rather than keeping strictly to the goal on the level of month-to-month or quarter-to-quarter results, as well as the flexibility to consider other factors, such as exchange rates or output. It was thus, in effect, a lot like the generalized goal of supporting decent growth while not provoking bad inflation.

inflation. If inflation is too low, they expand the money supply and/or lower interest rates, and do the opposite if inflation is too high.

An advantage over monetary targeting is that it goes directly at the goal of an inflation rate that is low and stable. Monetary targeting had the same goal but was premised on the idea that velocity was stable. In fact, as Mishkin [12] points out, the German implementation of monetary targeting included a forecast of the trend of velocity, precisely because of the recognition that velocity could change. Inflation targeting acknowledges the unstable link between inflation and growth in the money supply and tells you to do what you have to with the money supply in order to have stable.

The idea behind inflation targeting is that monetary policy can't affect anything real in the long run, and even in the short run, when it arguably *does* have an impact, its use is likely to introduce harmful uncertainty into the economy. So instead of having multiple, amorphous goals, monetary policy should simply aim at the one thing that it is thought to be able to reliably influence in the long run, and that is the price level.

An additional motivation is to constrain government spending. If the inflation-targeting policy is chosen by a country's government, it implies that government's almost contractual obligation not to run deficits that would create undue inflation for the monetary authority to fight. On a more direct level, it raises the cost of borrowing to finance the budget if the government does choose to run large deficits: deficits will tend to be inflationary, and so the central bank will be forced to raise interest rates, rather than making deficit spending easy for the government by keeping rates low.[6]

Another popular idea is a Taylor Rule, which is somewhat like a formalized version of the generalized policy guidance for a central bank: boost GDP from slumps while not letting inflation get out of hand. The formulation from Taylor's original article setting out the rule [14, Eq. 1, p. 202] can be written as

$$i = \pi^a + 0.5 \cdot \frac{Y - Y^*}{Y^*} + 0.5 \cdot (\pi^a - 0.02) + 0.02, \tag{12.2}$$

where i stands for the Federal Funds rate, π^a is inflation (averaged over the most recent four quarters), and Y and Y^* are actual and potential GDP, respectively.

The -0.02 in the parentheses with π^a means that there is an inflation target of 2%; if inflation is higher than that, you will raise your policy interest rate.

The two terms of 0.5 mean that equal weight is given to deviations from potential GDP and deviations from targeted inflation.

These deviations from potential GDP are known as the **output gap**. The most consistent way to express it is as a percentage above or below potential GDP. If potential GDP is \$14.5 trillion and actual GDP is \$14.3 trillion, then the output gap is -1.4%.

[6] See [10].

The 0.02 on the end means that your "equilibrium" policy interest rate—the level you should choose when GDP and inflation are both right where you want them—is *2% in real terms* (notice that the first item on the right-hand side is the inflation rate, so the 0.02 at the end is added on to that). This "neutral" interest rate of 2% is chosen for its combination of simplicity and closeness to an assumed long-run real GDP growth rate of 2.2%.

The article introducing this formulation talks about "discretion vs. policy rules," and that's an important part of how to think about it. The rule's guidance on how to respond to output gaps and inflation implies a more active role for monetary policy than what monetary targeting would suggest, but by setting out a rule on how to respond, the monetary authority makes its actions more predictable: nobody knows what the Federal Funds rate will be in the future, because we don't know future levels of GDP or inflation, but if the monetary authority adopts the Taylor Rule we *do* know how it will respond to whatever path of inflation and GDP we end up seeing.

In addition to the predictability that such a rule provides, the particular version laid out in Eq. 12.2 embodies specific assumptions (the 2.2% long-run growth rate mentioned above) and policy choices (2% inflation being a good target; equal weight given to output gaps and inflation). There's no reason in principle we couldn't change any of those choices.

The predictability provided by such a rule, with whatever parameters it contains, may have some benefits, but the Federal Reserve's adoption of quantitative easing in various flavors suggests that it may not be sufficient in all cases. A more general policy guideline is the idea of targeting nominal GDP (e.g., [13]). Like a Taylor Rule, this has the effect of balancing GDP growth and inflation: if nominal GDP is higher than your target because of inflation, or because of worryingly fast growth in real GDP, the central bank is asked to pull back; if nominal GDP is below the target, whether because real GDP growth has been slow or because inflation is below target (possibly even negative), then stimulus is called for.

As Sumner [13, p. 321] points out, in addition to opening up to more tools than just the interest rate, a policy of targeting a level of nominal GDP has the advantage over a Taylor Rule that it doesn't rely on knowing the level of potential GDP, a quantity that can never be observed. On the other hand, it does require us to decide what we think is a reasonable, desirable growth rate of nominal GDP.

12.7 Conclusion

This chapter has been about the goals and tools of monetary policy. An assessment of how well it works is deferred until Chap. 17, when it can be considered together with fiscal policy and with the benefit of the analytical tools developed in Chaps. 14 through 16.

Appendix: An Open-Market Operation

Let's actually start not with an open-market operation, but just with a regular private transaction. Alice is a depositor at Bank A, so her savings is a part of the line labeled "Deposits" on Bank A's balance sheet (I've simplified the balance sheet to focus on just the parts that are important for this example). Similarly, Bob is a depositor at Bank B.

Bank A		
	Assets	L & E
Reserves	500	
Deposits		5,000
Other	4,800	300
Total	5,300	5,300

Bank B		
	Assets	L & E
Reserves	600	
Deposits		6,000
Other	5,850	450
Total	6,450	6,450

Let's say Alice has a Treasury bond that she'd like to sell; either she wants to spend the money on some goods or services, or she wants to buy some other asset (a different bond, or some stocks) that she thinks better suits her current needs. Alice and Bob agree on a price of $40.

Bob writes Alice a check for $40 and she sends him the bond (or some valid electronic documentation of ownership). We don't have to worry about the bond anymore, because it wasn't on either bank's balance sheet (it was wealth that Alice had, but not wealth that was stored in a bank account). But we can track what happens to the check.

When Alice gets the check, she'll take it to Bank A and deposit it. That will increase "Deposits" at Bank A by $40. Then Bank A will bring the check to Bank B and say, "Your customer Bob wrote this to our customer Alice, so give us $40." Bank B will transfer $40 worth of reserves to Bank A, and it will reduce Bob's account (and thus its total of "Deposits") by $40.

Once the transaction is completed, the new balance sheets will look like this:

Bank A		
	Assets	L & E
Reserves	540	
Deposits		5,040
Other	4,800	300
Total	5,340	5,340

Bank B		
	Assets	L & E
Reserves	560	
Deposits		5,960
Other	5,850	450
Total	6,410	6,410

Bank A does indeed have more reserves, but Bank B has fewer, and so the quantity of reserves in the banking system as a whole is unchanged.

In an open-market operation, one side of the transaction is not a private individual like Alice or Bob, nor is it a regular bank; it's the Federal Reserve. Say Alice decides to sell another bond, but this time to the Fed, which is carrying out an open-market transaction. Alice gets another $40 check and deposits it. Bank A's "Deposits" line goes up by another $40. But now it takes the check to the Federal Reserve instead of to Bank B. The Fed honors the check by increasing Bank A's reserves, and it doesn't have to decrease reserves at Bank B or anywhere else.

The balance sheets below show the situation after this second transaction; comparing to the previous table, you can see the increase in total reserves of the two banks together. If the Fed were to sell a bond rather than buying it, the process would operate in reverse: the money received by the Fed for the sale would end up coming out of the total reserves of the banking system.

Bank A		
	Assets	L & E
Reserves	580	
Deposits		5,080
Other	4,800	300
Total	5,380	5,380

Bank B		
	Assets	L & E
Reserves	560	
Deposits		5,960
Other	5,850	450
Total	6,410	6,410

Problems

Problem 12.1 Figure 12.6 shows the effective Federal Funds rate for 1954 through 1984, with the shaded bars indicating U.S. recessions; Fig. 12.7 shows the same thing for 1985 into 2015.

Compare the two figures. What has changed in the relationship between the Federal Funds rate and the onset of recession?

Problem 12.2 Figures 12.8 and 12.9 show excess reserves as a share of potential GDP, for two different time spans.

(a) In Fig. 12.8, the sharp spike in the chart is during September, 2001. What happened at that time that might have caused that phenomenon and why might it have been a good idea for the Federal Reserve to provide banks with a large quantity of additional reserves, suddenly and for only a short time?

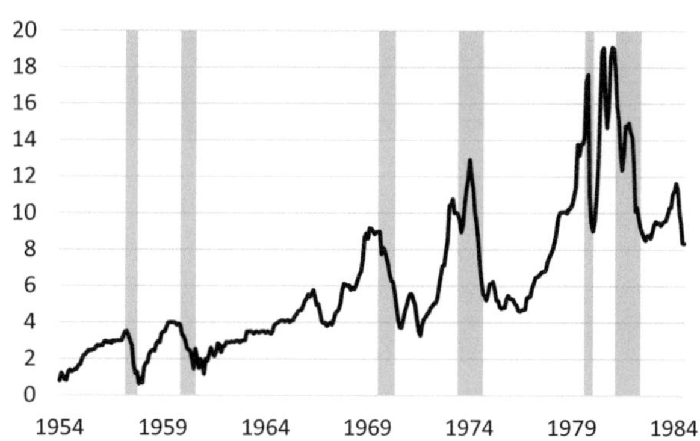

Fig. 12.6 The effective Federal Funds rate, in percent, 1954–1984; from Federal Reserve Board of Governors (Shaded areas show U.S. recessions)

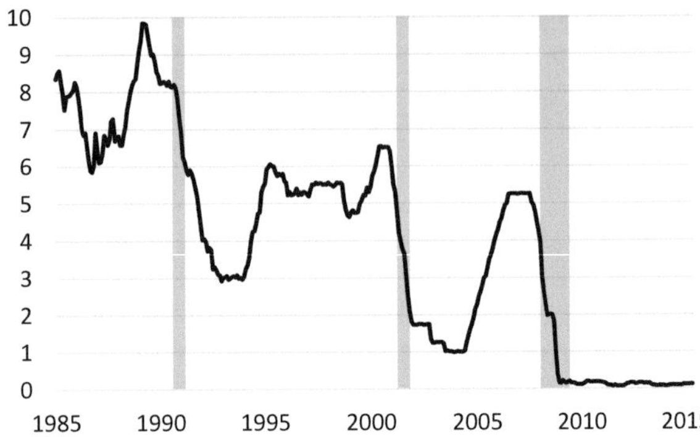

Fig. 12.7 The effective Federal Funds rate, in percent, 1985–2015; from Federal Reserve Board of Governors (Shaded areas show U.S. recessions)

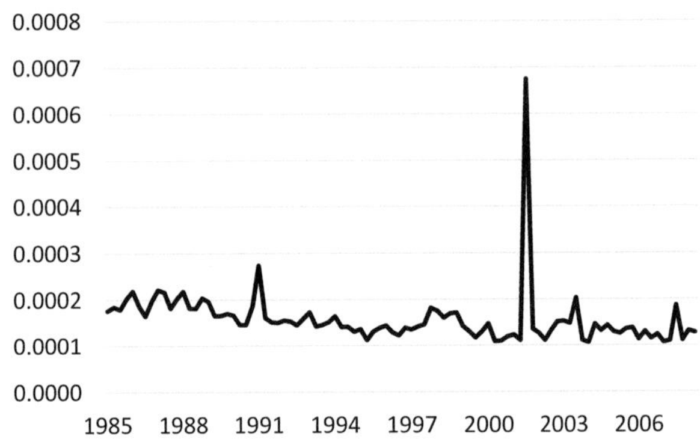

Fig. 12.8 Excess reserves of depository institutions, as portion of potential GDP, 1985.I – 2008.II (Data from Federal Reserve Bank of St. Louis (reserves) and Congressional Budget Office (potential GDP))

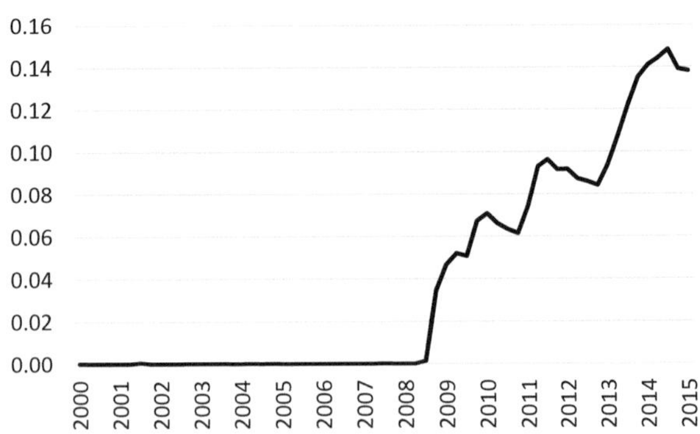

Fig. 12.9 Excess reserves of depository institutions, as portion of potential GDP, 2000.I – 2015.I (Data from Federal Reserve Bank of St. Louis (reserves) and Congressional Budget Office (potential GDP))

(b) The first eight-and-a-half years shown in Fig. 12.8 are the same as the last eight-and-a-half years of the span covered in Fig. 12.9, yet that span (January, 2000 through July, 2008) look very different in Fig. 12.9 than in Fig. 12.8. Why is that?

(c) Comparing the two charts, what is the approximate ratio between excess reserves in 2015 and excess reserves during the mid-2000's, when both are expressed as shares of potential GDP?
(d) What does your answer to (c) suggest about where the money for quantitative-easing purchases has been going?

Problem 12.3 Assume your central bank is operating under a modified Taylor Rule: your assumed long-run neutral interest rate is 1.8%, your inflation target is 2.5%, and you put equal weight on the output gap and inflation.

(a) Your average recent inflation is 2.8% and your estimated output gap $[(Y - Y^*)/Y^*]$ is 0.4%. What interest rate would you choose based on this version of the Taylor Rule?
(b) Is your answer in (a) a rate that is likely to hold back growth or spur it higher? Explain.
(c) Recalculate the Taylor-Rule interest rate with recent inflation of 2.2% and an output gap of −0.5%.
(d) Is your answer in (c) a rate that is likely to hold back growth or spur it higher? Explain.
(e) Calculate once more, with an output gap of −1% and recent inflation of 3.2%.
(f) How does your *real* interest rate in (e) compare to the assumed neutral rate? Explain why that is.

References

1. Federal Open Markets Committee. Press release, December 16th 2008.
2. Federal Open Markets Committee. Press release, April 29th 2009.
3. Federal Open Markets Committee. Press release, November 3rd 2010.
4. Federal Open Markets Committee. Press release, 2011.
5. Federal Open Markets Committee. Press release, September 13th 2012.
6. Federal Open Markets Committee. Press release, December 12th 2012.
7. Federal Open Markets Committee. Press release, October 29th 2014.
8. Federal Open Markets Committee. Press release, June 17th 2015.
9. Monetary Trends. Federal Reserve Bank of St. Louis, July 2015.
10. Fischer, A. M. (1993). Inflation targeting: the [N]ew [Z]ealand and [C]anadian cases. *Cato Journal, 13*, 1–27. Spring-Summer.
11. Madigan, B. F. & Nelson, W. R. (2002). Proposed revision to the Federal Reserve's discount window lending programs. In *Federal Reserve Bulletin* (pp. 313–319). The article is available at https://www.federalreserve.gov/pubs/bulletin/2002/0702lead.pdf.
12. Mishkin, F. S. (2000). From monetary targeting to inflation targeting: lessons from the industrialized countries. In Presentation at Bank of Mexico Conference, "Stabilization and Monetary Policy: The International Experience", November 14–15, 2000. https://www0.gsb.columbia.edu/faculty/fmishkin/PDFpapers/00BOMEX.pdf. Accessed June 17th, 2015.
13. Sumner, S. (2014). Nominal GDP targeting: a simple rule to improve Fed performance. *Cato Journal, 34*, 315–337. Spring/Summer
14. Taylor, J. B. (1993). Discretion versus policy rules in practice. *Carnegie-Rochester Conference Series on Public Policy, 39*, 195–214.
15. Wray, R. L. (2012). *Modern money theory: A primer on macroeconomics for sovereign monetary systems*. New York: Palgrave Macmillan.

Chapter 13
Fiscal Policy

Abstract After the treatment of multipliers in Chap. 11 and the discussion of monetary policy in Chap. 12, the mechanics of fiscal policy are relatively straightforward. This chapter addresses those briefly, distinguishing between automatic stabilizers and active policy, then addresses questions of how well fiscal policy works and factors that are likely to make it more or less effective. An exercise walks the reader through the rough contours of the 2009 stimulus bill.

13.1 The Aims of Fiscal Policy

As with monetary policy, the aim of fiscal policy is to keep the economy at a place that is considered "good," or to get it *back* to such a place if you think you're not there. In principle, fiscal policy can concern itself with inflation. In practice, people are more likely to advocate active fiscal policy in response to a situation of high unemployment than out of concern over the level of prices.

13.2 Mechanics of Fiscal Policy

The core idea of fiscal policy flows from the way the multiplier works, as developed in Chap. 11. All else being equal, when government increases its expenditure, that new expenditure represents an increase in someone's income, and to the extent that they respend some of the increased income, there's a multiplier effect that should cause GDP to grow by something more than just the increase in government expenditure. Similarly, when there's a reduction in taxes collected, that leaves more purchasing power with households, and to the extent that some of that increased purchasing power is spent, the tax cut should stimulate an increase in GDP. The expenditure and tax multipliers summarize the cumulative predicted impacts of the chain of spending and respending. Of course, the multiplier model suggests that *cuts* in government expenditure or *increases* in taxes collected should result in a *smaller* GDP.

Within that basic structure, it's important to distinguish between automatic stabilizers and active fiscal policy.

K. Seeley, *Macroeconomics in Ecological Context*, Studies in Ecological Economics 5, DOI 10.1007/978-3-319-51757-5_13

13.2.1 Automatic Stabilizers

In a recession there are very predictable changes in government revenue and outlays as a result of the condition of the business cycle—things that happen without any change in policy. First, the government collects less revenue, because fewer people have jobs, business profits are down, and taxable sales are down. Second, government outlays go up—not necessarily expenditures, but several programs involving transfer payments: unemployment insurance, food stamps, and so on. Both of these are exactly what you want in a recession: the decreased tax collection and the increased outlays will both tend to boost GDP, just when a business-cycle contraction is dragging it down. Because they happen without any need for a new policy, they're called "automatic stabilizers".

13.2.2 Active Fiscal Policy

As the name suggests, active fiscal policy is when you *do* implement a change in policy. Instead of just collecting less in taxes because fewer people have jobs, you actually cut tax rates. And instead of just having spending go up because social-insurance programs have more people who qualify, you can:

- Increase benefit payments or extend benefit payments past their usual expiration.
- Pay for more teachers, or police officers, or soldiers, etc.
- Pay for additional infrastructure spending.
- Reduce tax rates.
- Give tax rebates.

As a practical matter, in the U.S. it's only the federal government that can operate stimulative fiscal policy, and there are two reasons for that.

1. Most states and cities within the U.S. require themselves to run balanced budgets. It's not that they can't borrow—after all, there's a whole market specifically in municipal bonds. But that borrowing has to be for capital expenses, like a highway, a school bus, or a sewage treatment plant.[1]

   What states and municipalities generally can't do is borrow to run an operating deficit. If your tax revenues are less than your expenditures (including payments you owe on any past borrowing), then you have to dip into your rain-day fund, if you have one. If you exhaust your rainy-day fund, then you have to either collect more in taxes or cut spending somewhere.

[1]Note that this is not deficit spending; it's a rational and fair way of financing capital expenditures. If you build a new sewage facility, it benefits people for the next 30 years. So it makes sense to have taxpayers pay for it over 30 years by repaying a loan, rather than having this year's taxpayers shoulder the whole thing while future taxpayers get a free ride.

So states have no practical option of stimulating their economies by increasing spending without raising taxes, or cutting taxes without reducing spending.

2. States would be vulnerable to "leakage" of any stimulus they did manage to provide. Remember that in the expenditure and tax multipliers of Chap. 11, the parameter IM_Y was in the denominator, as a part of MPE. A bigger IM_Y means a smaller MPE, which in turn means smaller expenditure and tax multipliers.

   Now think about how much an individual state "imports" from the rest of the country. Cars are bought all over the country, but produced in only a few states. Produce is purchased all over, but for many crops the majority is grown in California. And so on. For the purposes of the multiplier, a state within the U.S. can be thought of a country with a very high IM_Y, and therefore a very low ability to get much bang for its buck if it were to try using fiscal stimulus.

13.3 Who Makes Fiscal Policy

In Chap. 12 we saw that monetary policy is carried out by a country's central bank, which usually has a degree of independence from the government. Fiscal policy concerns how much money the government pays out and how much it collects in taxes, and those decisions are made directly by a country's legislative and executive branches. In the U.S. that means Congress and the president.

Taxes and government outlays are the result of laws directing people to pay certain taxes and authorizing the government to spend certain amounts of money for various purposes. The president is free to *propose* anything he (or she) wants, but a potential law has to be introduced by a member of Congress before it can even be voted on to become a law. Similarly, Congress can pass anything it wants, but after Congress passes a measure the president has a chance to veto it to stop it from becoming law. Congress in turn can try to override a veto, which requires two thirds of the members of each house to vote in favor of an override. All of this occurs against the background of particular laws needing to get passed by Congress and signed by the president, or the Federal government won't have the authority to pay most of its workers and the government will shut down, as happened in Fall, 2013.

The system gives varying amounts of policy-making power to various groups and individuals, based on factors such as how much unity different groups can muster within their own ranks, the players' perceptions of who will be blamed for a failure (such as a shutdown), and the willingness of Congress and the president to engage in brinksmanship in pursuit of their goals.

It's a fascinating process if you're into that sort of thing, but a messy one. The policies it produces are unlikely to match anyone's vision of ideal; they may not even be in spitting distance of rationality, but it's how fiscal policy is made.

13.4 Fiscal Policy, the Multiplier(s), and Timing

The exercises in Chap. 11 made things look relatively simple: you look at the expenditure functions, take C_Y, IM_Y, and t, and just do your calculations. If the values of those parameters end up telling you that $\mu_E = 1.5$, then you can predict that raising G by $10 million will raise Y by $15 million.

Which all sounds simple enough, except that it's very hard to estimate the actual multiplier. Terms like C_Y and IM_Y are not immutable constants of the universe, like the speed of light. They are nothing more than behavioral regularities, ways that people *tend* to behave. The economist Robert Solow has observed, "We should not be trying to find 'the' multiplier: the effects of fiscal policy are highly regime dependent."[2] That means that the effect of any given fiscal policy doesn't depend only on the policy itself, but on broader factors in the economic environment.

There are two big sources of instability in the multiplier, things that will make it different in one situation than in another. One of those sources is the kind of consideration introduced in Chap. 11, looking at whether firms are both *able* and *willing* to respond to increased expenditure with increased output. The second factor is monetary policy. Let's say the government undertakes a stimulative fiscal policy, but the central bank is worried about how that policy will increase inflation. So the central bank introduces a restrictive monetary policy of higher interest rates, cancelling out the stimulative effect of the fiscal policy.

In addition, it can be hard to know what to count as "fiscal stimulus." The American Recovery and Reinvestment Act of February, 2009, was billed explicitly as an attempt at boosting the economy out of the recession that was already at that point quite deep (though it would get worse). In contrast, the tax cuts of 1981 were not sold as efforts to stimulate the economy out of a recession, but as supply-side improvements. Think of them in terms of the long-run model of Part II. Remember that tax cuts or increases in government expenditure don't *directly* change Y in that model, but taxes are a disincentive to work. So if taxes are reduced, the equilibrium level of employment should go up, and output with it. In that model the economy is never out of equilibrium, but it can put its productive forces to work more effectively if the government gets out of the way. In other words, lower taxes are seen as a way of achieving a higher long-run level of output.

However, the way a tax cut is described and the way it acts may be two different things. Supply side theory said that the government should get out of the way not only by reducing taxes, but by reducing expenditure as well. The tax cuts happened, but the expenditure cuts didn't. The net impact (along with the effect of the recession itself) was a government budget deficit that was large by peacetime standards (recent budget deficits have been larger still). So although it was called something else, the 1981 suite of tax cuts may in practice have been a stimulus package.

---

[2] Quoted in [1].

Another issue is the question of timing.It's not a simple matter to read the economy's performance. Unemployment and inflation data come in pretty quickly—for example, the February unemployment figures are released in early March. Many other signals show up pretty close to real-time, such as weekly unemployment claims, hiring data, figures on sales of houses, etc. The GDP itself, however, is only calculated quarterly. We get our first estimate of GDP about a month after the quarter ends, and it takes another few months for the Bureau of Economic Analysis to come to a more stable view of what the most reliable number is.

Then by the time we know we're in recession and some stimulus might be warranted, it's not necessarily easy to get it passed and implemented. As explained in Sect. 13.3, the government's spending and taxing actions are based on bills passed by Congress and signed by the president. If those two can't agree, adoption of a stimulus program will be slow. Then the tax provisions might not even apply to the current year, but will be implemented for the year *after* the stimulus program is passed. And expenditure provisions might take a few months to get ramped up and actually have the money going out the door. If the recession is a mild one, it's possible that it will have ended on its own before active fiscal policy has had any chance to have an impact.

13.5 Conclusion

The mechanics of fiscal policy are relatively simple, particulary in comparison to the details of monetary policy. The difficulties in implementing it are similarly straightforward. A look at the arguments and evidence about whether it works is deferred to Chap. 17, where the two types of policy are considered together.

Problems

Problem 13.1 The stimulus bill of 2009 can be looked at as having three big parts:

1. $355 billion in increased federal expenditure, everything from highways, to Amtrak, to purchase of electric cars for the federal government's vehicle fleet.
2. $144 billion in "fiscal relief" to state and local governments, to enable them to avoid cuts in education and health or to avoid tax increases
3. $288 billion in a wide range of reduced tax collections.

Say the state and local fiscal relief goes half to avoided spending cuts and half to avoided tax hikes. That $72 billion in avoided spending can be in a sense added to the $355 billion in increased federal expenditure, for total expenditure of $427 billion. Similarly, the $72 billion in avoided tax hikes can be added to the federal $288 billion in tax reductions to get a total of $360 billion in tax cuts.

(a) Assume the expenditure multiplier is 1.5 and the tax multiplier is 0.5. What does that imply about the total expected impact of the stimulus package on GDP?
(b) The stimulus wasn't all carried out in one year. If the bulk of it was carried out over two years, how much stimulus effect was there per year?
(c) When the American Recovery and Reinvestment Act (ARRA) was being debated, the most recent available GDP data concerned the 4th quarter of 2008. The nominal GDP was around $14,550 billion dollars, while nominal *potential* GDP was around $15,330 billion. Based on those numbers, how much stimulus would be needed in a year to close the gap between actual and potential GDP?

Reference

1. Romer, D. (2011). What have we learned about fiscal policy from the crisis? In *IMF Conference on Macro and Growth Policies in the Wake of the Crisis*. https://www.imf.org/external/np/seminars/eng/2011/res/pdf/DR3presentation.pdf. Accessed June 12, 2014.

Chapter 14
The IS and LM Curves

Abstract The IS-LM model is a tool for understanding the effects of monetary and fiscal policy when interest rates are allowed to vary. This chapter derives the IS and LM curves and addresses the factors that determine their shape. For each one, a graphical explanation is followed by an algebraic derivation that allows a quantitative description of how far a curve will move in response to a given change in the economy.

14.1 Overview of the IS-LM Model

In the earlier model of aggregate expenditure and Keynesian multipliers, interest rates and prices were implicitly held constant. But changes in fiscal or monetary policy, or in investor outlook, consumer confidence, or the balance of trade clearly *should* affect interest rates and prices.

The IS-LM model leaves prices fixed (for now) but provides a way of understanding the interaction between changes in the interest rate and changes in output.

The underlying idea is that there are two markets: the output market and the money market. If each of them is in equilibrium, then the economy as a whole is at its overall equilibrium.[1]

The IS curve describes equilibrium in the goods market; the LM curve describes equilibrium in the money market. The intersection of these two curves is, therefore, the one combination of r and Y where the whole economy is in equilibrium.

[1] An alternative way of explaining this is to see money demand as based on a choice between storing your wealth as money or as non-money assets (simplify by calling those "bonds"), so there are *three* markets: output, money, and bonds. But equilibrium in the market for money implies equilibrium in the market for bonds, so we can get away with only considering two markets: output and money.

K. Seeley, *Macroeconomics in Ecological Context*, Studies in Ecological Economics 5, DOI 10.1007/978-3-319-51757-5_14

14.2 Overview of the IS Curve

The IS curve captures equilibrium in the output market, where goods and services are produced and bought. (The derivation of the term "IS" is explained in the appendix on "The meaning of 'IS' and 'LM'.") Every point along the IS curve represents a combination of an interest rate and a level of output at which the output market is in equilibrium.[2]

The IS curve slopes down to the right (in Cartesian terms, its slope is negative).

The IS curve is shifted by fiscal policies and by "autonomous" changes in investment and consumption behavior or net exports.

In Fig. 14.1, interest rate r_1 and output level Y_1 are consistent with equilibrium in the output market, so together they define a point on the IS curve. If the interest rate drops to r_2, the output market will be out of equilibrium unless output increases to Y_2, so the point (r_2, Y_2) is another point on the IS curve.

14.3 The Shape of the IS Curve

The basic things we need to know about the IS curve are why it slopes down, and what factors make it either flat or steep.

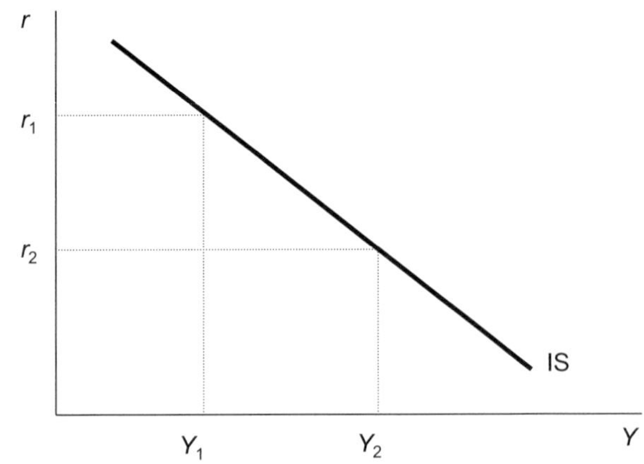

Fig. 14.1 The IS curve

[2]In John R. Hicks' original formulation in the 1930s (see description in [2]), this was the "goods" market. Changing the terminology to "output" avoids potential confusion in an era when so much of our GDP and employment is linked to services rather than goods.

14.3.1 Why Does it Slope Down

First a little intuition. When interest rates are lower, people want to spend more money. If they're trying to spend more money, there had better be more things for them to buy, so a lower interest rate requires higher output for equilibrium to be maintained.

Now get a little more technical: for the output market to be in equilibrium, everything made must be sold. If the economy produces something and it goes unsold, the output market is out of equilibrium; output has to go down or expenditure come up for equilibrium to be restored. Similarly, if people want to buy things that have not been produced, the output market is out of equilibrium; output has to be increased or expenditure decreased in order for us to once again be at equilibrium.

In even more technical terms, equilibrium means that output (which is the same as income) is equal to expenditure. Denoting output as Y and expenditure as EX, we have:

$$EX = Y.$$

The next step is to be more specific about what constitutes expenditure. The four sectors buying the economy's output are: consumers (C), businesses making investments (I), the government (G), and net exports (NX):

$$EX = C + I + G + NX. \tag{14.1}$$

So far, this is the same approach as was taken to get the expenditure multipliers in Chap. 11. But in this case we're going to focus on the interest-sensitive components, rather than the parts that are functions of Y, as we did in that earlier instance.

Interest rates potentially affect all four of these components, but the really important ones, as suggested by the functions in Chap. 5 on "Composition of output," are investment and net exports. All else being equal, the lower the interest rate, the more that businesses will be willing to spend money on new capital. All else being equal, the lower the interest rate the higher the real exchange rate and therefore the greater are our gross exports and our net exports as well.[3] To show this dependence of I and NX on the interest rate, we can rewrite Eq. 14.1:

$$EX = C + I(r) + G + NX(r). \tag{14.2}$$

In the end, this is a fancy way of saying what the intuition at the beginning of this section said: when interest rates go down, people want to spend more. (The notation will also be useful further down.) A lower interest rate means higher expenditure.

[3]Interest rates also have a pretty clear effect on consumption. When interest rates go down, it's more attractive to borrow money to spend on consumption; or, if you have money you were thinking of saving, saving becomes a little less attractive relative to consumption. In either case, a lower interest rate, *ceteris paribus*, should encourage more consumption. But the effect is in the same direction as with investment (lower interest $\Rightarrow$ more spending), so bringing it up doesn't qualitatively change the story.

And looking back at Eq. 14.1, if there's more expenditure, there has to be more output for the goods market to stay in equilibrium.

A last note for this section. A lower interest rate doesn't magically, instantaneously call more output into existence. Let's say we're at the equilibrium (r_1, Y_1) depicted above in Fig. 14.1. Now the interest rate drops down to r_2. Output in the economy does not suddenly jump up to Y_2, but people do instantaneously start *trying* to buy more; *EX* goes up but *Y* doesn't. The output market is out of equilibrium. But it is unlikely to stay there. As people buy more than is being produced, inventories start getting drawn down. Firms notice this and take it as a signal to produce more, so there is a pull towards the equilibrium level of output Y_2. The increased spending in general acts as a spur to increase output. And if we were to look at a situation where the interest rate was rising and expenditure was falling, firms would respond (with a lag) to the decreased spending by decreasing their output.

14.3.2 *What Makes it Steep or Flat*

The question of "steep or flat" has to do with how sensitive investment demand and gross exports are to the interest rate. When the interest rate falls, do firms want to build a lot more capital, or only a little more? In technical terms, this is the interest-rate elasticity of investment demand. If a given change in interest rates leads to a relatively large change in investment demand, then this demand is relatively elastic; if the same change leads to a relatively small change in demand, then demand is relatively inelastic. Similarly, how sensitive are gross exports to changes in *r* via changes in the real exchange rate?

Take the same drop in *r* as depicted above in Fig. 14.1, from r_1 down to r_2. If investment demand is elastic, and/or gross exports are highly sensitive to the interest rate, desired expenditure goes up a lot. For equilibrium to be restored, output has to go up a lot. The change in *r* is associated with a relatively large change in *Y*. This amounts to a relatively flat IS curve, as illustrated in Fig. 14.2a.

For inelastic investment demand and/or low interest-sensitivity of gross exports, the argument simply turns around. The same change in *r* doesn't elicit that much

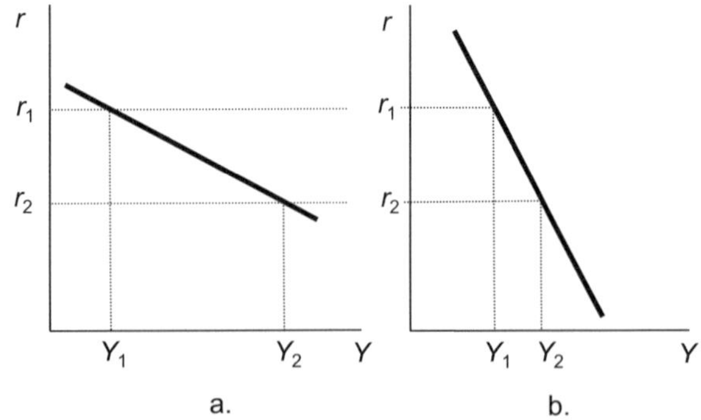

Fig. 14.2 A flat IS curve (**a**) and a steep one (**b**)

more investment demand or exports; that means there's not much more expenditure, so it only takes a small increase in Y to restore equilibrium. This results in a relatively steep IS curve, as shown in Fig. 14.2b.

14.4 What Moves the IS Curve

To track down the forces that move the IS curve, it will help to add a little more detail to Eq. 14.2 from above, reproduced here:

$$EX = C + I(r) + G + NX(r).$$

These things that move the curve (sometimes called "shifters") are factors **other than** Y **or** r that change EX. Because the IS curve graphs Y against r, direct changes in those things are movements **along** a particular IS curve; only other things that change EX have the effect of **moving** the IS curve.

Just as with the multiplier in Chap. 11, we're going to substitute in the consumption function specified in Chap. 5:

$$C = C_0 + C_Y \cdot (1 - t) \cdot Y.$$

The next detail concerns investment demand, which Chap. 5 explained could be represented as:

$$I = I_0 - I_r \cdot r.$$

Lastly, net exports are $GX - IM$. Within that, gross exports depend both on foreign income Y^f and on the real exchange rate ε, and the real exchange rate depends in turn on the real interest rate r, so we have

$$\begin{aligned} GX &= GX_Y \cdot Y^f + GX_\varepsilon \cdot \varepsilon \\ &= GX_Y \cdot Y^f + GX_\varepsilon \cdot \{\varepsilon_0 - \varepsilon_r \cdot (r - r^f)\} \qquad (14.3) \\ &= GX_Y \cdot Y^f + GX_\varepsilon \cdot \varepsilon_0 - GX_\varepsilon \cdot \varepsilon_r \cdot r + GX_\varepsilon \cdot \varepsilon_r \cdot r^f. \end{aligned}$$

If your algebra is rusty, it's not a bad idea to work through those last two lines to make sure you understand what is happening at each step.

Imports depend on our income, Y, so net exports become:

$$\begin{aligned} NX &= GX - IM \\ &= GX_Y \cdot Y^f + GX_\varepsilon \cdot \varepsilon_0 - GX_\varepsilon \cdot \varepsilon_r \cdot r + GX_\varepsilon \cdot \varepsilon_r \cdot r^f - IM_Y \cdot Y. \end{aligned}$$

If we put these back into Eq. 14.2, we get:

$$EX = C_0 + C_Y \cdot (1-t) \cdot Y + I_0 - I_r \cdot r + G$$
$$+ GX_Y \cdot Y^f + GX_\varepsilon \cdot \varepsilon_0 - GX_\varepsilon \cdot \varepsilon_r \cdot r + GX_\varepsilon \cdot \varepsilon_r \cdot r^f - IM_Y \cdot Y. \quad (14.4)$$

That gives us all of our shifters spelled out in one place:

- fiscal policy (t and G)
- autonomous consumption (C_0)
- autonomous investment (I_0), and
- changes in gross exports due to
  - foreign income (Y^f)
  - changes in perception of the "correct" real exchange rate (ε_0), and
  - changes in foreign interest rates (r^f).

Now let's see how they act.

As mentioned above, an important distinction to keep in mind is the difference between a change in r or Y and a change in anything else. Remember that the IS curve graphs r against Y. The implication of that is that a change in r or Y does not move the IS curve—rather, it moves us along the IS curve. A change in anything else, on the other hand, does move the curve.

Start with a cut in taxes (a negative change in t). Looking at Eq. 14.4, a drop in t increases expenditure (in more intuitive terms, if your taxes go down, you have more disposable income, so you'll spend more). If expenditure goes up, Y has to increase to maintain equilibrium. If t drops without a change in r, then the only way to have Y increase is for the IS curve to shift to the right.

(Note that we're not saying that interest rates won't increase, we're just following the algebra. Look at Eq. 14.4 and see what changes as t is increased but r is held constant. The actual effect on the interest rate can be seen later, once we put the IS curve together with its cousin, the LM curve.)

How much does the IS curve shift to the right? It's our old friend, the tax-change multiplier from Eq. 11.12 in Sect. 11.3.3. That multiplier is:

$$\frac{-C_Y}{1 - \text{MPE}}.$$

So if $C_Y = 0.8$ and $IM_Y = 0.2$, the tax-change multiplier is

$$-0.8/(1 - [0.8 - 0.2]) = -0.8/(1 - 0.6) = -0.8/0.4 = -2. \quad (14.5)$$

This implies that a reduction in the tax rate t that leads to tax collection falling by \$100 will then shift the IS curve to the right by \$200.

Now on to the other arm of fiscal policy, government expenditure. An increase in G has qualitatively the same effect as a decrease in t: expenditure goes up, so Y must be higher at a given level of r to maintain equilibrium, meaning, again, that the IS curve shifts to the right. In this case, the IS curve shifts by the government-expenditure multiplier from Sect. 11.3, or $1/(1 - \text{MPE})$.

Autonomous consumption (denoted here as C_0), autonomous investment (I_0), and the parts of gross exports that don't depend on our interest rates ($GX_Y \cdot Y^f$, $GX_\varepsilon \cdot \varepsilon_0$, $GX_\varepsilon \cdot \varepsilon_r \cdot r^f$) have exactly the same effects as an increase in G. If you're comfortable with algebra, this falls right out of Eq. 14.4: notice that whether you add \$100 to C_0, or \$100 to I_0, or to G, you have exactly the same effect on the right-hand-side of Eq. 14.4, so you should expect any of these situations to have the same effect on the equilibrium. Staying away from algebra, the model says that it doesn't matter whether extra spending comes from consumers arbitrarily deciding to spend more, investors arbitrarily deciding to build more capital, or the government suddenly increasing its outlays; all of it is increased expenditure, and all of it has the same effect.

14.5 Algebraic Derivation of IS Curve

What follows looks a lot like the derivation of the tax and expenditure multipliers in Chap. 11, except that now investment and gross exports are given as functions of the real interest rate.

The IS curve can be derived from Eq. 14.4 by putting Y on the left-hand side, to represent equilibrium in the output market:

$$\begin{aligned} Y = {} & C_0 + C_Y \cdot (1 - t) \cdot Y + I_0 - I_r \cdot r + G \\ & + GX_Y \cdot Y^f + GX_\varepsilon \cdot \varepsilon_0 - GX_\varepsilon \cdot \varepsilon_r \cdot r + GX_\varepsilon \cdot \varepsilon_r \cdot r^f - IM_Y \cdot Y. \end{aligned}$$

From the right-hand side, bring terms that have Y over to the left:

$$\begin{aligned} Y - C_Y \cdot (1 - t) \cdot Y + IM_Y \cdot Y = {} & C_0 + I_0 - I_r \cdot r + G + GX_Y \cdot Y^f \\ & + GX_\varepsilon \cdot \varepsilon_0 - GX_\varepsilon \cdot \varepsilon_r \cdot r + GX_\varepsilon \cdot \varepsilon_r \cdot r^f. \end{aligned}$$

On the left we can group the terms that are with Y, and on the right, the terms that are with r:

$$\begin{aligned} Y \cdot (1 - (C_Y \cdot (1 - t) - IM_Y)) = {} & C_0 + I_0 + G + GX_Y \cdot Y^f + GX_\varepsilon \cdot \varepsilon_0 \\ & + GX_\varepsilon \cdot \varepsilon_r \cdot r^f - (GX_\varepsilon \cdot \varepsilon_r \cdot r + I_r \cdot r). \end{aligned}$$

Now note that some of the terms on the left make up MPE (marginal propensity to expend) and on the right we can pull an r out of the last two terms:

$$\begin{aligned} Y \cdot (1 - \text{MPE}) = {} & C_0 + I_0 + G + GX_Y \cdot Y^f + GX_\varepsilon \cdot \varepsilon_0 \\ & + GX_\varepsilon \cdot \varepsilon_r \cdot r^f - (GX_\varepsilon \cdot \varepsilon_r + I_r) \cdot r. \end{aligned}$$

If we divide through by $(1-\text{MPE})$, we have Y as a function of r along with other terms:

$$Y = \frac{C_0 + I_0 + G + GX_Y Y^f + GX_\varepsilon \varepsilon_0 + GX_\varepsilon \varepsilon_r r^f}{1-\text{MPE}} - \frac{GX_\varepsilon \varepsilon_r + I_r}{1-\text{MPE}} \cdot r. \quad (14.6)$$

The second term on the right-hand side determines the slope of the IS curve, while the first term controls its shifts leftward and rightward.

An increase in any item in the numerator of the first term (C_0, etc.) will shift the IS curve to the right, and the size of the shift will be modified by the autonomous expenditure multiplier $[\,1/(1-\text{MPE})\,]$.

An increase in anything in the second term ($X_\varepsilon \cdot \varepsilon_r$ or I_r) will cause a given change in r to be associated with a larger change in Y, thus producing an IS curve with a flatter slope.

Note what is in the numerator of that second term. $GX_\varepsilon \cdot \varepsilon_r$ is the **interest-rate sensitivity of gross exports**. It combines the interest-rate sensitivity of the exchange rate and the exchange-rate elasticity of gross exports. The term I_r is the **interest elasticity of investment**, familiar from Chap. 5.

Lastly, note the role of the tax rate, t. It is part of MPE, so it is in the denominator of both parts of the IS curve. If t goes down, the MPE goes up, so the denominators get smaller. That combines the effect of shifting the IS curve to the right and making it flatter.

14.6 LM Overview

The LM curve captures equilibrium in the money market. (The derivation of "LM" is explained in the appendix on "The meaning of 'IS' and 'LM'.") Every point along the LM curve represents a combination of an interest rate and a level of output at which the money market is in equilibrium.

The LM curve slopes up to the right (in Cartesian terms, its slope is positive).

The LM curve is shifted by changes in the money supply or in the money demand function.

In Fig. 14.3, interest rate i_1 and output level Y_1 are consistent with equilibrium in the money market, so they are a point on the LM curve. (Note that the LM curve, for reasons explained below, uses the nominal interest rate i rather than the real interest rate r.) If the interest rate rises to i_2, the money market will be out of equilibrium unless output increases to Y_2, so the point (i_2, Y_2) is another point on the LM curve.

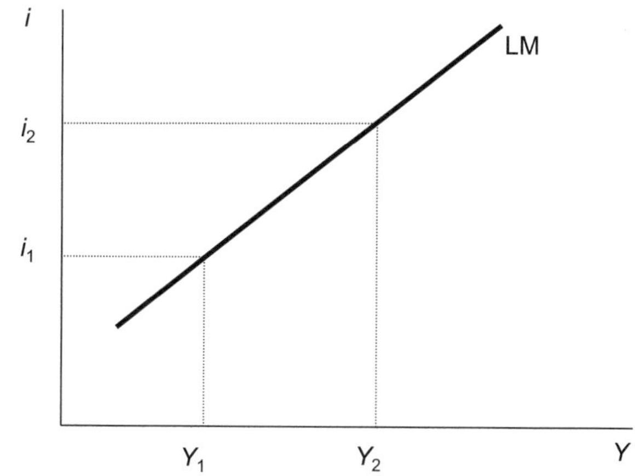

Fig. 14.3 The LM curve

14.7 The Shape of the LM Curve

Analogously to the IS curve, we want to explain why the LM curve slopes up, and what makes it steep or flat.

14.7.1 Why Does it Slope Up

First the intuition. The bigger the economy, the more liquidity people want, in order to carry out business. On the other hand, the higher the interest rate, the less willing people are to keep their wealth in liquid form, because they're sacrificing the interest they could be earning on that wealth. These tradeoffs drive the behavior of the money market. If Y gets bigger and the money supply doesn't increase, the money market will be out of equilibrium (the quantity of liquidity people demand will exceed the supply), unless something happens to reduce the quantity demanded. That "something" is a rise in the interest rate. So along the LM curve, an increase in Y must be accompanied by an increase in i in order to maintain equilibrium.

Note that the relevant interest rate here is the nominal rate i rather than the real rate r. That's because it's the nominal rate that determines how much you're giving up by holding your wealth in liquid form rather than as some interest-earning asset. The nominal rate is (approximately) the real rate plus expected inflation: $i = r + \pi^e$, where π^e is expected inflation. And whether it's because the real return is high and you're losing that by not lending your money out, or because your money's value will be eaten away by high inflation, a high nominal rate implies a large loss from holding cash.

In mathematical terms, we can describe money demand as a function of income and the interest rate:

$$M^D = L(Y, i).$$

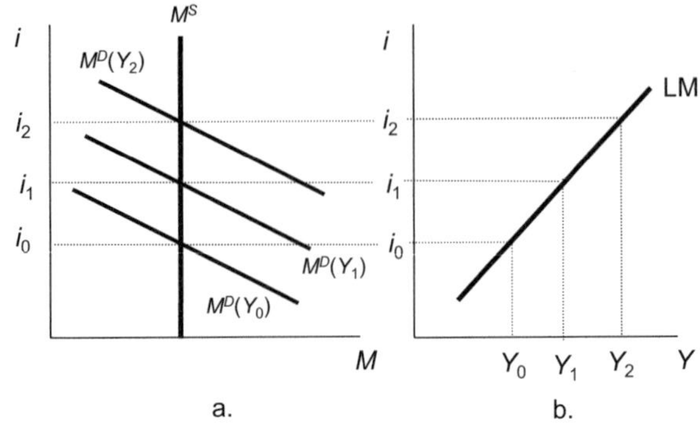

Fig. 14.4 Money-market equilibrium and the LM curve

Embodying the discussion above, this function should have the properties that as Y increases, M^D goes up, and as i increases, M^D goes down. A simple, linear example of such a function is:

$$M^D = m_0 + m_1 \cdot Y - m_2 \cdot i, \quad (14.7)$$

which captures exactly the behavior described above.[4]

Figure 14.4a shows this linear money demand function graphed with the quantity of money on the horizontal axis and the interest rate on the vertical. The money supply (M^S) is a vertical line, because it is not a function of the interest rate. It doesn't respond automatically to changes in either Y or i—rather, it moves only if the money-creation process moves it.[5]

On this diagram, because income (Y) is not represented on the graph, a change in Y causes the money demand curve to move—specifically, to shift to the right (an increase). So as income increases from Y_0 to Y_1 to Y_2, the money demand curve shifts right (or up).

With M^S a fixed, vertical line, and M^D shifting up, the interest rate is driven up—from i_0 to i_1 to i_2—to keep the quantity of money people want to hold in line with how much money there is. These pairs of Y and i trace out the LM curve, shown in Fig. 14.4b.

14.7.2 What Determines the Steepness

The steepness of the LM curve is determined by the **interest elasticity of money demand**: when the interest rate goes up by a certain amount, do people try to hold

[4]This particular specification of the demand for money follows [1].

[5]This is a useful simplification. As Chap. 10 explains, the money supply is more subtle than just an exogenously determined quantity.

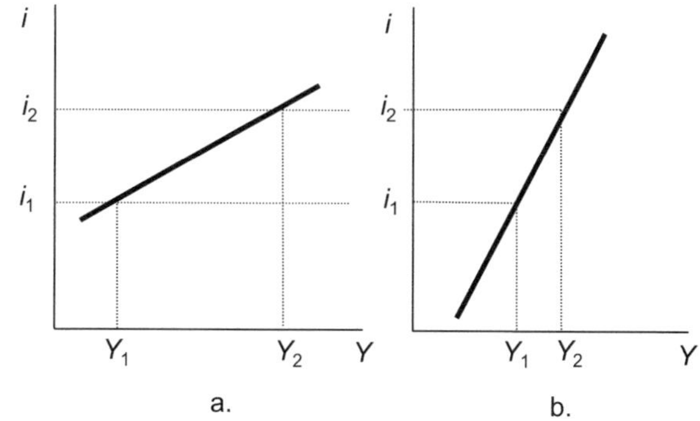

Fig. 14.5 A flat LM curve (**a**) and a steep one (**b**)

a lot less money (relatively elastic money demand), or only a little less money (relatively inelastic demand)?

Figure 14.5a shows a fairly flat LM curve, corresponding to a money-demand curve that is relatively elastic. As the interest rate rises from i_1 to i_2, people want to hold a lot less money. For the money market to stay in equilibrium, there has to be a large increase in Y to induce people to want to hold as much money as there is in the economy.

Figure 14.5b shows a steep LM curve, corresponding to relatively interest-inelastic money demand. For the same rise from i_1 to i_2, people's desire to hold money is not much diminished, so only a small increase in Y is required to keep the money market in equilibrium.

As Footnote 5 says, it's a simplification to say that the money supply is fixed exogenously and therefore should be represented as a vertical line when graphed against i. Indeed, to the extent that contemporary monetary policy focuses on interest rates, the situation should be exactly the opposite: the interest rate is the exogenous factor and the central bank does what it has to with the money supply so as to establish the interest rate it has chosen. That would be represented by a horizontal money-supply curve, leading in turn to a horizontal LM curve. However, the interest rate that the Fed directly targets is the Federal Funds rate, not the interest rates earned by savers or paid by borrowers. It is those latter interest rates that shape the behavior of people in the money market. The Federal Funds rate *affects* that i but does not determine it. Problem 14.6 explores further implications of these ideas.

14.8 What Moves the LM Curve

Two factors can move the LM curve: a change in the money supply, which is partly a policy variable, partly a function of private decisions; and a change in the underlying money demand function, or liquidity preference, which is entirely outside the policy makers' control.

Fig. 14.6 The LM curve with an increase in the money supply

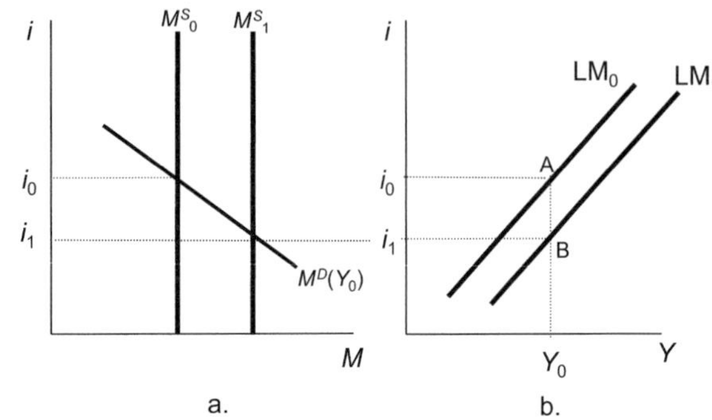

Figure 14.6 shows the effect on the LM curve of an increase in the money supply. With the original money supply of $M^S{}_0$ and income of Y_0, the equilibrium interest rate is i_0, at the point A on the curve LM_0 in Fig. 14.6b. Suppose now the money supply increases to $M^S{}_1$. To find the effect on the LM curve, look at what must happen if income stays at Y_0. That means that the money-demand curve in Fig. 14.6a doesn't move, so for equilibrium to be maintained, the interest rate must drop: there's more money available, and people will only be willing to hold onto that extra money if the interest rate is lower.

Translating that over to Fig. 14.6b, we're still at income level Y_0, but we're now at interest rate i_1, so point B must be a point on the new curve, LM_1.

The other factor capable of shifting the LM curve is a change in people's underlying liquidity preference. Note that this is different from the shifts in money demand *in response to* increases in income depicted in Fig. 14.4a. In that case, the underlying liquidity preference, *given a certain interest rate and a certain level of income*, was unchanged, but as income rose, the demand for money at each level of interest also rose. Here, we're considering a change in the amount of money people want to hold, *even though the interest rate and the income level are unchanged.*

In general, increased uncertainty will increase people's liquidity preference.[6] Conditions that might increase the risk of bond default or corporate bankruptcy will make people less willing to hold their wealth in those less-liquid forms. On the other hand, a lack of confidence in the government issuing a currency would make people shy away from liquidity in favor of other forms of wealth.

Figure 14.7 illustrates an increase in liquidity preference: with the original demand function $M^D{}_0$ and income level Y_0, an interest rate of i_0 kept the money market in equilibrium with the fixed money supply M^S, making A a point on the original curve LM_0 in Fig. 14.7b. With the increased liquidity preference $M^D{}_1$, even if income is still at Y_0, people want to hold more money than M^S, until the interest rate rises to i_1. So point B, with the original income Y_0 and the new interest rate i_1, is a point on the new curve LM_1.

[6]John R. Hicks, one of the original creators of the IS-LM framework, observed that without uncertainty regarding one's expectations, there's little need for liquidity. [2, p. 152]

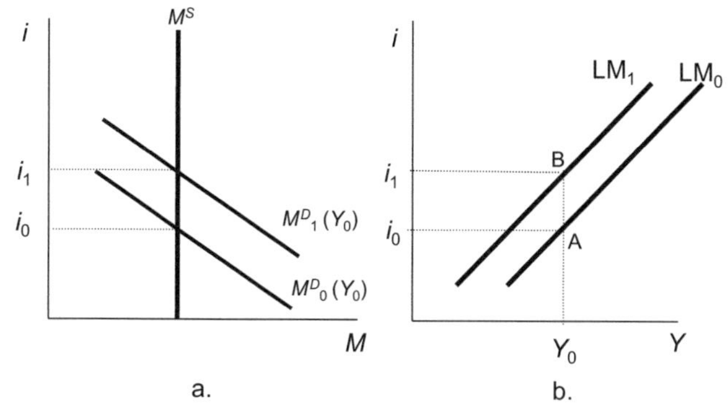

Fig. 14.7 The LM curve with an increase in liquidity preference

14.9 The Money-Supply Multiplier

Just as with the IS curve, it may be useful to be able to tell how much the LM curve moves in response to a policy choice—in this case, a change in the money supply. That answer can be found in the algebra of the LM curve.

Start with Eq. 14.7 above describing money demand, M^D. Remember that the LM curve is defined as the set of combinations of i and Y such that the money market is in equilibrium, and that equilibrium in the money market is where the quantity of money demanded equals the money supply, that is,

$$M^D = M^S.$$

Then if we replace M^D in Eq. 14.7 with M^S, we have an equation for the LM curve:

$$M^S = m_0 + m_1 \cdot Y - m_2 \cdot i.$$

If you rearrange this equation, solving it for Y, it becomes

$$Y = \frac{M^S}{m_1} - \frac{m_0}{m_1} + \frac{m_2}{m_1} i. \tag{14.8}$$

The horizontal shift of the LM curve is described by a change in Y with i held constant. If M^S is changed by some amount and i is held constant, then the change in Y is the change in M^S, times $1/m_1$. If $m_1 = 0.4$, then $1/m_1 = 2.5$; increasing the money supply by \$100 will shift the LM curve to the right by \$250.

Similarly, if there's an increase in money demand, captured by an increase in m_0, the right=hand side of 14.8 is smaller, so i has to be higher in order to balance it out. In other words, the LM curve has shifted up, or leftward.

There is a major caveat to this. Chapter 12 distinguished between the monetary base, which is an exogenous choice in the hands of the central bank, and the money supply, which is not.[7] Nonetheless, we can simplify and think about the central bank acting so as to encourage a particular increase or decrease in the money supply.

Appendix: The Meaning of "IS" and "LM"

"IS" is an acronym for "investment-savings." In a conceptually simplified economy with no government or foreign sector, equilibrium is only possible when investment equals savings ($I = S$). In this simple economy, the only two things that can be done with output are that it can be consumed or saved: $Y = C + S$. And the only two things that it can be spent on are consumption and investment: $EX = C + I$. Equilibrium means that output (that is, income) equals expenditure: $Y = EX$. That means that

$$C + I = EX = Y = C + S,$$

which amounts to

$$C + I = C + S,$$

or

$$I = S. \tag{14.9}$$

So the IS curve is the "investment-savings equilibrium" curve.

The "M" in LM stands for the money supply, while the "L" stands for "liquidity," since the demand for money can also be thought of as the demand for a very "liquid" form of wealth. That's also why the demand for money is often written as $M^D = L(Y, i)$.

Problems

Problem 14.1 The diagrams in Fig. 14.8 show two different IS curves. Assume the IS curve changed from the one shown in (a) to the one shown in (b). For each of the following items, answer whether it could have caused that change and explain why or why not.

---

[7]This distinction is related to the concept of the "money multiplier," as opposed to the "money-supply" multiplier discussed here. This other sense of "money multiplier" describes a relationship in which bank reserves are multiplied up into money. As pointed out in [3], that's not how it works.

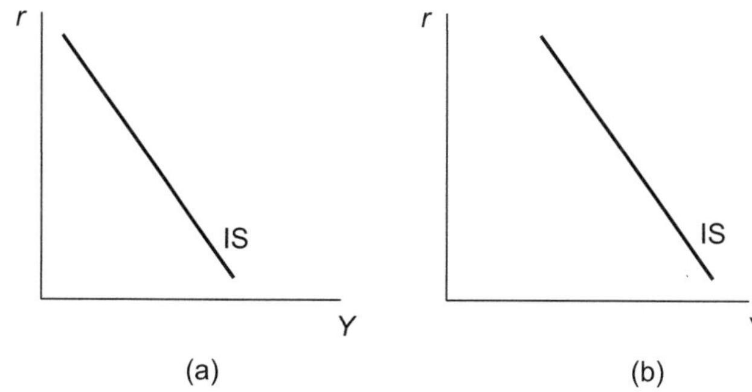

Fig. 14.8 A change in the IS curve

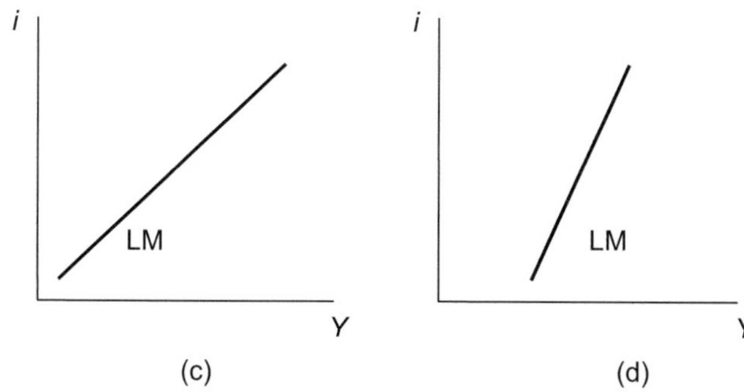

Fig. 14.9 A change in the LM curve

(a) Decreased interest-rate sensitivity of investment
(b) A decrease in Y
(c) Increased foreign income
(d) A decrease in G
(e) Decreased interest-rate sensitivity of gross exports
(f) A decrease in autonomous investment (i.e., I_0)
(g) A decrease in the money-supply multiplier

Problem 14.2 The diagrams in Fig. 14.9 show two different LM curves. Assume the LM curve changed from the one shown in (c) to the one shown in (d). For each of the following items, answer whether it could have caused that change and explain why or why not.

(a) An increase in Y
(b) A decrease in the interest-rate sensitivity of money demand
(c) An increase in G
(d) A decrease in t
(e) A decrease in money supply
(f) An increase in the foreign interest rate

Problem 14.3 (a) If m_0 falls by $20, which curve is affected, IS or LM?
(b) In qualitative terms, what happens to the curve that is affected?
(c) If the starting values of the terms in the money-demand function are $m_0 = 700$, $m_1 = 0.2$, and $m_2 = 3,000$, how big is the money-supply multiplier?
(d) Given your answer to (c), how much does the affected curve move when m_0 falls by $20 as described in (a)?

Problem 14.4 Assume an economy with a marginal propensity to consume of 0.9, a tax rate of 20%, and an import rate of 10%. Assume that government spending in this economy increases by $100. In the multiplier model, how much does GDP increase?

Problem 14.5 In the IS-LM model, will the increase in GDP be the same as your answer to question 14.4, more than that, or less than that? **Explain.**

Problem 14.6 In Fig. 14.4 the money supply is shown as a vertical line, reflecting an assumption that it is insensitive to the nominal interest rate.

(a) Given how money is created in the lending process (Chap. 10), make a case for the money supply curve to be sloped, specifying whether it is a positive slope or a negative one.
(b) Using the slope you chose in part a., redraw both parts of Fig. 14.4. How has the LM curve changed as a result of giving the M^S line a slope?

References

1. Froyen, R. T. (2001). *Macroeconomics: Theories and policies* (7th ed.). Upper Saddle River: Prentice Hall.
2. Hicks, J. (1980). IS-LM: an explanation. *Journal of Post Keynesian Economics, 3*, 139–154.
3. McLeay, M. Radia, A. & Thomas, R. (2014). Money creation in the modern economy. *Quarterly Bulletin, Q1*, 1–14.

Chapter 15
Policy and Shocks in the IS-LM World

Abstract We put together the behaviors of the IS and LM curves laid out in Chap. 14 to see what predictions the IS-LM model makes about different policy actions and external shocks and how they affect output and interest rates. The goal of policy is defined as keeping actual output close to potential output. Depending on the relative slopes of the two curves, we may be able to say that fiscal policy is particularly effective or, with other slopes, that monetary policy is particularly effective.

15.1 Overview

Fiscal policy shifts the IS curve. An expansionary fiscal policy (tax cuts or increased government spending) moves the IS curve to the right. This results in higher output and higher interest rates.

Monetary policy moves the LM curve. An expansionary monetary policy (increasing the money supply) moves the LM curve to the right. This results in higher output and lower interest rates.

Fiscal policy loses its effectiveness when the IS curve is relatively flat (which implies intended investment being very sensitive to interest rates) or when the LM curve is relatively steep (which implies that money demand is not very sensitive to interest rates).

Monetary policy loses its effectiveness when the LM curve is relatively flat (which implies that money demand is very sensitive to interest rates) or when the IS curve is relatively steep (which implies that intended investment is not very sensitive to changes in the interest rate).

15.2 Combining the Two Curves

The IS curve is drawn in terms of the *real* interest rate, r, while the LM curve is drawn in terms of the *nominal* interest rate, i. In order to put them on a single diagram, one of them has to be recast.

K. Seeley, *Macroeconomics in Ecological Context*, Studies in Ecological Economics 5, DOI 10.1007/978-3-319-51757-5_15

As explained in Sect. 3.5 on "Interest rates," the real interest rate is approximately the nominal interest rate minus expected inflation. For example, if the nominal interest rate is 8%, then \$100 put in the bank now will turn into \$108 a year from now. At the same time, if inflation is 5%, you'll need \$105 a year from now to buy what \$100 buys now, so only \$3 of the \$8 that your money earned will actually be increased purchasing power. 3% real = 8% nominal minus 5% inflation. (It's actually a little less than that, but this is a close enough approximation when real interest and inflation are low). And the aspect of inflation that's relevant here is expected inflation, because when you buy a bond you know what nominal interest you'll earn over the bond's life, whereas the only thing you know about inflation over that same period is what you *expect* it to be, not what it actually will be.

The implication for the LM curve and the real interest rate is that, for any given value of expected inflation, we can just as well draw the LM curve with the real interest rate r as with the nominal rate i. The algebra of this is in Appendix I, "The LM curve and the real interest rate."

15.3 Effect of Fiscal Policy

Chapter 14 showed that fiscal policy—changes in the level of taxation and/or government expenditure—moves the IS curve. An expansionary fiscal policy (cutting taxes or increasing government expenditure) moves the IS curve to the right. The size of the shift is determined by the multipliers worked out in the basic aggregate-demand model. But there's an important difference from the effect there.

In the aggregate-demand model, interest rates are implicitly held constant. Assume an MPC of 0.7, a tax rate of 25%, and a marginal propensity to import of 0.125. This results in a marginal propensity to expend (MPE) of 0.4, implying that the government expenditure multiplier is 1.67, and a \$100 million increase in G will lead to a \$167 million increase in Y. With the interest rate unchanged, there's no reason for there to be a change in I, or in any other part of aggregate demand, so the \$167 million increase is the end of the story.

The IS-LM model, in contrast, allows the interest rate to move. In this case, it moves up, so intended investment goes down a little bit. There's still an increase in output, but not by the full \$167 million that the simple aggregate-demand model predicts.

Figure 15.1 illustrates the effect of fiscal policy in the IS-LM model. The fiscal stimulus shifts the IS curve from IS_0 to IS_1. The size of the shift is the horizontal distance from point A to point B indicated on the graph. This is the amount that comes from the multiplier in the simple aggregate-demand model: if the government expenditure multiplier is 1.67 and G increases by \$100 million, then the move from A to B is a distance of \$167 million.

Notice on the horizontal axis that this is also the distance from Y_0, our initial level of GDP, to Y_{AD}, the new level of GDP predicted by the simple aggregate-demand model.

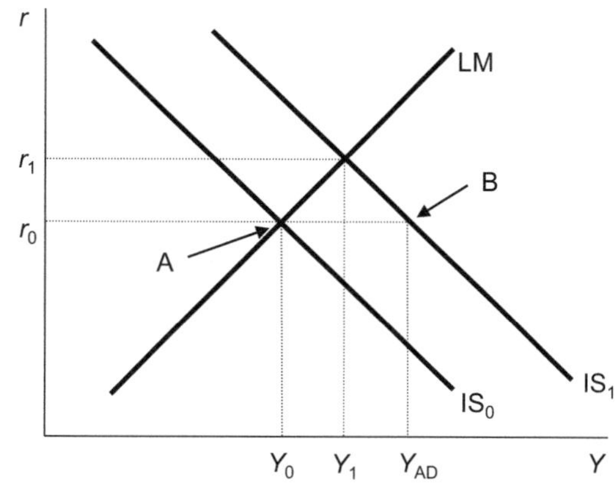

Fig. 15.1 Expansionary fiscal policy

But this large a change only happens if the interest rate remains unchanged at r_0; in reality, the government's borrowing to fund its expenditure does put some upward pressure on interest rates. The increase in r isn't as big as in the classical model, so the expansionary effect of increased G isn't entirely wiped out, but it is reduced. The interest rate rises from r_0 to r_1, causing intended investment to decline somewhat, and gross exports to decline somewhat. The net effect is that output goes up, but only to Y_1 rather than all the way up to Y_{AD}.

Regardless of what causes the IS curve to move, the effects are the same. With an MPE of 0.4 and an MPC of 0.7 as above, the tax multiplier will be -1.1667, so a tax cut of $100 million will cause the IS curve to shift right by $116.67 million. Just as with the effect of an increase in government expenditure, the interest rate will rise from its initial level of r_0 (though not as high as in the case of a $100 million increase in G, because the IS shift isn't as large), so GDP will go up by less than $116.67 million.

Similarly, increases in autonomous investment or net exports will move the IS curve by whatever amount the aggregate-demand multiplier says, with some smaller net effect on GDP after taking account of the rise in interest rates and resulting decline in that part of investment that depends on the interest rate.

The model can be used just as well to look at leftward shifts of the IS curve. Policy makers might cut G or increase T, either to deal with a deficit they feel is too large or to "cool off" an economy they think is growing too fast. Either of these actions would shift IS to the left. Similarly, a drop in autonomous investment or in exports, or a rise in imports, would shift IS to the left. Whatever the cause, the result would be a reduction in GDP and a lower interest rate.

So far we've been vague about the size of the offsetting effect where the higher interest rate leads to a reduction in investment: the size of the offsetting effect is discussed below in Sect. 15.6.

15.4 Effect of Monetary Policy

On the LM side, Chap. 14 explained that monetary policy is the factor under policy-makers' control that affects the LM curve. An expansionary monetary policy moves the LM curve to the right.

Recall how the shift of the LM curve was demonstrated. For a fixed level of income (Y_0), a greater money supply requires a lower interest rate if people are going to be induced to hold the extra money that is now available. In Fig. 15.2, that is represented by the drop from r_0 to r_M, over the level of income Y_0.

But income is not actually constant. As the interest rate starts to fall to keep the money market in equilibrium, intended investment increases in response to the lower interest rate, and gross exports go up for the same reason. And as intended investment and gross exports go up, income goes up with it. The last step in this chain is that, with higher incomes, people's demand for money goes up, so the interest rate doesn't have to fall as far as when we pretended that income was constant.

If you compare Figs. 15.3 to 15.2, the interest rate drop from r_0 to r_1 is smaller than the fall from r_0 to r_M, and income has increased from Y_0 to Y_1.

Appendix II, "Algebraic solution of IS-LM," puts the whole model in more concrete terms.

15.5 The Goal of Policy

We have these tools that, in principle, can move the IS and LM curves in the direction that policy-makers want.[1] The next question is, What is it you're trying to accomplish? The short answer is that you're trying to keep actual output not too far from potential output.

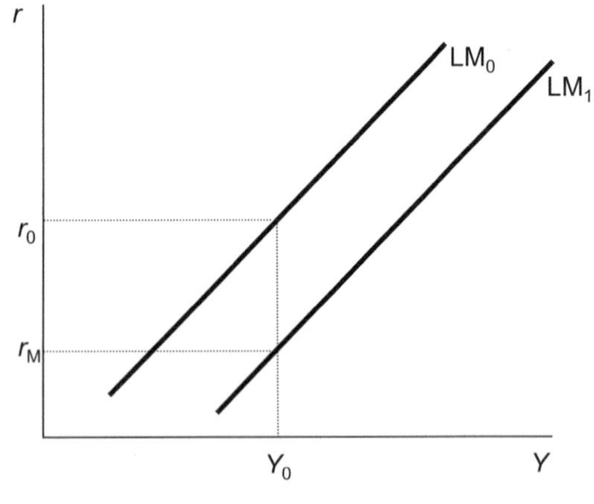

Fig. 15.2 Shifting the LM curve

[1]Chapters 16 and 18 discuss limits on the efficacy of such efforts, but they are still sometimes effective.

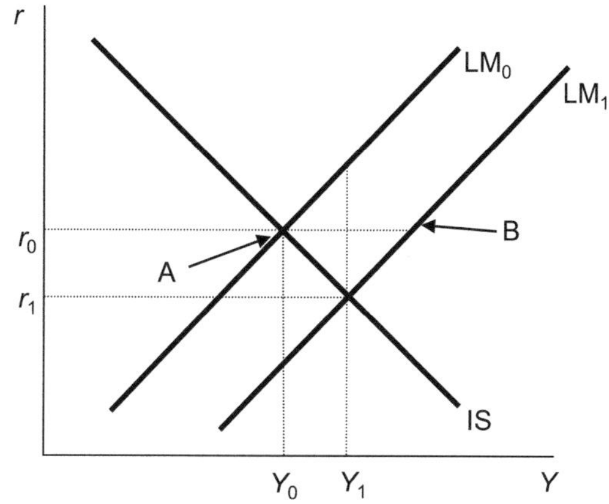

Fig. 15.3 Expansionary monetary policy

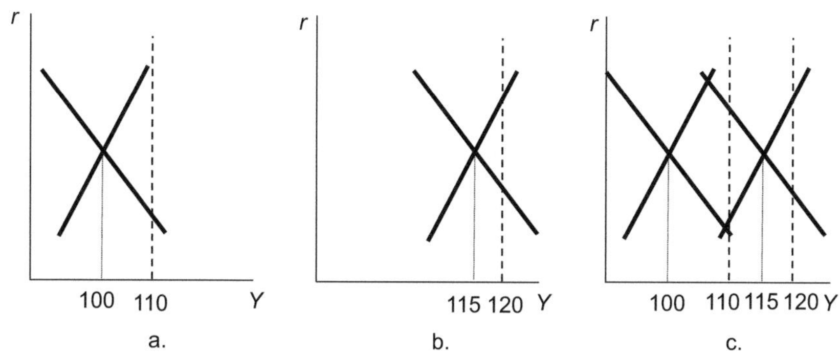

Fig. 15.4 Growth and policy action in absolute terms

In order to understand that in the context of IS-LM, it helps to re-cast the model in terms relative to potential output. As a start, consider a pair of curves on a diagram with specific numbers and a level of potential output. To show the effect of your policy, your curves will be moving, let's say to the right. But over time, as your policy takes effect, potential output would be growing, since that's what it normally does. You're passing from Fig. 15.4a to 15.4b. If you try to portray the situation over time in a single diagram, you get the confusing mess of Fig. 15.4c. So consider two questions that are tempting but misleading, and the alternative questions that point in a more useful direction.

The misleading questions are

1. How much is GDP?
2. How much did GDP change as a result of a shock or a policy move?

The better questions are

1. Where does actual GDP stand relative to potential GDP? In percent terms, how much is actual GDP above or below potential?

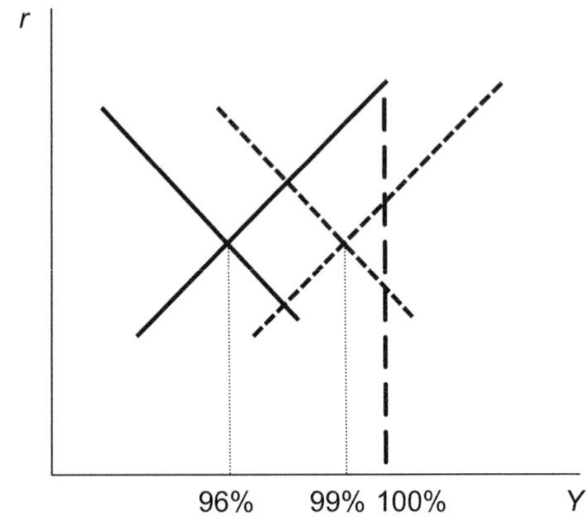

Fig. 15.5 IS and LM curves relative to potential GDP

2. Is actual GDP growing more slowly than potential (falling behind, or further behind)? Or is it growing faster than potential (catching up to potential or rising above it)?

Figure 15.4 can now be interpreted as shown in Fig. 15.5. The vertical line for potential output doesn't move, because it's always simply 100% of its own level at a given time. This means that underlying long-term growth has been stripped out of the IS and LM curves and any change in them reflects their movements relative to potential output.

Now we can go back to the question of what it is we're trying to accomplish through macro stabilization policy. In Fig. 15.5 the solid IS and LM curves portray an economy performing significantly below potential, with an output gap of −4%. If stimulative policy moves you to the dashed curves, then the policy was fairly effective, reducing the output gap to −1%. If you find an economy already in the situation described by the dashed curves, then you may want to leave well enough alone and not try to goose GDP any further.

Having identified our goal, the next thing to consider is the conditions under which we expect policy to be effective or ineffective.

15.6 When Fiscal Policy Is Ineffective

Two conditions can make fiscal policy ineffective in the IS-LM model. Each will be presented graphically, followed by an explanation of the intuition behind the outcome.

Figure 15.6 shows a relatively flat IS curve, corresponding to investment demand and gross exports that are highly sensitive to the interest rate. The horizontal shift of the IS curve from IS_0 to IS_1 is the same as in Fig. 15.1 above (compare the distance from A to B in each graph), but the increase in *Y* is considerably smaller than in that "generic" case. (The increase in *r* is also smaller than in the previous case, but this

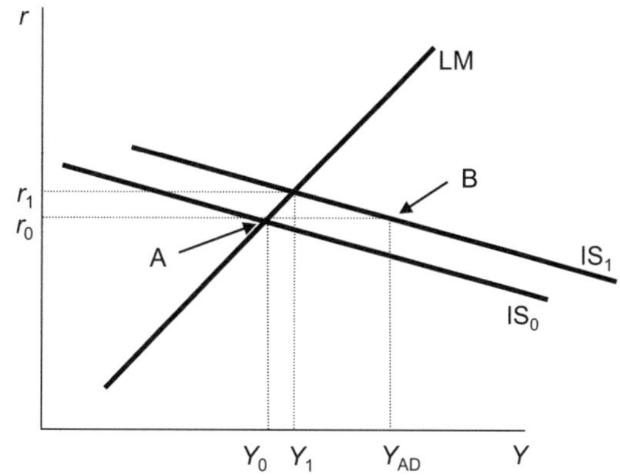

Fig. 15.6 Ineffective fiscal policy (I)

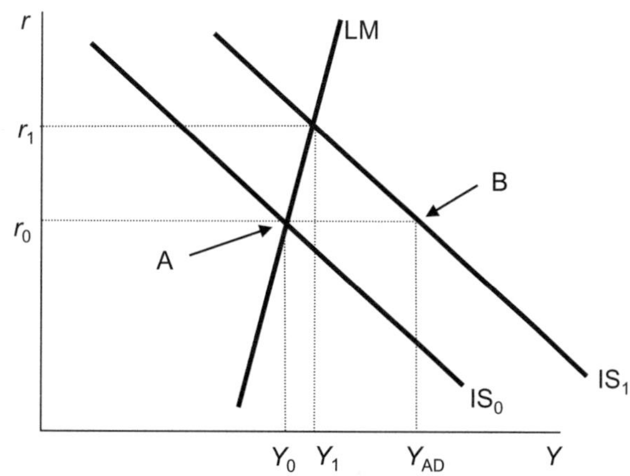

Fig. 15.7 Ineffective fiscal policy (II)

is less important, since the ultimate goal of fiscal policy is to affect Y, and effects on r are merely part of the mechanism by which Y is affected.)

As the increase in government spending drives up income (Y), people want to hold more money. But the money supply, M, has not increased, so r has to go up to keep the money market in equilibrium. Because I is very sensitive to r, it goes down a lot, offsetting much of the effect of the government-expenditure multiplier.

Figure 15.7 shows a pair of generic IS curves (neither very flat nor very steep), but the LM curve is fairly steep. As with Fig. 15.6, the horizontal shift of the IS curve is unchanged from Fig. 15.1, but the resulting increase in Y is again less than in the case when the two curves are similarly sloped. Money demand is not very sensitive to the interest rate, which means that r has to rise a lot in order to maintain money-market equilibrium. So even though the interest-elasticity of investment is only moderate, the large rise in r still drives I and GX down significantly.

Where fiscal policy is hamstrung by curves with the slopes shown in Figs. 15.6 and 15.7, monetary policy has the potential to have a large impact.

15.7 When Monetary Policy Is Ineffective

As with fiscal policy, two conditions make monetary policy ineffective—and they're the opposite two conditions from the fiscal case.

Figure 15.8 illustrates a scenario with a "neutral" LM curve and a steep IS curve (which reflects very interest-inelastic investment demand and gross exports). As the LM curve shifts to the right, the interest rate drops, but because investment demand and gross exports are inelastic, there isn't much increase in expenditure. It follows that there isn't much increase in income. In the earlier "neutral" case in Fig. 15.3, equilibrium in the money market is restored by a mix of some increased income and some lowered interest rate. In the case here, equilibrium is restored primarily through a lowered interest rate, with only a small increase in income.

Figure 15.9 above shows a "neutral" IS curve with a flat LM curve (reflecting an underlying money-demand curve that is highly interest-elastic). The increase in the money supply moves the LM curve the same horizontal distance as in Figs. 15.3

Fig. 15.8 Ineffective monetary policy (I)

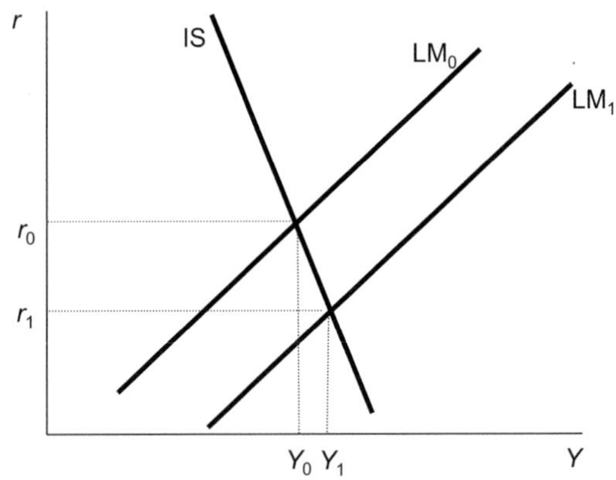

Fig. 15.9 Ineffective monetary policy (II)

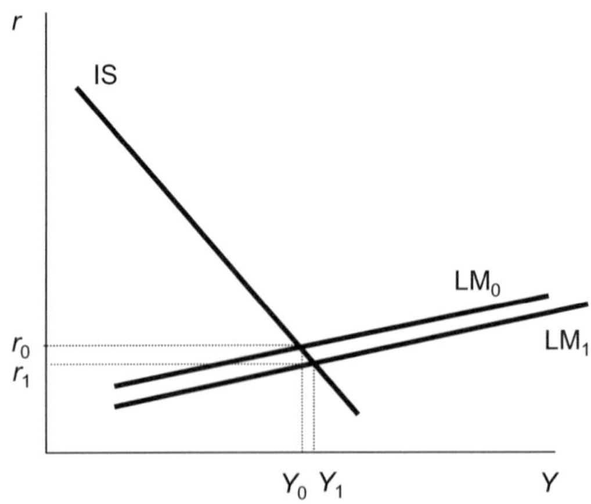

and 15.8, but the effect on income is much smaller than in the "neutral" case. As the money supply increases, the interest rate drops to keep the money market in equilibrium. But because money demand is so interest-elastic, r doesn't have to fall very far. And because there's only a small drop in r, there's also only a small increase in intended investment or in gross exports, which in turn means only a small increase in income. Instead of falling interest rates leading to increased investment, the stimulus of the increased money supply gets "soaked up" by people holding more money.

This situation is often known as a "liquidity trap," a term popularized by Keynes. The idea is that in an extreme economic meltdown, such as the Great Depression, people develop a very high preference for liquidity, and interest rates are often quite low. The central bank can try pumping up the money supply (note that the horizontal shift of LM in Fig. 15.9 is fairly large; the curves are close together *vertically* because of their small slope), but people just suck it up without requiring there to be much of a drop in interest rates to make them willing to hold it. When you lend money to someone so they can spend money on investment (or even on consumption), you're trading a highly liquid asset (money) for a much less liquid asset (the borrower's promise to repay). In a liquidity trap, nobody wants the illiquid assets, so everyone holds onto the money themselves rather than lending it to be spent. As a result, the monetary authority can increase liquidity without there being much change in Y. The effect is compounded if investors are convinced that market conditions are poor and therefore are not very responsive to the interest rate, resulting in a steep IS curve.

Because of this liquidity preference, the economy can get "trapped" below potential output, with monetary policy unable to accomplish anything. This was famously summed up in the expression, "You cannot push on a string." [1, p. 377] The flip side, of course, is that fiscal policy is *particularly* effective in this setting.

15.8 The Uses of the IS-LM Framework

For several years the IS-LM model has been an object of controversy among economists. As an example of a very critical view, one could cite John Cochrane from the University of Chicago: "Static ISLM / ASAD modeling and thinking really did pretty much disappear from academic research economics around 1980. You won't find it taught in any PhD programs, you won't find it at any conferences (except the occasional lunchtime 'keynote speech' where an Important Person from the policy world comes in to enlighten us), you won't find it in any academic journals (AER, JPE, QJE, Econometrica, etc.)." [2]. Even the model's co-creator wrote in 1980 of the model's limitations as anything more than a "classroom gadget." ([3], p. 152)

Yet even as a classroom gadget, it remains useful in helping bridge the gap between the supply-driven perspective of the long-run model a demand-oriented explanation of the business cycle. And in skilled hands, it can still shed light on issues of current interest (e.g., Brad DeLong's discussion of different monetary regimes in [4]). Like any model, it has its limitations, but as *part* of your mental toolkit it can still play a useful role.

Appendix I: The LM Curve and the Real Interest Rate

Chapter 14 introduced the algebraic representation of the LM curve in terms of GDP and the *nominal* interest rate:

$$Y = \frac{1}{m_1}M^S - \frac{m_0}{m_1} + \frac{m_2}{m_1}i. \tag{15.1}$$

When you lend or borrow money, the *actual* real interest rate that you will receive or pay is unknown, because you don't know what inflation will turn out to be over the duration of the loan. All that you know is the *expected* real interest rate, which is the (known) nominal rate i and the expected inflation rate π^e:

$$r \cong i - \pi^e.$$

We can use this relationship to take the nominal interest rate out of Eq. 15.1 above describing the LM curve:

$$Y = \frac{1}{m_1}M^S - \frac{m_0}{m_1} + \frac{m_2}{m_1}(r + \pi^e).$$

Now if we regroup the inflation expectation, we get an equation for the LM curve in Y and r, showing the position of the curve as a function of both the money supply and the expected level of inflation:

$$Y = \left(\frac{1}{m_1}M^S - \frac{m_0}{m_1} + \frac{m_2}{m_1}\pi^e\right) + \frac{m_2}{m_1}r \tag{15.2}$$

Appendix II: Algebraic Solution of IS-LM

We now have equations for the IS and LM curves, both of them expressing Y as a function of the real interest rate, and other stuff.

The LM curve is above, at the end of Appendix I, and the IS curve (derived in Chap. 14) is:

$$Y = \frac{C_0 + I_0 + G + GX_Y Y^f + GX_\varepsilon \varepsilon_0 + GX_\varepsilon \varepsilon_r r^f}{1 - \text{MPE}} - \frac{GX_\varepsilon \varepsilon_r + I_r}{1 - \text{MPE}} \cdot r.$$

Equilibrium for the economy as a whole is where there is equilibrium in both the money market and the goods market—the pair of values of Y and r that are on both the IS and the LM curve simultaneously. In other words, equilibrium for the economy as a whole is when IS = LM:

$$\frac{C_0 + I_0 + G + GX_Y Y^f + GX_\varepsilon \varepsilon_0 + GX_\varepsilon \varepsilon_r r^f}{1 - \text{MPE}} - \frac{GX_\varepsilon \varepsilon_r + I_r}{1 - \text{MPE}} \cdot r$$
$$= \left(\frac{1}{m_1} M^S - \frac{m_0}{m_1} + \frac{m_2}{m_1} \pi^e \right) + \frac{m_2}{m_1} r$$

This is now a single linear equation in one unknown (that is, r). If you bring the r terms over to one side, then divide by the items that are multiplied by r, you can solve for the equilibrium level of r.

Once you know the equilibrium value of r, you can plug it back into either the IS or the LM curve to find the corresponding equilibrium level of Y.

Problems

Problem 15.1 Consider an economy with the following parameters:

Government:	$G = 200$, $t = 18\%$
Consumption:	$C_0 = 20$, $C_Y = 0.8$
Imports:	$IM_Y = 0.07$
Exchange rate:	$\varepsilon_0 = 1$, $\varepsilon_r = 1{,}500$, $r^f = 3\%$
Gross exports:	$GX_Y = 0.2$, $Y^f = 200$, $GX_\varepsilon = 6$
Investment:	$I_0 = 140$, $I_r = 200$
Money demand:	$M^d = 1{,}200 + 0.1 \times Y - 20{,}000 \times i$
Inflation:	$\pi^e = 3\%$
Money supply:	$M^s = 250$

Assume potential output is 1,117.

(a) Determine the equation for the IS curve.
(b) Determine the equation for the LM curve.
(c) Use your IS and LM curves to determine the economy's short-run equilibrium output y and real interest rate r.
(d) In percentage terms, what is the size of the output gap?

Problem 15.2 Except where specified, use the same parameters as in Problem 15.1.

(a) If government expenditure falls from \$200 to \$194, how much of a change in Y do you expect, based simply on the expenditure multiplier of Chap. 11?
(b) Which curve (IS or LM) is affected by the change in G?
(c) Rewrite the curve you identified in (b), to reflect the change in G.

(d) What are the new equilibrium values of Y and r? How much did Y actually change?
(e) What is the new size of the output gap?

Problem 15.3 Go back to the parameters provided in Problem 15.1, with $G =$ \$200.

(a) If M^s is increased to \$270, which curve is affected?
(b) Rewrite the curve you identified in (a), to reflect the new value of M^s.
(c) Solve for the new equilibrium values of Y and r.
(d) Qualitatively, how has this outcome been similar to and different from the outcome in Problem 15.2?

Problem 15.4 Once again, go back to the parameters of Problem 15.1. This time, consider expected inflation π^e falling from 3% to 2.9%.

(a) Which curve is affected?
(b) Rewrite the curve you identified in (a), to reflect the new value of π^e.
(c) Solve for the new equilibrium values of Y and r.
(d) Explain conceptually why the fall in expected inflation had the effects on output and real interest that you identified in (c).

Problem 15.5 Revisit Problem 14.6.

(a) How do your answers there change your view of the efficacy of fiscal policy?
(b) How do your answers to Problem 14.6 change your view of the efficacy of monetary policy?

References

1. U.S. Congress House Banking Currency Committee. (1935). Hearings, banking act of 1935.
2. What's wrong with macro? "The grumpy economist" Blog. http://johnhcochrane.blogspot.com/2014/12/whats-wrong-with-macro.html. Accessed Aug 13, 2015, Dec 4 2014.
3. Hicks, J. (1980). IS-LM: an explanation. *Journal of Post Keynesian Economics, 3*, 139–154.
4. Bradford deLong, J. (2012). The changing multiplier since 1925 .... Blog post, Mar 2012. http://delong.typepad.com/sdj/2012/03/the-changing-multiplier-since-1925.html. Accessed June 27, 2012.

Chapter 16
Short-Run Aggregate Supply/Aggregate Demand and Policy

Abstract This chapter deals with relationships between the price level and real output. A higher price level is linked with a reduced level of aggregate demand (AD), but with an increased level of aggregate supply (AS). The curves for AD and AS are first explained in conventional Keynesian terms, where a change in the price level causes a change in the quantity demanded and the quantity supplied; AD is shaped by the central bank's response to inflation, while AS is driven by stories of sticky wages or worker misperceptions. These are followed by alternative explanations: AD is shaped by the uncertain transition from *planned* expenditure to achieved *real* demand. AS results from the varying degree of firms' willingness and ability to respond to increased demand by increasing output. The chapter ends with a discussion of the Lucas critique and an extension of that insight to broader issues of how policy is perceived.

16.1 Overview

The previous two chapters on the IS-LM framework gave us a way to relax the earlier implicit assumption that r was fixed; in the IS-LM model, changes in r are balanced with changes in Y. Our next step is to relax the assumption that prices are fixed. To do that, we'll develop a pair of relationships between the price level and the level of output, relationships known as "aggregate demand" (AD) and "aggregate supply" (AS).

We'll start by laying out the conventional Keynesian explanations of these relationships, which have the property that they function like standard demand and supply curves from microeconomics: if you tell me the price level, I can tell you the quantity demanded, or the quantity supplied. Note that to build up the supply side of this explanation, we will need to invoke something being out of equilibrium, either the wage or workers' views of what's happening with the price level.

That is followed by an alternative explanation grounded in the view of money and banks laid out in Chaps. 8 through 10 and the relationship between expenditure and output in Chap. 9 and the first part of Chap. 11.

The IS-LM framework already chipped away at the effectiveness of macroeconomic stabilization policy: when interest rates are flexible, any attempt to goose the economy through fiscal stimulus is at least partially offset by lower investment

K. Seeley, *Macroeconomics in Ecological Context*, Studies in Ecological Economics 5, DOI 10.1007/978-3-319-51757-5_16

expenditure and gross exports, as a result of higher interest rates. The AD-AS model adds to that by allowing prices to rise as well as interest in response to a stimulative policy. The Lucas critique (see Sect. 16.6) casts doubt on the enterprise at a deeper level, by calling into question the stability of the parameters we build into our models, but that insight has ambiguous effects, as discussed in Sect. 16.6.1.

16.2 Aggregate Demand the Standard Way

In the simple aggregate-expenditure/multiplier model, the level of output is flexible, but the price level, the wage, and the interest rate are all assumed to be constant. The IS-LM model keeps the price level and the wage constant but allows the interest rate to vary in response to policy changes or other shocks to the economy. To see the relationship between aggregate demand and the price level, we take the next step and let the price level change.

As explained in Chap. 14, one of the things that shifts the LM curve is a change in the money supply, with a decreased money supply moving the curve to the left. When prices are constant, there's no need to distinguish between the nominal money supply (the amount of dollars out there) and the *real* money supply (the actual amount of goods and services those dollars will buy). But the real money supply is what people actually care about, not the nominal. Liquidity—the reason you hold money at all—is only meaningful in terms of what you can buy, not some ultimately arbitrary number on the bills in your wallet.

Figure 16.1a below shows the effect in the money market of a decrease in the *real* money supply. The nominal money supply, M^S, is unchanged, but because the price level rises from P_0 to P_1, the real money supply, M^S/P, has gone down. This drop in the real money supply moves the LM curve to the left, as shown in Fig. 16.1b. And as the LM curve shifts left, the quantity of aggregate demand decreases. So a higher

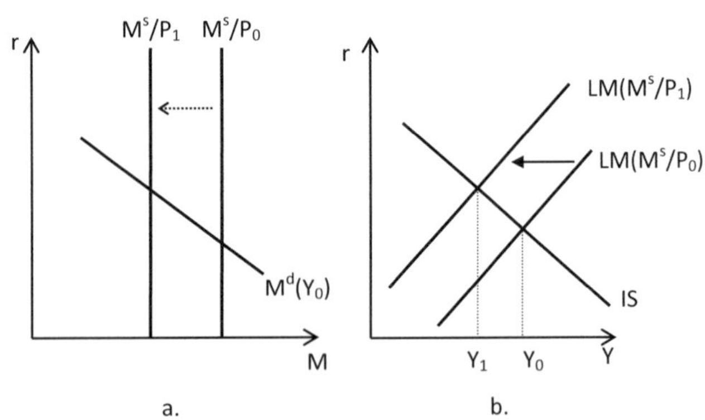

Fig. 16.1 Expansionary fiscal policy

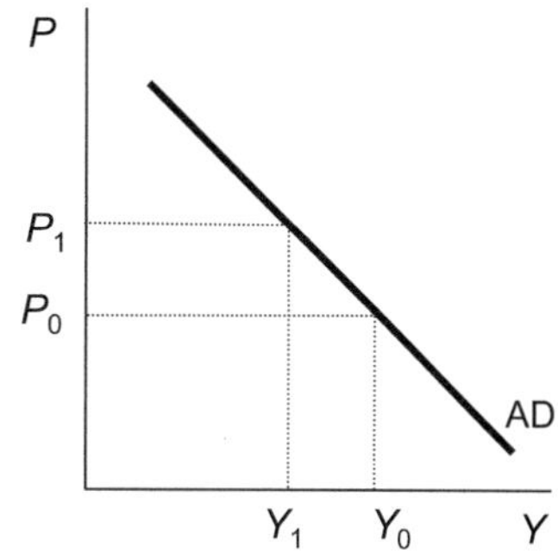

Fig. 16.2 An aggregate demand curve

price level (P_1 instead of P_0) leads to a lower quantity of aggregate expenditure (Y_1 instead of Y_0). Figure 16.2 shows the resulting downward sloping aggregate demand curve.

16.2.1 Interest-Rate Targeting

The aggregate demand curve, as explained above, depends on the central bank keeping the money supply fixed, so that changes in the price level move the LM curve. But what happens when the bank targets the interest rate, changing the money supply as needed to keep the interest rate at the desired level?

The aggregate demand curve in this case is based on the strength of the central bank's intention to fight inflation. As prices rise, the bank raises its target interest rate in order to keep inflation from getting out of hand. The more prices rise, the more severe the bank's raising of the target interest rate. This action on the bank's part raises the LM curve, resulting in lower aggregate expenditure.

16.3 Aggregate Supply the Standard Way

Just as in the classical model, the Keynesian model derives the amount of output from the production function: given a certain amount of capital and a certain level of technology, the output level is determined by the amount of labor actually employed. But the two models end up with different results because of different views about the labor market.[1]

In the classical model, the labor market is always in equilibrium. Firms and workers are both perfectly informed about the price level, and of course both sides know the nominal wage, so everybody knows the real wage. And the nominal wage

[1]This section follows [3].

adjusts as it needs to so that the real wage is always at its market-clearing level. If the price level goes up by 5%, everyone sees the change and the nominal wage goes up by 5%. The real wage hasn't changed at all, so the amount of labor used is unchanged and the economy's output is also unaffected. If prices drop 3%, that is rapidly matched by a 3% drop in the nominal wage, again leaving unchanged the real parts of the economy: the real wage, the level of employment and the amount of output.

There are two conventional stories that change the workings of the model and lead to changes in the price level having effects on the real side of the economy. One is sticky wages, and the other is worker misperceptions of the price level.

16.3.1 Sticky Wages

The idea of "sticky" wages is that the wage can get "stuck" at some level above the market-clearing, equilibrium price. Workers are being paid more than the value of their marginal product, so fewer people are employed than at equilibrium. More specifically, it's the *nominal* wage that's stuck—workers won't accept a reduction in the number of dollars they take home. But if prices rise, the real wage will come down even if the nominal wage doesn't budge. There are two questions this idea may raise: does it make any sense, and is there any evidence for it. The answers are: yes, and yes. There are also a couple of problems with the story, but we'll get to those in Sect. 16.4.

There's a somewhat plausible explanation for why workers might accept a cut in real wages through price hikes while rejecting the same real outcome through a reduction in their nominal wage. Suppose your boss comes to you and your workmates and explains that your wages are too high for current conditions, so it'd be best for everyone if you took a 10% pay cut. And let's say you agree with him about current economic conditions and you see that your wage is above equilibrium. (No, it's unlikely that most workers in any part of the economy actually think about whether their wage is at, above, or below equilibrium, but play along with me here.)

The problem is that you don't know what workers at other companies or in other industries are going to do. Let's say workers across the economy agree to a 10% pay cut. Real wages are restored to equilibrium and, while you'd rather be making more money, everyone is doing as well as they can under current conditions. But what if only *your* company or your industry agrees to the pay cut? For the most part, wages in the economy are still too high. Eventually, the price level will *have to* rise to restore equilibrium in the labor market. That will cut into your wages just as much as into the wages of everyone else—but you already took the 10% hit in your nominal wage, whereas the others only have the erosion of their purchasing power through inflation.

Consider the alternative, where you—and workers across the economy—refuse to take a cut in nominal pay. This time, when equilibrium is restored through

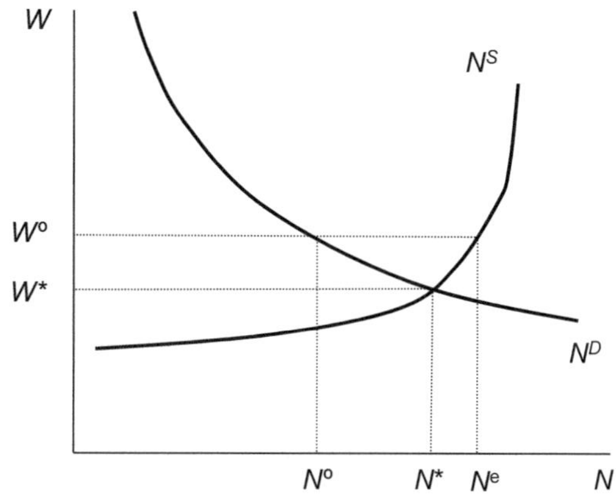

Fig. 16.3 Labor market with a stuck nominal wage

inflation, the reduction in real wages affects everyone equally. So it may well be rational for workers to resist cuts in real wages even if they know that market conditions suggest their real wage is too high.

There's also some empirical evidence that this happens. Most dramatically, during the Great Depression nominal wages did fall, but not by nearly as much as prices did, so that real wages went up significantly. With unemployment rates of 15%, 20%, or even 25%, your basic supply-and-demand intuition would suggest that real wages were too high and needed to come down, yet employers weren't able to achieve the size of nominal-wage reductions that would have been needed to clear the labor market.

With our sticky-wage story in place, we turn now to examine the effects of price changes in such a world. Figure 16.3 shows a labor market with a nominal wage that is "stuck" above its equilibrium level. (Notice that the vertical axis now shows the nominal wage, W, rather than the real wage, W/P, as was the case in the labor-market diagrams in Part II.)

For simplicity, this shows only a single labor supply curve, rather than labor supply and resource-augmented labor supply, as in Chap. 6. You can think of that single curve as either the resource-augmented labor supply from Chap. 6, or as labor supply in a model that doesn't include resources.

The equilibrium wage is W^*, where labor supply and labor demand intersect, but the nominal wage is up at W° (the "stuck" level). At that wage, the amount of labor employed is only N°, since firms can't be forced to hire more people than they want to at the prevailing wage. At the same time, the amount of people who would like to work at that wage is N^e, so there is involuntary unemployment covering the span from N° to N^e.

Now consider the effect of a rise in the price level. Whatever a firm produces, it will be able to sell at a higher price. In nominal terms, the value of the firm's marginal product has gone up. Since the demand for labor is based on the value of labor's marginal product, and our labor-market diagram here is in nominal terms, a rise in the price level causes the labor-demand curve to shift to the right. When

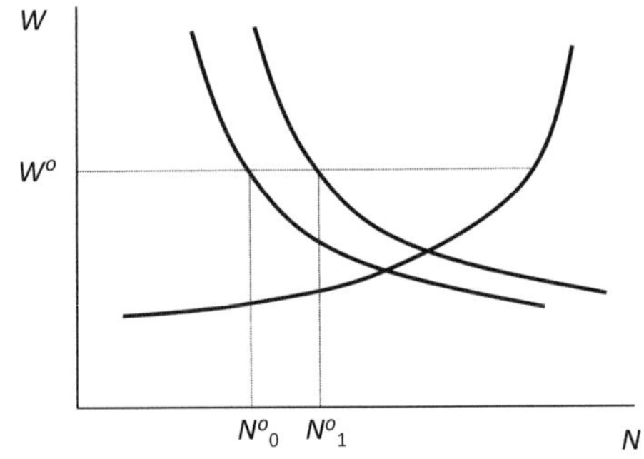

Fig. 16.4 A price increase in the sticky-wage model

that happens, more labor is hired even though the nominal wage hasn't come down. With more labor hired, more is produced, so a higher price level leads to increased output.

In Fig. 16.4, the price level rises from P_0 to P_1, causing the labor-demand curve to shift to the right. This moves the employment level from $N^\circ{}_0$ to $N^\circ{}_1$. Unemployment is down, output is up, it's a beautiful world.

(Note that, if the workers are aware of the change in price level, the labor *supply* curve should move to the left as well, so that workers are continuing to offer the same amount of labor for a given level of real compensation. But if employment was being held down by the real wage being higher than employers wanted to pay, rather than lower than workers wanted to accept, the effect on the labor market will be the same.)

16.3.2 Flexible Wages

If we want to move beyond sticky wages and allow nominal wages to change, we can still get to a similar result of an upward-sloping aggregate supply curve by a different route. The key assumption here is that workers don't know the *actual* price level, but instead form some expectation (or guess) about what the price level is. As in the classical model, they're concerned with the level of real wages, but unlike in that model they can be systematically wrong about what that level is.

Let's say workers form a guess about the price level, P^e. That means they perceive the real wage to be W/P^e. On the other side of the labor market, employers are assumed not to be guessing at the price level, but to know what it truly is.

So when prices go up, labor demand increases for exactly the same reason as in the sticky-wage model: firms can sell their output for more dollars, so they're willing to hire more workers for any given level of nominal wages. This increased demand for labor drives up nominal wages, but labor doesn't (yet) perceive the increase in the price level, they only see the increase in the nominal wage. If you see your nominal wage going up and you think prices are holding steady, you'll naturally think that your real wage is going up. This makes you more willing to work than before.

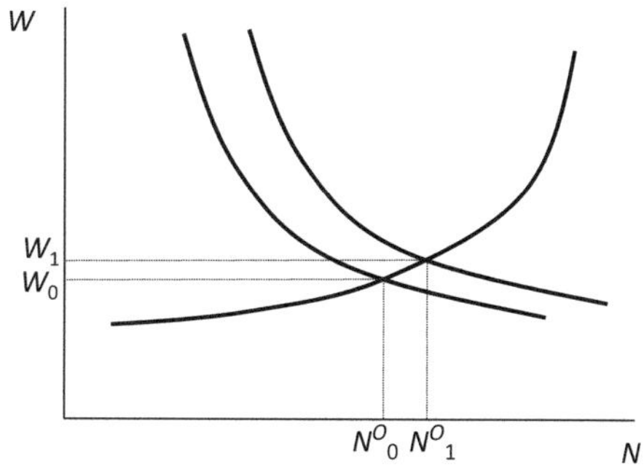

Fig. 16.5 A price increase in the flexible-wage model

Figure 16.5 shows the effect of a price increase in the flexible-wage model. Prices rise from P_0 to P_1. This pushes labor demand to the right, as firms are willing to pay more (in nominal terms) and hire more workers. Workers see the rise from W_0 to W_1, while their guess of the price level remains at P^e, so they're willing to supply more labor. Employment goes up from N_0 to N_1. With more labor employed, output increases.

One difference to note between the sticky-wage and flexible-wage models is the treatment of equilibrium. In the sticky-wage story, the labor market is out of equilibrium because of the wage being stuck at the wrong level; the level of employment is determined by the intersection of the labor demand curve and the nominal wage, rather than labor demand and labor supply. In the flexible-wage story, the actual level of employment is determined by the intersection of supply and demand; the disequilibrium element comes from the assumption that the workers have an inaccurate perception of the price level and so, in a sense, the labor supply curve is in the "wrong" place—if employees knew the true price level, they wouldn't be willing to offer as much labor.

16.3.3 Sticky vs. Flexible

Both of these explanations of the aggregate supply curve account for an increase in output as a result of an increase in the price level—in other words, both models can support an upward-sloping aggregate supply curve, as opposed to the perfectly vertical supply curve of the classical model, or the perfectly horizontal supply curve of the simple aggregate-demand model. But there is a key difference between the two, which is that the flexible-wage model results in a steeper aggregate supply curve.

In the sticky-wage model, the entire rightward shift of the labor demand curve gets translated into increased employment, precisely because the wage is stuck. What drives the model is that the wage doesn't fall down toward its equilibrium level, but there's also no reason for it to go up so long as it is still above equilibrium. In the flexible-wage model, the nominal wage rises somewhat, so firms don't add as

Fig. 16.6 Four versions of aggregate supply

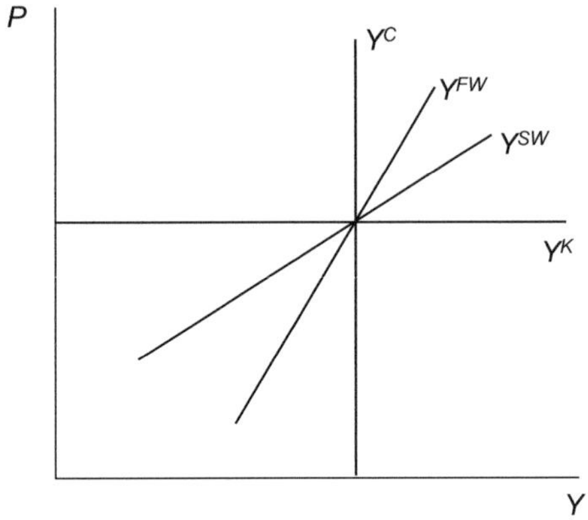

many workers as in the sticky-wage version. So the same increase in prices leads to a smaller increase in employment when wages are flexible, and that smaller increase in employment means, in turn, a smaller increase in output. The less output increases for a given increase in the price level, the steeper the aggregate supply curve.

Figure 16.6 shows four versions of the aggregate supply curve.

- Y^K is the curve implicit in the simple Keynesian aggregate-demand-multiplier model: prices are fixed and output will expand in response to demand.
- Y^C is the classical aggregate supply curve: tell me the quantity of capital and the labor supply curve, and I'll tell you the quantity of output. Price has nothing to do with determining output, as any stimulus to aggregate demand will just be converted into price increases.
- Y^{SW} is the sticky-wage aggregate supply curve. Output goes up with an increase in prices.
- Y^{FW} is the flexible-wage aggregate supply curve. As with the sticky-wage version, output goes up with an increase in prices, but not by as much, making for a steeper supply curve.

16.4 "Fool Me Twice": Alternatives to the Standard Explanation

The sticky-wage and flexible-wage models have a certain internal logic to them, but they also have dissatisfying traits. In the case of the sticky-wage model, it's not clear what puts the nominal wage up above the market-clearing level in the first place. Presumably the wage *was* at equilibrium and then aggregate demand fell, drawing down the equilibrium wage and leaving the nominal wage "stranded" at its excessively high level. But then, why did aggregate demand fall?

There are some efforts to answer this, such as "efficiency-wage" theory. In the simple model, your labor has a marginal product; you and I both know what that marginal product is; you and I both know that I have no reason to pay you anything more than that, so that's what you get paid.

In the real world, marginal products aren't so cleanly visible. And people work differently depending on their motivation, and hiring someone to replace you isn't free. If I pay you $15/hr instead of $12/hr, maybe you'll work much better, and your marginal product will justify the higher wage. And if I pay you that higher wage, you're less likely to jump to some other company the first chance you get, so I don't have the expense of finding and training someone to replace you. A simple-minded view of efficiency says the employer should pay the marginal product, not a penny more; the theory of the "efficiency wage" suggests that employers can do better by paying somewhat more.

So there are stories that can get the nominal wage up above its equilibrium level, but in some ways they just lead to more questions. (Such as, "Why don't those same 'efficiency-wage' factors cause the nominal wage to adjust right along with prices, rather than being stuck at one particular, high level?")

The flexible-wage model has a weakness that is possibly more troubling, which is the information asymmetry between firms and labor: firms are assumed to *know* the price level, while workers are operating on their *best guess*, and they are routinely wrong. They see an increase in the nominal wage and mistake it for an increase in the real wage, since they haven't yet noticed that prices have increased. And they make this mistake *again and again*, even though that increase in prices is the only reason firms are willing to pay more. As the old saying goes, Fool me once, shame on you; fool me twice, shame on me. It seems odd that labor as a whole should be consistently duped without learning from its experience.

One last problem is common to both these forms of the aggregate-supply story. Notice that in both cases the quantity of labor employed is ultimately determined by the demand for labor, and the reason firms are willing to hire more people when prices go up is that a higher price elvel means that *real* wages are down. Economic recovery, by definition, means more output, which shows up in Figs. 16.9 and 16.10 as an increase in Y. But remember that all output is somebody's income. If total income has gone up and wages have gone down, what happened? Employment has also increased (after all, that's what created the increased output), so one possibility is that total compensation to labor has gone up, it's just spread over so many more people that the average wage has gone down. The other possibility is that the increase in employment *doesn't* offset the drop in the real wage level, so the recovery is good for firms' profits while hurting the average worker substantially. If you were unemployed and now have a job, you gained; but if you were already employed and now have to accept a drop in your real wage, you've been set back. In either case, a scenario of falling real wages for most workers doesn't feel a lot like "recovery" or "prosperity" as most people understand those things.

For a different view—perhaps a more intuitive one—we'll turn to the understanding of money, expenditure, and response to expenditure built up earlier in Part III.

16.4.1 Aggregate Supply as a Result of Spending

An alternative approach to aggregate supply avoids the troubling implications of the sticky-wage and flexible-wage stories told so far. Those were both inspired by supply curves in microeconomics, where the price can be treated as the cause, and suppliers respond by producing and selling more. Analogously, the stories told above treated increased inflation or a higher price level as the *cause*, and tried to explain why that would lead to a higher level of production.

The alternative story goes the other way, starting from the level of expenditure coming out of the aggregate demand curve. As expenditure goes up, producers try to increase production. They go to buy more inputs; if there's been a *large* increase in expenditure, they look to hire more workers, or have their current workforce put in longer hours. But they're not always successful. If makers of smart phones and game consoles both need microchips, the chip-makers' capacity may soon be tapped out, and the companies that buy the chips end up in a bidding war, pushing up the price without getting much in the way of increased chip production. If unemployment is already low, firms may find they have to pay higher wages to get the employees they want. Or they may be able to keep the wage the same but have to settle for lower-quality workers, meaning they're getting less work done for the same amount of money—their cost per unit of *effective* labor has gone up.

This explanation of the aggregate supply curve doesn't have a definitive relationship to the sticky-wage and flexible-wage stories: if we tell a story of flexible wages, then we know we're looking at a steeper AS curve than if we tell a story of sticky wages; but if we tell a story of expenditure first and supply responding, we can't say whether that's steeper than with flexible wages, flatter than with sticky wages, or somewhere in between. Sometimes there will be lots of "slack" in the economy and firms will be able to increase output without significantly raising prices, so the AS curve will be fairly flat. In other instances, raising output will be impossible, or firms will be unwilling to incur the expense of producing the extra output, and so the extra expenditure will turn into higher prices.

There's one more point in favor of this way of understanding aggregate supply, which is that it ties in better with the nature of money as laid out in Chap. 9. The sticky- and flexible-wage stories are closely grounded in the long-run model from Chap. 4 through 7, which is in essence a model of barter. Real labor is exchanged for real output. Money exists, but it's merely a tool for transactions, a convenience to get around the barter problem of a "double-coincidence of wants."

One of the key points in Chap. 9 was that newly created money could result in new *real*, *physical* activity in the economy. It didn't have to happen one-for-one (a dollar of new expenditure resulting in a dollar of *new* output), and it didn't even have to happen at all. But it *could* happen, and it could be one-for-one, and it could even have a multiplier effect, as explained in Chap. 11. It all depends on the economy's physical *ability* to produce the additional output, together with the *willingness* of producers to meet increased expenditure with increased output.

16.4.2 Aggregate Demand as a Result of Decentralized Reactions to Inflation

On the AD side, the problems with the conventional explanation are less severe than with AS, but the story is somewhat unsatisfactory. It ultimately depends entirely on a policy action by the central bank in response to changes in inflation or price levels. That's not wrong, but it overlooks the possibility of an AD-type behavior based on decentralized responses to people's economic environment.

Consider a concrete example: the price level is at 150, and households, firms, and governments choose expenditures that add up to $250. (You can add a bunch of zeros and call it $250 billion if you like). In real terms, they're planning to buy $167 worth of stuff.

If the price level stays at 150, then spending $250 nominal dollars will actually get you $167 of stuff in real terms.

But what if that expenditure causes the price level to rise to 160? In that case, spending $250 nominal dollars only gets you $156 worth of stuff in real terms. On the other hand, if the price level falls to 140, then aggregate expenditure of $250 will result in the purchase of $179 worth of stuff in real terms.

Figure 16.7 shows this relationship, which is our first cut at the aggregate demand curve. We start with expenditure determined in nominal terms: a certain number of dollars. And that means that a higher price level is associated with a lower level of expenditure in real terms. And it's this real expenditure that we call "aggregate demand."

We need one last modification before aggregate demand is finished: we have to go beyond the simple mathematical relationship among nominal expenditure, price level, and real expenditure, and consider people's reaction to higher or lower prices.

As presented above, it sounds as though people commit to spending a certain number of dollars, then something happens to the price level, and people find out

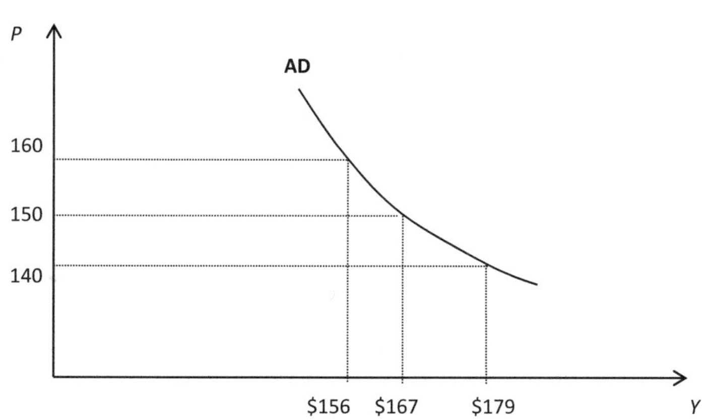

Fig. 16.7 Aggregate demand with fixed nominal expenditure

how much those dollars actually bought and don't change the number of dollars they spend. But of course the price level is a continually evolving thing, and people can change the number of dollars they spend in response to the price level.

Say you want to open up a store, and you think you will need to spend $100,000 *in real terms* to do it. At a price level of 150, you'll need $150,000 to get it done. You go to the bank for a loan and they approve it, so they extend you $150,000 worth of credit.

You start into the project, but it turns out that the price level has risen to 160. That $150,000 loan will now only buy you $93,750 in real terms, instead of the $100,000 that you were planning on. If you want to carry out your original plans, you'll need an extra $10,000. What to do?

Maybe you do stick to your original plans. Perhaps you dig into your own savings. Or you go back to the bank and explain the situation, and they extend you an extra $10,000 credit.

Another option is to only spend the original $150,000 in nominal terms, and find ways to do a little less. Maybe you use some lower-quality materials. Or you were planning a big display window in front and you make it a smaller window (windows are more expensive than walls).

Or you can go somewhere in the middle: spend $155,000 instead of $150,000, and therefore in real terms get $96,875 instead of either $100,000 or $93,750.

An extreme response would be to just throw in the towel. You budgeted for $100,000 in real terms; if you can't afford that, you're not going to do it at all. But that's usually not a good idea. You've already spent some of the borrowed money, and if you never open the store, you'll never have a way of earning the money to pay it back. If the new inflation makes your whole business plan no longer viable, then maybe this is the way to go, but in general you'll probably want to proceed in some way or other.

The less extreme version of this is not to throw in the towel, but to reduce your nominal spending below $150,000. You were planning to buy $100,000 worth of stuff in real terms. Prices went up, so you can only afford $93,750 in real terms, still spending $150,000 nominal. But the price change itself worries you, and so out of caution you reduce your nominal spending to $140,000, thereby reducing your real spending to $87,500.

The same logic applies if prices are falling. You borrowed $150,000 when the price level was 150, and now it turns out the price level is only 140. You thought you were going to be buying $100,000 worth of stuff in real terms, but now you can buy $107,143.

As with the price increase, you could stick to your original plans: buy $100,000 in real terms, which will only cost you $140,000 in nominal dollars. So there's $10,000 of your loan that you won't spend and therefore won't have to earn back.

Or you could spend the whole $150,000 and get to some things you'd earlier decided not to do—maybe you upgrade to higher quality materials, or spend some extra money on your original supplies for the store.

Or you could go somewhere in between, spending slightly fewer dollars than you expected but buying slightly nicer or more stuff.

These behavioral responses have an effect on the shape of the aggregate demand curve. At one extreme, everyone sticks to their real plans. You wanted to buy $100,000 worth of stuff to open a store and that's what you do, regardless of the price level. If the price level is at 150, you spend $150,000; if it's at 130, you spend $130,000; if it's at 200, you spend $200,000. The result would be a perfectly vertical aggregate demand curve: regardless of the price level, people try to buy the same amount of stuff in real terms.

The other extreme (and it truly is an "extreme") is kind of hard to imagine. Visually, it would be a perfectly flat (horizontal) aggregate demand curve. That would reflect a situation where everybody just threw in the towel when prices went up. You were planning to buy $100,000 worth of stuff with a CPI of 150, but now that the CPI has gone up to 151, you scrap the whole project and buy $0 worth of stuff. And if the price level fell to 149, you'd ... buy an infinite amount of stuff?

That extreme case is hard to even make sense of, and the other extreme (a vertical aggregate demand curve) is conceivable but not realistic. The underlying point, however, is that the strictly arithmetical relationship depicted in Fig. 16.7 is not the only possible aggregate-demand relationship. As Fig. 16.8 shows, people in general can be somewhat insensitive to the price level, making the AD curve steeper (the dotted line in Fig. 16.8, labeled "AD_1"). They could react to higher prices by cutting back on their nominal expenditure, resulting in a flatter AD curve (the dashed line, labeled "AD_2"). Or they could stick to their nominal spending plans, and spend more or less in real terms, depending on the price level (the solid AD curve, "AD_0", the same curve as shown in Fig. 16.7).

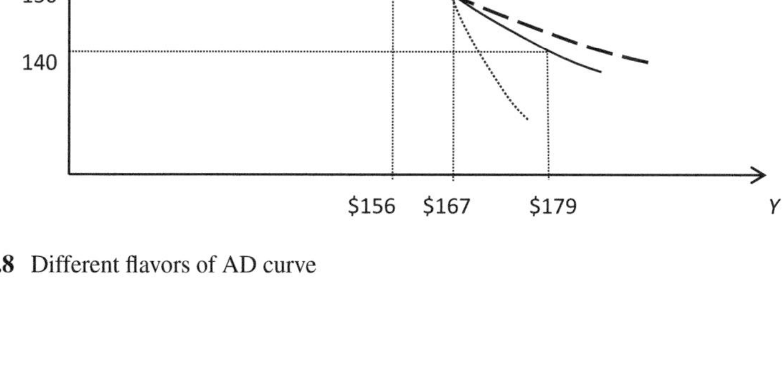

Fig. 16.8 Different flavors of AD curve

16.4.3 Combining AD and AS

Now we have an AS curve that maps out a set of production possibilities, with varying tradeoffs between increased output and a higher price level, and an AD curve that reflects people's expenditure plans, their access to purchasing (including via credit), and their behavioral response to changes in the price level.

A change in productive possibilities moves the AS curve. A change in planned expenditure moves the AD curve. The two curves interact, and their slopes determine how much of each curve's movement gets translated into changes in output and how much shows up as changes in the price level.

Note that on the supply side, the direction of the relationship has been turned around. In a microeconomic supply curve—and in the conventional aggregate supply curve laid out in Sect. 16.3—we start from a price level and find out what level of output goes with it. In the alternative explanation presented here, that's not actually the right question. We don't have a situation where a particular price level will result in a particular level of output. Rather, when firms face increased expenditure on their products, in principle they try to increase output. At lower levels of output, they're more successful and/or willing; at higher levels, they have less ability and/or willingness to actually produce more, so the increased expenditure turns into higher prices.

On the demand side, one could think of the relationship as being from price levels to different quantities of real purchases, but it may be more helpful to stay with the chain of reasoning from *planned* real expenditure to possibly altered *actual* expenditure in the face of changed price levels.

This alternative story leaves out the policy role of the central bank, but it more easily reflects the role of the banking system in enabling expenditure through the provision of credit.

16.4.4 Demand Shifters

As with the normal sort of demand curve in microeconomics, it's useful to know what shifts aggregate demand. The first thing is to rule out changes in the price level—as with microeconomic demand curves, a change in price represents a move *along* a demand curve, rather than a shift of the curve itself.

That leaves all the things that change aggregate expenditure in the simpler model of Chap. 11. Tax cuts and increases in government spending will shift the curve to the right. A decrease in gross exports will move it to the left. A drop in autonomous consumption (captured by the C_0 in the consumption function) or a drop in autonomous investment, will likewise cause aggregate demand to shift to the left.

16.5 Policy Effects

As with the IS-LM model, part of the point of having the model at all is to try to understand the effects of policy. These can be seen by combining the IS-LM model with the aggregate-supply/aggregate-demand model.

In Fig. 16.9, the government pursues an expansionary fiscal policy of increasing government expenditure, from G_0 to G_1, shifting the IS curve to the right as shown in Fig. 16.9a. The effect is an increase in aggregate demand, which shows up in Fig. 16.9b. The increase in aggregate demand leads to an increase both in output and in prices. The increase in the price level in turn has an effect on the IS-LM model, because the LM curve is determined by the *real* money supply, and the higher prices reduce the real money supply, moving the LM curve to the left. The LM shift doesn't completely counteract the IS shift—that would be a "classical" result, where fiscal policy had no effect on real output—but it does result in a smaller increase in output than in the IS-LM model on its own. The economy starts out at point A; the policy aims it toward point B; but with the increase in the price level, it ends up at point C instead.

A similar effect shows up with monetary policy, as illustrated in Fig. 16.10. An increase in the money supply initially shifts the LM curve significantly to the right, in an effort to move the economy from its starting point at A to point B. This translates into an increase in aggregate demand, with output and the price level both increasing. As in the case of fiscal policy, the increased price level ends up shifting the LM curve partway back to the left—again, not all the way, or we would be back in a classical world, but the effect of the aggregate-demand shift is blunted by the increase in the price level, leaving us at point C.

Note that the steeper the aggregate supply curve, the stronger is this blunting effect. In the sticky-wage model, there's a substantial increase in output, accompanied by a moderate increase in prices. In the flexible-wage model, the aggregate supply curve is steeper, so you get more of a price hike and not as much of an

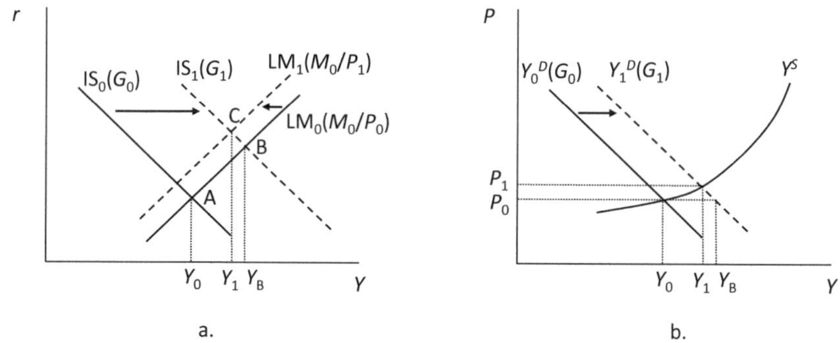

Fig. 16.9 Fiscal policy with flexible prices

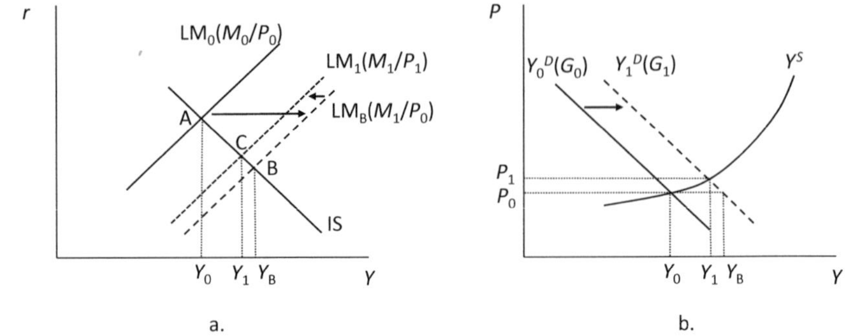

Fig. 16.10 Monetary policy with flexible prices

increase in output. In the classical case, prices go up so much that the LM curve shifts strongly to the left—just enough to keep output from going up at all.

16.6 The Lucas Critique

So here's this wonderful tool. All we need is some estimates of what the world looks like, and we can go ahead and make policy. Referring back to the IS-LM model in Chap. 15, are we in the "neutral" case where both curves are "average" rather than being extremely steep or extremely flat? Then either fiscal or monetary policy should be about equally effective. Do we have a steep LM curve or a flat IS curve? Then monetary policy is the way to go. Or if we have a flat LM curve or a steep IS curve, we need to rely on fiscal policy.

And we can even get a sense of how large the policy should be. If we're in the "neutral" case, we might need a moderately large fiscal stimulus; if reality has a relatively steep IS curve (see Chap. 14), then fiscal policy is highly effective and we can get the same result with a smaller stimulus.[2] Combine all this with an estimate of the slopes of the AS and AD curves, and we can be even more accurate. If we're in a flat section of the AS curve, then stimulative policy will be highly effective; if we're in the steep part, not so much.

So we send out some econometricians to do studies of the interest-elasticity of investment and of money demand, and of the marginal propensity to consume, and to estimate how much more inflation we can expect from a 1% increase in aggregate expenditure. We translate that into IS and LM curves of the right steepness, and we can then calculate how much our policies will move each curve and what the

[2]Remember from Chap. 15 that the reason it's effective is that investment isn't very interest-elastic; the fiscal stimulus drives up interest rates, but this has little effect on investment, so there's little offsetting drop in investment activity.

ultimate effect will be on income and interest. Modify it by the effect on prices from the AS/AD framework, and we're all done. It's as easy as following a cookbook.

All of this depends, however, on the parameters of the model being stable. That is, our policy will only work the way we expect it to if the MPC doesn't change and if the interest-elasticities of investment and gross exports and money demand don't change. If these things *do* change, then all bets are off. Let's say we've calculated an MPE of 0.75, so we have a government expenditure multiplier of 4. We expect our \$100 billion spending package to shift the IS curve by \$400 million, but suddenly the MPE drops, so the IS curve doesn't move as far as we thought it would and our policy is less effective than we expected.

Or we've estimated very interest-elastic investment demand, so we think monetary policy will be effective. But as we implement the policy, investment demand becomes less interest-elastic, so our policy ends up being less effective.

This idea—that the parameters of our model may not be stable—is often referred to as the "Lucas critique," named for the economist Robert Lucas, who developed it in [4].

The Lucas critique isn't merely that it's possible to incorrectly estimate these parameters. Rather, the critique is the idea that there may be systematic reasons for getting this stuff wrong. Lucas observed that the parameters of a macroeconomic model— things like interest elasticities and the MPC—are behavioral regularities that are shaped by many factors, *including policy*. So if you change policy, it would be naïve not to expect behaviors to change at the same time.

It would be one thing if such behavioral adaptation were random, but (in Lucas's view) it's more likely that the adaptation works against the efficacy of fiscal or monetary "management" of the economy. Consider the two cases presented here. If the government tries to stimulate the economy with extra spending, forward-looking people might predict increased taxes or decreased government spending in the future in order to pay back the debt incurred. And at least some of them will respond to that insight by saving a greater portion of their extra income than they would have otherwise, so as to avoid too large a drop in consumption when that tax hike or government cut happens.[3] In other words, people might rationally respond to fiscal stimulus by cutting their MPC, undercutting the effect of the stimulus.

Something similar could lie behind the second example. An expansionary monetary policy could raise fears of future inflation, discouraging investment in general and making it less interest-elastic. As in the previous case, the policy itself changes the parameters of the model that the policy was meant to take advantage of.

Another way of thinking about this is that there *are* stable parameters out there in the world, but they're hidden down underneath the parameters in our model—the things we used our econometric studies to estimate, such as GX_Y, C_0, I_r. Between

[3]This is an idea known as Ricardian equivalence. The claim is that the path of government spending determines the amount of taxes that will need to be collected eventually, and people's behavior shouldn't be much influenced by whether they need to pay those taxes now or later; households will save or borrow as needed to protect their spending from changes in the tax rate.

the parameters in our model and the stable parameters underneath them, there are people's perceptions about the world, such as their expectations about inflation, and what they think future fiscal and monetary policy are going to be. But we can't see those stable parameters, nor can we see the steps that link them to the parameters in our model.

So the result is the same: A change in policy doesn't just change, say, M^S, or G, or t. It also changes people's views of future inflation and future fiscal and monetary policy. As their views change, the processes that translate those views into C_0, or I_0, or IM_Y, etc. start to produce different results, and so our estimates of those values turn out to be wrong.

16.6.1 Extending the Lucas Critique

In its simplest form, the Lucas critique looks just at the size of the change in the money supply or the size of the fiscal stimulus (that is, the size of the tax cut or increase in G). But, intuitively, some subtler details should matter as well. If you cut taxes, *whose* taxes precisely are you cutting? Different parts of the population are likely to have different MPCs, so it should make a difference whose hands your tax cut gets into first.

And a wealth of variety is covered under the simple little variable G. Consider two different "public works" projects: $50 billion spent on new highways vs. $50 billion spent on new passenger-rail capacity. The first difference is that you'll get different amounts of passenger-moving capacity for the same $50 billion. If you're in a situation where rail is more efficient, but the government spends the money on highways, the effect of the policy is likely to be diluted, because people will see the government wasting money and form a more pessimistic estimate of future economic conditions. (On the other hand, the highway system requires the further purchase of cars and gasoline in order for people to use it, so while more of society's resources are being used up by this choice, in some sense making society poorer, it may stimulate more economic activity.) Also, highways and rail-transit also serve somewhat different constituencies and lead to different patterns of settlement and urban growth, so different kinds of businesses will be stimulated, depending on where the government puts its money.

And the differences are not limited to varieties of public works. More money on transit—whether roads or rails—should affect the economy differently than the same amount of increased spending on education, which in turn should be different from increased spending on the military or homeland security. Rational people will respond not merely to the size of government efforts to manage the economy, but also to their perception of the underlying economic value of activities the government funds or the taxes it cuts.

Schelling [7] has an interesting meditation on the interaction between belief and the effectiveness of policy. As summarized by Tesfatsion [8, p. 14], this is "the distinction between trying to get people to believe a proposition that is *unconditionally true* and trying to get people to believe a proposition that *would* be true if (and perhaps only if) enough people believed it were true." As an extension of those ideas, if people see government expenditure going to things that they think will benefit them, or the economy in general, that should increase their confidence and thus their willingness to consume and invest.

The converse should also hold: some policies may fail—even objectively "good" policies—if enough people think they're flawed. If people see government expenditure directed at things they think will be of no use to them, or that may even harm the economy in general, then it's more reasonable to expect that they will reduce their own spending just as the government ramps up. And of course there are many areas of government spending where people don't agree whether it's harmful or helpful.

Lastly, there's the question not just of specific policies, but of overall policy environments. Lucas's interpretation of his insight led him to a recommendation that policy generally not focus to much on smoothing out the business cycle (see, e.g., [5]). Because of the difficulty of doing it right, such "active" macroeconomic policy tends to introduce more uncertainty into the economy. It's hard enough to figure out what the economy is doing on its own and try to react intelligently based on that understanding. Now if you throw in stabilization policy, people have to also try to guess at the bumbling actions of the government, and at how their fellow-citizens will respond to those bumbling actions.

An alternative story is that, even if macroeconomic management is imperfect, it's still better than simply letting the business cycle run its course. When it's done reasonably well, such management of the business cycle can shorten downturns, resulting in a "safer" business climate, one where any given firm's chance of bankruptcy is lower, and where the penalty for launching a business venture at the "wrong" time (right at the beginning of a downturn) is reduced.[4]

This leads to the observation that the meaning of the Lucas critique depends on what people generally think is true of the underlying economy. If people agree with Lucas that macroeconomic management is futile, then people will react badly when they see such management being tried; it will be a signal to them that the government is making things worse. But the whole situation turns around if people think that a certain amount of competent management is better than none. In this case, when people see the government responding (rationally) to an economic slowdown, it gives them confidence, and makes them more likely to spend (whether on consumption or on investment). In this scenario, what discourages people and makes them hug their wallets close is exactly the hands-off policy that Lucas advocates.

[4]This idea is explored more in Chap. 18.

Appendix: The Phillips Curve

In 1958, the economist A.W.H. Phillips published a paper looking at the connection between the rate of unemployment and the rate of growth of nominal wages [6]. As James Forder [2] documents, there was already a literature on the role of the unemployment rate in determining wages, but somehow the name "Phillips curve" got attached to it, and then used in a variety of subtly different meanings, including a common textbook version (e.g., DeLong [1]), in which it's a relationship between unemployment and the rate of inflation.

This version of the Phillips Curve is anchored by expected inflation and the natural rate of unemployment.

Expected inflation is straightforward: the rate of inflation that people in the economy expect over the coming time, perhaps a year.

The natural rate of unemployment is also known in this context as the NAIRU, or the non-accelerating inflation rate of unemployment. The name is awkward, but the concept is fairly intuitive. If unemployment is very low, that's a sign of there being little "slack" in the economy, few productive inputs that aren't being put to use. The price of those inputs—particularly the wage to pay labor—will be pushed up, feeding inflation. As people observe *actual* inflation that's higher than what they expected, eventually their perceptions will shift and they'll start to expect higher inflation. Those expectations will get built into future price-setting behavior, making the expectation reality. If unemployment remains low, there will still be a lack of slack in the economy, and so prices will continue to get pushed up, but now from the higher base of people's higher expectations, leading to continually rising inflation. The NAIRU is the lowest rate of unemployment that won't cause this phenomenon. Above the NAIRU, inflation is stable or even falling; below it, you eventually trigger the continual rise described here.[5]

Figure 16.11 shows a representation of the Phillips curve (the downward-sloping line labeled "PC"), anchored at the expected-inflation rate π^e and natural rate of unemployment u^*.

The Phillips curve can be seen as a kind of aggregate supply curve, just flipped around. In the normal aggregate supply curve, higher prices go with higher output; in the Phillips curve, higher inflation goes with lower unemployment, which implies higher output.

In this framework, if the Phillips curve is a type of aggregate supply curve, then the aggregate demand curve is something known as the monetary policy reaction function, or MPRF. The idea is that the monetary authority is concerned about inflation. At higher levels of inflation, it will be more concerned and so is more likely to raise the interest rates it controls. That in turn should slow down expenditure,

---

[5]In theoretical terms, the NAIRU or the natural rate of unemployment can also be thought of as corresponding to the equilibrium rate of employment determined by the long-run factors that were the focus of Part II, and the corresponding level of output can be thought of as potential GDP, as discussed in 6.10.

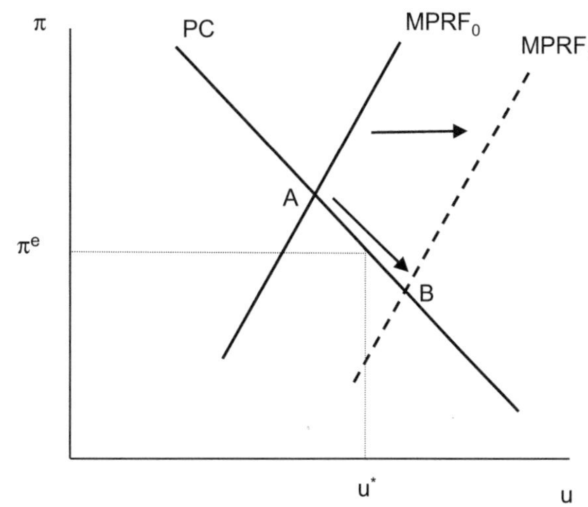

Fig. 16.11 A drop in aggregate demand

leading to lower GDP (or lower *growth* of GDP) and the the higher unemployment associated with that. So the MPRF is an upward-sloping line, as shown in Fig. 16.11. Equilibrium in the economy is at their intersection (see point "A" in Fig. 16.11). An exogenous decrease in aggregate demand (say, a loss of consumer confidence) would cause the MPRF to shift to the right, moving equilibrium to point "B".

A limitation of the Phillips curve is that its two anchor points—expected inflation and the NAIRU—are things we can't actually observe in the world. We are instead forced to work with proxies for them or other ways of estimating them. Still, it can be a useful tool in thinking about expectations and how they influence economic outcomes, somewhat analogously to the role played by perceptions of how good policy is, described in Sect. 16.6.1. If inflation expectations are "anchored," that implies that they don't change too easily and policy makers can tolerate a modest period of somewhat elevated inflation without triggering a change in expectations and a movement of the Phillips curve in an unfortunate direction. In contrast, if inflation expectations are not well anchored, much more caution is in order, so as not to spook the public into expecting higher inflation, which would leave future policy-makers with less favorable tradeoffs.

Problems

Problem 16.1 (a) Use the parameters in this table to solve for the IS and LM curves.

Government: $G = 400$, $t = 19\%$
Consumption: $C_0 = 50$, $C_Y = 0.75$

Imports:	$IM_Y = 0.08$
Exchange rate:	$\varepsilon_0 = 1.5$, $\varepsilon_r = 1400$, $r^f = 4\%$
Gross exports:	$GX_Y = 0.002$, $Y^f = 20,000$, $GX_\varepsilon = 8$
Investment:	$I_0 = 280$, $I_r = 500$
Money parameters:	$m_0 = 1000$, $m_1 = 0.15$, $m_2 = 8,000$
Money supply:	$M^S{}_{nominal} = 318$
Price level and inflation:	$P = 39.75$, $\pi^e = 3\%$

(b) Use the IS and LM curves from (a) to solve for r and Y.

(c) Now consider an increase in G from 400 to 425. Which curve moves? Which way does it move? How far does it move?

(d) Using the new curve from (c), solve for the new values of r and Y. (e) How did the actual change in Y (from (b) to (d) differ from the size of the shift of the curve that you identified in (c)? *Why* is it different, and why is it different in the way it is (i.e., smaller or larger)?

(f) Use the parameters below to solve for output Y and the price level P.

AD: $Y = 4,839.5 - 72P$

AS: $Y = 388 + 40P$

(g) When G increases from 400 to 425, as in (c), which of these two curves (AD or AS) is affected, which way does it move, and how far does it move?

(h) Use your new curve from (g) to calculate new values of Y and P.

(i) How does your answer to (h) change either the IS or the LM curve?

(j) Use the updated curve from (c) and the updated curve from (i) to solve for r and Y.

(k) How does the change from (b) to (j) compare with the earlier changes (part (b) to part (d), and part (b) to part (e))? *Why* is the (b)-to-(j) change different in the way that it is?

References

1. Bradford deLong, J. (2002). *Macroeconomics*. Boston: McGraw-Hill/Irwin.
2. Forder, J. (2014). Nine views of the Phillips curve: Eight authentic and one inauthentic. University of Oxford Department of Economics Discussion Paper Series, September 2014. http://www.economics.ox.ac.uk/materials/papers/13451/paper724.pdf. Accessed September 5, 2015.
3. Froyen, R. T. (2001). *Macroeconomics: theories and policies* (7th ed.). Upper Saddle River: Prentice Hall.
4. Lucas, R. (1976). Econometric policy evaluation: A critique. *Carnegie-Rochester Conference Series on Public Policy, 1*, 19–46.
5. Lucas, R. (2013). Macroeconomic priorities. *American Economic Review, 93*, 1–14.
6. Phillips, A. W. H. (1958). The relation between unemployment and the rate of change of money wage rates in the United Kingdom, 1861–1957. *Economica, 25*, 283–299.
7. Schelling, T. C. (1982). Establishing credibility: Strategic considerations. *American Economic Review, 72*, 77–80.
8. Tesfatsion, L. (2013). Notes on the Lucas critique, time inconsistency, and related issues, November 2013. http://www2.econ.iastate.edu/tesfatsi/luccrit.pdf, Accessed April 1, 2016.

Chapter 17
Policy Assessment

Abstract This chapter looks at the evidence and argument over how well fiscal and monetary policy has worked. This is an inherently inconclusive exercise, given that the reference point for "success" is an alternative reality in which different policies were pursued. The chapter also includes a taxonomy of arguments against the efficacy of stimulus policy, addressed in the framework developed earlier in the book of a biophysical perspective on long-run growth and money as part of the real economy.

17.1 Introduction

Starting from the explanation of what money is and how it works, Part III has worked through different aspects of business cycles and the basic policy tools for trying to smooth them out. A natural question is, Do those tools work?

That turns out to be a very hard question to answer. As a first pass, you might think to look at the implementation of a policy and then see what happened after that. For example, the model presented here, like any flavor of Keynesian model, suggests that cutting taxes should raise GDP, at least in the short run. So look at a tax cut and see if it is followed by faster GDP growth.

There is a big problem with that, which is that there are lots of things going on besides the fiscal or monetary policy that was implemented. Perhaps a stimulative policy was enacted, but the underlying situation was worse than people understood, or the economy was hit with a new negative shock, and so the policy was followed by no improvement, or even a worsening of economic performance. But it's possible that things would have been worse still without policy action.

And the confounding factors can run the other way as well. If you see improvement following a stimulative policy, that doesn't prove that stimulus works, because the economy could have been repairing itself just when policy was implemented, or a positive shock other than your stimulative policy may have come along that was actually responsible for the improvement.

The underlying problem is that we're not interested simply in what happens after a policy is implemented, but in what happened after the policy *compared to what would have happened in the absence of stimulus*, and that second thing is something we can't observe. By its nature, stimulative policy is adopted in response

K. Seeley, *Macroeconomics in Ecological Context*, Studies in Ecological Economics 5, DOI 10.1007/978-3-319-51757-5_17

to unsatisfying economic performance. If we're not sure how quickly the economy should respond to stimulus, it becomes tricky to tease out the possible positive impact from the underlying reality that policy is implemented when things aren't going well.

As I'll discuss in Sect. 17.3, there are ways of partially getting around that difficulty of not being able to observe the counterfactual of the "no-policy outcome," though even there we wind up with contradictory results.

Before getting there, Sect. 17.2 will look at arguments that stimulus can't work *even in principle*, and discuss the weakness of that position. Section 17.3 then discusses a selection of studies trying to determine how big an impact stimulative policy has had.

17.2 Theory and the Anti-stimulus Charge

What if stimulus just couldn't work at all, merely by the logic of things? That would simplify matters, because we wouldn't have to bother with careful econometric work to try and suss out the actual impact of fiscal and monetary policy. And of course the long-run model in Part II provides a framework to reach exactly this theoretical conclusion: output is determined by the factors of supply; fiscal policy rearranges how much of the output is used for what purposes, but it doesn't change GDP; it's not clear what monetary policy does at all, since the loanable funds market wasn't about money, but was actually in terms of quantities of real output saved and borrowed.

And there is a portion of the economics profession—and even more, a portion of the political and public discourse—dedicated to the proposition that effective stimulus is impossible *as a matter of economic logic*. For a statement of this position in the context of the recent recession, and from a reputable source, we can turn to Nobel laureate Robert Lucas, who said in 2009, "there's nothing to apply a multiplier to." [10] The argument is that the money has to come from somewhere. If government decides to spend \$1 million building a bridge, it has to either collect an extra \$1 million in taxes, or borrow an extra \$1 million. If it borrows the money, then the lender is either not spending that money herself, or not lending that money to someone else who would spend it. If the government raises taxes, then the taxpayers are doing some combination of reducing their own spending and reducing their saving, and the reduction in saving means there's less for others to borrow and spend. So the government can choose to spend \$1 million on the bridge, but that has to entail a reduction of \$1 million elsewhere in the economy.

This line of argument can be restated as, "The money has to come from *somewhere*."[1] And once it's stated in those terms, perhaps you can see the problem

[1]For example, economics columnist Robert J. Samuelson, discussing the money to fund government jobs, wrote, "it must come from somewhere." [18].

with it. Remember that an important point of Chaps. 9 and 10 is that money *doesn't* have to come from somewhere. It can be called into existence by credible promises—i.e., loans. What's more, the fact that you put money into a bank doesn't necessarily mean that money will be lent out for someone else to spend. The bank could be hesitant to lend; the public could be hesitant to borrow.

The identity $S \equiv I$ says that savings must be equal to investment, and it would seem to support the idea that the money has to come from somewhere. But it actually applies to the flow of funds in national income accounting, not to what happens when you put savings in a bank. The money that one person borrowed doesn't have to be money that someone else relinquished. And the money that one person puts in the bank through saving doesn't have to go out the door, lent to someone else for them to spend.

Indeed, the statement that the money has to come from somewhere does too much work: it explains why fiscal stimulus is logically impossible, but that explanation applies just as well to increases in expenditure for consumption or investment by the private sector. If money for increased government expenditure has to come from somewhere, then the same is true of the money for increased private consumption or increased private investment. If more spending by the government means less spending by someone else, then more spending by *any* actor in the economy means less spending by someone else. In other words, the argument that public spending can't move aggregate demand also means that private spending can't move aggregate demand. This in turn implies that arguments about the economy being held back by low spending due to uncertainty[2] are equally baseless: if changes in government spending can't move the economy (because "the money has to come from somewhere"), then changes in private spending can't move it either, so a lack of private spending due to uncertainty should have no economic impact.

Despite its logical flaw, there's an intuitive appeal in the argument that fiscal stimulus can't work because of the need for the money to come from somewhere. You can arrive at an even stronger position against stimulus if you pair that idea with an assertion of government's inherent inefficiency.

Perhaps the furthest point on the spectrum of denying the usefulness of government is positions such as Ryan P. Long [9], who doesn't seem to recognize any value in government at all: "the impact of paying government employees is to transfer economic resources from the production of economic goods and services to the performing of services for which there is no market demand." The conclusion is that people employed by the government are simply not productive.

The first thing to say about this is to have you go up to a teacher making sure kids can read, or a city employee fixing a pothole so that you don't break an axle, and ask them whether what they do is real work. For extra fun, try this with a fire fighter or a police officer. Or a marine. You'll be glad you asked.

Long sums up his argument: "The Austrian perspective argues that all government jobs divert resources into the production of goods and services that would

[2]e.g., [8]

either never exist in free-market conditions or would exist to a much lesser extent." And that's undoubtedly true. But it's also true that markets don't do everything we want done, they don't accomplish everything we think is useful. In some sense, the whole point of government action is that the end result is different from what we would witness in the absence of government action. If we run government with at least a little intelligence and with a sense of what it can and can't accomplish, the end result is *better*.

Toning it down a bit from Long [9], Ahlseen [1] admits some useful functions of government, such as national defense, police, administration of courts, but he assumes the fundamental inefficiency of government: "Government needs to reduce spending and taxes in order to leave income in the hands of individuals who earned it and who can spend it much more efficiently than the government can."

Of course, the government is capable of inefficiency. But the same is true of the private sector as well; for instance, [12, p. 102] finds excess administrative costs of $190 million per year in the health sector of the U.S. economy, most of them involving the private sector, not the government.

We could even say that the efficiency of the private sector depends on inefficiency. Friedrich Hayek explains that the price system allows private markets to adjust automatically to changed conditions. "Even the large and highly mechanized plant keeps going largely because of an environment upon which it can draw for all sorts of unexpected needs; tiles for its roof, stationery for its forms, and all the thousand and one kinds of equipment in which it cannot be self-contained and which the plans for the operation of the plant require to be readily available in the market." [6, p. 524] But if all those thousand and one items are to be there, ready and waiting when a given plant manager unexpectedly shows up to buy them, it must be true that they might not have been needed. Hayek is the great apostle of the power and efficiency of the price system, and his own observation is that the smooth operation of the price system requires slack—or in another view, a kind of waste.

So inefficiency is not the unique province of government work. It is, rather, a question of degree.

It is also a question of defining the proper role of government. While Ahlseen [1] acknowledges some of the government's traditional roles in national defense and domestic security, he questions the wisdom of having the government in the business of delivering first-class mail; it is worth noting that similar postal questions arise in Leonard E. Read's famous essay, "I, pencil" [15].

On the one hand, it's quite plausible that a private mail service could deliver mail within a city more cheaply than is accomplished by the U.S. Post Office, and also that, as Read claims, the private market delivers four pounds of oil from the Middle East to the US for less than the post office charges to deliver a one-ounce letter across the street.

But this is overlooking one of the fundamental features of a postal system, which is the flat rate over the whole country. Mailing your water bill to city hall costs so much partly because it costs the same as mailing a Christmas card from Florida to Alaska. Users of local mail are, in effect, subsidizing people who send letters across the country. There's an economic argument in favor of that system, but even more, there's a political and social argument in its support. You don't need to agree with those arguments, but you do need to understand that a private carrier would be unable to provide flat rate service across the whole country—anyone who tried would be undercut in the local market by a competitor willing to charge only the cost of local service. And so *if* we believe that flat-rate service is worth having, the government will have to be involved. It is worth noting that when opponents of government action cite the postal service as an example of something the market could do just as well or better, it seems as if they haven't actually looked at the way a postal service functions.

The situation is summed up nicely by Harvey [5]: "not everything that is profitable is truly of social value and not everything of social value is profitable." Going further, if we understand the government as part of an evolving human economy, as suggested by Chap. 8, then we should expect shifts over time in the balance between what makes sense for government to do as opposed to the private sector. Harvey [5] may be right when he says of arguments like that of [9], "their true goal isn't to generate a scientific understanding of the manner in which the macroeconomy operates, but to make a moral statement."

The rest of this chapter will assume that government has a useful role in the economy as in the society conceived more broadly (indeed, the book as a whole has made that assumption). It will also assume that stimulus can be effective in principle, and will now turn to evidence regarding whether it actually is or not.

17.3 Empirical Assessments of Stimulus

Each of the two basic types of stimulus—fiscal and monetary—tend to be handled separately in the literature, so we'll also handle them one by one, starting with fiscal policy. The idea here is not a comprehensive discussion, but a general overview with some illustrative examples.

17.3.1 Has Fiscal Policy Worked?

Given the amount of money involved and the political charge around issues of taxes, government spending, and deficits, it's not surprising that there are many papers trying to measure whether fiscal stimulus has worked. This can either be in the form of estimating the size of the fiscal multiplier, or in terms of connecting a particular stimulus move to an effect on GDP and/or employment. Both Whalen and Reichling [22] and Ramey [14] provide broad surveys of empirical estimates of fiscal multipliers. While they differ in tone (Whalen and Reichling are more positive, while Ramey is more skeptical), they end up making a similar point: your quantitative estimate of the fiscal multiplier (or of a set of fiscal multipliers) will depend on a range of decisions:

- What model you use
- What assumptions you make
- Underlying conditions (economy with slack or at full employment?)
- *Can* monetary policy respond, either to offset or enhance fiscal policy
- *Does* monetary policy respond
- Was the downturn triggered by a crisis in the financial system
- What spending are you increasing and/or what taxes are you decreasing

As an example of the importance of models, Oh and Reis [13] use a very "classical" model. In particular, they assume that consumers look at increased government deficits today, foresee the implied higher taxes or lower government spending in the future, and respond by saving more today to buffer themselves against those future negatives. This is a set of ideas known as "Ricardian equivalence," named for the early-19th-century English economist David Ricardo, and it implies that fiscal policy can't work.[3] Unsurprisingly, Oh and Reis find multipliers of around 0.

Coming at stimulus-skepticism from a different angle, John B. Taylor [19] doesn't look for an impact on output, but on spending, reasoning that if the American Recovery and Reinvestment Act (ARRA) of 2009 didn't have much impact on spending, it couldn't have had much impact on GDP. And indeed he finds that there was little impact on spending. The increase in direct federal purchase of goods and services peaked at only 0.26% of GDP. Lucas [10] said there was nothing to multiply because by theory he assumed that any spending would come with offsetting tax increases or borrowing that would push aside private spending. Taylor doesn't make that assumption, but simply looks at the numbers and observes that, in terms of how much federal purchasing there was, there simply was nothing to multiply.

Most of the ARRA *was* a combination of tax credits and transfers to individuals and grants to state governments, but in considering the impacts of those outlays, Taylor doesn't seem to take into account the counterfactual. In the case of state and local spending, he finds that those government bodies didn't increase much spending, but instead increased "other expenditure" and decreased their net borrowing. It's true that, by Taylor's reckoning, state and local government purchases didn't increase much during the ARRA,[4] but by his own data, such spending had been on a downward trajectory, and it recovered slightly then leveled off after the stimulus grants kicked in. Perhaps it would have continued down in the absence of the ARRA.

Second, Taylor's finding of little response to the tax credits and transfers is based on a "counterfactual" of looking at disposable income that wasn't from those ARRA components. But higher consumption expenditure leads to higher disposable income, all else being equal, so if the various parts of the ARRA *did*

[3]Ricardian equivalence was mentioned in Sect. 16.6.

[4]The data in his Fig. 17.4 are inconsistent with data from the National Income and Product Accounts of the Bureau of Economic Analysis, if Taylor's "Government purchases" are the BEA's "[Government] Consumption expenditures" and his "Other expenditures" are "social benefit payments", "interest payments", and "subsidies" from the BEA's Table 3.3.

cause spending to stop falling and then rise, that means that a portion of Taylor's calculated disposable income "without stimulus" is in fact the indirect result of the stimulus. He has implicitly assumed away the multiplier, then found that increased transfers and reduced taxes had little effect on consumption.

Two other papers illustrate a different approach to the question. As explained earlier in the chapter, the basic challenge in actually measuring the effect of stimulus is to separate out the way that the stimulus is affecting the economy from the way that the poor state of the economy is causing you to undertake stimulus in the first place. The key is to find some aspect of the spending that varies from one place to another but that is plausibly independent of the reason you undertook the stimulus. Chodorow-Reich et al. [2] look at Medicaid spending, because it was increased by the ARRA and some of that increase was based on how much each state had been spending before the ARRA was passed; those amounts in turn were based on policies adopted before the recession hit, so they were unrelated to how hard a state was hit by the recession. They found that states that got more of that additional Medicaid money had stronger recoveries.

An expanded version of the same technique was adopted by Wilson [24], who added highway funding and school funding to the Medicaid funding considered in [2], since these categories likewise had elements (number of miles of federal highway, and number of school-age people, respectively) that were not functions of how hard each state had been hit by the recession. His results were in line with those of [2], though smaller, because he considered not only money already spent, but money promised as well.

17.3.2 Has Monetary Policy Worked?

Turning to the monetary side, there's the same problem of comparing the world as it actually turned out to be with the world as we think it would have been without the policy we're studying. And of course just as the efficacy of fiscal policy depends in part on how the monetary authority acts (including its responses to changes in fiscal policy), so the impact of monetary policy is related to whatever fiscal moves are happening at the same time.

Chung et al. [3] find a suggestion that "the Fed's large-scale asset purchase program is providing significant support to real economic activity and the labor market." That result, however, is based on the outputs of a model, rather than econometric analysis.

Williamson [23] reviews 17 studies of large-scale asset purchases by central banks (i.e., some form of quantitative easing) reaching back as far as 1966, but including several carried out after the financial crisis of the late 2000s. He sums up their findings by observing that, "although individual estimates differ, this analysis consistently finds that asset purchases have sizable effects on yields on longer-term securities," (in other words, quantitative easing has a real effect on interest rates) but also that, “there remains a great deal of uncertainty about the magnitude of these effects and their impact on the overall economy” (that is, we don’t know how big the impact was, nor whether it affected the GDP). [23, p. 10]

An interesting laboratory for monetary (and fiscal) policy after 1990 was Japan, which had suffered the collapse of an enormous real-estate bubble followed by years of slow GDP growth. Writing in 2007, before the global financial crisis, Ugai [21] surveyed studies of the quantitative easing policy carried out by the Bank of Japan between 2001 and 2006, and found that it had little effect on GDP, but that was attributed to simultaneous changes on bank balance sheets which tended to offset the central bank’s efforts.

If we think that the period since the financial crisis is different than what came before, we face a data problem, which is that there hasn’t been much time since the financial crisis to generate new data, and only one such crisis of its size. Like Williamson [23], Gambacorta et al. [4] deal with that by looking at multiple countries. They find that a “shock,” in the form of a period when the central bank is engaged in unconventional monetary policy, leads to a modest, temporary rise in GDP. It would seem to follow that a policy carried out over many periods, such as the 100% increase in the Federal Reserve’s balance sheet from July, 2009 to July, 2014 (see Fig. 12.5) is consistent with an increase of a few percentage points of GDP over what would have otherwise been true.

17.4 Conclusion

As these examples from the literature suggest, it is hard to be sure whether fiscal and monetary policies have their intended effect. On balance, I think they do. Cutting taxes, increasing expenditure, or lowering central-bank interest rates can increase output, under the right conditions, such as “slack” in the economy, characterized most of all by high unemployment. And when the economy is at the zero lower bound (the central bank’s key interest rate has already been reduced essentially to zero), unconventional policies like quantitative easing can also have an impact.

Figure 17.1 gives impressionist support to that position. It shows the U.S. output gap, calculated with three different “vintages” of potential GDP. Remember that the output gap is $(Y - Y^*)/Y^*$, where Y is actual GDP and Y^* is potential GDP. Remember further that potential GDP is not something we can observe directly; rather, the Congressional Budget Office calculates it based on a model of how the economy works, and one of its key inputs is an assumption about what the long-run equilibrium rate of unemployment is. If you change your view of that “normal” level of unemployment, then you’ll also change your estimate of potential GDP, which in turn results in a change in how big you think the output gap is. The figure shows

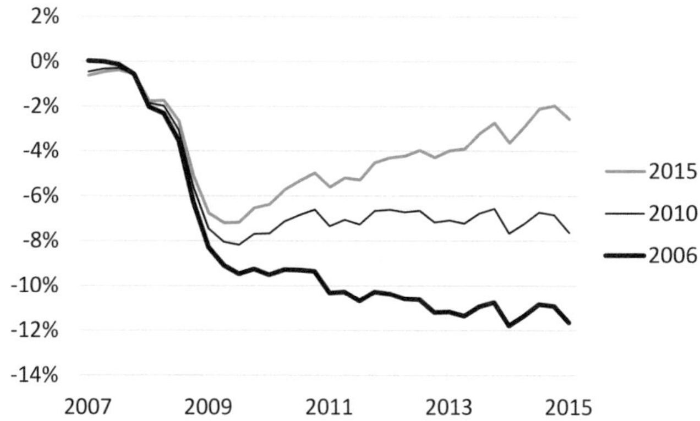

Fig. 17.1 Output gap, based on three different "vintages" of potential GDP. Actual GDP from Bureau of Economic Analysis; vintages of potential GDP from Congressional Budget Office, via ALFRED, Archival economic data of the St. Louis Federal Reserve

the output gap measured against potential GDP as it was estimated in January 2006, January 2010, and January 2015.[5]

There are three things to observe about the figure. First, the middle of 2009 is a turning point of sorts, regardless of which potential GDP you're looking at; the gap either turns around and starts getting smaller, or it stabilizes, or at least it comes out of free-fall and starts a pattern of falling only slowly. Either the economy's direction just happened to change at the same time as the fiscal stimulus was implemented, or the stimulus actually had a positive effect on the growth of GDP. And the economy continues on its path of improvement (or only slowly deteriorating) even in 2011 and after, when the stimulus of the 2009 ARRA was almost all spent, which suggests the positive impact of the quantitative easing that continued at the time.

Second, the Congressional Budget Office got progressively more pessimistic about potential GDP: their estimate in 2015 was considerably lower than their estimate looking forward from 2006, so if you calculate the output gap using the 2015 "vintage" of potential GDP, you get a much smaller output gap.[6]

Third, the story told using the 2006 estimate is striking. Instead of an output gap of "only" -7.2%, then recovering to -2%, the gap falls in two years to -9.5%, then arrests its free-fall but continues on down through the end of the data in early 2015, where it is flirting with -12%. If the stimulus did work, it still wasn't enough to get

[5]There is no obvious best way of making different vintages commensurable. The period-to-period growth rates are broadly similar across different vintages, but even for the 1950s and 1960s they're not identical, and so no single price index will convert one series to another with a perfect fit, even in the older data. Figure 17.1 is constructed by adopting the -0.57% output gap that the 2015 vintage produces for the fourth quarter of 2007 and using that for all the other vintages. The rest of the path for each vintage is constructed using that vintage's period-to-period growth rate.

[6]There are additional vintages in between the three shown here; they fall in line with the trend portrayed, toward more pessimistic estimates over time.

us catching up with where we thought we would be—it merely slowed the rate at which we fell behind.

There is a camp that argues that the stimulus was too small. Mian and Sufi [11] argue that the economy is still being held back by the high level of household debt run up during the housing bubble (and that we should have addressed the downturn with a significant amount of debt forgiveness). Jordà et al. [7] and Reinhart and Rogoff [16] both point to the tendency for recessions after financial crises to be severe and the recoveries to be slow. Jordà et al. calculate that the U.S. is doing as well as can be expected, or slightly better, given the condition of the financial system when the recession hit. [7, p. 25][7]

Another possible explanation for the weak performance visible in Fig. 17.1 is based in the role of resources in macroeconomic outcomes. In Part IV we return to that issue to look at how a failure to increase resource supply affects both the business cycle and the economy's long-run path.

For now, all in all we could do worse than to go with David Romer's conclusion [17] that the crisis of 2007–09 taught us that monetary policy on its own is limited in situations like those the global economy faced at that time, and there is still a role for fiscal stimulus.

Problems

Problem 17.1 Figure 17.2 shows the change in jobs (the gray bars) along with four components of the federal fiscal situation: the deficit (D/S), consumption and investment (C/I), transfers and subsidies (T/S) and revenues (R). (The budget numbers are presented as shares of potential GDP.)

(a) What does this figure suggest about fiscal stimulus and its impact on the economy?
(b) What caution do you need to attach to your conclusion from (a)?

Problem 17.2 Figure 17.3 shows discount rates, government deficits, and unemployment for the Eurozone (solid lines) and the U.S. (dashed lines).

(a) What does this figure suggest about the combined impact of fiscal and monetary stimulus on the economy?
(b) What caution do you need to attach to your conclusion from (a)?

Problem 17.3 Figure 17.4 shows the debt of various sectors, added together and portrayed relative to potential GDP. Figure 17.5 shows the same data, but this time without the federal government.

[7] Taylor [20] argues that recovery from finance-led recessions is no more arduous than from others, but he uses a different categorization of recessions than Jordà et al. [7] and confines his analysis to the U.S. rather than the other authors' multi-country analysis.

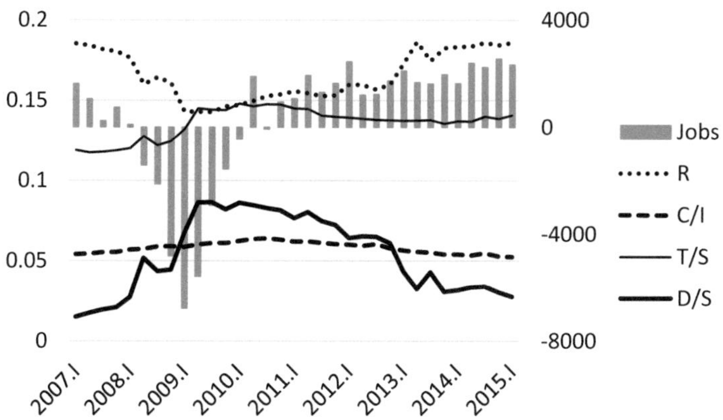

Fig. 17.2 Federal fiscal position and change in jobs; fiscal figures are as percentages of potential GDP, measured on the *left* axis; jobs are quarterly changes in the number of jobs, in thousands, measured on the *right* axis; fiscal figures are from the Bureau of Economic Analysis; jobs are based on the Current Establishment Survey

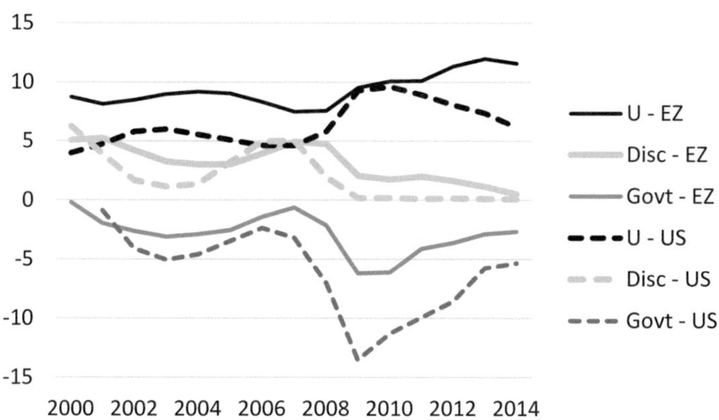

Fig. 17.3 Unemployment, budget deficit (as percentage of GDP) and discount rate, Eurozone and U.S.; Data from International Monetary Fund

(a) In Fig. 17.4 identify three different phases in the evolution of debt in the U.S. economy.
(b) What does Fig. 17.4 suggest about the role of changes in debt in the Great Recession?
(c) Comparing Fig. 17.5 to Fig. 17.4, how did Federal fiscal policy change the evolution of debt during the course of the Great Recession?
(d) Building on your answer to (c), what impact might Federal fiscal policy have had on the course of the recession?

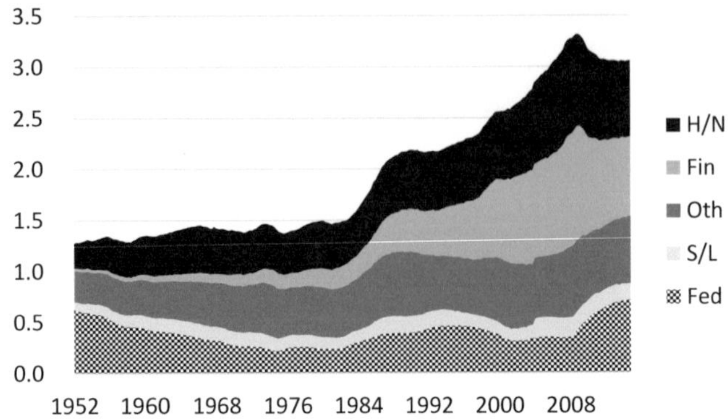

Fig. 17.4 Private and public debt in the U.S. as ratio of potential GDP. H/N = households and non-profits, Fin = financial corporations, S/L = state and local governments, Fed = federal government, Oth = other. Data from Congressional Budget Office (potential GDP) and Board of Governors of the Federal Reserve System

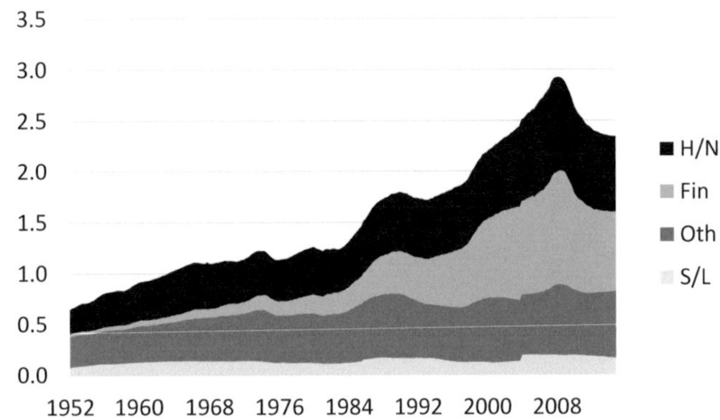

Fig. 17.5 Private and public debt in the U.S. as ratio of potential GDP, excluding federal government debt. H/N = households and non-profits, Fin = financial corporations, S/L = state and local governments, Oth = other. Data from Congressional Budget Office (potential GDP) and Board of Governors of the Federal Reserve System

References

1. Ahlseen, M. (1993). Why government can't create jobs. The Freeman, Oct 1, 1993. http://fee.org/freeman/detail/why-government-cant-create-jobs. Accessed June 11, 2015.
2. Chodorow-Reich, G., Feiveson, L., Liscow, Z., & Gui Woolston, W. (2012). Does state fiscal relief during recessions increase employment? Evidence from the American recovery and reinvestment act. *American Economic Journal: Economic Policy, 4*, 118–145.
3. Chung, H., Laforte, J.-P., Reifschneider, D., & Williams, J. C. (2011). Estimating the macroeconomic effects of the Fed's asset purchases. *FRBSF Economic Letter*, Jan 31, 2011. http://www.frbsf.org/economic-research/publications/economic-letter/2011/january/macroeconomic-effects-fed-asset-purchases/. Accessed July 1, 2015.

4. Gambacorta, L., Hofmann, B., & Peersman, G. (2014). The effectiveness of unconventional monetary policy at the zero lower bound: A cross-country analysis. *Journal of Money, Credit and Banking, 46*, 615–642.
5. Harvey, J. T. (2012). Why government should not be run like a business. Forbes.com. http://www.forbes.com/sites/johntharvey/2012/10/05/government-vs-business/, October 5th, 2012. Accessed July 2, 2015.
6. Hayek, F. A. (1945). The use of knowledge in society. *American Economic Review, 35*, 519–530.
7. Jordà, Ò., Schularick, M., & Taylor, A. M. (2013). When credit bites back. *Journal of Money, Credit and Banking, 45*(s2), 3–28.
8. Kliesen, K. L. (2013). Uncertainty and the economy. *The Regional Economist*, Apr 2013. https://www.stlouisfed.org/Publications/Regional-Economist/April-2013/Uncertainty-and-the-Economy. Accessed June 8, 2015.
9. Long, R. P. (2011). Are government jobs productive? Mises Daily, Nov 1, 2011. https://mises.org/library/are-government-jobs-productive. Accessed June 11, 2015.
10. Lucas, R. (2009). Why a second look matters. Transcript from the CFR Symposium on a Second Look at the Great Depression and the New Deal. http://www.cfr.org/economics/why-second-look-matters/p18996. Accessed July 7, 2012.
11. Mian, A. & Sufi, A. (2014). *How they (and You) caused the great recession, and how we can prevent it from happening again*. Chicago/London: University Of Chicago Press.
12. [IOM] (Institute of Medicine). (2013). *Best care at lower cost: The path to continuously learning health care in America*. Washington, DC: The National Academies Press.
13. Oh, H. & Reis, R. (2011). Targeted transfers and the fiscal response to the Great Recession. National Bureua of Economic Research, working paper 16775, February 2011. http://www.nber.org/papers/w16775.pdf. Accessed July 1, (2015).
14. Ramey, V. A. (2011). Can government purchases stimulate the economy? *Journal of Economic Literature, 49*, 673–685.
15. Read, L. E. (1958). I, pencil: my family tree as told to [l]eonard [e]. [r]ead. Originally in *The Freeman*, republished 2008 as pamphlet. http://fee.org/files/doclib/20121114_IPencilUpdatedCover2012.pdf. Accessed June 15, 2015.
16. Reinhart, C. M. & Rogoff, K. S. (2014). Recovery from financial crises: Evidence from 100 episodes. *American Economic Review, 104*, 50–55.
17. Romer, D. (2011). What have we learned about fiscal policy from the crisis? IMF conference on Macro and Growth Policies in the wake of the crisis, March 2011. https://www.imf.org/external/np/seminars/eng/2011/res/pdf/DR3presentation.pdf. Accessed June 12, 2014.
18. Samuelson, R. J. (2012). The flat-earth theory of job creation. Washington Post, Oct 25, 2012. http://www.washingtonpost.com/opinions/the-flat-earth-theory-of-job-creation/2012/10/25/2c922630-1eb1-11e2-ba31-3083ca97c314_story.html. Accessed June 11, 2015.
19. Taylor, J. B. (2011). An empirical analysis of the revival of fiscal activism in the 2000s. *Journal of Economic Literature, 49*, 686–702.
20. Taylor, J. B. (2014). The role of policy in the great recession and the weak recovery. *American Economic Review, 104*, 61–66.
21. Ugai, H. (2007). Effects of the quantitative easing policy: A survey of empirical analyses. *Monetary and Economic Studies, 25*(1), 1–48.
22. Whalen, C. J. & Reichling, F. (2015). The fiscal multiplier and economic policy analysis in the United States. Congressional Budget Office, Working Paper 2015-02, February 2015. https://www.cbo.gov/sites/default/files/114th-congress-2015-2016/workingpaper/49925-FiscalMultiplier.pdf. Accessed July 3, 2015.
23. Williamson, J. C. (2014). Monetary policy at the zero lower bound: Putting theory into practice. Working paper, Hutchins Center on Fiscal and Monetary Policy at Brookings, Jan 16, 2014. http://www.brookings.edu/~/media/research/files/papers/2014/01/16.%20monetary%20policy%20zero%20lower%20bound/16%20monetary%20policy%20zero%20lower%20bound%20williams. Accessed July 8, 2015.
24. Wilson, D. J. (2012). Fiscal spending jobs multipliers: Evidence from the 2009 American Recovery and Reinvestment Act. *American Economic Journal: Economic Policy, 4*, 251–282.

Part IV
Macroeconomics in a Constrained World

This is a tour through unusual precincts of economics. Chapter 18 starts with a twist on what can be thought of as the standard model of macroeconomics, tying together the long-run perspective of Part II with the short-run dynamics of Part III, then visits some other ways of thinking about business cycles.

Chapter 19 reviews the evidence that we may be facing a fundamentally different situation of resource availability than was true for the last 200 years. In Chap. 20 we look at the effects that binding resource constraints have on long-run growth, while Chap. 21 does the same for the business cycle.

Chapter 22 clarifies the relationship between how this book views the macroeconomy and a more conventional approach that leaves out resources; it highlights the elements that carry over while showing how they get slightly reinterpreted. It ends with a look in the direction of much broader ways of thinking about the economy and its relationship to the environment, society, and our well-being.

Chapter 18
The Standard Model and Alternative Perspectives

Abstract Part III made a connection between the short run and the long run, but only in a superficial way. The long run was just "given," as if by some natural evolution of the economy's productive inputs. The economy's "actual" output then varied around the "potential" output, depending on whether we were in a booming or recessionary phase of the business cycle. This chapter looks at the ways that business cycles and the policy responses to them may affect the path of long-run growth and considers different ways that influence could run. The rest of the chapter looks at a small selection of alternatives to this neoclassical synthesis.

18.1 The Standard Model

We now have a model of how the economy grows over the long run and a set of tools for understanding its short-run fluctuations. It's time to knit those two sets of ideas more closely together and then look briefly at alternatives to the whole edifice. It bears a resemblance to the structure of other textbooks (e.g., DeLong [4], Krugman and Wells [6]). The long run is fairly neoclassical (see Part II), with a focus on the factors of long-run growth and a model of equilibrium in the labor market. Then Part III was about short-run phenomena, including, implicitly, the possibility of GDP being either above or below the equilibrium indicated by the long-run model. That way of describing things suggests a one-way relationship between the two types of models: long-run factors set the equilibrium potential GDP, and then short-run determinants of aggregate demand shape the output gap, showing how far the actual is from the potential.

But the pursuit of macroeconomic stabilization policy can affect more than just how much of the current potential the economy is actually achieving. By influencing decisions about expenditure on investment and innovation, short-run stabilization policy can affect the future capital stock and level (and type) of technology, thereby having an effect on the future level of potential output.

Having said that much, there are two basic stories you can tell about the nature of that relationship. One is that stabilization policy dissuades useful investment, and so it sets up a trap for itself. The other story is that competent stabilization policy encourages useful investment and thus allows you to simultaneously minimize recessions and promote long-run growth. The difference between the outcomes

K. Seeley, *Macroeconomics in Ecological Context*, Studies in Ecological Economics 5, DOI 10.1007/978-3-319-51757-5_18

depends on how you think businesses view policy. To set up the narration of the two stories, let's start with a scenario where long-run growth is exogenous to short-run policy—that is, short-run policy doesn't have an effect on long-run growth.

18.1.1 Exogenous Growth

Figure 18.1 shows stylized data for potential and actual GDP. The heavier dashed line shows potential GDP, which grows at 3% per year for a while, then slows down to 2%, before returning to 3% growth. The light dashed line shows a trend that continues growing at 3% per year. The solid line shows actual GDP, which displays a negative output gap around the area labeled "A," a positive one just around "B," then hovers close to potential for the area labeled "C". In other words, there's some variability in this economy, but by the region of "C", the policy makers are either very lucky, or very good at their jobs, keeping the output gap so close to zero.

But of course we don't observe potential GDP directly; we calculate it based on models of what we think the economy should be doing. In the wake of the 2007–2008 financial crisis, the Congressional Budget Office went back and revised downward its estimate for what potential GDP would be in the future, and also what it had been in the recent past. But when politicians and central bankers are making stabilization policy, they don't know what the Congressional Budget Office (CBO) will eventually decide the potential output was. Let's say they assume a continuation of the recent trend, so their estimate of potential GDP is something like the light dashed line in Fig. 18.1. The double-headed arrow on the diagram shows what they *think* is a very large, negative output gap.

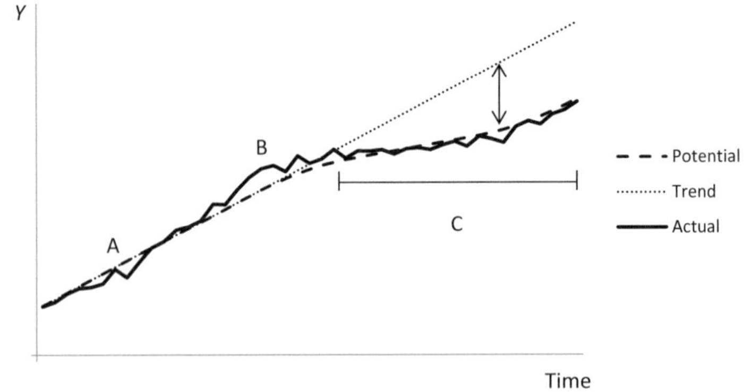

Fig. 18.1 Potential GDP with period of reduced growth; unchanging trend; and actual GDP

18.1.2 *Keynesian Policy as Misguided, or Even a Trap*

If you're inclined toward a relatively classical view of the economy, in line with the model of Part II, you may well come to see Keynesian policy as a worthless tool, or even as a counterproductive one. Whether you go with the first, weaker form of this argument or the second, stronger one, may depend on whether you see growth as exogenous (happening for its own reasons, independently of your business-cycle policy choices), or endogenous (influenced by whatever set of policies you choose to adopt in the face of macroeconomic fluctuations).

18.1.2.1 With Exogenous Growth

The first observation about the limits of stabilization policy concerns the lag between the onset of a contraction and the recognition that it's happening, and then the lag between that recognition and the implementation of policy to deal with the situation. The idea is that the economy may have a tendency to recover on its own, so that by the time the policy starts to have an effect, it's no longer needed. Instead of helping the economy recover from recession, the policy pushes GDP up above potential and just contributes to inflation.

Or look again at Fig. 18.1. Now imagine that rather than a temporary downturn that will fix itself before we can do any good, we're dealing with a slow-down in long-run growth. We've left that higher trend line and are now on the lower path of potential GDP in the region labeled "C", but policy makers don't know that. Based on what they think is true, the appropriate policy is a strong dose of stimulus. But the economy is already pretty much at potential GDP. If the money supply is increased or government expenditure is raised or taxes are cut, the most likely outcome is that the economy will be overstimulated, leading to inflation and to growth that can't be kept up.

This phenomenon could be a problem even in a world of exogenous growth. But if short-run stabilization policy tends to be a drag on growth, then the situation is worse, as the next section explains.

18.1.2.2 With Endogenous Growth

There are multiple components to the argument that stabilization policy is bad for growth.

- The most fundamental is the idea that stimulative spending *does* crowd out investment expenditure (see Chap. 6). So a world with a counter-cyclical fiscal policy will end up with lower levels of K, Z, and ρ (or in conventional terms, K and A) than a world without stimulative policy.
- If fiscal policy is accomplished through automatic stabilizers rather than through active policy, that implies a more extensive social safety net. The safety net itself

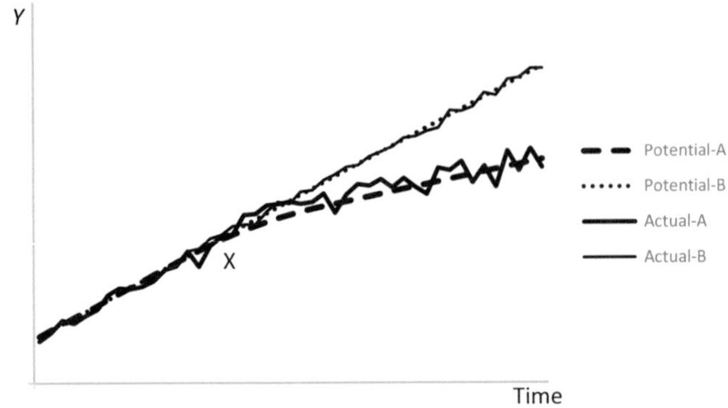

Fig. 18.2 Potential and actual GDP growth, under interventionist policy (*path A*) and non-interventionist (*path B*), if intervention is bad for long-run growth

is seen as a significant disincentive to work for those who can receive benefits without working, and a disincentive to work *hard* for those whose taxes support the safety net. People slacking off on their work effort in turn implies lower output than otherwise.[1]

- Lower output means a smaller pool of savings, which means less investment activity.[2]
- Active monetary policy is seen as unable to effectively smooth out the business cycle; rather, it simply introduces additional uncertainty, because not only will the economy itself be producing a certain amount of turbulence, but the incompetent efforts of the central bank will add to that as well. The increased uncertainty is a further disincentive to invest.

When you put it all together, you have an argument that efforts to actively manage the macroeconomy end up cutting into long-run growth. And that opens up what can be thought of as the "trap" of Keynesianism.

Start by granting the arguments laid out above. Now imagine an economy under two different scenarios. Figure 18.2 shows such an imaginary economy with a choice of possible futures. It starts at the left edge of the diagram with a non-interventionist approach to policy. Around point "X" it can either continue the non-intervention, or it can switch to a more active approach to stabilization. The view explained above suggests that the interventionist economy will follow the path labeled "A," with a noisier path around a lower level of potential GDP, while the non-interventionist future would take the economy along path "B," with a smoother path around a higher level of potential GDP.

In a strongly classical economic perspective, this is where we arrive at the trap that Keynesianism digs for itself. Macroeconomic stabilization policy leads

[1] See Lucas [10].

[2] ibid.

to slower long-run growth. The slow growth is interpreted as a sign that more stimulus is needed (remember the lesson of Fig. 18.1). The combination of slowly growing potential output and a constant pressure for stimulus means that you're likely pushing output above potential, which is inflationary, and that in turn acts as a further drag on growth, which increases the pressure for more stimulus, and so on.

It's not a happy story.

18.1.3 Keynesian Policy as an Aid to Long-Run Growth

But as with many issues in economics, it's possible to build a theoretical argument that runs exactly the opposite way.

This position agrees that business doesn't like uncertainty, but it also thinks that stabilization policies can actually be effective, and thus that they can reduce uncertainty rather than increasing it. The idea is that, without intervention, severe downturns are inevitable. Those represent not only periods of lost profits, but instances that crush the return on investments made shortly before the downturn. So investment will be higher in an economy where the government enacts reasonably competent stabilization policy than in one that follows a more hands-off approach.

Automatic stabilizers (see Chap. 13) play a role as well. During a recession, people who've lost their jobs make large cuts in expenditure, causing a reduction in firms' revenues. A generous safety net leads to smaller cuts in expenditure, cutting the bottom off of downturns. At the same time, the safety net requires a somewhat higher level of taxation, which dampens the "boom" effect from increased spending during good times.

The result of stabilization policy—whether active or passive—is shown in Fig. 18.3, where the economy starts off along a non-intervention path. At around "X" it can go one of two ways. Along path A, the government starts to carry out competent macro-stabilization policies. As a result, potential growth accelerates

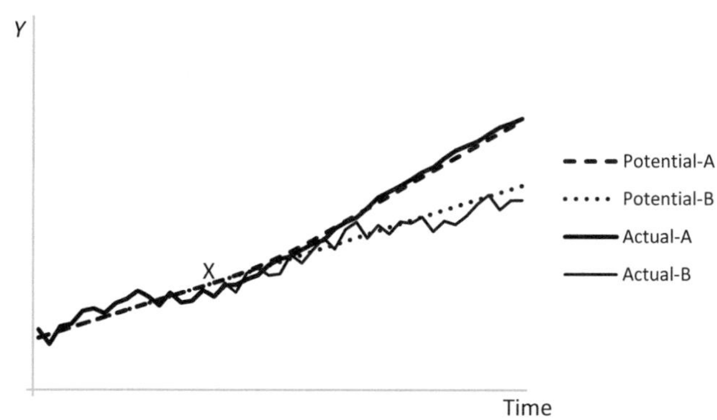

Fig. 18.3 Potential and actual GDP growth, under interventionist policy (path A) and non-interventionist (path B), if intervention is good for long-run growth

and the business cycle smooths out; along path B, macro-stabilization is shunned, so potential growth stays at its lower, initial rate, and there continues to be considerable instability in the economy.

Does stabilization policy reduced the volatility of the economy? As Christina Romer [15, p. 314] observes, "industrial production, unemployment, and Gross National Product all show larger cyclical fluctuations in the late 1800s and early 1900s than after World War II." But on a more detailed look at the data, both in [15] and in [16], she provides evidence that there is at best a mild increase in the stability of the U.S. economy in the postwar, Keynesian era, compared to the period before World War I, when there were neither Keynesian efforts at stabilization nor the massive shocks of the 1930s.

However, Moazzami and Dadgostar [12] look at Canada, Sweden, and the United States and find that economic policy has reduced the volatility of the business cycle. "The main difference between the present study and the existing studies is that this study covers the period of 1990s when central banks were successful in reducing inflationary pressures and interest rates in all three countries." [12, p. 23] Of course, publishing in 2008, they were likely writing in 2007 and early 2008, right on the cusp of the most massive economic destabilization since the catastrophe of the Great Depression. So let's just say the jury is still out.

We thus have competing stories about the possible link between short-run stabilization policy and long-run growth. They share a concern with how short-run policy affects investment expenditure, and thus how it affects long-run growth. They differ in how they see that effect. We'll consider the evidence for one side or the other in Sect. 18.2.1 below on real business cycle theory.

18.2 Alternative Perspectives

This section is far from a comprehensive look at alternative ways of thinking about the macroeconomy. Its goal is simply to illustrate some representative points along a spectrum.

18.2.1 Real Business Cycle Theory

The theory of real business cycles, or RBC, says that business cycles arise from "real" shocks to the economy, as opposed to "nominal" ones having to do with monetary policy. In one sense this is unremarkable, since real shocks include changes in government expenditure or exports, things that many macro theories agree would affect an economy's performance. What distinguishes RBC, however, is its emphasis on real shocks to the supply side specifically: changes in the production function or in labor supply.[3]

[3]For seminal works, see Finn E. Kydland and Edward C. Prescott [7] and Charles I. Plosser [14].

Recall from the end of Chap. 6 that the long-run model as laid out in Part II was not very good at explaining the economy's quite visible fluctuations in employment and rate of growth. RBC asserts that model actually *can* account for what we observe. An argument based on changes in labor supply may have something of an ad hoc feel to it, but there's more substance in the argument from technological changes. Recall the problem of explaining how technology could go backwards—getting worse—which would seem to be necessary in order to explain recessions. But a series of uneven forward movements could potentially lead not just to uneven growth, but to periods of contraction.

Start from the saying that you should "make hay while the sun shines." The idea is that a farmer should not work the same amount of hours every day, regardless of conditions. Rather, when the weather is good for cutting the crop and bringing in the hay, you should work as long as you can; take your rest on days with less favorable conditions.

Something similar could happen with technology shocks. An innovation spurs a need for investment in the new technology. The new capital creates a period when the marginal product of labor—and thus the wage—is unusually high. Workers should rationally shift some of their willingness to work into that period of high returns to labor, and away from periods without a particularly elevated MPN. Formally, this is known as intertemporal labor-leisure substitution: you're shifting your allocation of time between labor and leisure in one direction at first, and then back the other way later.

This can, in principle, produce the fluctuations in economic growth that are characteristic of the business cycle, and it does it without having to invoke monetary factors. It also implies that business cycles are optimal—not *good*, but preferable to the outcome if the government tried to smooth them out. By assumption, the market is in equilibrium; people are responding optimally, as they see it. In this case, what they're responding to is a bad technology shock. If the government were to stimulate people into working more than they are, that would be moving them away from what they themselves view as their best response to the plain reality of the situation.

There are, however, a couple of problems with this line of argument. The first of these is the persistence of downturns, in the U.S. most spectacularly from 1929 to 1933. Related to this is the implication that being out of work is voluntary, a choice to take more leisure now in expectation of doing more work later, or in response to having done more work in the past. This fails spectacularly to match up with the lived experience of the unemployed, as portrayed in Fig. 18.4.

More recently the tremendous spike in long-run unemployment, unprecedented in the era of consistent data starting in 1948, seems hard to reconcile with an explanation of millions of people deciding that right now would be an ideal time to take a year or two or three off from work. Numerous profiles of individuals who have been out of work for a long stretch (see, e.g., [5] and [17]) similarly fail to support the implications of RBC as to the nature of unemployment.

Fig. 18.4 People in the Great Depression freely exercising their labor-leisure choice, and choosing leisure, year after year after year ... (Sources clockwise from top: [13], [1], [2])

18.2.2 Minsky's Unstable World

Where RBC theorists see the economy as inherently self-correcting, Hyman Minsky saw it as inherently producing damaging business cycles, not because of unavoidable changes in technology, but due to the nature of finance. Minsky's work was considerably off the beaten path during his lifetime, but the financial crisis that started developing in 2007 brought renewed positive attention to his ideas.

His financial-instability hypothesis starts with the observation that we live in a monetary economy where "money is connected with financing through time." [11, p. 3]. Entrepreneurs borrow money to buy goods and services in order to make a profit in the future. This leaves them with a set of definite obligations to pay money in the future, and a set of conjectural, uncertain opportunities to earn the money to meet their obligations.

Not only firms, but households as well, have these future obligations. If spending in the future is high, then earnings will be high (profits for firms; wages and salary for households), and people will be able to meet their obligations; if spending in the future is low, then future income will not support the obligations. "[T]hus, whether or not liabilities are validated depends upon investment. Investment takes place now because businessmen and their bankers expect investment to take place in the future." [11, p. 6]

Minsky puts entities into three categories, based on the relationship between their cash flows and their credit obligations. "Hedge" finance units can pay both interest and principal out of their expected cash flows; "speculative" finance units can pay interest out of their expected cash flows, but need to "roll over" at least some of their principal, getting into new borrowing arrangements to pay off old ones. "Ponzi" units[4] can't meet either principal or interest out of their expected cash flow, and so they are forced to meet both those obligations by either the sale of assets or additional borrowing; this second option, of course, only digs them into a deeper hole.

Minsky saw an economy dominated by "hedge" finance units as being stable. But virtue sows the seeds of its own demise, because a protracted period of stability and good times would encourage borrowers and lenders to move from hedge finance to speculative arrangements and Ponzi schemes. That sets up a situation where a small event—say, the monetary authority trying to reduce inflationary pressure in the economy—is capable of triggering a chain reaction in which speculative units become Ponzi units, Ponzi units become insolvent, and there's a widespread drop in asset values and output.

Minsky suggests that the central bank could try to avoid economic downturns by acting to "validate" even the claims of Ponzi units. That is, as long as the central bank issues enough new money, there will be enough new money so that Ponzi schemes turn out to pay off for their investors. But Minsky recognized that at some point this would run into the physical reality that it wasn't possible to put real economic activity behind all that money being created, and so the result would be runaway inflation. Furthermore, as we've seen with the Great Recession of 2008, the monetary authority's ability to create money may be severely limited by banks' unwillingness to lend and customers' unwillingness to borrow, whatever the central bank may want to bring about.

In the end, Minsky gives a convincing explanation for how the workings of finance can produce macroeconomic instability, but doesn't provide a clear sense of what can safely be done to limit it.

18.2.3 The Prospect of Agent-Based Modeling

The technique of agent-based modeling (ABM) is a departure not from the perspectives of any particular school of macroeconomics, but from the techniques. Whether classical or Keynesian, new classical, or new Keynesian, the standard approach is to write a set of equations that describe the behavior of economic aggregates: the consumption expenditure of *all* consumers, in one equation; the investment expenditure of *all* firms in another single equation, and so on. In ABM, you write equations that describe the behavior of individual agents—how they

[4]Named for the infamous Boston financial swindler Charles Ponzi.

behave and how they interact with each other. Then you set lots of these agents loose in your computer, and you observe the results.

The technique has applications outside economics, such as in modeling traffic flow, flocking behavior of birds, or chemical reactions. In macroeconomics, you can do things like create a bank, several firms, and a lot of households that both work for the firms and buy their goods. You can change rules about, say, the minimum wage, and see what happens to output, unemployment, and wage levels.[5]

But this change in technique can lead to significant changes in how one sees the economy. This book has presented the standard view that business cycles are deviations around a long-run growth path. But it's possible to build an ABM model in which a business cycle is "a cyclical deviation *below* the full employment level that is due to coordination failure of the interacting agents." [9, p. 111] Also, like Minsky's financial instability hypothesis, ABM modeling is capable of generating business-cycle fluctuations within the economy, rather than needing to impose exogenous shocks, such as changes in technology, or costs, or information [8].

18.3 Heterodoxy in Perspective

The ABM modelers are not the only ones who set aside the very idea of equilibrium. The writer and former banker Frances Coppola talks about "the essential non-linearity of a monetary economy whose heart is a financial system that is not occasionally but NORMALLY far from equilibrium. Until macroeconomists understand this, their models will remain inadequate." [3]

In fact, we can look at the role that equilibrium plays in each school of thought and use that to construct a spectrum of ways of thinking about the economy.

- RBC explains business-cycle fluctuations as changes in the economy's long-run equilibrium.
- The standard model at the core of this book takes the long-run equilibrium as defining potential output, and then sees the business cycle as deviations around that long-run trend.
- Minsky's financial instability hypothesis has a stable equilibrium when most entities are engaged in hedge finance, and then observes that the equilibrium becomes less and less stable as more firms move toward speculative and ultimately Ponzi finance.
- ABM doesn't necessarily have an equilibrium at all. There are no equations that describe the system as a whole and which could therefore be analyzed for their equilibrium properties. There are only the behaviors of individual agents whose interactions then create the condition of the economy, but there's not really an equilibrium.

[5]See [18].

Perhaps it's disorienting to have so many ways of thinking about the macroeconomy, but it shouldn't be a surprise that unanimity is hard to find. We're dealing with an entity as complex as an ecosystem, tied together by social structures, and populated by individuals who, when you try to study them, might just know that you're watching.

Plurality is in the nature of macroeconomics. Accept that, and get used to thinking about the same topic in different ways.

Having made a brief tour through other perspectives on the field, in Chap. 19 we look at the evidence for new limits on resource availability, then in the remaining chapters turn back to the main model of this book, this time assuming conditions of more limited resources, and see what conclusions from Parts II and III are changed, and what elements of continuity there are.

Problems

Problem 18.1 Write a function for I_0 and/or I_r that shows its response to policy under the classical view of stabilization policy's effect. Use the variable q to denote the degree of policy intervention, with $q = 0$ corresponding to a laissez faire, hands-off approach, and $q = 1$ being a maximally interventionist stance. Explain how your function reflects the classical view of how stabilization policy affects behavior.

Problem 18.2 Write a function for I_0 and/or I_r that shows its response to policy under a more Keynesian view of stabilization policy's effect. Use the variable q in the same way as in Problem 18.1, and as in that problem, explain how the function you created reflects a Keynesian view of how stabilization policy affects behavior.

Problem 18.3 Start with your answer to *either* Problem 18.1 or Problem 18.2. Whichever you chose, plug it into the long-run model of Part II. Use the modified model to derive the effect of changes in q on investment and consumption.

Problem 18.4 Start with your answer to *either* Problem 18.1 or Problem 18.2. Whichever you chose, plug it into either the IS curve or the LM curve, as appropriate. Use the modified curve to discuss the effect of changes in q on investment and consumption.

References

1. Abbott, B. (2015). Huts and unemployed, West Houston and Mercer St., Manhattan. Image ID: 482853. Wikimedia Commons, https://commons.wikimedia.org/wiki/File:Huts_and_unemployed_in_West_Houston_and_Mercer_St_by_Berenice_Abbott_in_Manhattan_in_1935.jpg. Accessed July 5, 2015.
2. City of Toronto Archives (2015). Unemployed men hop train. Canada. Wikimedia Commons, https://commons.wikimedia.org/wiki/File:UnemployedMenHopTrain.jpg. Accessed July 5, 2015.

3. Coppola, F. (2015). The failure of macroeconomics, 2014. *Coppola comment: Finance economics and music*, posted February 26, 2015. Accessed April 12, 2015, at http://coppolacomment.blogspot.co.uk/2015/02/the-failure-of-macroeconomics.html.
4. deLong, J. B. (2002). *Macroeconomics*. New York: McGraw-Hill/Irwin.
5. Hu, W. (2013). When being jobless is a barrier to finding a job. *New York Times*, February 17, 2013.
6. Krugman, P., & Wells, R. (2012). *Economics: Second edition in modules*. New York: Worth Publishers.
7. Kydland, F. E., & Prescott, E. C. (1982). Time to build and aggregate fluctuations. *Econometrica, 50*, 1345–1370.
8. Lengnick, M. (2011). Agent-based macroeconomics – A baseline model. Economics working paper/Christian-Albrechts-Universit at Kiel, Department of Economics, No. 2011,04.
9. Lengnick, M. (2013). Agent-based macroeconomics: A baseline model. *Journal of Economic Behavior & Organization, 86*, 102–120.
10. Lucas, R. (2013). Macroeconomic priorities. *American Economic Review, 93*, 1–14.
11. Minsky, H. (1992). The financial instability hypothesis. Working paper no. 74, Levy Economics Institute of Bard College. www.levyinstitute.org/pubs/wp74.pdf. Accessed July 2, 2015.
12. Moazzami, B., & Dadgostar, B. (2008). Has the business cycle been dampened? the case of Canada, Sweden and the United States. *The Journal of Applied Business Research, 24*(4), 23–27.
13. National Archives and Records Administration (2015). Unemployed men queued outside a depression soup kitchen opened in Chicago by Al Capone. Wikimedia Commons, http://commons.wikimedia.org/wiki/File:Unemployed_men_queued_outside_a_depression_soup_kitchen_opened_in_Chicago_by_Al_Capone,_02-1931_-_NARA_-_541927.jpg. Accessed July 5, 2015.
14. Plosser, C. I. (1989). Understanding real business cycles. *Journal of Economic Perspectives, 3*, 51–77.
15. Romer, C. D. (1986). Is the stabilization of the postwar economy a figment of the data? *American Economic Review, 76*, 314–334.
16. Romer, C. D. (1991). The cyclical behavior of individual production series, 1889–1984. *Quarterly Journal of Economics, 106*, 1–31.
17. Semuels, A. (2015). A better way to help the long-term unemployed. *The Atlantic*, February 10, 2015.
18. Seppecher, P. (2010). Flexibility of wages and macroeconomic instability in an agentbased computational model with endogenous money. In *Workshop on economic heterogeneous interacting agents ESHIA/WEHIA 2010*, Ancona.

Chapter 19
Resource Constraints

Abstract This chapter extends the material from Chap. 2 on the use of resources and introduces the models of Howard Hotelling, John Hartwick, and M. King Hubbert. It then discusses the evidence that our resource situation is getting fundamentally tighter and introduces the concept of energy return on energy invested, or EROI.

19.1 What to Do with a Treasure Chest?

Chapter 2 mentioned the basic puzzle of how to use a non-renewable resource. With a renewable resource, it's tempting to say we should use things "sustainably," and it's easy to define what that would mean: use only as much as can be used year after year, without impairing the ability to use the same amount the year after. But if we start thinking in similar terms about nonrenewable resources, we run into a particular kind of economic puzzle.

In one sense, there is no "sustainable" level of exhaustible resource use, because such resources are—well, exhaustible. Any level of use, continued for long enough, will result in the resource being used up, and if the economy has come to depend on it, you've got a big problem. On the other hand, as Chap. 2 explained, these are incredibly useful resources. They have high energy-to-weight ratios, they're found in large deposits so it's easy to get a lot from one place, and our ability to extract them is limited more by our technology and capital for extraction rather than by the flow rate, as happens with resources we derive from the current solar flow.

Given all these virtues, it hardly seems to make sense to simply ignore non-renewables, so we need to think about how the rates at which they *are* or *should* be extracted. Three important perspectives on this problem come from what you can think of as the Three H's: Hotelling, Hartwick, and Hubbert.

19.1.1 The Hotelling Rule

Concerns about running out of fossil fuels go back at least to William Stanley Jevons' examination of Britain's coal supplies in the 1860s [11]. Wouldn't it be

K. Seeley, *Macroeconomics in Ecological Context*, Studies in Ecological Economics 5, DOI 10.1007/978-3-319-51757-5_19

nice if the economy would somehow act in a way that made sure that "running out" wasn't a problem? In the 1930s, American economist Harold Hotelling had an insight that suggested that maybe economies *did* have the potential for such desirable behavior, that the economy would naturally take care of impending resource scarcity by gradually raising the price long before exhaustion made itself felt directly; this pattern of rising prices would force the discovery of alternatives and cause us to gently taper off our use of the diminishing resource. In other words, the Hotelling Rule is descriptive rather than prescriptive (it says what it claims the world is like, rather than pointing to what it *should* be like), and it is optimistic (markets will handle the problem just fine).

Hotelling's idea can be understood by imagining an owner of a unit of the resource in the ground (in situ) and the decision she has to make each period of time [7]. In each period, she could pull her unit out of the ground and sell it (at the going price), or she could leave it in the ground. If she leaves it in the ground, then next period she'll face the same decision. What should she do?

Hotelling reasoned that the resource is an asset like any other. If the owner extracts the resource and sells it, she can take the money (net of any extraction costs) and buy something else, like some shares of stock, or some bonds. If she does that, she'll earn some interest—exactly how much interest depends on exactly which financial asset she chose to buy, but you can simplify it and think about her earning "*the* interest rate" available in the economy. Let's say her profit from extracting and selling the resource this period would be $100 and the interest rate in the economy is 5%. If she goes ahead and sells the resource, she can have $100 now, which she can turn into $105 next year by buying a stock or bond that will grow by 5% over the year. And that option tells you what she should do now.

If she expects next year's resource price to be $110, she should keep it in the ground, since the value of the oil she owns will grow more quickly than would the value of financial stocks she might buy. If she expects next year's price to be $100, she should extract and sell, because she'll do better that way. And if she expects next year's price to be $105, she's indifferent between selling and holding, which indirectly tells you what the price path actually *should* be.

Hotelling's explanation of the resource situation depends on a kind of arbitrage process. Arbitrage is when trades happen in order to take advantage of price differences that shouldn't exist. Let's say next period's price is expected to be $100, so the return on holding the resource is 0%. In that case, a lot of owners will sell now, and when they do that, the current price will fall below $100. Once the price gets down to $95.24, the growth from that to next year's price of $100 would be 5%. At that point owners would become indifferent between selling and holding, and the price would stabilize.

In the opposite situation, if owners expected the price to be $110, they'd all want to hold on to the resource as the best way to increase their wealth. And with fewer people selling, the current price would rise above $100. Once it got to $104.76, the growth from there to $110 would be 5% and owners would once again be indifferent. Arbitrage is this set of decisions to either sell or hold, depending on how the price path of the exhaustible resource compares with "the interest rate" in the rest of the

Fig. 19.1 Hotelling paths for price and quantity

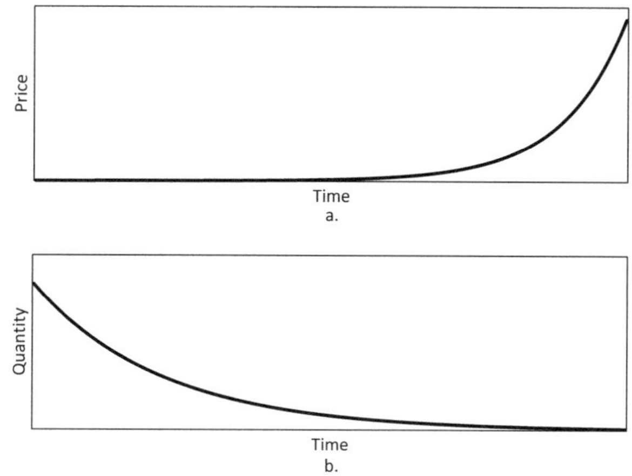

economy, and the net result of that arbitrage is that the price of a nonrenewable resource (net of extraction costs) should rise at the rate of interest.

This is a powerful result for an intellectual tradition that places a high premium on decentralized solutions. Because as Hotelling explains, you don't need any explicit coordination to make this happen. Let's say you know the total size of the resource (or have a pretty good guess about it), and let's say you know some cutoff price above which you won't be able to sell the resource (maybe there's some "backstop" technology, a substitute that becomes worth using once you reach that price). Then the self-interested decisions of rational, private actors will put you on this "Hotelling path," which turns out to be the optimal path from society's perspective as well. The resource gets used up in an orderly way, a signal is given for the development of alternatives, and the interests of present and future are balanced in the way standard economics says they should be.

The two parts of Fig. 19.1 illustrate a sort of idealized Hotelling path with price increasing at an exponential rate and quantity declining at an exponential rate.[1]

Compare these predictions of the Hotelling model with the actual behavior of the most famous nonrenewable resource, conventional crude oil. Figure 19.2 shows historical prices starting in 1861.

The price certainly does jump up at the end of the chart, but there's a long period where the price was actually tending to fall rather than rise. And what about quantity? As Fig. 19.3 shows, there hasn't yet been much sign of an exponential decrease in production of oil, and Fig. 19.4 goes further back and includes a period with an exponential *increase* of use, never mind a decline, corresponding to the period of stable or falling prices.

---

[1]This assumes constant demand for the resource. You can model increasing demand, and if the increase is strong enough, the quantity used will actually increase over time, but the theoretically correct price path is still the exponential increase shown in the upper graph, just starting from a higher price in order to preserve more of the resource for later expanded output.

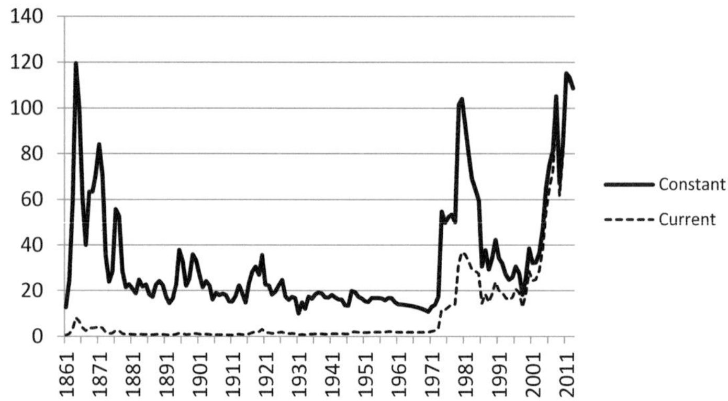

Fig. 19.2 The price of oil, annual average, current dollars and 2013 dollars (Source: BP *Statistical review of world energy 2013*, downloaded July 1, 2014, from http://www.bp.com/en/global/corporate/about-bp/energy-economics/statistical-review-of-world-energy/statistical-review-downloads.html)

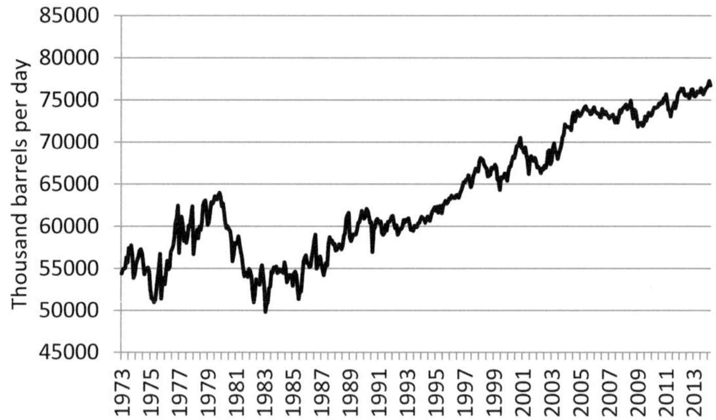

Fig. 19.3 Global crude oil production, Jan 1973 – March 2014 (Source: Department of Energy Information Administration, *Monthly Energy Review*, Table 11.1b, downloaded July 1, 2014)

The logic of the Hotelling Rule is very compelling to many economists, yet its predictions seem fundamentally falsified. Why doesn't it work? Three big problems with it include:

- Uncertainty
- Cash-flow motivations
- Endogeneity

Uncertainty Remember that the Hotelling argument depends on having a pretty good estimate of the total size of the resource. In the 2000s, there were estimates of the remaining oil reserve from credible sources that ranged from 1 trillion barrels to 3 trillion barrels. If you were to try to apply the Hotelling logic using one of those

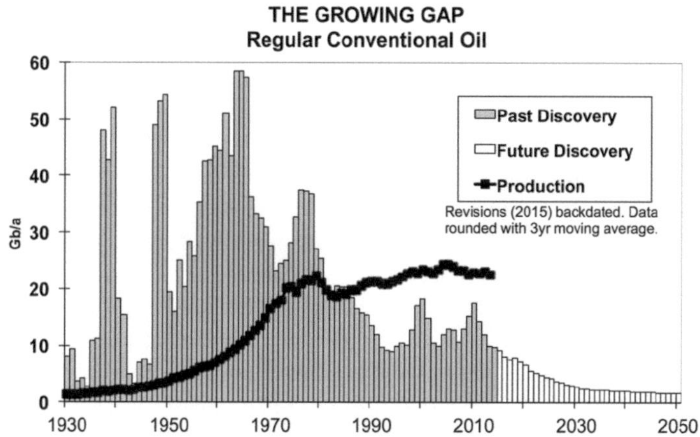

Fig. 19.4 Production, Past discovery, Predicted discovery of conventional oil (Source: Colin Campbell, 2015)

two numbers rather than the other, you'd get two very different answers. If you have a lot of uncertainty as to the right number that will ultimately be extracted, maybe you shouldn't spend a lot of time trying to work out the consequences for you today of what that number ultimately will be.

Earlier in the twentieth century, estimates of the size of the total resource kept rising as additional oil fields were found. If you were trying to follow a Hotelling price path and geologists kept increasing the amount of oil they thought there was, you would keep having to "reset" your price path, and so the path as a whole would look nothing like the idealized path of a price that rises at the rate of interest.

Similarly, what exactly *is* the "backstop" technology for petroleum? It's not clear that we yet know of anything that can play the role that oil plays in our economy, much less have a clear idea at what price that would become available in sufficient quantity to make us uninterested in oil.

Cash-flow motivations The Hotelling Rule assumes owners of the resource who maximize the present value of all future profits they get from extracting and selling the resource. Sometimes that requires selling less (and accepting less revenue) now, in exchange for more revenue later. That may sound good in theory, but what if the resource owner is a government that is trying to curry favor through the proceeds of oil sales? This could be an elected government, such as the UK, that would like to be elected again and so is happy to use oil revenue to reduce taxes on the general populace, or some sort of dictatorship, that would like people not to revolt, and so is desperate to use oil revenue to provide services that will keep people from rioting in the streets.

An owner in either of those situations is more concerned with current cash flow than with the present value of the resource profit over infinite time. If it doesn't play the cash-flow game right, the future becomes rather irrelevant to it.

Endogeneity The logic of the Hotelling Rule has a fixed level of demand, or if demand grows, it grows exogenously (that is, for reasons determined outside the model). But this doesn't look like a good description of the demand for oil.

Society can develop its infrastructure in various ways. It can build settlements that are spread out across the landscape, where almost all travel has to be by automobile, and those cars get relatively few miles per gallon, and tourism and business activities are built around the idea that passenger flight is common, and farming is concentrated in massive operations using lots of machinery and requiring that all food then be shipped relatively large distances.

Or it could build more focused settlements where walking, biking, and public transit are realistic options, what cars there are get higher miles per gallon, trains are more important than flight, and food is grown and delivered to consumers in less energy-intensive ways. At a given price of oil, this second world will clearly try to buy a smaller quantity of oil than the first world—in other words, its oil demand curve will be further to the left. In terms of the model of this book, its path has led it to a lower level of ρ.

But being dropped into one of these worlds rather than the other isn't a random occurrence. If we've had decades of *low* oil prices, we're likely to find ourselves in the first one, with high demand for oil. If instead, starting from the same point, we'd had decades of *high* oil prices, we're more likely to end up in the second world, where oil demand is low. And maybe our economy will be smaller overall, not having been goosed by the stimulant of cheap energy.

In other words, the demand for oil is arguably *endogenous*: it is not a fact determined outside the model, something to which owners of oil are simply responding. It is, rather, determined within the model, shaped in part by the resource-owners' decisions about how much to sell year after year.

But the endogeneity extends to the interest rate as well. At the micro level, the interest rate is simply a bargain between someone who wants to consume more now and someone who wants to consume more later. But at the macro level, in the aggregate, the interest rate is tied to the rate of growth. A fast-growing economy can afford to pay higher interest rates on investments than can a slow-growing economy. If more use of oil speeds up the growth of the economy, and the growth of the economy affects the average interest rate over the long term, and the interest rate shapes the extraction path of oil, what then? It turns out we've got a circular argument on our hands, and the Hotelling Rule can't help us much.

Overall, the Hotelling Rule is an intellectually interesting construct, but it may be of limited value in actually understanding the role of resources in an economy.

19.1.2 The Hartwick Rule

Where Hotelling took a descriptive approach, saying what he expected to happen in a market with perfect competition and perfect information, John Hartwick reflected the concerns of the 1970s with his more prescriptive approach, explaining how society *should* take advantage of the economic wealth stored in fossil fuels [6].

Hartwick recognized that fossil fuels were a particularly potent resource, and since using them at any rate meant eventually using them up, there were interesting questions about how to fairly allocate their use to people alive at different times. Using them now with no thought for the future is hardly fair to later generations, but saving them now so that future generations have some isn't a clean solution either: How *much* do you save, since there's *no* amount you can assign to the present generation and still enable every future generation to have the same amount?

Hartwick's solution had two components. The first was the realization that we're not interested in oil for itself, we're interested in oil for the benefits it confers. The other was the claim that there's significant substitutability between oil (or other resource inputs) and capital (machinery, etc.). Though this claim is fairly standard in economics, it is at least questionable, but if you accept this idea of strong substitutability, then Hartwick provides clear advice. As you use exhaustible natural resources, you should take some of the wealth they provide and use it to build up a capital stock that will fill in for the exhaustible resource as it runs down. The present will have a large flow of resources and a relatively small capital stock; the future will have a small flow of resources and a relatively large capital stock; and both will have roughly equivalent standards of living.

Despite the elegance of Hartwick's prescription, it's not clear that it would actually be possible to follow his advice in practice, for two reasons. The first is that generalized "capital" is not necessarily a substitute for resources. A windmill can substitute in principle for coal burned in a power plant. And if you convert cars and diesel trains to electricity, the windmill can substitute for petroleum. So there's a piece of capital (the windmill) substituting for finite resources (coal and oil). But "capital" includes cars, trucks, airplanes, roads, airports, coal-burning power stations, internet capacity, and on and on. As mentioned above, some of these things could operate without fossil fuel, as long as there is *some* other energy source, but none of them in themselves *provide* that energy source. They are *complements* to energy in general, rather than *substitutes* for exhaustible energy resources.

Second, it's not clear that there even are adequate substitutes that can match the efficacy of fossil fuels. For the thermodynamic reasons discussed in Chap. 2, sources such as biofuels may perform some of the same functions as petroleum, but only at significantly higher cost. And functions like aviation do not yet have *any* alternatives to petroleum-based fuel (though of course it's hard to rule out the possibility of developing something along those lines in the future).

And beyond whether the Hartwick Rule is even possible to follow, it's clear that we've spent the vast majority of the time since 1977 (when Hartwick's original paper was published) not really trying. In 1977 the U.S. economy got 71 quadrillion Btus (or "quads") of energy from fossil fuels, and 4.2 quads from renewables. By 2015, renewables had grown to 9.7 quads, expanding their share from 3.5% of the primary energy supply, to 8.5%. But fossil fuels had grown in absolute terms to 79.4 quads, and still made up 81.3% of our primary energy supply.[2]

[2]See Table 1.1 "Primary energy overview" from [2].

So where the Hotelling Rule could be described as optimistically descriptive, the Hartwick Rule is optimistically prescriptive—optimistic because it thinks we might adopt such a policy of self-restraint, and even more so because it assumes that a technologically viable substitute for fossil fuels exists.

19.1.3 Hubbert Curves

In contrast to Hotelling and Hartwick, who approached the issue from a very abstractly economic perspective, M. King Hubbert was a geologist who spent much of his career in the oil industry and who mixed some economic reasoning into his understanding of the question from the perspective of the natural sciences.

First, he observed that, in a given region, extraction of oil seemed to lag discovery by a few decades (see Fig. 19.5).

Second, he noted that discovery would tend to follow a bell-shaped curve, with early exploration in an area quickly leading us to the biggest, most accessible deposits, while at some point discoveries would have to decline and taper off to zero (oil is, after all, a finite resource). Extraction would follow roughly the same path, with a lag, rising exponentially at first, then more slowly, and finally peaking before heading back down toward zero, as illustrated in Fig. 19.6.

When Hubbert first proposed this idea he was widely dismissed, particularly for his 1956 prediction that U.S. oil production would peak in the late 1960s [8]. (Remember that oil production had been increasing pretty steadily since 1859, and people treated that increase as practically a law of nature.) After the oil discovery at

Fig. 19.5 Lag between discovery and extraction

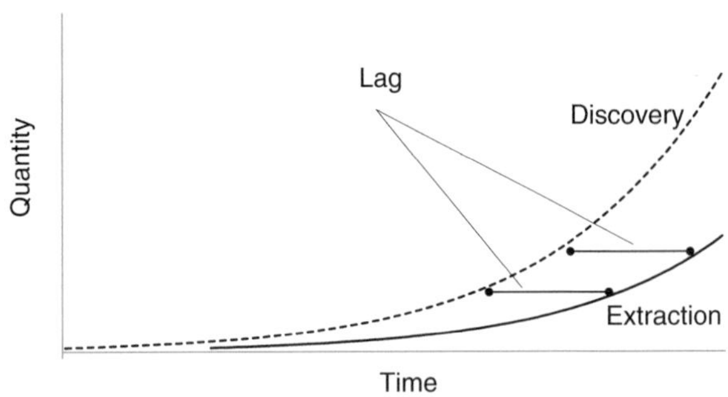

Fig. 19.6 Idealized Hubbert curves showing peaks of discovery and extraction

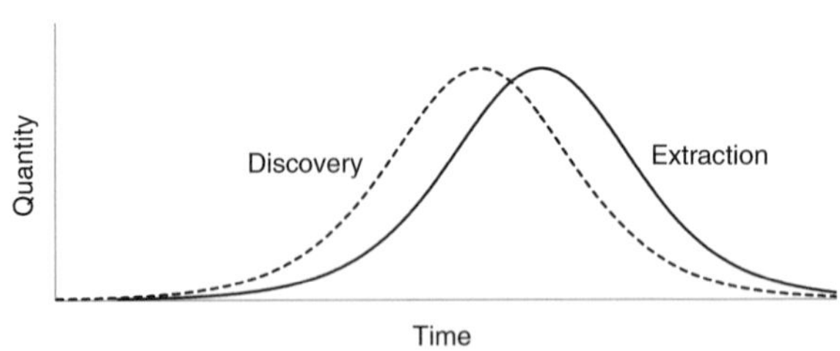

Prudhoe Bay in Alaska, he revised his prediction to say that U.S. production would peak in 1970. As it turned out, that's exactly what happened, and people still don't take him seriously.

Hubbert reasoned that, since the world was made up of a lot of individual regions, the world as a whole should display the same type of behavior as its individual regions. He applied his methodology and predicted that global oil production would peak in the 1990s. This point, whenever it comes, is often referred to as "peak oil."

There are two problems with this forecast. First, it didn't happen. Global crude oil production was 73,865,606 barrels per day in 2005, and after a dip it rose to 74,049,195 barrels per day in 2008, compared to 67 million barrels per day in 1998, the highest level for the 1990s. As part of the global economic crisis in 2008, production fell again, but in 2011 it reached a new high, and by 2015 it was up to 80,073,182 barrels per day.[3]

The second problem is conceptual. When a single region experiences peak and decline of oil *production*, that doesn't necessarily imply anything about that region's oil *consumption*. Oil produced in the U.S. has an incredibly close substitute: oil produced anywhere else. U.S. oil *production* peaked in 1970, but U.S. oil *consumption* kept right on rising. We'd been importing an ever-larger portion of our oil use starting after World War II, and we just kept right on doing that as our production not only failed to rise as fast as consumption but actually started decreasing.

In contrast, global oil has no such close substitute. So while French or U.S. production can peak and the French and U.S. economies can continue on their merry ways as if nothing had happened, the global economy can't necessarily do the same thing. An individual region can follow the roughly symmetrical shape predicted by Hubbert's model by switching to imports. But since the world as a whole can't import oil, what does it do? Does it keep increasing extraction far past the peak predicted in Hubbert's model, because there's no good alternative? That implies at some point a very rapid decline in extraction (see Fig. 19.7). And if that's what to expect, *when* will it happen? And what happens to the global economy then?

19.1.4 Hotelling Behavior with Endogenous Demand

My personal view among these three leans more toward the Hubbert approach. The Hartwick Rule is interesting in theory, but as explained earlier, we don't seem to be following it, and it's not clear that we *can* follow it. Hotelling's idea has the elegance characteristic of much of neoclassical economics, but it has some big problems, too:

[3]Table 11.1b "World Crude Oil Production: Persian Gulf Nations, Non-OPEC, and World," [2]. Some analyses break out "conventional" oil vs. more exotic sources, such as shale oil. In that view, the production of conventional oil has been relatively flat since 2005, with the increase in overall production of petroleum coming from other forms of oil. See, e.g., [13].

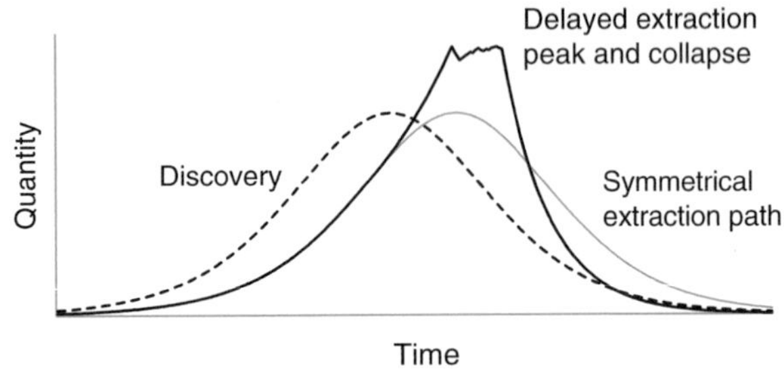

Fig. 19.7 Delayed extraction peak followed by collapse

earlier, the chapter discussed the issues of uncertainty, cash-flow motivations, and endogeneity. That last one is worth another look after the speculation above about what a Hubbert curve will look like on a global scale.

Remember the essence of the endogeneity argument: in an environment of low energy prices, people will build an economy where demand for energy is high, and they'll act differently if they experience decades of expensive energy. The Hotelling Rule has a neoclassical elegance: natural market forces will lead private owners of an exhaustible resource to extract the resource in a way that is good for society, slowly raising the price and tapering off the quantity. But if we make this one little change—energy demand is endogenous, and it depends on the past path of energy prices—that same neoclassical logic leads to a very different result.

The reason is that owners face a different set of choices than when demand is exogenous. When your actions don't affect future demand, Hotelling's logic on prices is valid. When you *do* affect future demand, it goes out the window.

Now you have a choice between:

- A price that rises at the rate of interest, thus quickly choking off demand and limiting the amount that you can sell in the future; or
- A price that stays low or even falls, netting you a little less in the present but guaranteeing you the ability to sell *much larger* quantities in the future, at a decent price.

Given those choices, it's perfectly reasonable to choose the second path. The result is output that keeps rising just as long as it can, until it collapses catastrophically (see Fig. 19.8).

In other words, it looks a lot like that last picture of the Hubbert Curve in Fig. 19.7.

But even this model is too simple. For instance, it doesn't account for the capital costs of building extraction capacity. More seriously, it abstracts from the increasing difficulty of getting to the resource after you use up the stuff that's easy to reach. Such considerations, combined with endogenous demand, may actually lead Hotelling's logic back to a path very much like the one Hubbert described, with a roughly symmetrical curve of extraction even on the global scale.

This chapter does not aim to settle the issue. As a practical matter, I doubt that we humans have enough information to apply the Hotelling Rule, or the technological

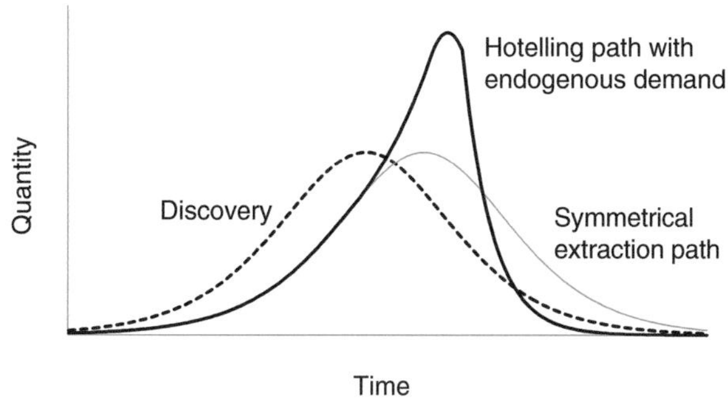

Fig. 19.8 Hotelling logic applied to endogenous demand

alternatives and the willpower to apply the Hartwick Rule. Roughly speaking, we pull oil up at the rate we can profitably sell it *now*, and we let the market set the price. This is the world described with the resource supply curves in Chap. 4.

We're not about to "run out" of oil. There are probably at least 1 trillion barrels in the ground, and substantially more if we loosen our description of what counts as "oil." What we may well be at the end of is the age of *cheap* oil. We've spent more than a century in a world where we could very reliably move the resource supply curve to the right. It would occasionally happen that our exploration and development efforts would fall a bit behind, and demand for oil would push a little bit up onto the more steeply rising part of the supply curve, but not for long. Or geopolitical events would pull the supply curve back to the left, and we'd find ourselves pretty far up that steeply rising part of the curve. But not for long.

We may now be in a different world. We may now be in a world where we reside pretty much permanently on the rising slope of the oil supply curve, with occasional excursions into much higher territory. Oil prices may fall significantly, as during 2015, but that will coincide with periods of weak global growth, and it will spur concern that low prices will shut off the investment needed to keep arduously expanding oil supplies. Indeed, the Canadian province of Alberta saw large drops in employment in 2015 as production of the province's expensive shale oil declines in the face of low prices [1]. It may be that there simply isn't much oil left that can be profitably sold at $20 a barrel—not enough, anyway, to power a robustly growing global economy.

The resource-inclusive long-run model from Chap. 4 through 7 was built to accommodate exactly this type of possibility. Chapter 20 revisits the long-run model in an environment of resource constraint, and Chap. 21 extends the implications to the short-run model.

But before turning to that, we have two more resource issues to address: the deeper meaning of a resource being "expensive,"; and the "resource" of the environment's ability to absorb our wastes.

19.2 EROI and Energy Cost

What does it mean for energy to be "expensive"? The simplest answer is that the price has gone up. But since energy goes into everything, if the price of energy goes up, won't the price of *everything* go up? Which means the price index will have gone up, and when you apply that price index to the price of oil to get its real price, you find there's been little change.

The way out of this conundrum is through the concept of "energy return on investment" (EROI; sometimes called "energy return on energy invested", or EROEI).

The gasoline in the tank of your car has a certain energy content, which can be quantified. That's the energy return.

What did it take to get that gasoline from the ground to your car?

- Exploration to find the oil
- Drilling and pumping to extract it
- Refining to turn the oil into gasoline (and other products, like diesel and aviation fuel)
- Transporting the oil to the refinery and the gasoline from the refinery to the gas station (a combination of tankers, pipelines, trucks, and trains)

All of those activities involve some use of energy, which can also be quantified, though there are tricky questions of where to draw the boundaries. (You certainly include the energy used to pump the oil out of the ground, but do you include the energy used to make the pump equipment? What about the energy used to make the metal in the pump equipment? What about the energy used to make the steel mill that made the metal? Etc., etc.)

When you have an acceptable calculation of the energy used, you can create the following fraction:

$$\frac{\text{Energy contained in the gasoline}}{\text{Energy consumed in making the gasoline available}}. \tag{19.1}$$

That fraction is the EROI.

The EROI is a useful concept because it's a way of describing the cost of energy without getting into the confusion over money, inflation, and aggregate price levels. When the EROI is high, energy is cheap in physical terms. When you spend a unit of energy, you get lots of energy back. Obviously then, when EROI is low, energy is fundamentally expensive: every time you use up a unit of energy to make more energy available, you don't get that much back.

The history of the Industrial Revolution was a history of progressing from wood to coal to oil and gas. It was also a history of progressing from lower to higher levels of EROI. In the 1930s, oil produced in the U.S. had an EROI of about 100: each barrel of oil was produced using the energy contained in just 1/100th of a barrel. In the 1970s, the EROI was down to roughly 30. Today it's under 20.

Offshore oil has a lower EROI than onshore oil. Deep-sea oil has a lower EROI than offshore in shallow water.

Nuclear power is somewhere around 10 (it's tricky to measure it, because you have to make decisions about how to count the cost of storing spent fuel and decommissioning a retired power plant).

Windmills are roughly 10–20. Photovoltaics are around 10. Biofuels (biodiesel, ethanol—vehicle fuels made from biological materials instead of from petroleum) come in around 1–6, depending on the fuel you're making and the feedstock you're using.[4]

The concern is not that we're literally running out of energy. It's that we're running out of *cheap* energy. Having low-EROI energy is better than having none at all, but it's not the same as having high-EROI energy.

And since we've never tried to run a modern, globalized, industrial economy on low-EROI energy sources, we don't know if there's some EROI threshold below which a modern economy doesn't really function. Obviously at EROI = 1, you're using all your energy just to get more energy, which means you're not growing food, heating houses, moving cars, or doing anything except obtaining more energy. And if the only reason to use energy is in order to obtain more energy, the whole enterprise is pointless. The question is, how far above and EROI of 1 do you need to be to have a viable economy. This is not a question that the field of economics has spent any serious time investigating.[5]

19.3 Limits on Absorptive Capacity

The end of Sect. 2.4 mentioned the biosphere's capacity to absorb the stuff we dump into it, under the larger heading of "renewable resources," but the legitimacy of categorizing it that way depends on a combination of the specific resource you're talking about and your time frame.

The most prominent waste as of 2016 is the collection of greenhouse gases we emit, with carbon dioxide (CO_2) getting the most attention. Higher atmospheric concentrations of greenhouse gases raise the equilibrium average temperature of the Earth (hence the term "global warming"), with diverse and far-ranging consequences for the climate. Among the predicted effects are increased extremes, including both flooding and more intense droughts. The possible social effects include disruptions to agriculture, expanded ranges of disease vectors (such as mosquitos that carry malaria), and some regions becoming simply uninhabitable by people due to extreme heat. A reasonably likely consequence of these disruptions

[4]A quick visual summary of EROI's of a range of energy sources, see the "bubble graph" by Charlie Hall in [5]. A discussion of EROI issues relatively up-to-date estimates is in [4]; other papers in that issue provide relatively up-to-date estimates of fuel-specific EROI's.

[5]David Murphy [14] provides a two-part discussion of the issue; additional information is in [12].

is mass migration, as people flee areas where climate disruption has made daily life increasingly difficult. These problems can be compounded by civil war or other unrest fed, in part, by increased population pushing on dwindling productivity of local ecosystems. Some locations may see benefits, at least for a while, such as areas in Canada or Russia that currently have very short growing seasons but will become better places for agriculture, but those improvements are expected to be minor—and temporary—compared to the damages incurred in other places.

CO_2 is a byproduct of any fossil-fuel combustion. It also comes from burning wood or other recently-harvested plant matter. An additional significant flow comes from the process of making cement.

When you burn fossil fuel, you're increasing the atmospheric concentration of CO_2 by taking carbon that had been stored underground for the previous millions of years (often hundreds of millions of years) and putting it in the atmosphere. Some of it is taken up by growing plants, and some is absorbed into the ocean, but a significant part remains in the atmosphere, where it contributes to raising the planet's equilibrium temperature. The portion that's absorbed into the ocean does prevent faster buildup in the atmosphere, but it is far from harmless. With increased CO_2, the seawater becomes more acidic, which harms the growth of some small forms of sea life, including ones that are important for the base of the marine food chain.

If you grow a tree, then cut it down and burn it, or grow grass then harvest it and burn it, the net effect on atmospheric carbon is essentially zero, because the carbon released when you burn the tree is about the same as the carbon the tree absorbed while it was growing. In contrast, taking land that has been in forest for ages and converting it to some other use does generally cause an increase in atmospheric carbon, partly from carbon released from the soil of the former forest as it loses organic matter, and additionally from the burning of the trees that used to be on the land.

There are widely varying estimates of the size of the economic impact from continued climate change. The Stern Report commissioned by the government of the United Kingdom estimated that "if we don't act, the overall costs and risks of climate change will be equivalent to losing at least 5% of global GDP each year, now and forever. If a wider range of risks and impacts is taken into account, the estimates of damage could rise to 20% of GDP or more." [17, p. vi]. A more sanguine view is taken by Nordhaus and Sztorc [15], who find that a continuation of policies as they were in 2010 would leave the world only about 1% poorer in 2100 than it would be under what they consider to the optimal amount of limiting carbon emissions, implemented through intelligent policy tools. At the other end is the possibility that the disruptions will be so severe that they undermine the foundations of civilization itself, making their cost either meaningless to estimate or essentially infinite. As Weitzman [18, p. 1] writes, "the planetary welfare effect of climate changes that might accompany mean temperature increases from 10°C up to 20°C with probabilities anything remotely resembling 5% down to 1% implies a nonnegligible probability of worldwide catastrophe."

The cost of *limiting* climate change is, for now, the cost of giving up some of the benefit we get from burning fossil fuels and from clearing forests for agriculture or other purposes. Perhaps in the future there will be a way to capture and "sequester" CO_2 (storing it away in some manner that we're confident will not be rapidly undone). But such technologies don't yet exist in a form that is viable on a large scale, so limiting our emissions means burning less fossil fuel.

A naïve way of figuring the cost of foregoing fossil fuel is to look at its contribution to our well-being, measured in terms of the portion of GDP made up by final purchases of energy, or the value added in the energy sector. Either of those approaches suggests that fossil fuels account for something between 3% and 5.5% of the economy in wealthy countries, so even reducing our use of fossil fuel by, say 20%, with no offsetting increase in cleaner sources of energy, would only amount to a GDP reduction of around 1%, at most.[6] Stabilizing atmospheric CO_2 at 450 parts per million (ppm), would require emissions in 2150 to be 75% lower than in 2006, when the Stern Review was published [17, p. 200]. But if you're using a naïve look at the energy share in GDP, that's still only about 4% of GDP.

The Stern Report itself does not use such a simple-minded approach. Rather, it assumes both the arrival of new technology for development of energy sources with less impact on the climate, and tools such as tradable rights to emit carbon so that there are economic incentives to make efficient use of a limited ability to put CO_2 into the atmosphere. As a result, it reaches the conclusion that, "the costs of action—reducing greenhouse gas emissions to avoid the worst impacts of climate change—can be limited to around 1% of global GDP each year" [17, p. vi].

On the other hand, the 3%–5.5% estimate is surely an underestimate of the importance of fossil fuels in the absence of highly effective substitutes. As a thought experiment, consider rapid, total elimination of fossil-fuel use in the U.S. As mentioned above, in 2015, fossil fuels accounted for 81% of our energy use. The economic effect of a 100% reduction in fossil fuels would surely be a lot closer to 81% than to 5.5%. So reducing fossil fuel use by 20%, rather than 100%, would likely bring economic impacts considerably larger than 1% of GDP.

The Intergovernmental Panel on Climate Change (IPCC), a UN body that represents the global consensus view on the issue, estimated in 2007, that stabilizing atmospheric concentrations at 445–535 ppm would mean slowing down GDP growth by less than 0.12%, for a GDP in 2050 perhaps 5% lower than without mitigation [9].

In the end, it doesn't make a lot of sense to obsess over simple estimates of how much our GDP might be affected by efforts to reduce emissions. As observed by the IPCC, emissions reductions can be achieved in various ways, and the path we choose affects not simply GDP in this or that country, but the path of economic

---

[6]Energy's share of GDP is calculated as the final expenditure on "Petroleum and coal products" and "Utilities" in the Bureau of Economic Analysis's 71-sector division of the economy, while the value-added figures are the sum of the same two sectors, as well as "Mining". These approaches are arguably overestimates of fossil fuel's share, since they include activities that are not directly based on those energy sources.

development and quality of life in many countries. Done right, climate mitigation could work in tandem with efforts to reduce other forms of pollution and ameliorate poverty; done wrong, it will make both those problems worse [10, Box 3.4, p. 91].

Problems

Problem 19.1 Use the resource market as modeled in Chap. 4 to illustrate the effect of policy aimed at significantly reducing emissions of CO_2.

(a) How does that play out in the long-run model of Part II?
(b) What effect does it have in the IS-LM and AS-AD framework of Chap. 14 through 16?

Problem 19.2 Table 19.1 provides four different years of figures for the output of energy products by the U.S. oil and gas industry, the direct and indirect energy used to obtain that output, and the spot price of crude oil.

(a) Calculate the EROI for each of the years given.
(b) Do the figures in the table display a positive or negative relationship between price and EROI?
(c) Given what EROI represents, why does the relationship you identified in (b) make sense? Which way is the causality—from price to EROI, or from EROI to price?
(d) (*Advanced*) The indirect energy inputs are calculated via input-output tables, with the indirect purchases of the oil and gas industry translated into estimated amounts of energy via energy prices. How might this help explain the relationship you identified in (b), but with the causality going in the other direction?

Problem 19.3 Chapter 4 introduced the production function that has been used throughout this book: $Y = K^{\alpha} \cdot (Z \cdot N)^{\delta} \cdot (\rho \cdot N)^{\gamma}$. In that function, do resources have a complementary relationship to labor, or are the two inputs substitutes? Explain how you know.

Table 19.1 Numbers for Problem 19.2; energy figures are in petajoules, from [3, Table 6]; prices are in constant 2015 dollars, from [16]

Year	Production	Direct energy used	Indirect energy used	EROI	Price
1954	25,980	53.9	193.0		17.00
1982	41,330	1,618.6	3,727.0		80.98
2002	38,750	1,336.2	1,212.0		32.97
2007	37,990	1,084.6	2,485.0		82.75

Problem 19.4 For this problem, refer again to the production function displayed in Problem 19.3.

(a) Are capital and resources substitutes or complements? Explain your argument.
(b) What is the implication of your answer in (a) for our ability to reduce resource use?

References

1. Bickis, I. (2016). *Alberta's oil and gas veterans look elsewhere for jobs after layoffs*. January 27, 2016.
2. Energy Information Agency (2016). *Monthly energy review*, March 2016.
3. Guilford, M. C., Hall, C. A. S., O'Connor, P., & Cleveland, C. J. (2011). A new long term assessment of energy return on investment (EROI) for U.S. oil and gas discovery and production. *Sustainability, 3*, 1866–1887.
4. Gupta, A., & Hall, C. A. S. (2011). A review of the past and current state of EROI data. *Sustainability, 3*, 1796–1809.
5. Hagens, N. (2008). Why EROI matters (part 1 of 6). http://www.theoildrum.com/node/3786. Accessed April 18, 2016, April 1, 2008.
6. Hartwick, J. M. (1977). Intergenerational equity and the investing of rents from exhaustible resources. *American Economic Review, 67*(5), 972–974.
7. Hotelling, H. (1931). The economics of exhaustible resources. *Journal of Political Economy, 39*, 137–175.
8. Hubbert, M. K. (1956). *Nuclear energy and the fossil fuels*. Shell Development Co., Exploration and Production Research Division, Houston, publication no. 95.
9. Intergovernmental Panel on Climate Change (2007). Climate change 2007: Synthesis report; 5.6: Costs of mitigation and long-term stabilisation targets. https://www.ipcc.ch/publications_and_data/ar4/syr/en/mains5-6.html. Accessed June 29, 2015.
10. Intergovernmental Panel on Climate Change. (2014). Climate change 2014: synthesis report. http://www.ipcc.ch/pdf/assessment-report/ar5/syr/AR5_SYR_FINAL_All_Topics.pdf. Accessed June 29, 2015.
11. Jevons, W. S. (1865). *The coal question: An inquiry concerning the progress of the nation and the probable exhaustion of our coal mines*. London/Cambridge: Macmillan & Co.
12. Lambert, J. G., Hall, C. A. S., Balogh, S., Gupta, A., & Arnold, M. (2014). Energy, eroi and quality of life. *Energy Policy, 64*, 153–167.
13. Mearns, E. (2015). A new peak in conventional crude oil production, June 8, 2015.
14. Murphy, D. (2010). What is the minimum EROI that a sustainable society must have? The oil drum: net energy. Part I: http://netenergy.theoildrum.com/node/6284; Part II: http://netenergy.theoildrum.com/node/6318. Accessed April 13, 2014.
15. Nordhaus, W., & Sztorc, P. (2013). Dice 2013R: Introduction and user's manual, October 13, 2013. http://www.econ.yale.edu/~nordhaus/homepage/documents/DICE_Manual_103113r2.pdf. Accessed June 26, 2015.
16. Statistical review of world energy 2016 (2016). Historical data from "Oil – crude prices since 1861,". In http://www.bp.com/content/dam/bp/excel/energy-economics/statistical-review-2016/bp-statistical-review-of-world-energy-2016-workbook.xlsx, downloaded June 21, 2016.
17. Stern, N. (2006). The economics of climate change. http://mudancasclimaticas.cptec.inpe.br/~rmclima/pdfs/destaques/sternreview_report_complete.pdf. Accessed June 18, 2015.
18. Weitzmann, M. L. (2009). On modeling and interpreting the economics of catastrophic climate change. *Review of Economics and Statistics, 41*, 1–19.

Chapter 20
Growth Under Resource Constraints

Abstract This chapter revisits the growth model from Part II, focusing attention first on the role of resources in the history of growth, then looking forward to understand possible implications of increased difficulty obtaining resources in the future. Highlights of past growth are the "Discoveries", when Europe realized the rest of the world was out there and gained control over a vastly increased supply of largely renewable resources, and the "Discovery", when technological progress made the vast energy storehouse of fossil fuels available for human use. The chapter ends with a consideration of three possible futures in a world of constrained resources.

20.1 Growth in the Resources Model

Growth in the standard model comes from investment and innovation, resulting in a larger capital stock that embodies more advanced technology.

In the resource-inclusive model, investment and innovation are still essential, but resource supply matters as well. We start here by reviewing the "normal" process of growth when resources are abundant, then look at what happens when resource availability can't be easily expanded. The transition to the modern world is marked by a change to a situation where resource availability *is* easily expanded.

20.1.1 Normal Growth

If you look at the marginal product of labor (see Eq. 4.8), which is also the labor demand function, you see that it is influenced by changes in K, Z, and ρ. Specifically, if those three things change such that $K^{\alpha} Z^{\delta} \rho^{\gamma}$ goes up, then labor demand will increase.

If that happens with no change in ρ (K and/or Z increased but ρ didn't), then that implies an increase in demand for resources: higher demand for labor results in more labor being employed, and so $R = \rho N$ must go up.

But the history of many technologies that make labor more productive is that at least part of how they do that is by allowing the average worker to control a greater

K. Seeley, *Macroeconomics in Ecological Context*, Studies in Ecological Economics 5, DOI 10.1007/978-3-319-51757-5_20

flow of resources—in other words, many technological innovations help workers accomplish more by increasing ρ. Which means that resource demand goes up even more. Not only is there more demand for labor, but each unit of labor is using a greater quantity of resources.

If the resource supply does not expand, sooner or later the increasing demand for resources will run into the steep part of the resource-supply curve (see Sect. 4.5, pushing the price up significantly. When the price gets high enough, it outweighs the improvements in labor productivity brought about by increased K, Z, and ρ: yes, labor is more productive, but the resources those workers need are so expensive that it's not worth hiring that many people.

This has an implication for the normal growth process:

Unless ρ is actually shrinking, sustained growth is only possible when R^S is moving continually to the right.

20.1.2 *Preindustrial Growth*

In a preindustrial setting, exhaustible resources play a secondary role. There's some use of metal ores, and even a little coal or peat for heat. But power comes from people and animals; clothes come from animals and plants; and heat mostly comes from trees. In terms of the resource-inclusive model, that means that η (the share of resources derived from exhaustible supplies) is very low (see Sect. 4.5.2)—for simplicity, we can say $\eta = 0$, which means the economy is entirely dependent on renewable resources.

This has the advantage that there is a sustainable level of resource use (in contrast to the situation with exhaustible resources, as explained in Chap. 19). But many renewable resources have a certain "fragility" about them. You can increase food harvests by working the land harder, but you run the risk of exhausting the soil. You can increase the number of trees you cut, but at the risk of exceeding the forest's growth rate, resulting in fewer trees in the future. You can build more boats to catch more fish, but at the risk of depleting the fish stock, and thus having fewer fish to catch in the future.

In other words, investment and innovation can shift the renewables supply curve to the right, supporting growth for a while. But there's a significant chance that, before too long, your extraction efforts will cause the curve to shift back to the left, perhaps even to the left of where you started. When that happens, much or all of your growth will be undone.

So, *if* there's some innovation and investment, the resulting growth is likely to peter out. But the effect goes deeper than that. To some extent, the spur for innovation and investment is the prospect of future gain. And the growth from one wave of investment provides the wealth and the launching point in terms of technology and infrastructure that supports the next wave. In a world where the resource supply curve doesn't consistently move to the right, you can't start up this "virtuous cycle" of growth begetting growth, since a wave will likely die out before its fruit can ripen. In fact, there is a large obstacle to the initial wave happening at all, since there are poor odds of it making you rich.

The only option for continual growth in the pre-industrial world is technologies that reduce ρ while significantly increasing Z, but given their rarity, they seem to be hard to come by. So what we get is the long history in the pre-modern age of almost no lasting growth.

20.1.3 The "Discoveries"

Something important changes after about 1500. The European "discovery" of the rest of the world, and Europe's capacity for lopsided influence, resulted in a new pattern of resource supply, at least from the perspective of Europe's economies. We can think of the lands over which Europe gained control as additions to its "effective acreage"; Europe itself didn't get bigger, but the land providing the resources that supported Europe's economy was augmented by the addition of control over other places. Europe's effective acreage started increasing, and was able to keep on increasing for centuries.

Sugar was produced on the islands and coastal areas of the Caribbean and sent back to Europe. Trees were cut down and sent back. Tobacco was grown and sent back. Fish were caught and dried or pickled and sent back. Grain was shipped, as was cotton. And as lands along the seaboard were "played out" by hard farming or over-eager tree-cutting, supply could be maintained or even expanded by moving inland.

There were a whole two continents whose existing inhabitants could be dominated or driven to the edge of extermination, making way for those who would increase the harvest of renewable resources and send the results back to Europe, or else supply the Europe-like economy developing within the U.S. itself. Throughout the nineteenth century there were still people carving out new farms in the Americas, planting new orchards, reaching additional virgin stands of trees that could be cut down.

That's 400 years, from the beginning of the "Age of Discovery" to the end of the nineteenth century, four centuries during which the European economy and its offshoots could expand by pushing on, pushing inland. That's probably a long enough time for the dynamic of growth to change from what it was in the pre-modern world. As Eric L. Jones described it, "The Discoveries were the first positive economic shock ... of a magnitude capable of promoting system-wide growth." [6, p. 82]

People had been used to the idea that the returns to innovation and investment would be throttled by resource constraints. Now there were generations' worth of time to get used to the idea that, if you invested in a new piece of capital, and that capital required increased resource flow to make it profitable, then the resource flow would in fact appear.

So now you have investment and innovation (both kinds: Z and ρ), but in the context of resource abundance created by the "Discoveries," these now lead to *continued* high profitability, simultaneously encouraging further efforts and making those efforts easier to support.

The "Discoveries" gave Europe access to a seemingly bottomless barrel of renewable resources, and this teamed up with Europe's dynamic institutions to shift the continent—and eventually the world—from the Malthusian stagnation of almost all prior history to the modern perspective where we take economic growth as the "normal" condition while the failure to grow looks like deviations from that normal.

20.1.4 The "Discovery"

Over the course of the eighteenth century, makers of iron and steel in Britain experimented with the use of coal. As described in Chap. 2, ferrous metals had depended on charcoal, which you make by using one batch of wood to heat a second batch of wood, getting rid of most of what's not carbon. The process consumes lots of wood, but the resulting charcoal burns hot enough to melt iron, and has few enough impurities that it could be used in the steel-making process of the time.

Steel is iron with just the right amount of carbon. Iron and charcoal would be combined in time-tested ratios and put into vessels together. The whole mass would be fired, with the charcoal providing not only the heat to drive the process, but the necessary amount of carbon as well. Steel makers in various regions learned what combination of inputs worked reasonably well given the ores and the wood available in their locale.

It was tempting to use coal in place of charcoal, since it was a cheaper fuel, but pulling it off was a big technological problem. It took a century of experimentation and the redesign of the entire iron-and-steel-making process before it could be done reliably. But as the process improved, the supply of iron and steel kept expanding. The constraint on the ferrous industry hadn't been the supply of iron ore—it had been the supply of energy. And in eighteenth-century Britain, coal was a source of energy that could be expanded far more than wood.[1]

During that same century, there was a revolution in the ability to make things move. The early steam engines were horrible wasters of fuel, turning less than 1% of the fuel energy into actual work; the rest escaped as waste heat. But coal mines provided an environment where these impractical beasts could thrive and evolve into more effective machines.

[1] J.R. Harris [5] provides a good narrative of how and why coal was incorporated into the ferrous-metals industry.

Mines—including coal mines—were reaching deeper into the ground, and running into the water table at depths where pumping out the water was a daunting task. Gathering together enough men or animals to do the work would be a logistical nightmare, as well as being very expensive because of all the food or feed that would have been needed. The early steam engines *were* horribly inefficient, but if you fed them enough coal they could deliver more power to the pumps than man or beast could provide. So they served a useful purpose.

And look where they were: right at the mine. Transport to anywhere else was expensive, which made the coal at the mouth of the mine relatively cheap. So if you threw some of it into your steam engine, that didn't cost you very much. And by doing that and pumping out the water, you were able to get at even more coal. The result was that the early steam engines, inefficient as they were, were economically viable.

Once they had an environment where they could survive, an environment where they could do real work and not just be idle curiosities, people naturally tinkered with them and found ways to make them better. The coal consumption per unit of work went down, and the power went up; it started becoming practical to install steam engines in factories, taking the place of water wheels. Technological innovations went hand in hand with improvements in the quality of making metal and working with it; the result was steam engines that could work at higher pressures, allowing a smaller and lighter engine to provide more power. A big, heavy, inefficient, weak engine would be no use on a boat—by the time you made room for the engine and all its fuel, there'd be no room left for cargo. With improved engines, steam became practical in shipping. With further improvements in the weight-to-power ratio, it became possible to put a steam engine on wheels and have a railroad.[2]

The railroad made land transit relatively cheap and closed the circle. It was now easy to move coal from the mine to wherever you wanted it, so mines didn't have an automatic cheap source of fuel. But the steam engine had outgrown its cradle and no longer needed that sheltered environment in order to survive. At the same time, railroads were one of the industries pushing demand for steel, and thus for the coal to make the steel.

The cumulative effect can be seen in the exponential growth of British coal consumption from 1751 to 1899, illustrated in Fig. 20.1.

Coal provided industrializing economies with a resource that had far more room to expand than any renewable thing it replaced, and applicable in many branches of the economy. The result was global growth of about 1% per year during the nineteenth century, compared to growth of about 0.1% per year from 1500 to 1800 [1].

In the 1860s petroleum started to be produced in meaningful quantities. Its first important use was as a lubricant and a fuel for illumination (in both roles, it replaced

[2]This incident and the basic narrative here of the Industrial Revolution draw heavily on David S. Landes [7].

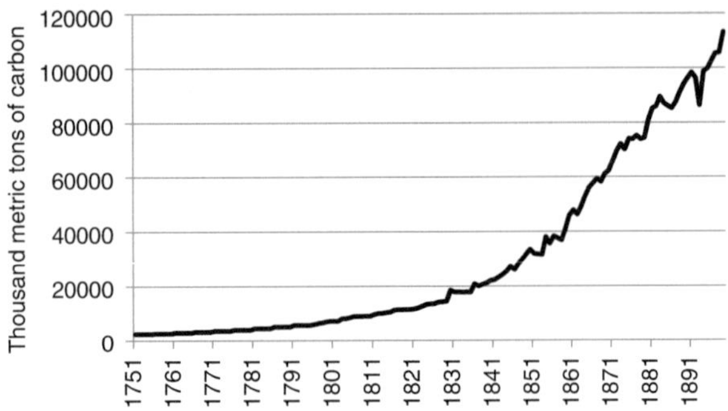

Fig. 20.1 UK emissions from fossil fuels, 1751–1899 (Source: [3])

Fig. 20.2 Global carbon dioxide emissions, 1751–2010, millions of metric tons of carbon (Source: [4])

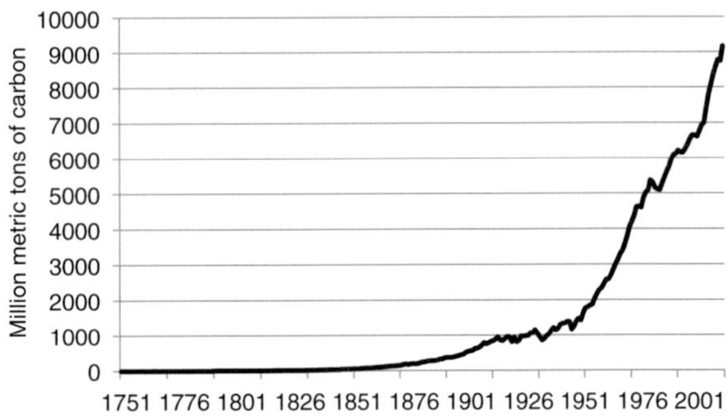

whale oil, which was getting expensive as hunting drove down whale numbers) [11, Chap. 1]. Gasoline was an annoying byproduct, a fluid that too easily converted to vapors. Of course, that turned out to be its key to success, as inventors figured out how to use it in a new kind of engine: the internal combustion engine, where the fuel was burned directly in the pistons, rather than burned in an external boiler to create steam to drive the pistons.

The internal combustion engine is what's under the hood of almost every car, truck, and bus on the road today.

In terms of the weight-to-power ratio, the internal combustion engine was an advance over even the best steam engine, and thus it made flight possible. After a few decades of flight, experimentation led to the jet engine, which was a new, more powerful way of burning oil. And that, in turn, led to the expansion of flight into the commonplace activity it is today.

Oil dominated the twentieth century, while coal continued to be an important fuel and natural gas became significant in its own right. The effect of all three together can be seen in Fig. 20.2. The growth of fossil-fuel use through 1899 looks like nothing compared to what the twentieth century brought us.

The "Discoveries" at the beginning of the modern age gave Europe access to an expandable resource supply like no economy had ever had before, and the result was

300 years of growth—the formation of the modern world itself. In the nineteenth century, the baton was passed to fossil fuels, and the growth accelerated.[3]

By the beginning of the twenty-first century, the limitations of the pre-industrial age had been relegated to the status of ancient history. They were not generally treated as being relevant to how an economy works in the modern world. But if we're heading back to a time of more binding resource constraints, we need to have a view of the economy more general than the one that developed during the time of environmental abundance.

20.2 The Long-Run Impact of Resource Constraints

Through most of the twentieth century, the price of oil was about $20 a barrel (in inflation-adjusted terms). This happy state was interrupted in the 1970s and early 1980s, but in 1986 we went back toward the twentieth-century norm. In 1998, in the wake of the economic meltdown of southeast Asia, the price fell to $10 and the *Economist* had a cover story about how we might see $5 prices. [2] 1998 was also the last time we saw prices anything like that. There was an uneven rise to the spectacular peak of $147 in July, 2008, followed by economic turbulence around the world which helped bring the price back into the $30s, before it once again worked its way up to the range of $80 to $100. Even with a slide from mid-2014 to the end of 2015, oil prices have stayed above what was normal for most of the twentieth century.

This is the new normal. The traders who make their money by being more right than wrong about the economy aren't worried about running out of oil, because there are still plenty of profitable opportunities for pulling oil out of the ground—as long as the price stays above $70![4]

It's possible that the smart-money guys are wrong and that a new age of cheap oil awaits us. It's possible that scientists will be able to make renewable resources far more potent than they are today—there's already been progress, and maybe there's much more in store. It's possible that there is some other resource waiting to be discovered, maybe even something right under our noses, if not under our feet; after all, people *knew about* oil for millennia, but it was only in the late 1800s that they realized what it was good for.

And yet, even if there *is* another cheap-oil age in our future, there's a further problem: climate change. Recall the discussion about the atmosphere's absorptive capacity (Chap. 4) and the evidence that we've been significantly exceeding that for a while now (Chap. 18). The negative effects are starting to appear already and are only forecast to get seriously worse.

---

[3]Problem 20.4 looks at various aspects of the relationship between fossil-fuel use and the market for renewable resources.

[4]Personal communication.

So we can't be certain that we *are* in a new age of resource scarcity. But there's no evidence to *reject* that possibility either, and even if we're not, we would be well advised to get onto a path of declining fossil-fuel use. Either way, we need to think through the economic implications of reducing our resource use after centuries of expanding it.

In the terms of our model, resource scarcity simply means that the resource supply curve no longer responds as readily to investment and innovation. We can keep drilling new wells and coming up with new ways of getting at oil, but a given amount of investment doesn't move the supply curve to the right as effectively as it used to. If we *choose* scarcity in order to avoid more extreme climate change, that could look similar: a quantitative limit on fossil-fuel use, or a tax on fossil fuel high enough that it shifts the supply curve significantly leftward.

The model of Part II was built to deal with specifically this kind of variation. How does the model respond to this scenario of limited resource supply? In a way it's not that different from how things work out in pre-modern setting. You have a period of growth with expanding resource supplies, and then resource supply curves stop shifting right, or even start shifting left. There are three big differences, however.

1. The period of growth wasn't a few decades, it was a few centuries. Our institutions are very much built around the assumption that growth will continue.
2. Even before the Industrial Revolution (which could be thought of as the Fossil Revolution), modern growth seems to have involved an increase in ρ—an increase in the amount of resources used per worker. The fossil age involved a much bigger increase in ρ, along with an increase in η (the share of resources coming from exhaustibles) as we shifted from agriculture to industry powered by fossil fuels. So in contrast to pre-modern societies that hit growth limits, we've built up an awfully large appetite for resources.
3. Europe's access to resources from elsewhere allowed its population to grow [9]. The introduction of New World crops like maize and sweet potato allowed China's already-large population to grow more [8]. And then fossil fuels further relaxed Malthusian constraints, improving the transportation of food from low-density areas to high, and then allowing the production of more food per acre. So not only have we inherited a ρ that is very high by historical standards, we've also inherited a very large population so that, all else being equal, we'll tend to continue putting a lot of pressure on resources.

That's a full plate of complications. Let's look at what the model we've built says about how to approach them.

20.3 Paths Toward a Resource-Constrained Future

To start, think about what technology parameters we want to have in the future, 30 or 50 years from now, if we are in fact heading for a future where exhaustible resources are starting to actually act, well, exhaustible.

As far as technology, it's obviously desirable to have as low a value of ρ as possible. To some extent, we could do that today. We could dig building foundations with shovels and wheelbarrows, instead of with backhoes and dump trucks. We could farm using horses to draw our ploughs, or even pull them ourselves, and harvest with scythes instead of combines. We could convert our airplanes to pedal power—Wait, no, we couldn't do *that*.

Clearly a reduction in ρ with no other change is not a recipe for a future that would look anything like prosperity. The key is to increase Z a great deal at the same time.

For any reduction in ρ, there's some increase in Z that fully offsets the effect on labor productivity. Resource intensity of labor can go down as much as we want and labor productivity won't be hurt, so long as $\dot{Z}^{\delta}\rho^{\gamma}$ doesn't drop. So we want:

Big Z, little ρ.

Turning to the question of what *kind* of resources to focus on, it may be tempting to look for a decrease in η, the share of resource use that comes from exhaustibles. After all, if the problem is that the supply of exhaustible resources is no longer expanding in the way to which we've become accustomed, wouldn't it help to shift our dependence away from them?

The problem is that we've never had such a high average level of prosperity to support, and we've never had 7 billion people and climbing. Fossil fuels allowed us to escape Malthusian constraints from overusing renewable resources back when there were 1 billion people in the world. If we simply try to substitute renewables for exhaustibles at our current level of output and our current population, we'll very quickly drive the supply of renewables (B^S) strongly leftward.

Turning to renewables is only a viable strategy if we have new technologies that effectively increase B^S in a sustainable way. A massive expansion of biofuels based on current technology would be a disaster. It's a different story if we have innovations that allow plants to capture more sunlight without big "subsidies" from fossil fuel (which they currently receive via pesticides and fertilizers—see Fig. 2.8 in Chap. 2) and without exhausting the soil. Wind and solar photovoltaic may have promise, though currently their capital cost relative to fossil alternatives is relatively high. In sum, we want:

Low η (if B^S will support the demand for renewables).

This strategy is actually complementary to reducing resource intensity of labor, ρ, because if resource demand in general is reduced, then increasing our relative reliance on renewables is less risky.

Lastly, what can we do about the supply of exhaustibles, E^S? The assumption behind this whole exercise is that the supply of exhaustible resources is shrinking, or at least not growing at the rate to which we've become accustomed. So if we simply assume that E^S *isn't* shrinking, then we solve the problem, but only by assuming it away. But it turns out there is something we can do to increase the future supply of exhaustible resources *relative to what they would otherwise be*.

Remember that E^S is shaped by:

- discovery, innovation, and investment, which shift the curve to the right; and
- extraction, which shifts the curve to the left.

Our premise is that discovery, innovation, and investment are failing to shift the curve rightward the way we would like. However, we still have a measure of control over how far the curve moves leftward, and how fast. The less we extract today, the more there will be tomorrow.

This flies in the face of a conventional economic perspective. Clearly we'll need significant investment in new technology in order to increase Z and decrease ρ. Such investment is funded out of current output. If we cut back on extraction of exhaustible resources, that is likely to reduce current output and thus reduce investment, making conservation counterproductive.[5]

This argument has more force if you think that capital and resources are substitutes. In that case, one way out of a resource constraint is investment in other capital (in other words, some version of the Hartwick Rule—see Chap. 19). In that case, reducing resource use really is harmful if it leads to less investment. But if resources and capital are actually more like complements than substitutes, conservation becomes part of a strategy that looks out for the future. So we have the third piece of our desired future:

As high a level of E^S as possible *in the future*, implying reduced use *now*.

Bringing it together,

The optimal future in the face of constrained supplies of exhaustible resources is characterized by:

- Big Z, little ρ
- Low η (if B^S will support the relative increase in demand for renewables)
- As high a level of E^S as possible *in the future*, implying reduced use *now*

These traits are the background for considering three basic paths into the future:

- Business As Usual (BAU);
- weak foresight; and
- strong foresight.

Each of these will be described, and its outcomes characterized in terms of output and consumption in the short, medium, and long term.

[5] This is the case Robert M. Solow makes in [10].

20.3.1 Business as Usual

Along the BAU path, we give the same long-run policy advice as has applied for the last 200 years. The role of government is simply to encourage investment and innovation. It's possible that private firms will pick up signals of resource constraints, predict high resource prices, and start shifting to technologies embodying high Z and low ρ.

It's also possible that firms are limited by a first-mover disadvantage. Often, if you have a technology that is advantageous when resource prices are high, it competes poorly when resource prices are moderate or low. So even if firms foresee higher prices, concerns for profitability mean that they can't move heavily in a desirable direction until high prices are already upon us.

BAU Short-run outcome Because there's no change in investment activity and resource prices are not yet extremely high, the short run along this path is much like our current economy. Output and consumption continue growing.

BAU medium-run outcome For our purposes, we could describe the medium run as the period of time when increases in K and Z are still able to stave off a leftward shift in E^S—it's getting harder and harder to do it, but it's still possible. On the positive side, that means that output and consumption remain high (though perhaps consumption is being eaten into a bit by the heavy investments needed to support exhaustible resource supply.) On the negative side, keeping E^S from shifting left means that the price remains moderate, which in turn means that extraction remains high, and that sets up the bad outcome that follows.

BAU long-run outcome The long run in this setting is the point at which K and Z can no longer nudge E^S rightward. At that point, resource prices rise quite strongly. The economy is saddled with technologies requiring large amounts of resource use, but inadequate supplies of resources to go with them. Output, employment, and consumption fall disastrously.

20.3.2 Weak Foresight

In the scenario of weak foresight, policy moves us in the direction of creating only capital that has low ρ. That is, existing capital is left in place, but as things wear out and need to be replaced, the new capital has a lower ρ than what it replaces.

Weak foresight short-run outcome In the short run, this differs little from the BAU path. Most of the capital in the economy is still "legacy" capital that we've inherited from past investment. It has a high ρ and is fairly productive in the presence of decent resource supply. This means that output is "normal." And our aggregate quantity of investment hasn't changed, so consumption is also "normal."

Weak foresight medium-run outcome This is the time frame in which significant amounts of low-ρ capital have come on-line, some of it replacing older, more resource-using capital. Past technological history suggests that it's actually not easy to raise Z drastically, so if we insist on low ρ, we may have to accept that there won't be the compensating rise in Z that would maintain productivity.

So we get a slightly falling level of output, or at least slower growth than what we've come to expect in the modern world. At this point in the game, we may be worse off than in BAU.

Weak foresight long-run outcome All in all, this is not a very rosy picture. Exhaustible resource supply is really starting to tighten, pushing up prices and pushing down output. On the other hand, our resource use has been falling further and further below the path of resource use in BAU, so the supply hasn't shifted as far left. And we're finally really reaping the fruits of our efforts at reducing ρ. So with somewhat increased resource supplies and somewhat decreased ρ, we're better off than in BAU (higher output and higher consumption), even if we're doing poorly by today's standards (lower output, lower consumption).

20.3.3 Strong Foresight

The essence of this path is not only to focus on technologies with low ρ, but to push the level of investment above its normal rate, to bring new technologies on-line faster and also speed up the retirement of old, resource-intensive capital. It can be thought of as analogous to a war effort, where a great push is made toward a goal of clear importance.

Strong foresight short-run outcome In the short run, output may be high, due to the increased investment push. However, that same focus on investment suggests that consumption has been reduced.

Strong foresight medium-run outcome By this time you've significantly lowered ρ through accelerated replacement of older capital. How well you're doing in this time horizon depends on how much Z has managed to make up for the reduction in ρ. Unless it's done much better than the historical norm, there's likely to be a significant decrease in Y (low ρ having reduced labor productivity), bringing with it a meaningful reduction in C.

Strong foresight long-run outcome This is where the payoff comes in. Compared to either of the other paths, you have the lowest ρ. And if there's going to be at least partially offsetting increases in Z, they may more likely come along this path, where the focus has been on getting by without resources. And to top it off, the rapid reduction in ρ has conserved resources, an effect which was reinforced by the reduction in output (and thus resource use) in the medium run. So with the lowest levels of resource depletion among the three scenarios and a low value of ρ, we have levels of Y and C that ... aren't so bad, even if they're down from in the medium term.

This table summarizes the stylized outcomes.[6]

	Short run		Medium run		Long run	
	Y	C	Y	C	Y	C
BAU	High	High	High	High	Disaster	Disaster
Weak foresight	High	High	Moderate	Moderate	Bad	Bad
Strong foresight	High (higher?)	Reduced	Low	Low	Not so bad	Not so bad

Chapter 22 will look at the policy implications of these paths.

Problems

Problem 20.1 Why is it potentially problematic to deal with constraints on exhaustible resources by replacing them with renewable resources?

Problem 20.2 What's the argument for why conservation now leads to more resource availability in the future?

Problem 20.3 What's the argument for why conservation now *does not* lead to more resource availability in the future?

Problem 20.4 Exhaustible and renewable resources have a complicated relationship, as suggested in Sect. 20.1.4

(a) How are renewable and exhaustible resources substitutes? (You can answer with an example.)
(b) What does that relationship imply about the demand for renewables as the use of exhaustibles grows?
(c) How does greatly increased use of exhaustibles push demand for renewables in the opposite direction from what you answered in (b)?
(d) How does increased use of exhaustibles increase the *supply* of renewables?
(e) What is the limit on the process you identified in (d)?

References

1. deLong, J. B. (2008). Longest-run economic growth, once again. Blog post. http://delong.typepad.com/delongslides/2008/02/longest-run-eco.html. Accessed July 2, 2012.
2. Economist (1999). Drowning in oil. *The Economist, 350*(8109), 19.

[6]Chapter 1 mentioned in passing some economy-related things we also care about but that escape measurement in Y or C. They might also be relevant here.

3. Fossil-fuel CO_2 emissions by nation. Office of Science, U.S. Department of Energy. http://cdiac.esd.ornl.gov/trends/emis/tre_coun.html. Accessed July 1 2014.
4. Global fossil fuel CO_2 emissions. Carbon dioxide information analysis center, Office of Science, U.S. Department of Energy. http://cdiac.ornl.gov/trends/emis/tre_glob_2010.html. Accessed July 1 2014.
5. Harris, J. R. (1988). *The British iron industry, 1700–1850*. Macmillan Education. Prepared for the Economic History Society.
6. Jones, E. (2003). *The European miracle: Environments, economies and geopolitics in the history of Europe and Asia* (3rd ed.). Cambridge/New York: Cambridge University Press.
7. Landes, D. S. (1969). *The unbound Prometheus: Technological change and industrial development in Western Europe from 1750 to the present*. London: Cambridge University Press.
8. Mann, C. C. (2011). *1493: Uncovering the New World Columbus created*. New York: Vintage Books.
9. Pomeranz, K. (2000). *The great divergence: Europe, China, and the making of the modern world economy*. Princeton: Princeton University Press.
10. Solow, R. M. (1991). Sustainability: An economist's perspective. The Eighteenth J. Seward Johnson Lecture to the Marine Policy Center, Woods Hole Oceanographic Institution, printed in R. N. Stavins (ed.), *Economics of the environment* (4th ed., pp. 131–138). New York: Norton & Co., 2000.
11. Yergin, D. (1991). *The prize: The epic quest for oil, money, and power*. New York: Simon & Schuster.

Chapter 21
Business Cycles Under Resource Constraints

Abstract This chapter looks at the different relationships between resources and recessions, depending on whether the recession is caused by events in resource markets, or caused by something else, then having effects on resource markets. It also looks at the limitations on policy efficacy when recessions are driven by resource events.

21.1 Recessions and Resources

This section makes the connection between resources and the business cycle, with two different relationships, depending on the direction of causality. Some recessions are caused by "conventional" demand factors somewhere in the economy—say, a tightening of monetary policy, a loss of consumer confidence, a drop in exports—while others are caused by adverse changes in resource supply. Each type has very different implications for policy responses.

21.1.1 Conventional Recessions

Start with a normal recession. As mentioned above, there are various types of events that could result in a normal, demand-led recession. You would start your analysis with the IS-LM model, and which curve you moved would depend on the exact scenario you were considering. If the central bank were tightening monetary policy, you would represent that with a leftward shift of the LM curve. Firms losing confidence in medium-term profitability and therefore spending less on investment would be equivalent to a leftward shift of the IS curve. You could translate your scenario to the AS-AD model with a leftward shift of AD showing the effects on output and inflation.

To see the effect on resources, note that the reduced output is accompanied by reduced employment, and since resource use R is equivalent to ρN, this lower level of N corresponds to a lower level of R. As we move leftward along the resource supply curve, the prices of resources should fall, as shown in Fig. 21.1.

K. Seeley, *Macroeconomics in Ecological Context*, Studies in Ecological Economics 5, DOI 10.1007/978-3-319-51757-5_21

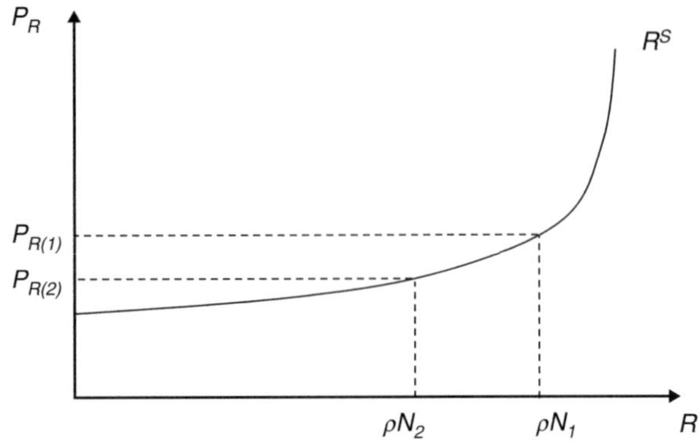

Fig. 21.1 Recession leads to lower employment (N_2 instead of N_1) and through that to lower resource prices (from $P_{R(1)}$ to $P_{R(2)}$)

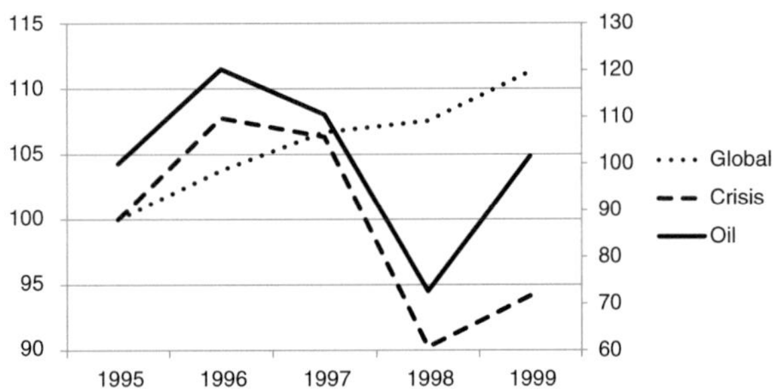

Fig. 21.2 Indexes (1995 = 100) of global GDP, GDP of crisis countries, and oil prices (oil price on right axis)

A prominent example would be the East Asian economic crisis of 1997–1998 (see Fig. 21.2). Among the countries of Indonesia, Thailand, Malaysia, Philippines, and South Korea, output in 1998 was 15% lower than in 1997. Globally, output had grown 3.8% in 1996 and 2.8% in 1997, and then grew only 0.8% in 1998. Meanwhile, oil prices fell from $20.71 per barrel in 1996, to $19.04 in 1997, all the way down to $12.52 in 1998, before rebounding to $17.51 in 1999.[1] If people's economies are imploding, their demand for resources will be down, and the price should fall.

21.1.2 Resource-Driven Recession

Things are different when resources themselves cause a recession. Such an event can itself take various forms:

- There could be a temporary disruption of supply.

[1]GDP data are "rgdpo"—"Output-side real GDP at chained PPPs" from [2]. Oil prices are Refiner Acquisition Cost of Crude Oil, Composite from [1], Table 9.1 "Crude oil price summary".

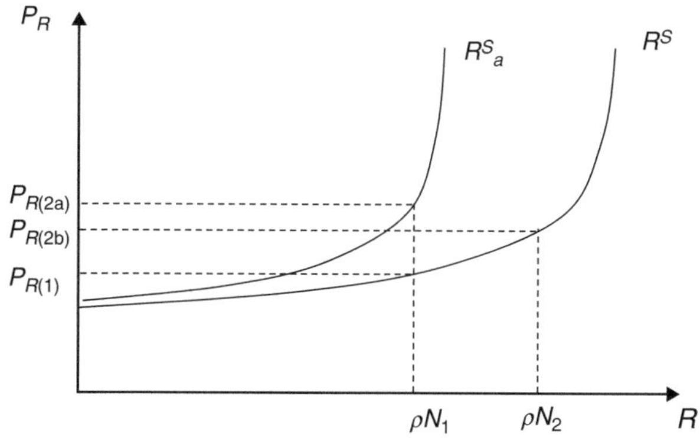

Fig. 21.3 High resource prices caused by reduced resource supply ($P_{R(2a)}$) and increased global demand ($P_{R(2b)}$)

  - War or other geopolitical factors could disrupt imports (e.g., the OPEC oil embargo of 1973 in connection with the Yom Kippur War).
  - Natural disasters could interfere with extraction or processing at home (e.g., Hurricane Katrina shutting down off-shore oil pumping and on-shore oil refining in Louisiana).

- Other economies could be expanding rapidly, increasing their demand for resources and pushing up the prices you have to pay.

A supply disruption means the resource supply curve is moving leftward, pushing up the resource price P_R (in Fig. 21.3 see the shift from R^S to R_a^S with the corresponding price rise from $P_{R(1)}$ to $P_{R(2a)}$). And the rapid expansion of other economies, as mentioned above, means *global* resource demand is moving rightward; without a commensurate increase in resource supply, this will again push up P_R (in Fig. 21.3 this is shown with the move from ρN_1 to ρN_2, which causes the price to rise from $P_{R(1)}$ to $P_{R(2b)}$). In the resource-inclusive labor market, the effect of a higher resource price is to widen the gap between N^S and $(N + R)^S$, which means that $(N + R)^S$ moves up or leftward. That means that equilibrium in the labor market gets shifted to the left: we have a lower equilibrium level of employment, which amounts to a lower level of potential output (see Fig. 21.4).

Translating that back into our tools for understanding business cycles, the reduction in potential output is a leftward shift and/or a steepening of the aggregate supply curve. If that's the only effect, then we expect to have a recession with lower output, lower employment, higher inflation, and higher resource prices (though the recession itself will somewhat mitigate those higher resource prices). This is shown in Fig. 21.5, with the shift labeled "a".

But the high resource price can have effects on demand as well. High energy prices are a strain on the budgets of households and businesses. Spending on energy may well increase, even as the quantity consumed goes down a little, but that means

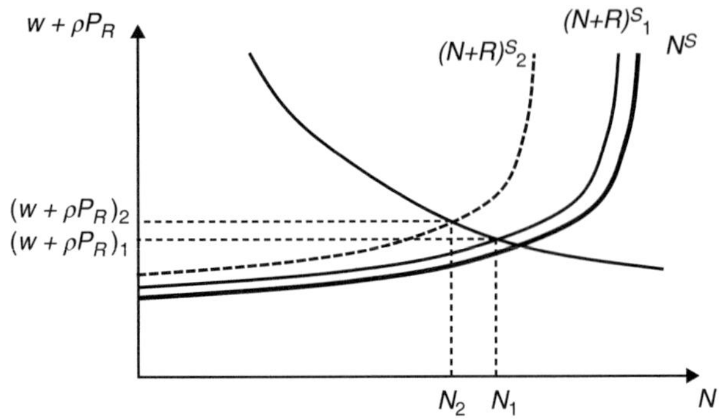

Fig. 21.4 Leftward shift of $(N+R)^S$, reducing employment from N_1 to N_2

Fig. 21.5 Leftward shift of aggregate supply ("a") and aggregate demand ("b"), resulting in lower output (Y)

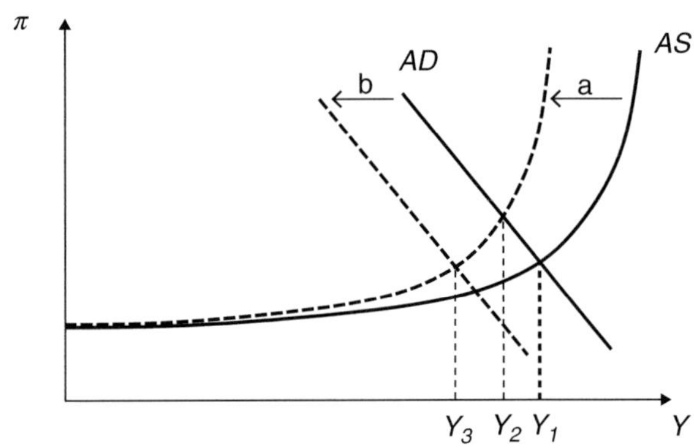

spending on other things will tend to go down. So consumer spending except for resources goes down, while firms outside the resource sector find their costs going up while demand for their goods and services goes down. To the extent that this engenders pessimism about future prospects, we'll see a decrease in expenditure on consumption and investment, which means that the IS curve moves leftward. The budgetary strain may also slow down loan repayments and increase the rate of defaults, which in turn may lead to less lending and less growth of the money supply. That possibility is represented by a leftward shift in the LM curve.[2]

To the extent that either the IS or LM curve moves, we have a leftward shift of the aggregate demand curve in addition to the leftward shift of the aggregate supply curve; the AD shift is illustrated with shift "b" in 21.5.

So the economy is in recession. What's the role of policy in this situation?

[2]A related phenomenon is described in James D. Hamilton [3].

21.2 Policy in a Resource-Driven Recession

The most important point about policy response to a resource-driven recession is this: our basic tools for macroeconomic management—fiscal policy and monetary policy—are tools for moving aggregate demand, not aggregate supply. And at the core of a resource-driven recession is a deterioration in aggregate supply.

As explained above, a resource-driven recession may include an AD component, and there is potential for stabilization policy to counteract that specific piece of the problem. But not necessarily. If supply conditions have worsened, making it harder to produce output, we may well *want* AD to be reduced somewhat: if demand stayed high while supply shifted left, we would be at risk of significantly higher inflation.

What follows from that is the economist's version of the Hippocratic Oath that doctors take: first, do no harm. If demand "overreacts" to the resource constraint and falls too far, then there's a role for conventional demand-side management, to counteract that overreaction. But policy-makers shouldn't be trying to maintain what they would have expected to be "normal" output or employment before the resource constraint bit.

The idea of a resource-driven recession shades into a longer-term contraction driven by resource limitations. Section 21.1 focused on scenarios in which the elevated resource price was plausibly a temporary phenomenon. If supply is interrupted by geopolitical factors, those shift all the time. If the price is being pushed up by higher demand elsewhere in the world, eventually those countries are likely to slow down, and even if they don't, resource supply may also shift to the right once resource suppliers have time to realize what's happening and respond to it.

But Chaps. 19 and 20 both looked at the possibility of high resource prices driven not by a spike in demand nor by a temporary interruption of the flow of resources, but a long-run shift of the resource supply curve to the left, or at least its failure to move to the right. This is the situation of resource constraints binding on the economy more quickly than technology Z is able to respond. Metaphorically, a parking brake has been applied to the economy. If policy tries to treat the situation like a typical recession, that's like hitting the accelerator. The inflationary aspects of a supply-driven recession will be exacerbated, but the leftward shift of the supply curve means you won't accomplish much in terms of increasing output.

In fact, the beginning of a long-term "secular" economic slowdown as a result of resource constraints may look at first like merely a resource-driven *recession*. And while we rightly dislike the effects of recession—in particular the increased unemployment it brings—in this instance there's one respect in which decreased economic activity is exactly what we want. Because decreased output also means, all else being equal, decreased use of resources. And if our long-run problem is resource availability, then there's a positive aspect to recession, in that it's reducing the "burn rate" at which we're using up our natural capital.

The impotence of traditional macro-stabilization policy in the face of a resource-driven recession means that our challenge in that situation is primarily a matter of patience: do no harm, wait until resource conditions improve, and the situation will fix itself. But if standard policy is largely impotent, and if longer-term resource problems give a recession an element of desirability, then we're taken outside the normal framework of economic analysis. We have to face deeper issues of what goals macroeconomic policy should pursue and even what questions it should ask. Those are addressed in Chap. 22.

Problems

Problem 21.1 In the labor market, consider the effect of a significant increase in P_R. How is w affected?

Problem 21.2 Model a decrease in ρ, undertaken in response to a resource-driven recession.

(a) Which diagrams do you have to work with in order to show the effects?
(b) How does a lower value of ρ help you?
(c) How does a lower value of ρ hurt you?
(d) Leaving aside your answers to (b) and (c), what is problematic about a reduction in ρ as a policy response to a resource-driven recession?

References

1. Energy Information Agency (2014). Monthly energy review, March 2014.
2. Feenstra, R. C., Inklaar, R., & Timmer, M. P. (2015). The next generation of the Penn World Table. Available for download at www.ggdc.net/pwt
3. Hamilton, J. D. (2009). Causes and consequences of the oil shock of 2007–08. *Brookings papers on economic activity*, Spring:215–283.

Chapter 22
Continuity and New Directions

Abstract We look back at the ways that the lessons of this book's resource-inclusive model are similar to those from a conventional model and how they differ. We conclude by asking what that suggests about different questions that macroeconomics should be asking and what new factors it should be taking into consideration.

22.1 Continuity and Difference

The model presented in this book has intentionally hewn close, in some ways, to a fairly conventional college-level macro model, while making the modifications necessary to tie it back to the physical processes underlying the economy. Not surprisingly, those modifications cause the model to reach different conclusions in some cases. Yet even where that's true, there's a deeper level of similarity in how the world looks through the prism of the conventional model and when looked at with resources in view as well. In the most general sense, the goals remain the same, it's just that there's a change in the specific content of what it means to achieve them.

22.1.1 The Long Run

The conventional model's view of desirable policy in the long run is based on fostering good underlying productive conditions. In practical terms, that means:

- Promoting innovation and the creation of human-made capital, and
- The efficient use of capital and labor, the economy's scarce inputs.

In different people's hands that can be interpreted somewhat differently, depending on how much you think different government actions help or impede the actions that promote a healthily growing economy. One economist might counsel an active stabilization policy to reduce the risk of recessions, and government support for certain R&D or investment activities that markets neglect. Someone of a more *laissez faire* orientation is likely suspicious of active stabilization and thinks the government will do a poor job of picking winners. But both those types

K. Seeley, *Macroeconomics in Ecological Context*, Studies in Ecological Economics 5, DOI 10.1007/978-3-319-51757-5_22

of economists would share the view that the goal is high growth; they only differ in what they think we need to do in order to get there.

When we turn our attention to the resource-inclusive model, the thread of continuity is that the policy-maker's goal is still to promote helpful underlying productive conditions. The difference is that, when resources are tight, that means:

- Promoting specifically *green* innovation and capital (high Z with low ρ) [a modified version of a standard goal];
- Encouraging efficient use not only of labor and capital but of resources as well [an extended version of a standard goal];
- Preserving the biosphere that provides some of your necessary resources [new criterion, entirely absent from the standard list].

To some extent, resource scarcity will lead to high resource prices which will in themselves push green technology and resource efficiency. But as explored in Chap. 20 there are problems of network effects and coordination that may cause such innovation to come later than optimal, suggesting a role for government action in moving the economy onto a green track earlier than markets alone would do so.

22.1.2 The Short Run

The traditional goal of short-run macroeconomic policy is to keep actual output close to potential output. If you're producing less than your potential, that's a waste of labor and other productive inputs that could be doing something useful; your economy is, in a sense, "leaving money on the table," because it is failing to produce output that could be used and enjoyed if only the economy were performing as it "should." In addition to these losses for the economy as a whole, the individuals who find themselves unemployed face high economic and personal costs. Output substantially *above* potential brings its own problems, namely the risk of inflation and bubbles.

From an ecological perspective, short-run policy is pretty similar. The goal is still (mostly) to keep actual output near its potential level. The big difference is that, as resource availability tightens, potential output isn't as high as you would estimate using a model that ignores the role of resources. So policy-makers in that environment should be more cautious about stimulus if they are including resources in their thinking. On top of that, they may even tolerate a period of output below potential because of the benefits it brings in terms of conserving resources for future use.

Chapter 18 laid out the interaction between the short- and long-run perspectives, and this is also somewhat modified by considering resources. The basic insight was that decisions about taxing, spending, and money supply should be viewed not only in terms of how they stimulate or restrain the economy in the present, but also for their effect on the long-run development of the economy. In the conventional model that can be boiled down to one question:

- Are your short-run policies encouraging more investment and innovation, or discouraging them?

In the resource-inclusive model, the right question is:

- Are your short-run policies are supporting *green* capital and also conservation, or are you simply stimulating more production?

There is a superficial resemblance here between the resource-inclusive model and the idea of the real business cycle. The essence of RBC theory is that recessions grow from conditions of supply, rather than demand, and that therefore stimulus policy is misguided (see Sect. 18.2.1). And the resource-inclusive model focuses attention on the idea that *some* recessions originate on the supply side (in the form of reductions in its resource supply), and that *in those case* it is misguided to try to return the economy to its former output level through demand-side policies.

But a conventional model does allow for supply-side recessions, even if it gives more attention to those that are caused by demand factors. And the resource-inclusive model, as laid out in this book, has plenty of room for recessions that start on the demand side as well, without trying to invoke indirect effects from supply shocks (see Part III). So while this book's model sometimes gives the same advice as an RBC model ("Don't reach for your demand-side toolkit!"), the spirit of the two approaches is not that similar.

22.1.3 Ecological Lucas, Ecological Keynesianism

Chapter 16 gave a very extended interpretation of the Lucas critique.[1] The takeaway was that rational actors will foresee the effects of policy; if they see stimulative policy as not being helpful, they will have a pessimistic view of the future, which will cause them to cut back on their spending, thus counteracting the effect of the stimulus program and making it in fact powerless.

If we apply that perspective to an ecological macroeconomic model, the lesson is that if policy is out of line with *perceived* ecological reality, then it won't work, and will in fact exacerbate other problems. And that applies whether the government is being "too green" or "not green enough."

In the case of a government pursuing green policy which most people view as pointless, they will see government involved in a wasteful, Quixotic quest and so will hold back on the private investment which is the necessary complement to the government's policy. On the other hand, if the public has internalized the idea of resource limitations while the government follows a conventional program of stimulus, paying no heed to the resource-efficiency of its actions, the public will

[1] "Extended" in the sense of going beyond what Lucas himself probably meant.

perceive that policy is not supporting a prosperous future and so people will hold back on investment, again undercutting the government's intention.

What sort of short-run policy would a government pursue in the face of acknowledged resource limitations? One piece would be a subsidy to green technology, to encourage faster development and adoption of capital with high Z and low ρ. That would be combined with a tax on resources. Not only would this tax discourage resource use, even as the green-tech subsidy made it easier to conserve; it would also counter the stimulative effect of the subsidy, to keep the economy from being too large and thus using resources at too fast a rate. Another component could be accommodative monetary policy to enable the private sector to undertake the green investment you're trying to elicit. And if that policy were deemed too stimulative, it could be balanced with a further increase in the resource tax.

Yet there are no guarantees. For a couple of centuries we have had astonishing growth based on modest increases in Z combined with massive increases in ρ—we have grown materially rich by figuring out how to extract and control a flow of energy and other resources that would boggle the minds of our ancestors. Continuing that level of material prosperity in a world of diminished *per capita* availability of resources will require a significantly lower value of ρ along with a much higher value of Z. It is unknowable whether that combination is something we can achieve. If it's not, then even the very best policy decisions will not allow us to continue enjoying the material prosperity that people in the developed countries have come to take for granted. Even more so, that would rule out the continued *growth* that standard macroeconomics considers to be the normal state of the world.

If ecological constraints continue biting and Z can't be raised faster than ρ is reduced, then the "ecological Keynesian" recipe spelled out above can't be counted on to provide rising employment, rising output, or rising wages. But in the long run, it's the best we can do (see the scenarios laid out in Sect. 20.3). And in the short run, if the public perceives the ecological constraints much like the policy-makers do, then no other short-run policy will do better.

And if policy makers see resource constraints but the general public doesn't? Then there are only bad options. Policy makers can go with traditional stimulative policy. Since that lines up with the public's perception, they get "buy-in" in the form of increased private spending in response to the stimulative policy. But reality will have its way in the end. Efforts at expanding output will run into high resource costs; in effect, the aggregate supply curve is sloped pretty steeply just to the right of where the stimulative policy was enacted, so the policy doesn't push the economy out to the right, it just pushes it up the steep part of the AS curve. And by encouraging more resource use now and investment in non-green capital, the policy is also stacking up additional costs for the long run. So traditional policy doesn't do much.

What about ecological Keynesianism? That doesn't work either. Since the public doesn't perceive the resource constraints, it views the "ecological" parts of the policy as wasteful and harmful, so the stimulative aspects of the policy fail to elicit the necessary private investment.

22.2 The *Very* Long View

Chapter 18 encouraged an attitude of openness to multiple ways of thinking about the macroeconomy. That approach is reinforced by a glance much further into the past than the steam engines of Chap. 2.

If we go all the way back to the prehistoric stone age and look at the hills surrounding the Fertile Crescent where civilization was born, we find communities that lived solely by mining rocks that were used for, literally, the cutting edge technology of their time (see Childe [3]). The archaeological evidence is that they grew little of their own food; rather, they mined obsidian and trade it with the farmers in the valley for the food they needed. In other words, even before there was writing, there was trade and there were economies that stretched far beyond the scope of a few villages. Without writing there was unlikely to have been money, and there certainly weren't banks, so those economies wouldn't have worked the same way as ours.

But economies are always changing. Clever humans find not only new ways to make things but also new ways to work with money and, more generally, to organize themselves. Cultural innovation helps shape how economies evolve, and as they evolve, our understanding of them needs to change as well.

The influence can go the other way was well, from the economy to the culture. The archaeologist David Anthony describes how ecological frontiers imposed different ways of making a living, and how those differences allowed for the persistence of cultural differentiation between neighboring societies. For example,

> The upland Kachin forest farmers, who lived in the hills of Burma (Myanmar), were distinct linguistically, and also in many aspects of ritual and material culture, from the Thai-speaking Shan paddy farmers who occupied the rich bottomlands in the river valleys. Some Kachin leaders adopted Shan identities on certain occasions, moving back and forth between the two systems. But the broader distinction between the two cultures, Kachin and Shan, persisted, a distinction rooted in different ecologies, for example, the contrasting reliability and predictability of crop surpluses, the resulting different potentials for surplus wealth, and the dissimilar social organizations required for upland forest and lowland paddy farming. [2, p. 115]

Our economies shape our cultures. The attributes and availability of resources shape our economies. In the modern world, human activity shapes the availability of resources to an unprecedented extent, but we still have not escaped the grip of the 1st and 2nd Laws of Thermodynamics (see Chap. 2); we may find new resources, and we may put known resources to new uses, but we still lack the means to conjure resources out of thin air.

From this swirl of interacting influences, something new is bound to emerge, as it always does. A few million years ago, our ancestors broke off from our primate relatives and started down the path toward being human. We humans organized ourselves in various ways, eventually developing things that could be called "economies." Going back the other way, before we were primates, we were mammals, and long before that, we were fish, and earlier still we were merely cells, or even just strands of RNA. Looked at in that way, "the economy" is nothing more than the latest thing in the 4-billion-year history of life on Earth. From that perspective, it makes sense to keep an open mind regarding what an economy is, what it's for, and how it works.

22.3 New Directions

As Sect. 22.1 suggested, in the face of binding ecological constraints, the best possible outcome may still be "not very good." In that case, what goals should policy try to achieve? How should we measure success? One approach is to start by thinking about what should be our ultimate concern, and I would posit that our deepest goal of all—really, the most important reason for trying to understand the economy—is to enable a high quality of life.

Many textbooks at least pay lip-service to the idea that quality of life comes from more than merely the material goods and services that the economy provides. But in practice, the fundamental measure of successful policy has been GDP growth. In the extreme, that would suggest that the discipline is implicitly working with a mental model like Fig. 22.1a. This diagram illustrates the view that while our quality of life is affected by more than just the economy, the various factors affect us independently. Whatever the state of our natural and social environments, an expanding economy merely creates additional options and opportunities, so a higher level of GDP and faster GDP growth are always desirable.

Increasing awareness of environmental issues—especially global warming and its link to economic activity—have added some subtlety to that picture. Indeed, the idea that we should accept at least a modest reduction in GDP in order to forestall catastrophic climate change is a recognition that there is a connection from the economy to the natural environment. What's more, the framing of the argument as giving up some GDP now in order to protect our GDP in the future is a recognition that the influence runs both ways. That does, however, have the effect of demoting the natural environment's direct effect on human well-being (we're only concerned with nature because of how its condition affects the economy, rather than how its condition affects *us*).

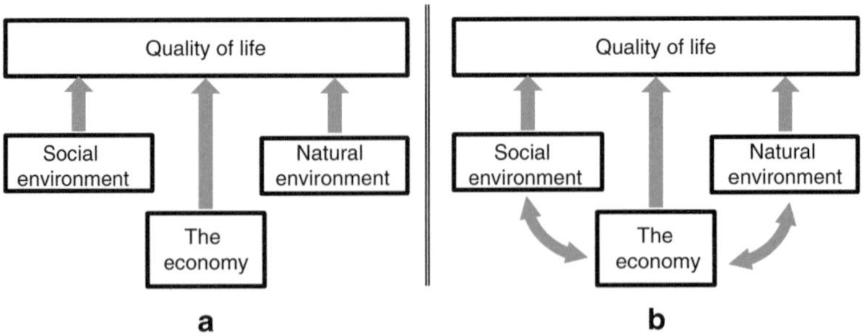

Fig. 22.1 Two ways of thinking about the relationship among quality of life, the economy, the social environment, and the natural environment

There is also a line of argument drawing a connection from the health of the economy to the health of the social environment, but much of this is in the vein of pointing out that a strong economy makes for a better social environment. Two examples would be the argument that democracy and an open society require not merely a high level of GDP but economic growth as well, [5] and the observation that useful institutions are easier to build in a rich society than in a poor one (e.g., Acemoglu et al. [1]).

The recognition of the role that social institutions play in economic performance is a recognition of a link from the social environment to the economy. What's missing is an awareness that it's possible for the pursuit of economic growth to come at the expense of the social environment.

During the 1930s unions successfully fought for the 40-h work week, displacing the old standard of 55 or 60 h and creating a new social reality, the weekend. But in recent decades white-collar workers have found work intruding ever more into what used to be the private sphere, while low-paid service workers cobble together two or three jobs to make ends meet. The GDP improves, but personal relationships fray and community organizations are starved of the time they need in order to function.[2] By this point we've moved from Fig. 22.1a to b. Importantly, the economy's effects on our social and natural environments can be both positive and negative.

One of the key lessons from this book's model of the economy is that economic growth is likely to be harder to come by in the future than we've come to expect. When we combine that with the reality that the pursuit of growth can damage not only the ecological web that sustains us but the social fabric that gives our life meaning, we see the need for a different definition of economic success.

We have to avoid the trap of "economism," of pursuing policies to help "the economy" regardless of their effect on anything else we care about. Because in the end, we shouldn't have any interest in the economy *for its own sake*. The economy should only concern us to the extent that it contributes to our overall well-being, either directly or through its impact on our social and natural environments.

Figuring out that alternative standard of success is beyond the scope of this book, but identifying the need is a good spot on which to end.

Problems

Problem 22.1 Look back at the view of the interconnections among the economy, the social environment, and the natural environment in Fig. 22.1b. Can you construct an argument against aiming to do economics in that way, rather than in the traditional way depicted in Fig. 22.1a? You could approach the question on theoretical or practical grounds, or on some other basis.

[2]See Daly and Cobb [4], especially Chap. 3, "Misplaced concreteness: measuring economic success".

Problem 22.2 Make an argument against the idea of an "alternative standard of success" proposed at the end of this chapter.

Problem 22.3 In contrast to Problem 22.2, accept the premise of the last line of this chapter, that we need different ways of measuring the success of our economic policies.

(a) What goals might you propose?
(b) What is there in favor of your proposed goal(s), from a theoretical perspective?
(c) Are there theoretical complications with your proposed goal(s)?
(d) What are the possibilities for, or obstacles to, implementing your proposed goal(s) as measures of successful economic policy?

References

1. Acemoglu, D., Johnson, S., & Robinson, J. A. (2001). The colonial origins of comparative development: An empirical investigation. *The American Economic Review, 91*(5), 1369-1401.
2. Anthony, D. W. (2007). *The Horse, the wheel, and language: How bronze-age riders from the Eurasian steppes shaped the modern world*. Princeton: Princeton University Press.
3. Childe, V. G. (1985). *What happened in history: The classic study which opened up new perspectives in history*. New York: Puffin.
4. Daly, H. E., & Cobb, J. B. (1994). *For the common good: Redirecting the economy toward community, the environment, and a sustainable future*. Boston: Beacon Press.
5. Friedman, B. M. (2006). *The moral consequences of economic growth*. New York: Vintage.

Index

K. Seeley, *Macroeconomics in Ecological Context*, Studies in Ecological Economics 5, DOI 10.1007/978-3-319-51757-5

R

S

T

U

MIX
Papier aus verantwortungsvollen Quellen
Paper from responsible sources
FSC® C105338
FSC
www.fsc.org

If you have any concerns about our products,
you can contact us on
ProductSafety@springernature.com

In case Publisher is established outside the EU,
the EU authorized representative is:
Springer Nature Customer Service Center GmbH
Europaplatz 3, 69115 Heidelberg, Germany

Printed by Libri Plureos GmbH
in Hamburg, Germany